Exam	Prentice Hall Title	MCSE Certification Credit	MCSE + Internet Certification Credit	MCDBA Certification Credit	MCSD Certification Credit	MCP + Site Building Certification Credit	MCP + Internet Certification Credit
70-079	*MCSE: Implementing and Supporting Microsoft Internet Explorer 4 by Using the Microsoft Internet Explorer Administration Kit*, Dell, 1999	1 of 2 Elective Requirements	1 of 7 Core Requirements	NA	NA	NA	NA
70-081	*MCSE: Implementing and Supporting Microsoft Exchange Server 5.5*, Goncalves, 1998	1 of 2 Elective Requirements	1 of 2 Elective Requirements	NA	NA	NA	NA
70-085	*MCSE: Implementing and Supporting Microsoft SNA Server 4*, Mariscal, 1999	1 of 2 Elective Requirements	1 of 2 Elective Requirements	NA	NA	NA	NA
70-086	*MCSE: Implementing and Supporting Microsoft Systems Management Server 2*, Vacca, 1999	1 of 2 Elective Requirements	NA	NA	NA	NA	NA
70-087	*MCSE: Implementing and Supporting Microsoft Internet Information Server 4*, Dell, 1999	1 of 2 Elective Requirements	1 of 7 Core Requirements	1 of 1 Elective Requirements	NA	NA	1 of 3 Requirements
70-088	*MCSE: Implementing and Supporting Microsoft Proxy Server 2*, Ryvkin, 1999	1 of 2 Elective Requirements	1 of 2 Elective Requirements	NA	NA	NA	NA
70-098	*Core MCSE*, Dell, 1998	1 of 4 Core Requirements	1 of 7 Core Requirements	NA	NA	NA	NA
70-175	*MCSD: Designing and Implementing Distributed Applications with Microsoft Visual Basic 6*, Houlette, 1999	NA	NA	1 of 4 Core Requirements and 1 of 1 Elective Requirements	1 of 1 Elective Requirements	NA	NA
70-176	*MCSD: Designing and Implementing Desktop Applications with Microsoft Visual Basic 6*, Holzner, 1999	NA	NA	NA	1 of 1 Elective Requirements	NA	NA

PRENTICE HALL SERIES ON MICROSOFT TECHNOLOGIES

DAVID KARLINS

MCSD: Designing and Implementing Web Sites Using Microsoft® FrontPage® 98

Prentice Hall PTR
Upper Saddle River, NJ 07458
http://www.phptr.com

ISBN 0-13-014117-8

90000

9 780130 141170

Library of Congress Cataloging-in-Publication Data

Karlins, David.
    MCSD: designing and implementing web sites using Microsoft FrontPage 98 / David Karlins.
       p. cm. -- (Microsoft technology series)
    Includes bibliographical references and index.
    ISBN 0 -13-014117-8
     1. Web sites -- Design--Examinations--Study guides. 2. Electronic data processing
   personnel--Certification. 3. Microsoft software--Examinations--Study guides. I. Title.
II. Series.

TK5105.888.K37 1999
005.7'221--dc21   99-040533

Editorial/Production Supervision: Nicholas Radhuber
Acquisitions Editor: Jill Pisoni
Development Editor: Jim Markham
Cover Design Director: Jerry Votta
Cover Designer: Anthony Gemmellaro
Manufacturing Manager: Maura Goldstaub
Series Design: Gail Cocker-Bogusz
Marketing Manager: Lisa Konzelmann

Prentice Hall books are widely used by corporations and government agencies for
training, marketing, and resale. The publisher offers discounts on this book when
ordered in bulk quantities. For more information, contact:

    Corporate Sales Department
    Prentice Hall PTR
    One Lake Street
    Upper Saddle River, NJ 07458
    Phone: 800-382-3419; FAX: 201-236-7141
    E-mail (Internet): corpsales@prenhall.com

Printed in the United States of America

10 9 8 7 6 5 4 3 2

ISBN 0-13-014117-8

Prentice-Hall International (UK) Limited, *London*
Prentice-Hall of Australia Pty. Limited, *Sydney*
Prentice-Hall Canada Inc., *Toronto*
Prentice-Hall Hispanoamericana, S.A., *Mexico*
Prentice-Hall of India Private Limited, *New Delhi*
Prentice-Hall of Japan, Inc., *Tokyo*
Prentice-Hall (Singapore) Pte. Ltd., *Singapore*
Editora Prentice-Hall do Brasil, Ltda., *Rio de Janeiro*

CONTENTS

David Karlins is a FrontPage Microsoft Certified Professional. In addition to this book, David is co-author with David Elderbrock of the *FrontPage 2000 Bible* (IDG). David's other recent books include *Teach Yourself FrontPage 98 in a Week* (Sams), *Create FrontPage Web Pages in a Weekend* (Prima), *Wild Web Graphics with Microsoft Image Composer* (Que), and *Teach Yourself CorelDRAW 9 in 24 Hours* (Sams).

David has also contributed chapters on publishing *FrontPage and Web Design to the Office 2000 Bible* (IDG), *Special Edition Using Microsoft Office 2000* (Que), *Platinum Edition Using Microsoft Office 2000* (Que), *Special Edition Using FrontPage 97* (Que), and *Platinum Edition Using Microsoft Office 97* (Que).

When David isn't writing about Web design or teaching FrontPage seminars, he hones his skills as an amateur, unpublished movie critic. Visit him anytime at www.ppinet.com.

ACKNOWLEDGMENTS

Jill Pisoni at Prentice Hall worked with my agent Lisa Swayne to create the opportunity for me to write this book. Jim Markham oversaw the entire development process, and provided sound advice and friendly encouragement. Suzanne Weixal supplied dedicated and vigilant technical editing, and Linda Ramagnano helped organize the book. The whole crew worked together to make this a fun project.

In writing this book, I drew on the collective experience of the many FrontPage developers who have posted problems and solutions at my Front-Page Forum at www.ppinet.com. I also incorporated many things I learned from working with students in my FrontPage seminars.

Finally, two people contributed especially helpful technical advice for this book. I frequently relied on Cat Hebert at the Virtual Drama Web site (http://www.virtualdrama.com/cat) for help with animation, media and browser challenges, and Stephanie Cottrell Bryant, at www.scottrell.com, helped me solve Web security and server probelms.

Thanks everyone!

....

#	Exam 70-055 Requirements: Designing and Implementing Web Sites using Microsoft® Frontpage® 98	Chapter/ Section No.	Question(s)
1.	Analyze Business Requirements	1/1.1, 1.2, 1.3	1.1-1.15
2.	Analyze Maintainability Requirements	2/2.1, 2.2, 2.3, 4/4.5	2.2-2.15 4.4, 4.6
3.	Defining Technical Architecture	3/3.1, 3.2, 3.3, 6/6.2, 10/10.4	3.1-3.10
4.	Developing the Conceptual and Logical Design |for a FrontPage 98 Web Site	4/4.1, 4.2, 4.3, 5/5.2	4.1-4.15
5.	Designing a User Interface and User Services for a FrontPage 98 Web Site	4/4.3 5/5/5.1	5.1- 5.15
6.	Evaluate methods of providing online user assistance	5/5.1 7/7.4	5.1, 5.11, 5.14
7.	Establishing the Development Environment Configuring Integration with Visual SourceSafe Installing Frontpage 98 with Server Extensions Installing Microsoft and FrontPage Personal Web Servers	6/6.1, 6.2, 6.3, 6.4	6.2-6.15
8.	Creating Use Services Alter Default Titles for Navigation Bar Create and use Frames Configure Shared Borders	4/4.3, 7/7.1, 7.2, 7.3	7.1-7.10
9.	Create Data Input Forms Add fields, set field properties, set form properties	8/8.1. 8.2, 8.3	8.1-8.15
10.	Validate User Input Validate Input using form field validation scripts	9/9.1, 9.2, 9.3	9.1-9.15
11.	Process User Input Send form results using e-mail Send form results to a file Display results in a frame	10/10.1, 10.2, 10.3	10.1-10.15
12.	Insert ActiveX Controls	11/11.2, 12/12.4	11.1, 11.6, 11.8, 11.9

MCSD Requirements Matrix, continued.

xix

#	Exam 70-055 Requirements: Designing and Implementing Web Sites using Microsoft® Frontpage® 98	Chapter/ Section No.	Question(s)
13.	Insert a Java Applet Insert a Java Applet onto a FrontPage Web Page	11/11.1	11.1, 11.2, 11.3, 11.5, 11.6, 11.7, 11.8, 11.10, 11.11, 11.14
14.	Create a Web Page that Uses Transitions, Animation and Dynamic HTML (DHTML)	11/11.3, 16/16.2	11.1, 11.4, 11.6, 11.9, 11,12, 11.15
15.	Use the Database Region Wizard	14/14.3	14.3, 14.4, 14.6, 14.7, 14.13, 14.14
16.	Insert a FrontPage Component	5/5.3	5.1, 5.4, 5.6, 5.9, 5.12, 5.14, 5.15
17.	Style Sheets and Templates	13/13.1, 13.2, 13.3, 13.4	13.1-13.15
18.	Tables, Graphics and Animation	12/12.1, 12.2, 12.3	12.1-12.15
19.	Testing a Frontpage Web Site Preview in Multiple Browsers	1/1.3, 2/2.2, 3/3.2, 5/5.4, 7/7.4, 9/9.1, 11/11/11.1, 11.2, 15/15.1, 15.3, 15.4, 16.2	1.13, 3.7, 5.3, 7.1, 7.5, 8.10, 9.15, 11.1, 11.3, 11.4, 11.7, 11.13, 13.3, 13.7, 16.1, 16.5, 16.6, 16.7, 16.8 16.9, 16.10, 16.11, 16.12, 16.13
20.	Publishing a FrontPage Web Site	14/14.1, 14.2	14.1, 14.2, 14.5, 14.7, 14.8, 14.9, 14.10, 14.11, 14.12
21.	Managing a Frontpage Web Site	4/4.2, 4.4, 4.5, 4.6, 5.3, 6.4, 16.1, 16.2 16.3, 16.4, 16.5	4.1, 4.4, 4.5, 4.6, 4.7, 4.14, 4.15, 5.12, 6.5, 6.8, 6.14, 6.15, 7.7, 7.8, 14.1, 14.11, 14.15, 15.1, 15.2, 15.3, 15.4, 15.5, 15.6, 15.7, 15.11, 15.12, 15.13
22.	Managing Access to a FrontPage 98 Web Site	15.1, 15.3, 15.4, 17.1, 17.2, 17.3, 17.4	17.1-17.15
23.	Adding Media Delivery Capabilities to a FrontPage Web Site	1/1.3, 3/3.1, 12/12.4	12.1, 12.3, 12.9, 12.10

INTRODUCTION

This book is designed primarily for people who need to pass Exam 70-055: *Designing and Implementing Web Sites Using Microsoft FrontPage 98*. When you pass Exam 70-055, you attain Microsoft Certified Professional status. You also earn credit toward Microsoft Certified Professional + Site Building (MCP+SB) certification and you earn elective credit towards Microsoft Certified Solution Developer (MCSD) certification.

This book will benefit any computing professional who is responsible for the management of FrontPage Web development environments. It is designed to be both a training guide and reference resource.

Who this book is for

This book serves three basic audiences: people who are already familiar with FrontPage and want to attain FrontPage MCP status, people who need to master FrontPage as a component of acheiving MCP+SB or MCSD certification, and finally, as a reference for FrontPage developers.

The book covers basic fundamentals of FrontPage development, but quickly, and with the expectation that the reader is either familiar with FrontPage or has a background in related Web development applications. Because the FrontPage Exam content matrix focuses on advanced level issues, this book emphasizes those area and problems. In that respect, I feel confident that this book will not only get you through the exam, but also provide a long-term resource for your FrontPage Web development challenges.

What you'll need

Through the use of numerous illustrations and CD-ROM-based training supplements, I have endeavored to make this book as self-contained as possible. Nevertheless, I acknowledge that there is no substitute for hands-on experience. To fully practice the concepts explained in this book, you will need to have FrontPage 98 installed on your computer. It is not necessary to have a network or Internet connection to work through the material in this book.

All that is required is that you either install a version of the Personal Web Server that is bundled with FrontPage 98, or Internet Explorer 4 or higher. At some points, there will be optional exercises that utilize Internet connections, and you will find you get more out of the book if you are able to work through those *Study Break* exercises connected to the Internet.

How this book is organized

This book is divided into 17 chapters which cover issues such as assessing Web development technologies, constructing workflow processes for Web development, designing user interfaces, integrating with servers, creating database regions, attaching external style sheets, controlling user access with user registration, incorporating Java, ActiveX and DHTML and publishing to Web servers.

The numbered sections in each chapter correspond to specific MCSD exam requirements, and each chapter concludes with a list of related study questions. All chapters have several hands-on *Study Break* section that permits you to practice what you learned. Appendix A contains the answer to all review questions.

Conventions used in this book

This book uses different features to help highlight key information.

Chapter Syllabus

The primary focus of this series is to address those topics that are to be tested in each exam. Therefore, each chapter opens with a syllabus that lists the topics to be covered. Each topic directly corresponds to the level 1 headings in the chapter. So if there are six level 1 headings in a chapter, there will be six topics listed under the chapter syllabus. If a syllabus topic and level 1 heading are MCSD-specific, they will be accompanied by an MCSD icon (see the following icon description.) However, there may be instances when the topics are not directly exam-specific. In these cases, the chapter syllabus highlights and corresponding level 1 headings appear with out the MCSD icon.

Icons

Icons alert you to called-out material that is of significance. Icons include:

Study Breaks

This icon is used to identify MCSD-specific chapter syllabus topics and appropriate MCSD sections in each chapter.

This icon calls out information that deserves special attention; one that the reader may otherwise run a highlight marker through.

This icon is used to flag particularly useful information that will save the reader time, highlight a valuable technique, or offer specific advice.

This icon flags information that may cause unexpected results or serious frustration.

These sidebars are designed to test your knowledge in a practical manner through the use of performance-based exercises. These exercises provide an opportunity to perform actual tasks that will undoubtedly be encountered in a working environment, and simulated in the Microsoft exam.

Chapter Review Questions

Each chapter ends with a series of review questions. These questions are designed to simulate a part of an actual exam and to reinforce what you have just learned. The number of questions will vary, depending on the length of the subject matter of the individual chapter. All of the questions are taken directly from the material covered in the chapter, and the answers can be found in Appendix A.

About the CD-ROM/Web Site

This book includes a CD-ROM that contains valuable self-paced training material, courtesy of CBT Systems. Please follow the installation instructions on the CD-ROM. Readers can find additional exam preparation aids and updates to the enclosed material by visiting the companion web site to this book. It is located at www.phptr.com/phptrinteractive.

For the latest exam information please go to www.microsoft.com/train_cert

Analyzing a Development Environment

Analyzing a development environment requires a survey of existing and required technical architecture, an assessment of the types of activity that will transpire over a Web site, and the ability to combine that understanding with a knowledge of what FrontPage can and cannot do. In Chapter 1, "Analyzing Business Requirements," we'll start with the methodology for surveying the business requirements of a Web site. In Chapter 2, "Analyzing Web Requirements," we'll explore maintenance requirements, including importing existing Web components into a FrontPage Web. In Chapter 3, "Defining the Technical Architecture for a FrontPage 98 Web Site," we'll survey a variety of technical architecture challenges, including integrating existing scripts, and working with different kinds of Web servers.

Analyzing Business Requirements

Scenario: An organization or corporation calls on you, a FrontPage 98 Microsoft Certified Professional, to install FrontPage as their development tool for creating and maintaining a Web site. You arrive at the client's site, flying through the window, "MCP" or "MCSD" on your chest and cape flowing in the wind. You land in the office of the Chief Information Officer. After promising to fix the window, you inform the awed CIO that in order to create a successful plan for implementing FrontPage 98, you need to learn two basic things:

- What are the technical requirements for the project?

- What are the business requirements for the project?

The bulk of this book will explore the capabilities of FrontPage, so that when you arrive at a client's site you will be ready to connect his or her needs with the ability and limitations of FrontPage 98. In this chapter we will focus on the second of these two elements, the client's site requirements. If you can make an accurate evaluation of a client's business and technical needs, you can then proceed to present a realistic plan for implementing FrontPage 98.

At the conclusion of this chapter you will be able to:

- Quantify the scope of a FrontPage Web site.
- Develop a plan for connecting project needs with the capabilities of the FrontPage development environment.
- Define business requirements for a FrontPage Web.
- Understand the basic role of FrontPage server extensions.
- Make a basic assessement of security requirements for a FrontPage Web.
- Understand the role of Secure Sockets Layer encryption.
- Identify performance requirements for a FrontPage Web.

Determining the Scope of a Project

The scope of a Web site development project is another way of describing the quantitative requirements of the site. Scope includes the number of visitors to the site, their capacity to download site information, and the amount and type of files to be provided at the Web site.

Your first task is to investigate, interview, and determine the purpose of your client's Web site. Will your client be presenting a few pages of mainly HTML text? Or will the site be loaded with audio and video files? Is the site expecting 20 hits a day, 200, or 200,000? Will your client be creating content that requires the latest versions of Internet Explorer and Netscape Navigator in order to be viewed by visitors? Or is the audience for the Web site expecting content that can be interpreted by older browsers?

Quantifying the Scope of a Web Site

One key element in determining the scope of a project is to itemize the kinds of content to be included in the site. Some site content requires tremendous amounts of server space. An AVI or MPEG video file can easily require as much server space as hundreds of pages of HTML text.

Bandwidth, or the capacity to move information in and out of your site, is a two-way street. If your client intends to provide heavy graphic or media content, this requires both sufficient storage space and speed at the server, as well as at the visitor's end. A Web site that provides sound or video content needs a large capacity server and sufficient bandwidth to send that content to visitors. A Web site laden with sound and video also requires that visitors have modems fast enough to handle large amounts of data quickly.

Interviewing clients and determining the scope of a project is as much an art as it is a science, but the following checklist provides a starting point for assessing the demands of a potential FrontPage 98 Web site:

- How many, and what type of content files will be stored at the client's Web site? Text pages? Pictures? Sound files? Video? Other Web elements?
- What kind of physical access to the site will visitors have? Modems? T1 lines?
- How many hits a day are expected at the site, both initially and long term?
- Is the site being deployed on the Internet or on a local intranet?
- What is the storage capacity of the server?

Small? Medium? Or Large?

The FrontPage MCP exam does not require that you prove expertise in server administration, but you are expected to be able to make a basic assessment of server requirement needs. As you investigate the potential scope of a client's Web site, you can organize scope needs into three basic categories:

- *Small:* An intranet in a small business or organization that will be accessed by 3–5 visitors at a time, with content that includes text, graphics and some media files. Such a site is a candidate for the Microsoft Personal Web Server installed on a Microsoft NT Server. A small site will typically require as little as 10 MB of disk space on the server, and 500 MB bandwidth.
- *Medium*: An intranet or Internet site that will be accessed by several hundred to ten thousand visitors per day, saved on an NT server using a T1 or faster connection line. A medium-sized Web site will typically require at least 50 MB of disk space, and at least 2.25 GB of bandwidth.
- *Large:* A commercial or large organization site that handles hundreds of thousands of hits per day. Large Web sites require more than 100 MB of server disk space, and at least 4.5 GB bandwidth. Large-and medium-sized Webs require a commercial Web server like Microsoft Internet Information Server.

Connecting Needs and Capacity

Once you determine the necessary requirements for a Web site, you can survey existing capabilities. For example, if a client is creating a small site, and has 100 MB of available space on an NT server, that will be sufficient to host his or her Web site. If a client needs a large commercial Web site, and has 100 MB of disk space on an NT server, you should advise them to shop for Web space from a commercial server provider.

If you are shopping for server space, Microsoft provides links to hundreds of Web site providers who offer sites that support FrontPage. Links to those sites are available from Microsoft's www.Microsoft.com Web site. The last time I checked, the direct link to the list of providers was found at: http://204.203.124.10/frontpage/wpp/list/intro.htm

Each of the links at that site leads to competing providers, most of whom display price lists right at their Web site, like the one in Figure 1.1.

Akorn Access specializes in low-cost virtual web hosting for small to large businesses. With Akorn, you can give your business the world wide advantage it needs to compete in the new global market.

If you already have a domain with another provider and need to make the switch to a faster more responsive provider, then we can do that for you, too. A one time transfer fee of $50 will get your current domain transferred to our server. Then using the FTP access we provide for you or Microsoft's FrontPage, you can copy your current web pages to us in just a matter of minutes.

For those users who want the flexibility of maintaining their own server but would rather not deal with the expense of a dedicated Internet connection, Akorn now offers **server co-location** services.

Putting your business on the Internet doesn't need to be expensive! At Akorn, we are dedicated to making the Web affordable -- and profitable.

Plan Type	Cost	Disc Space	Bandwidth
Plan I	$25	10MB	500MB
Plan II	$75	20MB	900MB
Plan III	$125	50MB	2.25GB
Plan IV	$175	100MB	4.5GB

Figure 1.1 *After you make an assessment of site requirements, you can comparison shop for Web server space.*

Surveying Web Capacity Options

Practice what you have learned by investigating available hosting options for Web sites.

First, log onto www.Microsoft.com and find the page that provides links to Web providers.

Next, identify the amount of server space and bandwidth different providers suggest for various types of Web sites.

Finally, familiarize yourself with other available options for Web sites, including domain name registration, database connectivity and e-mail.

MCSD 1.1 Defining Business Requirements

When you assess the business requirements for a Web site, you will need to connect those requirements to the capabilities of FrontPage 98. For example, if a client is developing a Web site for an intranet, you need to know that this is possible. You also need to know that a FrontPage intranet requires that the client have FrontPage 98 server extensions available on the server that will manage the intranet site.

Similarly, a business may need to include data input forms in their Web site. You can inform your client that this is possible in FrontPage, as shown in Figure 1.2. However, you also need to make your client aware that these forms require either that a Web site is published to a server with FrontPage extension files, or that these forms will require additional scripting from the Web site provider.

A Word About FrontPage Extensions

Many of the advanced features of FrontPage 98, including the ability to collect form input data, work only after a Web site is published (posted) to a Web site that has FrontPage extension files installed.

FrontPage extensions enable non-programmers to design and implement Web components that require programming or scripting. FrontPage extensions are available for all major Web servers, including UNIX-based Web servers.

Throughout this book, you will learn to identify features that require FrontPage extensions to work, and those that do not. See Chapter 6 for a complete discussion of FrontPage server extensions.

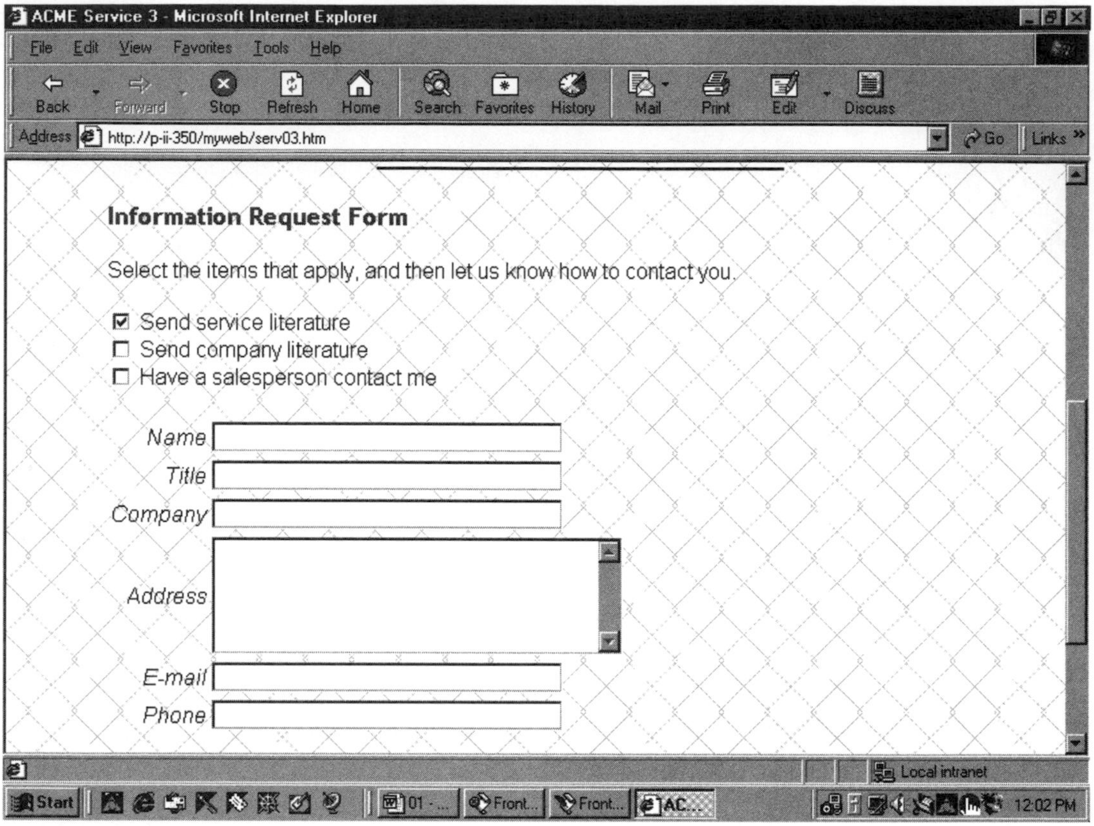

Figure 1.2   *FrontPage 98 will generate input forms, but they require either a server with FrontPage extension files, or additional scripting from the site provider.*

The bulk of this book is devoted to exploring the capabilities of FrontPage 98. Before you can really evaluate the business requirements of a Web site, it is helpful to know what FrontPage can and cannot do.

However, there is a particular art to analyzing what the requirements are for a Web site. Table 1.1 identifies key business requirements, and matches them with FrontPage's capacity to create those site elements. Where appropriate, the table includes the chapter in this book that explores the particular feature.

Table 1.1 *Identifying and Analyzing Business Web Requirements*

Business Requirement	FrontPage 98 Capabilities and Limitations
Search capability	Available (within a Web site) for sites published to servers with FrontPage 98 extensions. (Chapter 5)
Internet access	Available either by directly publishing to an Internet site, or via an intranet proxy server. (Chapter 17)
Electronic commerce	Available. FrontPage can publish to sites with Secured Socket Layers (SSL), including sites using Internet Information Server.
Database integration	Technically possible, but difficult in FrontPage. Requires a Web server that supports Active Server Pages (ASP). (Chapter 14)
Document integration	FrontPage can integrate text from almost any source, but the ability to interpret that text depends on the browsers and local software available to visitors.
Frames	Frames are easy to design in FrontPage 98, and include options for browsers that do not recognize frames. (Chapter 7).
Controlled accessibility	FrontPage allows password protection for Web sites and for developers. (Chapter 17)

Study Break

Assessing Business Requirements

Test your skills at assessing business requirements by determining the business requirements for a projected FrontPage Web site. Assume that the business environment demands data integration with a database, an internal search engine, encryption to protect online transactions, and 1000 MB of server space.

First, identify whether or not FrontPage can handle the business demands of this project. What warnings would you issue to the developers before they embark on designing a FrontPage Web that meets their business needs?

Then, identify for yourself what kind of technology is required to meet the security demands of this site.

Finally, identify a solution to the site's need for database access.

MCSD 1.2 Analyzing Security Requirements

There are different levels of Web security. They include:

- Defining who can access Web site content.
- Administering permission to edit Web site content.

- Assigning administration rights to control access to content and development of a site.
- Data protection with Security Sockets Layer (SSL) encryption.

FrontPage allows administrators to define who can visit sites, who can edit them, and who can administer them. These properties are defined in the FrontPage 98 Explorer. I'll discuss assigning SSL protection later in this chapter. FrontPage is also compatible with protecting data with Secure Sockets Layer (SSL) encryption. But before you dive into defining security for a Web site, the first step is to determine the level of security required. FrontPage provides three basic levels of control over Web site access:

- Browser permission allows visitors to view Web site content.
- Author permission allows a developer to edit site content.
- Administrator permission assigns control over browser- and author-level permission.

In order to make an assessment of what levels of permissions are required, you need to investigate and understand the content and purpose of a proposed Web site.

Controlling Access to Site Content

Most Web sites are designed and intended to welcome the broadest possible access to their content. If a company is building a Web site to promote its image and its products or services, there may well be no security considerations for who visits the site.

On the other hand, if a Web site is being developed to allow sales staff to check inventories, see wholesale prices, and read internal company bulletins, then access to that site should obviously be restricted.

One of your first tasks in evaluating the requirements of a Web site is to determine if any or all portions of a Web site should have access restricted. Unrestricted access for a site posted to the Internet means that anyone on the planet with access to the Web can visit the site, read content, copy it, and view or interact with components of the Web site. Unrestricted access on an intranet means that anyone who has access to an organization or company's intranet can access content on the site.

Access to an Internet or intranet Web site can be restricted to defined browsers. FrontPage does allow you to make some sections of a Web site unrestricted while restricting other areas.

If a developer elects to restrict access to all or part of a Web site, the site administrator can define users, assign them user names and passwords.

Controlling Access to Site Development

While many sites will welcome any and all visitors, no Web site administrator will want the general public altering the site content! Even within a company or organization, decisions will be made as to who can edit the content of a Web site.

FrontPage allows administrators to define author permission. Authors are assigned user names and passwords that allow them to open and edit FrontPage Web sites.

Assigning Administrator Privileges

The highest level of permission is administrator level. Administrators can assign (or remove) permission for both visitors and developers. Administrators have total authority over access to a Web site.

So, who defines the administrator? When you install FrontPage 98, you define an administrator and a password for the Personal Web Server. If you are using a Web server provided by an Internet service provider, or run by an intranet administrator, those Web administrators will assign initial FrontPage administrator status.

Defining Permissions in an Existing Web Site

To make this discussion more concrete, it is useful to look quickly at the procedure by which FrontPage assigns different levels of access to a Web site. This process is explored in more detail in Chapter 17, but for now you can experiment with the basic routine.

To define permissions for a FrontPage Web:

1. In the FrontPage Explorer, select File, Open FrontPage Web.
2. Select an existing Web, or click on the Create a New FrontPage Web options button in the Getting Started dialog box and create a new Web site.
3. With a Web site open, select Tools, Permissions. The Permissions dialog box opens. In the Settings tab of the dialog box, select the Use Unique Permissions for This Web options button. (Note: The FrontPage Personal Web Server is designed mainly for use by one individual developer, and therefore does not include Permission options. Other, more robust Web servers that have FrontPage extension files do include Permission options.)
4. In the Users tab, use the Add button to add a new user, the Edit button to edit a selected user, or the Remove button to remove a selected user from the list in the dialog box. The Add and Edit buttons open the Edit

Figure 1.3   *FrontPage 98 allows administrators to define access to a Web site.*

Users dialog box, where permissions are assigned. Figure 1.3 shows administrator privileges being defined for a FrontPage Web site.

5. To require users to register before visiting a site, click on the Only Registered Users Have Browse Access options button.

6. After defining permissions, click on the Apply button in the Permissions dialog box. You can change permission levels at any time.

If you elect to require users to register, you will have to individually add new users (using the Add button), and assign them user names and passwords. Figure 1.4 shows a user being assigned visitor privileges, with his own unique password.

Study Break

Assigning Permissions

Practice what you have learned by assigning author and editor privileges in FrontPage 98.

First, open an existing Web site, or create a new one. If you need help with this, skip ahead to Chapter 4, and return to this Study Break after you have created a FrontPage Web.

Next, use the Permissions dialog box to note existing Names and Access Rights.

Finally, add a new name, give that new user administrator, author and browser rights. Cancel the dialog box instead of clicking on Apply so you don't corrupt an existing Web.

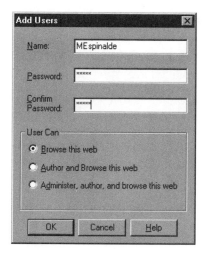

Figure 1.4 *Assigning browser permission for a password-protected Web site.*

Who Needs SSL?

Secure Sockets Layer (SSL) is an encryption system that protects the security of data exchanged over the Internet or an intranet. Determining whether a client needs SSL encryption for his or her site is a somewhat subjective decision.

Probably the single most sensitive area where SSL applies is when credit card data is collected over the Internet. Many credit card purchasers feel more comfortable knowing that the credit card information they transmit to a Web server is protected by an encryption system like SSL. Companies may have other reasons for protecting transmitted data from electronic eavesdropping. For example, they may need to protect confidential information from competitors.

If a client decides that a Web site should be protected with SSL, the site can be published directly from FrontPage to a site that supports SSL encryption. FrontPage itself does not assign SSL protection because that is a property of the Web server.

When FrontPage Web sites are published, you can indicate that the target Web server is equipped to handle SSL. To publish a Web site to an SSL Web server:

1. With a Web site open, in the FrontPage 98 Explorer select File, Publish FrontPage Web.
2. In the Publish FrontPage Web dialog box, enter the URL for the target Web server.

3. Select the Secure Connection Required check box, as shown in Figure 1.5.

4. Click on OK in the dialog box. If a user name and password are required by the server, you will be prompted to provide them.

A full discussion of the technical aspects of Web security is beyond the scope of this book, and you won't be grilled on the politics of SSL in the MCP/MCSD Exam. Ultimately, your role as a FrontPage expert is to make clients aware that FrontPage Web sites can be published to servers with SSL.

MCSD 1.3   Identifying Performance Requirements

So far, in discussing performance requirements for a Web site, we've focused on the requirements of the Web server. Is there enough drive space for the FrontPage Web? Does the server support FrontPage extensions? Does the server support SSL?

However, there is another side to identifying performance requirements. The content of a Web site must take into account the software and browser performance capacities of *visitors*.

Visitor capabilities also define what you can place in a Web site. Is the site going to be published to an intranet, where all visitors have the latest version of Microsoft Office and Internet Explorer? Or to the World Wide Web, where visitors may be browsing with older version of Netscape Navigator, and have Lotus SmartSuite software installed. Web site content that is appropriate for the first scenario won't work well in the second situation.

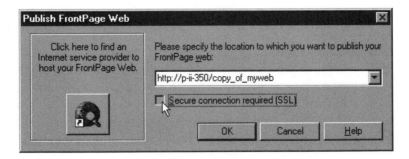

Figure 1.5 *Web sites can be published from FrontPage to servers with SSL encryption.*

Table 1.2 lists some of the elements of Web content that can be included in a FrontPage Web site, and the constraints on who will be able to view that content.

Table 1.2 *Matching Web Site Content with Visitor Capabilities*

Business Requirement	FrontPage 98 Capabilities and Limitations
HTML Web pages	Can be created in FrontPage 98, and accessed by all browsers.
Web compatible graphics	JPEG and GIF images can be created in FrontPage 98, and accessed by all browsers.
PowerPoint slide show files	Can be included in FrontPage 98 Web sites, requires either PowerPoint on a visitor's computer, or downloadable view program available free from Microsoft.
Microsoft Word files	Can be included in FrontPage 98 Web sites, requires either PowerPoint on a visitor's computer, or downloadable Word viewer program available free from Microsoft.
ActiveX content	Can be incorporated in FrontPage Web sites, requires Internet Explorer 4 or higher.
Java and JavaScript files	Can be incorporated in FrontPage Web sites, requires Internet Explorer or Netscape Navigator versions 4 or higher.
AVI video files	Can be included in FrontPage 98 Web sites, requires Windows operating system or downloaded plug-in program.
Tables	Tables can be imported into or created in FrontPage, and are interpreted by almost all browsers. However, some table attributes are displayed differently in Netscape Navigator and Internet Explorer, and not interpreted at all in browsers before version 3 of Navigator and IE.
Frames	Frames are interpreted by Netscape Navigator (version 2 and higher) and Internet Explorer (version 3 and higher). Tables can be created easily in FrontPage. Older browsers do not interpret frames, and some visitors do not like them. FrontPage can generate alternate pages for browsers that don't interpret frames.

Study Break

Identify Performance Requirements

Practice what you have learned by analyzing performance requirements for the following scenario: A developer wants SSL encryption, frames, ActiveX objects, JPEG and GIF files and PowerPoint slide shows in his or her Web site.

First, identify browser constraints for this scenario. Are there any concerns you should make the developers aware of in terms of visitors being able to access all the options in the Web?

Next, identify server issues involved in the proposed Web. What will be required of a server to support this Web site?

Finally, find a piece of scratch paper, and draw a grid like the one shown here, listing the elements identified in the scenario for this site. Fill in the missing information on browser requirements for each feature.

Feature	**Browser Requirements**
SSL encryption	
Frames	
ActiveX objects	
JPEG files	
GIF files	
PowerPoint slide shows	

■ Summary

You need to be good at two things to be a FrontPage expert. You need to know FrontPage; and you need to be able to analyze the requirements of a client's Web site.

Most of this book is about what FrontPage can do. But here, we've focused on identifying the requirements of a Web site. Those might include HTML Web pages, JPEG and GIF images, elements that require additional software on a visitor's computer to interpret (like PowerPoint or Microsoft Word files), cutting edge technology like ActiveX content, Java applets or JavaScript files, media like video files, tables, or frames.

FrontPage can handle all of these features, but the initial phase of coming up with a Web development plan includes identifying what a client needs in his or her FrontPage Web.

▲ CHAPTER REVIEW QUESTIONS

Here are a some practice questions relating to the material covered in the "Analyzing Business Requirements" area of Microsoft's *Designing and Implementing Web Sites Using Microsoft FrontPage 98* exam (70-055).

1. *Clients who want to include search capability within their Web sites will need to contract for additional programming since FrontPage does not generate working search boxes.*
    A. True
    B. False

2. *FrontPage Web sites work best when published to Web servers with*
    A. the Unix operating system
    B. the Windows NT operating system
    C. anonymous access
    D. FrontPage extension files
    E. Secure Sockets Layers

3. *FrontPage Web sites can be designed to restrict access to a set of users with assigned browser access.*
    A. True
    B. False

4. *SSL can be used to encrypt transactions over Web sites created with FrontPage.*
    A. True
    B. False

5. *FrontPage Web sites must be published to servers using the NT operating system.*
    A. True
    B. False

6. *Which of the following are factors in determining bandwidth requirements for a FrontPage created Web site? (Select as many as necessary.)*
    A. Multimedia content
    B. Expected hits
    C. SSL encryption
    D. Type of Web server
    E. Versions of browsers used by visitors

7. *Developers who are designing sites that will collect sensitive data might want to consider using which of the following (Select all correct answers.)*
    - **A.** Microsoft Internet Information Server version II or higher
    - **B.** Servers with FrontPage extensions
    - **C.** Microsoft certified Web site providers
    - **D.** Web servers that support sufficient bandwidth
    - **E.** SSL

8. *Many Web sites will need SSL to prevent unauthorized visitors from accessing Web site content.*
    - **A.** True
    - **B.** False

9. *The highest level of FrontPage administrative authority is Author permission.*
    - **A.** True
    - **B.** False

10. *FrontPage's Permissions dialog box allows you to require password authorization to access Web site content.*
    - **A.** True
    - **B.** False

11. *PowerPoint presentations can be incorporated in FrontPage Web sites.*
    - **A.** True
    - **B.** False

12. *Which of the following are considerations in incorporating AVI files in a FrontPage Web site? (Select all correct answers.)*
    - **A.** Server bandwidth
    - **B.** Server disk space
    - **C.** Server operating system
    - **D.** Permission settings
    - **E.** Visitor's browser types

13. *FrontPage Web sites require that visitors use Internet Explorer.*
    - **A.** True
    - **B.** False

14. *Which of the following types of content require current versions of Web browsers? (Select all correct answers.)*

    A. HTML Web pages

    B. ActiveX content

    C. Word files

    D. AVI video files

15. *FrontPage includes what feature for browsers that do not recognize frames? (Select all correct answers.)*

    A. Alternative images

    B. Alternative pages

    C. Public key encryption

    D. Java applets

Analyzing Web Requirements

In addition to analyzing business requirements for a Web site, the FrontPage MCP/MCSD Exam tests your ability to analyze a somewhat far-flung array of user requirements for FrontPage 98 Web sites.

The unifying theme is assessing how a Web site is going to be used, and figuring out how to integrate a new FrontPage Web site with existing people requirements and technical requirements.

At the conclusion of this chapter you will be able to:

- Identify many maintenance tasks for a FrontPage Web.

- Assign alternative text to images.

- Develop strategies for text-only sites.

- Modify tab order for data input forms.

- Integrate existing (non-FrontPage) Web content with a FrontPage Web.

- Preserve Active Server pages in a Web.

- Integrate a FrontPage Web with existing security systems.

21

MCSD 2.1   Analyzing Maintainability Requirements

One of the really exciting things about FrontPage 98 is the ability to automate the maintenance of a Web site. The key to doing this is the FrontPage Explorer, which, in its seven different views allows you to orchestrate and oversee different aspects of Web maintenance.

Throughout this book, we'll look at Maintaining FrontPage Webs from many different angles. For example, in Chapter 4, "Developing a Conceptual Design for a Web Site," I'll discuss how to use FrontPage's Tasks view to organize Web development. In Chapter 7, "Creating User Interfaces," we'll look at how FrontPage up-dates shared borders throughout an entire Web.

The details of many aspects of FrontPage Web maintenance are examined in detail in section 4.5 of this book, "Maintaining a Site." Here, I'll summarize Web maintenance tasks in table form. Table 2.1 lists various Web maintenance requirements, and how they are handled in FrontPage 98. This table will provide a quick introduction to the kinds of tasks involved in Web maintenance, and how they are accomplished in FrontPage.

Table 2.1 *Web Maintenance in FrontPage*

Web Maintenance Job	How FrontPage Does It
Keeping track of To Do tasks	Tasks view in the FrontPage Explorer.
Keeping track of and deleting Web files	Folders view and All Files view in the FrontPage Explorer.
Viewing, printing and changing the navigational structure of a Web	Navigation view in the FrontPage Explorer.
Viewing links to and from Web pages	Hyperlinks view in the FrontPage Explorer.
Testing the validity of internal hyperlinks	Tools, Recalculate Hyperlinks menu option in the FrontPage Explorer.
Testing and fixing external hyperlinks	Tools, Verify Hyperlinks in the FrontPage Explorer.
Publishing changed pages from a local server to a remote server	The Publish button in the FrontPage Explorer.
Locating orphan pages (pages with no links)	Click on the Orphan column heading in All Files view in the FrontPage Explorer to sort pages by those that are orphans and those that are not.
Check spelling throughout a Web	Click on the Cross File Spelling button in the FrontPage Explorer toolbar.
Locate a file	Click on the Cross File Find button in the FrontPage Explorer toolbar.
Change the content of Shared Borders used by all pages in a Web	Open any page in the FrontPage Editor, and edit the content of the Shared Border. The border changes for every page when the page is saved.
Change the assigned theme for an entire Web	Select a new Theme in Themes view in the FrontPage Explorer.
Refresh the connection between the FrontPage Explorer and a server	Press the F5 function key.

Table 2.1 *(Continued)*

Web Maintenance Job	How FrontPage Does It
Enable new administrators, page authors or users for a site	Select Tools, Permissions in the FrontPage Explorer.
Delete a FrontPage Web	Open the Web in the FrontPage Explorer, and select File, Delete FrontPage Web from the menu.
Manage different versions of Web objects	FrontPage integrates with Microsoft Visual SourceSafe, a program that tracks changes to files.

Study Break

Performing Basic Web Maintenance

Practice what you have learned by performing some basic Web tasks.

First, create a new Web using the Personal Web template. Assign a different Theme, and note changes to pages in the FrontPage Editor.

Next, examine the navigation structure. Look at all the files in the Web. How many are there? Look at the Hyperlink structure of the Web. Are there any external links? (There are.) Verify the external link.

Finally, delete the Web you just created.

MCSD 2.2 Assessing the Human Factor

Bad Scenario: You sit down with a client to discuss developing a Web site for an organization or company. You carefully analyze the technical requirements for the site—including server space, bandwidth, browsers that visitors will use, and the need for a search engine. You design and implement a plan for a FrontPage 98 Web site, but the client is unhappy.

Why? Well, to discourage ad displays and speed up downloading, one department has a policy that all browsers should be set to not display images. Other employees are visually impaired, and require Web page content that can be translated into audio speech by their browser. Because your plan neglected to provide alternate text for hidden images, employees and managers are up in arms.

The point is to avoid bad scenarios by analyzing the human factor before designing a plan to implement a FrontPage Web site.

Assigning Alternate Text

Alternate text is text that displays in a browser window when a visitor elects not to display images. Alternate text also displays while an image is downloading. There are many reasons, both functional and aesthetic, to provide alternate text for every image in your Web site. Because current browsers display alternate text when a cursor is moved over an image, alternate text can serve as an interactive image caption. Figure 2.1 shows alternate text displayed when a visitor points to an image in Netscape Navigator.

The content of alternate text may vary depending on the way it is going to be used. For example, if you are developing a plan to implement Front-Page for an intranet where some visitors will have images turned off in their browsers and some will not, you cannot count on images to convey content.

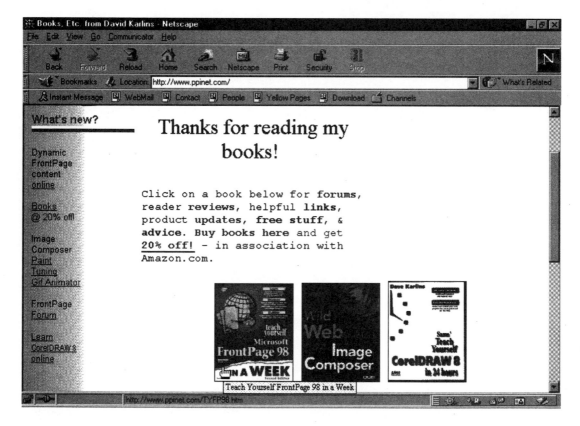

Figure 2.1 *Alternate text can serve as a caption for an image.*

You must provide an alternate way of communicating the message embodied in the image.

Additionally, as mentioned in the "Bad Scenario" at the beginning of this chapter, the Web is becoming increasingly accessible to partially-sighted people who rely on software to read Web page content to them out loud. This software cannot interpret images, but does "read" alternate text.

If everyone visiting a Web site has fast access to the Web and wants to see images, then alternate text can function simply as an interactive caption. But if, as is often the case, some visitors will not want to or be able to see images, alternate text plays a more critical role in conveying Web page content.

To assign alternate text to an image in FrontPage:

1. Click on an image in the FrontPage Editor to select it.
2. Right-click on the selected image, and choose Image Properties from the context menu. The Image Properties dialog box appears.
3. In the Text field of the General tab in the dialog box, enter alternate text, as shown in Figure 2.2.
4. OK the dialog box. You can test the alternate text by viewing the Web page in a browser with image display turned off.

Using Text-Only Sites

While the Internet mass media focus on streaming audio and interactive video, the reality on the ground is that many sites are still composed exclusively of text content.

One implication of a text-only environment is obvious: avoid images and image files. By avoiding images, you dramatically cut down on download time for visitors. Easier to forget is the need to provide text navigational links. For example, if you are incorporating FrontPage's ability to generate Navigation Bars, you will want to make sure those navigation bars use text links, not graphical buttons.

To insert Navigation Bars with text links:

1. In the FrontPage Editor, position your cursor where the links will be displayed. Often these links are positioned in a Shared Border. (For a full discussion of navigational strategies and combining Navigation Bars with Shared Borders, see Chapter 7.)
2. Select Insert, Navigation Bar. The Navigation Bar Properties dialog box appears.

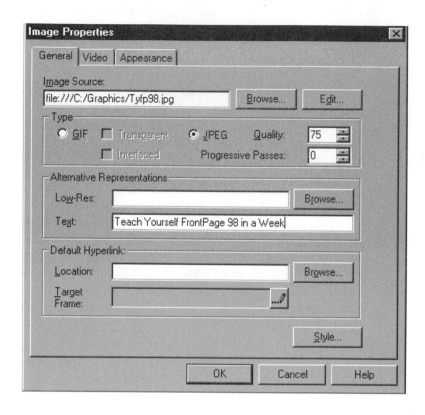

Figure 2.2 *Alternate text is assigned in the Image Properties dialog box.*

3. After selecting a navigational strategy, and a vertical or horizontal orientation for the Navigation Bar, click on the Text option button, as shown in Figure 2.3. Then click on OK. Navigation bars are generated.

Study Break

Creating a Text Web Page

Practice what you have learned by adding a text page to a Web site.

First, create a file in Word or another text editor, and save the file in any text format with a TXT filename extension.

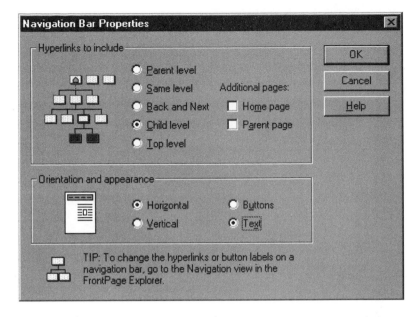

Figure 2.3 *Navigation Bars can conform to the constraints of a text-only environment.*

Next, import the file into an existing FrontPage Web site. Create a link to the TXT file from the site home page.

Finally, preview the site's home page in a Web browser. Test the link to the text page.

Another option, if visitors will be working in a text only environment, is to include *.txt text files in the Web site. These files can be viewed in browsers. They won't have the formatting features available in HTML Web pages. However, sometimes the purpose of a Web site is to make text files available to visitors in the fastest, rawest form possible.

Text files can be imported into FrontPage Web sites, and displayed in browsers. Text Files saved to TXT format with no line breaks will display in a browser without line breaks. They are harder to read, but easier to copy into a word processor for editing or printing. Text files saved to RTF format maintain much of their formatting.

The following set of steps can be used to move text documents from Word into a text-only Web site:

1. Open a text file in Word, and save it as either a text (TXT) or Rich Text Format (RTF) file.

2. With a FrontPage Web open, from the FrontPage Explorer select File, Import. The Import File to FrontPage Web dialog box appears.
3. Click on the Add File button in the dialog box, and navigate to the text file you wish to import into the Web, as shown in Figure 2.4.
4. Click on the Open button in the Add File to Import List dialog box.
5. Add additional files if appropriate, and then click on the OK button in the dialog box. The text files will be added to the Web.

After you import text files into your FrontPage 98 Web site, you can create navigational links to them, just as you would HTML files. Figure 2.5 shows a home page with links to two different types of text pages.

Text files display in browsers as no-frills text. They download quickly, and provide content while taking up very little space on a Web server. When you determine that text files are appropriate for a Web environment, you can use FrontPage to integrate them into a Web site. Figure 2.6 shows a text file displayed in a browser.

Modifying Tab Order

An often ignored sector of Web browsers are those who rely on keyboards to navigate a Web site. Keystroke navigation is not well known to users who have physical access to a mouse. But navigation keys are available in both

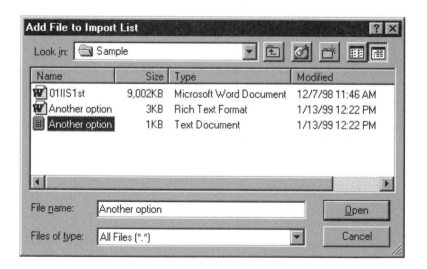

Figure 2.4 *Text files can be imported into FrontPage Webs.*

Netscape Navigator and Internet Explorer. For example, Alt+Left Arrow moves back, while Alt+Right Arrow moves forward in browsers.

Since input forms require some of the more intensive keystroking in Web browsing, it is particularly inconvenient to force visitors to reach for their mouse each time they wish to move from field to field.

The existence of mouseless web navigators, and the need to provide convenient keystroke access to input forms, compels Web designers to assign intuitive tab ordering to input forms. A visitor should be able to enter data in one form field, and then press the tab key to move intuitively to the next input field.

To assign tab order to form fields:

1. Open a FrontPage Web page with an input form. (For a full discussion of Input Forms, see Chapter 8.)

2 Right-click on an input form field, and select Form Field Properties from the context menu. Depending on the type of form field you have selected, an appropriate properties dialog box will appear.

3. In the Tab Order field of the dialog box, enter a number that will define the order in which a visitor will move to the selected field when he or she presses the tab key.

4. Continue to assign tab order values to the remaining fields in your input form.

Study Break

Assigning Tab Order to Form Fields

Practice what you have learned by assigning and testing tab order in form fields.

First, create an input form page for an existing Web site by selecting File, New and double-clicking on the template for the Feedback Form.

Next, assign tab orders to each of the fields in the form, starting by assigning 1 to the last field (the check box), and working backward so that the first field has tab order 12 assigned to it.

Finally, preview the site's home page in a Web browser. Test the assigned tab order by completing the form without using a mouse.

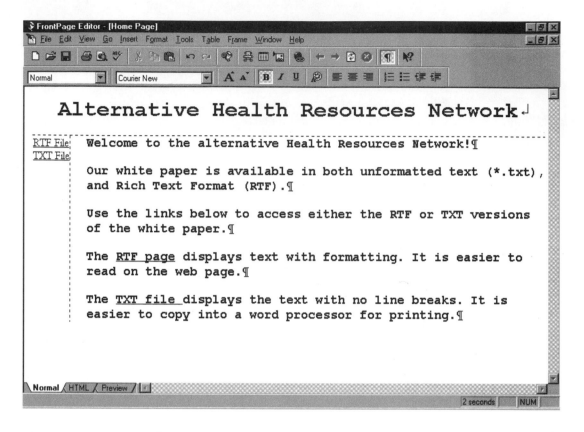

Figure 2.5 *Designing for a text-only Web environment.*

MCSD 2.3   Integrating with Existing Web Sites

Existing Web sites can be imported into FrontPage 98. When you do this, you make available all the ease of FrontPage Web development, including WYSIWYG HTML-less page design, codeless input forms, and the design features of Navigation view.

One challenge in converting an existing Web structure to FrontPage involves connecting existing databases with FrontPage. Topics include the relationship between existing databases and FrontPage Web sites, and meshing FrontPage Web sites with Active Server Pages. This is a somewhat uncharted element of FrontPage development, and a challenging set of ques-

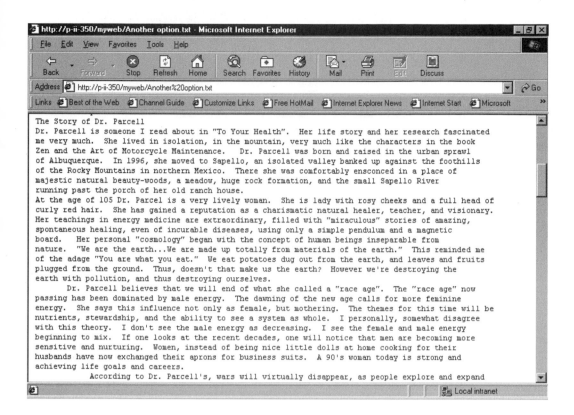

Figure 2.6 *Text files aren't pretty, but they convey content efficiently.*

tions in the test. It requires some knowledge of the world beyond FrontPage, and so this chapter will explore how FrontPage fits into existing business and organization environments.

Another challenge is to recognize and handle the constraints of an existing security system, particularly firewall protection that might prevent a developer from accessing and maintaining a site from a remote location.

You should be aware of potential pitfalls when integrating an existing Web site into FrontPage. Probably the most significant issue you will encounter is the existence of Active Server Page (ASP) scripts in an existing Web site. It is possible to integrate existing ASP pages with FrontPage, but you have to recognize them in an existing site, and make some adjustments in FrontPage to enable them.

FrontPage Webs—The Heart of FrontPage 98

Before I discuss the process for importing an existing Web site into Front-Page, you should understand how FrontPage organizes Web site files. Front-Page Webs are the method by which FrontPage 98 orchestrates all the files required for a FrontPage Web site to function. These files include not only HTML and image files, but other files as well. These additional files are generated by FrontPage and allow you to generate elements like input forms without resorting to CGI programming, PERL, Java, or other scripting languages.

In order to enable the features of FrontPage, all files in a Web site must be organized into a FrontPage Web. When you create a Web site from scratch in FrontPage 98, starting from the FrontPage Explorer, a FrontPage Web is automatically generated.

Importing Existing Web Sites

Before you can enjoy the benefits of using FrontPage to manage an existing Web site, you need to import that site into a FrontPage 98 Web. When you import existing Web site folders, FrontPage organizes them into a FrontPage Web. With the files imported into a FrontPage Web, you can begin to manage and edit the site in the FrontPage Explorer and the FrontPage Editor.

To import the files from an existing (non-FrontPage) Web site into a FrontPage 98 Web:

1. Open an existing FrontPage Web, or create a new one. You can use the Empty Web template to generate a FrontPage Web into which you will import an existing Web site.

2. Select File, Import to open the Import File to FrontPage Web dialog box.

3. Use the Add File button to add files to the file list in the dialog box, or use the Add Folder button to add entire folders from a local drive or Web server to the list. If you are importing a large number of files or folders, you may want to import them in batches instead of all at once just to reduce the risk of crashes.

4. After you have added all the files from an existing Web site to the list, click on the OK button in the dialog box to import the files into the open FrontPage Web.

Preserving Active Server Pages

Active Server Pages are Web pages that include built-in programming. ASP technology relies on files that are installed on the Web server. In that sense,

ASP technology is somewhat parallel to FrontPage 98, which also achieves much of its functionality by relying on extension files installed in servers. While many of the features of ASP are available through FrontPage, ASP technology includes additional features, the most significant of which is the ability to read and write database data to ODBC databases.

FrontPage allows you to integrate existing databases into Web sites utilizing both ASP pages, and ODBC registered databases. This process will be discussed in detail in the section "Using the Database Region Wizard" in Chapter 14 of this book. Here, I'll focus on how to integrate ASP technology when importing existing files into FrontPage 98.

FrontPage 98 does support ASP technology, but it requires some tweaking to get ASP and FrontPage to mesh. Files with an *.asp filename extension can be imported into FrontPage just like any other files. Then, you must install ASP to your server, and enable scripts to run in FrontPage. To install ASP to a server:

1. On the FrontPage 98 CD, locate the file
   E:\60 Minute Intranet Kit\60 Minute Intranet Kit\modules.
2. Double-click on the file to initiate the installation wizard.
3. The wizard will prompt you with the option of installing OBDC (including Microsoft Access and SQL server drivers). If these are not installed on your system, select this check box. The other option is to install online documentation, Adventure Works, and sample pages. If you are simply enabling existing Active Server Pages, you can skip this second option, but if you want to experiment with ASP and create Active Server Pages yourself, these are valuable options. Figure 2.7 shows both options selected in the installation wizard.
4. Complete the installation wizard, accepting or changing the default installation folders.

After installing ASP on your Web server, you need to enable scripting. FrontPage lets you turn (all) scripting on or off for selected folders. To do that:

1. In the FrontPage 98 Explorer, select Folders view.
2. Select the folder with the ASP files.
3. Select Edit, Properties (or press Alt+Enter). The Properties dialog box appears.
4. Select the Allow Scripts to Be Run check box, as shown in Figure 2.8, and click on Apply to enable scripting in the selected folder. Then, click on OK.

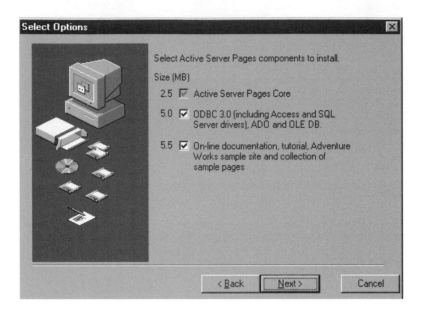

Figure 2.7 *The FrontPage 98 CD includes ASP files along with tutorials, samples and online documentation for ASP developers.*

Unique scripting properties can be assigned to specific folders within a Web. So, if you don't want to allow scripting in one folder, you can make that assignment in the Properties dialog box.

For more information on ASP, what it does, and how it works, you can visit: http://www.activeserverpages.com/.

Importing Non-FrontPage Web Pages into a FrontPage Web

Start this Study Break exercise by breaking one of the cardinal rules of FrontPage (you're an expert, it's OK for you to do this):

Create three different FrontPage Web pages in the FrontPage Editor without starting the FrontPage Explorer. Save them as HTML files to a file folder on your local drive.

Next, create a new FrontPage Web using the Empty Web template.

Then, import the two Web pages you saved as HTML files into the new Web.

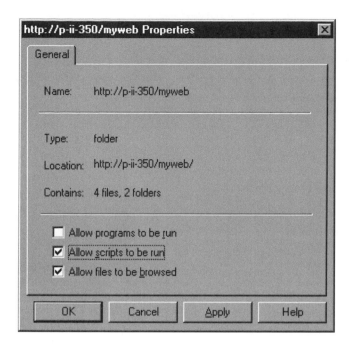

Figure 2.8 *Script enabling must be assigned to FrontPage Web folders that in-clude ASP files.*

Finally, examine the Web with the imported pages in Folder view. You can experiment with the three pages in the FrontPage Explorer Navigation view.

MCSD 2.4   Integrating with Existing Applications

As you investigate maintenance requirements for a FrontPage Web development project, you will want to identify and analyze major transition issues. Two of the most important of these are integrating with existing security systems, and integrating with existing databases.

If an organization, for example, is depending on its FrontPage-generated Web site to provide interactive online database querying, this is a major project. You will need to assess this, and make an informed decision on an approach to providing this query ability.

Security systems present a number of challenges to you as a FrontPage 98 Web developer. You may need permission to cross an internal firewall protecting a Web server in order to access and work on a Web from outside the organization. You will also need to navigate through firewall protection in order to test external links as you create a Web site in FrontPage.

The following two sections will provide an overview of security issues, and database connectivity. They will provide you with the information you need to make an initial assessment of development requirements. Chapter 14 will provide a more detailed explanation of approaches to integrating FrontPage 98 with databases.

Integrating with Existing Security Systems

Large servers utilize firewall software to prevent Web site visitors from penetrating into internal server files. If the development environment for your FrontPage Web site includes a firewall, you can configure FrontPage to use a Proxy Server to access the Internet through the firewall. A Proxy Server can also be used to access files protected by a firewall from a remote location. So, if your mission is to design and/or manage a Web site protected by a firewall from a different location, you will need to use a Proxy Server to get through firewall protection.

Actual addresses for Proxy access are assigned by a server administrator. They will typically be a URL address, and often followed by a port setting (like http//www.wxy.com:2010). If you are accessing internal servers, these too can be provided by a network administrator and defined in FrontPage.

In addition to allowing you to pass through a firewall to do Web development, defining a Proxy Server allows you to use the FrontPage Editor to test links outside of a firewall during Web development, and to open Web pages outside of the firewall. It also allows you to test external links as you develop your Web site using the Hyperlink Status view.

We'll examine Proxy Servers and their relationship to Web security in detail in Chapter 17. Here, I'll quickly walk you through the process of defining Proxy Server settings:

1. With your Web open, select Tools, Options.
2. Select the Proxies tab, as shown in Figure 2.9.
3. Enter the URL you will be using for Proxy access to the Web server.
4. Use the Lists of Hosts Without Proxy area of the dialog box to enter internal (intranet) servers that you will be using. The Do Not Use Proxy Server for Intranet Addresses check box disables the Proxy Server when you are connecting to internal Web servers.
5. After you define Proxy Server settings, click on OK.

Meshing with Existing Databases

FrontPage 98 can be used to access existing databases. For example, if you maintain an inventory of products in an Access database, you can import that database into your FrontPage Web, and allow visitors to view data that is drawn from that database.

The process is far from the friendliest feature of FrontPage 98. Still, if linking to an existing database is a critical element of your Web development project, FrontPage can manage the task.

The process of meshing a FrontPage Web site with an existing database is rather complex, but it can be done. For a step-by-step walkthrough of integrating an active database into a FrontPage Web, see the section "Using the Database Region Wizard" in Chapter 14.

The most complete discussion of connecting databases to FrontPage 98 Webs is found in Chapter 17 of *The FrontPage Bible*, by David Elderbrock with Paul Bodensiek.

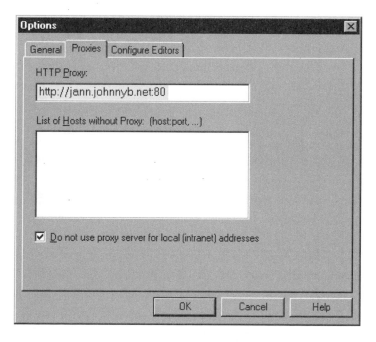

Figure 2.9 *You can define Proxy Settings to access the Internet through a firewall.*

Study Break

Connecting FrontPage Web via a Proxy Server

In Chapter 17 at the end of this book, I'll go more deeply into the role of Proxy servers, and how to set them up. For our purposes here, assume that you have walked into a FrontPage environment, and that the server administrator has informed you that the Proxy Server is connected at http://webcor.web.net:80.

Start by configuring the FrontPage Web to connect via the proxy server for which you were given a URL.

Then, set the Proxy connection so that FrontPage will not use the proxy server for a local (intranet) address.

Finally, OK the Proxy server settings. Then, go back into the Proxy Server settings and remove the Proxy.

■ Summary

In this chapter, we explored how FrontPage Web development requires you to assess and respond to a variety of specific requirements for particular browser and development environments. You can design FrontPage Webs for text-only browser environments. You can use FrontPage to define tab order for input forms. And you can make your site accessible to text-only browsers by assigning alternate text to images.

Along with responding to browser requirements, we also looked at particular development environments, and how they affect the process of creating FrontPage Webs. You can integrate existing Web content from non-FrontPage Webs by importing files into FrontPage Webs. Active Server Pages can be imported into a Web. And FrontPage Web development can be managed through existing, defined security systems including Proxy Servers.

▲ CHAPTER REVIEW QUESTIONS

Here are a some practice questions relating to the material covered in the "Analyzing Maintenance Web Requirements" area of Microsoft's Designing and Implementing Web Sites Using Microsoft FrontPage 98 exam (70-055).

1. *Firewall protection is best handled by assigning a Proxy Server.*
   A. True
   B. False

2. *Which of the following file formats are universally interpreted by browsers?*

    A. TXT format text files

    B. DOC format Word files

    C. HTML HyperText Markup Language files

    D. Adobe *.PDF files

    E. FTP files

3. *You can facilitate data input in a form fields by which of the following. (Select all correct answers.)*

    A. Hot keys

    B. Assigned tab key order

    C. Data entry macros

    D. All text page display

4. *The best way to convert an existing Web site to a FrontPage Web is to open the existing pages as files in the FrontPage Editor.*

    A. True

    B. False

5. *Importing a database through the Database Region Wizard requires that you first create a DSN file.*

    A. True

    B. False

6. *Which of the following are needed to complete the Database Region Wizard? (Select all correct answers.)*

    A. SQL queries

    B. TXT files

    C. SSL encryption

    D. Existing Active Server Pages

    E. Internet Explorer 4.0 or higher

7. *FrontPage Web pages can be published as Active Server Pages provided (select all correct answers):*

    A. The server has Microsoft Internet Information Server version II or higher.

    B. Scripting is enabled for the folder containing the pages.

    C. The page is going to be visited by browsers that interpret Java.

    D. The server to which the pages are published has ASP extensions.

    E. The browser used to visit the page is SQL enabled.

8. *ASP can be installed to a server from files on the FrontPage 98 CD.*
   A. True
   B. False

9. *ASP files can be edited in FrontPage 98.*
   A. True
   B. False

10. *The best way to circumvent a firewall when managing a FrontPage site from a remote location is to assign a Proxy Server.*
    A. True
    B. False

11. *Proxy Servers require that a Web site be published to a server with FrontPage extensions.*
    A. True
    B. False

12. *Where in FrontPage are Proxy Servers defined? (Select all correct answers.)*
    A. In the Options dialog box in the FrontPage Editor
    B. In the Options dialog box in the FrontPage Explorer
    C. In the Navigation area of the FrontPage Explorer
    D. In the Page Properties dialog box of the FrontPage Editor
    E. In the visitor's browser

13. *Scripting can be enabled for an entire Web, but not for individual folders.*
    A. True
    B. False

14. *An existing, off-line database can be queried interactively through a FrontPage Web site.*
    A. True
    B. False

15. *Which of the following are good reasons to provide alternate text for Web site images? (Select all correct answers.)*
    A. To assist sight-impaired browsers
    B. To provide online captions in modern browsers
    C. To provide links to image thumbnails
    D. To provide access to frameless browsers
    E. To provide content for browsers with pictures disabled

Defining the Technical Architecture for a FrontPage 98 Web Site

The exam for Microsoft Certified Professional status in FrontPage 98 puts a great deal of emphasis on the ability to make an overall assessment of the Web development environment in which FrontPage is being implemented.

Like a surveyor laying the groundwork for erecting a building, one of your first tasks is to identify the "terrain" on which FrontPage is being imposed. Under ideal circumstances, that terrain is a smooth, flat, empty field, free of other technologies. In many cases that may be true. Web development may begin and end with FrontPage. In that situation, it isn't as critical for developers to worry about Web elements that fall outside of those generated automatically by FrontPage.

In real life, FrontPage will often be implemented on top of a complex existing Web structure. In this chapter, we will focus on how to identify and assess other Web development technology with which you must mesh a FrontPage Web site.

Much of the material covered in this chapter will be explored in depth, and in other contexts, throughout this book. Here, I will be emphasizing the information necessary to make an overall assessment of how different development technologies integrate with FrontPage.

At the conclusion of this chapter you will be able to:

- Embed scripts in VBScript and JavaScript in FrontPage Web pages.
- Understand how Java and ActiveX integrate with FrontPage 98.
- Identify the relationship between FrontPage Components and other Web development technologies.
- Understand the role and limitations of the two versions of Personal Web Server.
- Integrate FrontPage Web development with Microsoft IIS.
- Mesh FrontPage Web development with competing server platforms like Apache and Netscape.

MCSD 3.1   Assessing the Use of Technologies in a Development Environment

The world of Web development is a chaotic stew of meshing and competing technologies. While our job is not to applaud or criticize Microsoft's strategic vision, it is helpful to step back from the technical side of things and understand the Microsoft vision in order to put some of what we are about to explore in perspective. Microsoft would like to see FrontPage 98 and its "big brother," InterDev, become development environments that encompass and integrate all these technologies under a big umbrella.

To take one possible scenario: You, the all-knowing FrontPage MCP/MCSD, are responsible for implementing FrontPage in an environment where existing Web pages use Java applets to process form data, media is delivered through Netscape Navigator compatible plug-ins, and the Web site resides on an Apache server that does not have FrontPage extensions. You need to be able to identify the conflicts posed by bringing all this activity into a FrontPage Web, and identify options for resolving those conflicts.

Table 3.1 identifies a variety of technologies, and how FrontPage handles them:

Table 3.1 *FrontPage and Web Technologies*

Web Technology	How FrontPage Handles It
VBScript	Can be embedded in pages using the Script dialog box (Insert, Advanced, Scripts). You cannot mix JavaScripts and VBScripts on the same page.
JavaScripts	Can be embedded in pages using the Script dialog box. You cannot mix JavaScripts and VBScripts on the same page.
Java Applets	Can be called from within a page in the FrontPage Editor using the Java Applet Properties dialog box (Insert, Advanced, Java Applet). You must first import the compiled *.class Java file(s) required for the applet.
Frames	FrontPage creates framed pages without the need of outside technologies.
Data input management	FrontPage server extensions eliminate the need for special CGI form management scripts. However, FrontPage input forms can be linked to ISAPI (Internet Server Application Programming Interface), NSAPI (Netscape Server Application Programming Interface), or CGI scripts.
DHTML	FrontPage generates Dynamic HyperText Markup Language (DHTML) that is compatible with Internet Explorer 4.0 and higher. Generating Netscape-friendly DHTML in FrontPage is, for practical purposes, impossible.
ActiveX controls	FrontPage allows you to define ActiveX controls.
Plug-ins	FrontPage makes it easy to embed plug-ins for any application (see chapter 12).

Study Break

Assessing the Practicality of Integrating Different Technologies in a FrontPage Web

For this study break, assume that you've walked into a room full of developers who want to know in a nutshell whether or not the technologies they want can be managed by FrontPage. Their "wish list" includes Java applets, Netscape-compatible DHTML, ActiveX controls to display multimedia content, and existing CGI form handling scripts at the Web server. And, they want to develop Web pages with both JavaScript and VBScript elements.

First, identify elements that can be relatively painlessly plugged into a FrontPage Web.

Then, identify elements in the developers' wish list that can be utilized with FrontPage, but for which FrontPage provides alternate ways of developing that work more smoothly with FrontPage Webs.

Finally, identify problem areas where the elements requested by the developers present major compatibility problems with FrontPage 98.

Integrating Scripts into FrontPage Webs

In this part of this chapter, we'll look at different scripting technologies and examine how they can be integrated into FrontPage. I wouldn't dare to attempt to provide even an introductory exploration of each scripting language here. What we'll do is assume that you walk into a development environment where there are existing scripts that you are expected to integrate into FrontPage 98 Webs.

- VB Script
- JavaScript
- Java
- ActiveX Controls
- FrontPage Components

All of these options allow you to smoothly integrate interactive elements into your Web site. What does interactive mean? In the context we are discussing, it means that the Web page interacts with the visitor, rather than presenting the same static information no matter what the visitor does. For example, Figure 3.1 illustrates three types of interactive scripting objects in a Web page. The page displays a greeting (either Good Morning, Good Evening, or in the figure, Good Afternoon), a dialog box that pops up when a button is pressed, and an online calculator.

The greeting in Figure 3.1 is interactive because it depends on the time at which the site is visited. The Dialog box is interactive in that it is activated only when the visitor presses a button on the page. And the calculator is interactive because it displays the results of a calculation entered by the visitor. Other interactive elements often include special effects like glowing or moving objects that react to a visitor's mouse movements or mouse clicks.

All the scripting methods available in FrontPage have much in common. They all create *client-side* programs that run on the visitor's browser, as opposed to a Web server. That means that they are browser dependent, and not all browsers interpret all scripts. In fact, probably the most significant difference between these scripting options is that VBScript and ActiveX controls are not interpreted by the Netscape Navigator 4.5. Java and JavaScript are the most universally interpreted scripting languages.

If scripts are being developed for a closed system, like an intranet where everyone is using IE as their browser, then you can confidently develop scripts using any of these languages. If not, there is an argument to be made for developing scripts using the more globally accepted Java and JavaScript.

Figure 3.1 *Interactive scripted elements in a Web page.*

Since all scripting options share the feature of creating client-side programs, they are all faster than programs that require interacting with a server. These scripts are easily visible to any visitor who elects to view a Web page's source code in his or her browser. Therefore, there are "no secrets" in terms of your scripting code. You are basically posting your code on the Web as well as the program, for all to see.

Does all this mean that scripts are never appropriate for a server? No, it does not. There are situations where saving a script to a server is appropriate. For example, if you want to protect the script from being viewed (or stolen) by a competitor, you can protect it by saving it to a server. This is rarely done, as it undercuts the speed necessary to make most scripts effective.

FrontPage allows you to implement scripts by writing (or copying) them into the Script dialog box. One limitation of FrontPage's ability to handle scripting languages is that you are constrained to one scripting language per page. So, if you are using JavaScript coding on a page, you can't mix in VBScript.

As a FrontPage expert, you should be prepared for an environment where it is necessary to integrate existing scripts into a FrontPage Web.

While we will take a quick look at ActiveX and Java here, these somewhat related ways of adding interactive elements to Web pages are discussed in more depth in Chapter 11.

Integrating VB Scripts

VBScript is an offshoot of Microsoft's Visual Basic. If your development environment is comfortable with Visual Basic, they will enjoy the ability to port those skills into Web development with VBScripts. VBScripts can range from a one-line script that displays the current date, to pages of code that create an ordering system that can be easily plugged into FrontPage Web pages.

Another advantage of VBScript is that it integrates smoothly with ActiveX components in FrontPage. ActiveX components are discussed in chapter 11. Microsoft uses VBScript for most of FrontPage's Components and Active Elements.

VBScript is compatible only with Internet Explorer version 3 or higher. As mentioned earlier, Netscape Navigator 4.5 will not interpret VBScript. However, a plug-in is available from NCompass Labs that allows Netscape browsers to implement VBScripts. That plug-in is available free from NCompass. If you are creating VBScripts and want to make them available to all visitors, you can include a link to the NCompass site at:

http://www.ncompasslabs.com

To embed VBScript in a FrontPage Web:

1. Create or open a FrontPage Web, and create or open a Web page in the FrontPage Editor.

Note   If you open an existing Web page in which you plan to embed **VBScript**ing, that page cannot have any other language scripts embedded in it.

2. Select Insert, Advanced, Script, and click on the VBScript options button, as shown in Figure 3.2.

Figure 3.2 *Embedding VBScript.*

3. Enter or copy your VBScript into the Script dialog box, then click on OK.

4. After you embed your VBScript, a [please insert VBSCRIPT.TIF] symbol will display in your Web page to indicate the location of the script. This icon only displays if the Show/Hide ¶ tool is selected in the Standard toolbar.

While the Script dialog box does not have an error-checking feature, you can test your script by viewing your page in the FrontPage Editor Preview tab. Script errors will be identified by a message in the status bar. You can also error check by viewing your page in Internet Explorer, where a similar error message displays in the status bar if your script has an error. Figure 3.3 shows the error dialog box that appears when you double-click in the status bar of Internet Explorer. Clicking the Details button in the dialog box provides hints as to where the errors are in your script.

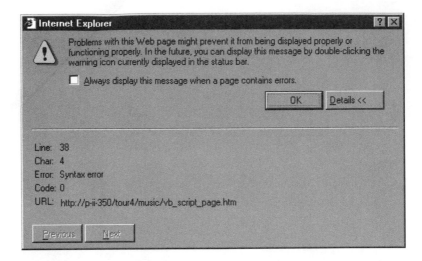

Figure 3.3 *Identifying script errors.*

A good source of sample (and useful) VBScripts is the VBScript area of Microsoft's Web site. At this writing, you can find a collection of scripts and tutorials at:

http://msdn.microsoft.com/scripting/default.htm?/scripting/vbscript/samples/vbssamp.htm

Other resources that provide a useful introduction to VBScript include:

- *The FrontPage 98 Bible* by David Elderbrock with Paul Bodensiek, chapter 15
- *FrontPage 98 for Dummies* by Asha Dornfest includes a bonus chapter on scripting on the CD that provides a good introduction to scripting in FrontPage
- *Special Edition Using FrontPage 98* by Neil Randall and Dennis Jones includes chapters on VBScript and JavaScript.

Study Break

Inserting a VBScript in a Web Page

Reinforce your understanding of embedding VBScripts by creating a page with a simple VBScript.

1. Open an existing FrontPage Web or create a new one, and create a new Web page.

2. Select Insert, Advanced, Script. In the Script dialog box, select the VBScript option button.

3. Enter the following code in the Script dialog box, as shown in Figure 3.4.

```
h = Hour(Now)
If h < 12 then
Document.Write "Good morning! "
ElseIf h < 17 then
Document.Write "Good afternoon! "
Else
Document.Write "Good evening! "
End If
```

4. Click on OK to close the dialog box, and test the script in the Preview tab of the FrontPage Editor.

If this script is entered correctly, and interpreted by a browser, it will display either "Good morning!" "Good afternoon!" or "Good evening!" depending on the time of day on a user's system clock.

Figure 3.4 *Embedded VBScript.*

Embedding JavaScripts

JavaScript is similar in syntax to Java, but is a separate and different scripting language. Its advantages are its global acceptance by browsers, and the fact that programmers who are comfortable with Java can quickly pick up JavaScript. Both Netscape Navigator and Internet Explorer versions 3 and higher interpret JavaScripts.

There are many online resources for JavaScript samples and free utilities. JavaScript seems to attract some really clever 15-year-olds who are obsessed with wild special effects and games. If you're in the mood for a *real* study break, you can jump online and do a quick search for JavaScript games. In Figure 3.5, I'm making a quick stop at http://plaza.harmonic.ne.jp/, where I've found an online video game. A few minutes at this site should increase my overall productivity.

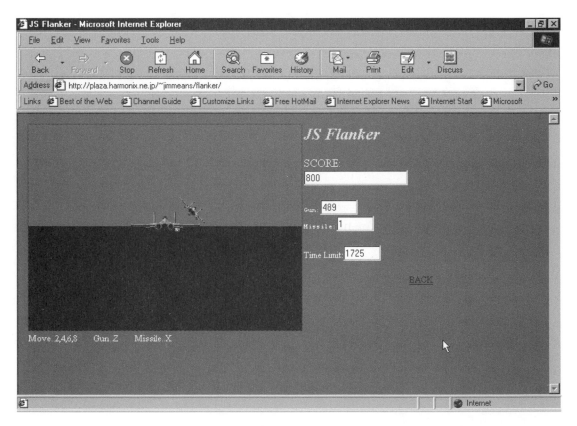

Figure 3.5 *JavaScript attracts creative coders who have filled the Internet with free online games.*

If you're looking for samples and tutorials that are more focused on functional JavaScript objects, you'll find a nice selection at these sites:

http://www.thefreesite.com/freejava.htm

http://javascript.internet.com

http://developer.netscape.com/tech

To embed a JavaScript in a FrontPage Web:

1. Create or open a FrontPage Web, and create or open a Web page in the FrontPage Editor.

Note

If you open an existing Web page in which you plan to embed JavaScript, that page cannot have any VBScripts or other (non JavaScript) coding embedded in it.

2. Select Insert, Advanced, Script, and click on the JavaScript options button.
3. Enter or copy your JavaScript code into the Script dialog box, as shown in Figure 3.6. Then click on OK.
4. After you embed your JavaScript, a [please insert JSCRIPT.TIF] symbol will display in your Web page to indicate the location of the script. This icon only displays if the Show/Hide ¶ tool is selected in the Standard toolbar.

As with VBScripts, you can test your JavaScript code by viewing your page in Internet Explorer. If IE detects an error, you can double-click on the error message in the status bar to see a detailed description of the error. Netscape Navagator has a similar error-trapping feature that notes faulty code in the Status bar.

Aside from entering embedded JavaScripts through the Script dialog box, you can embed JavaScript directly into a Web page through the HTML tab in the FrontPage Editor, or even by entering a line of JavaScript in the URL box in the Create or Edit Hyperlink dialog boxes. This is appropriate for a very short command, or for a JavaScript command that is inserted, for example, instead of a URL for a hyperlink. However, if you are placing a significant amount of script, it is more convenient to organize it in the Script dialog box where it can be kept track of, and easily edited.

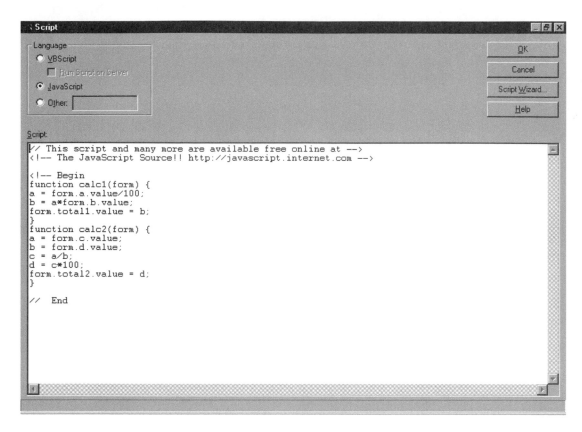

Figure 3.6 *Entering JavaScript.*

Study Break

Inserting JavaScript in a Hyperlink

Experiment with JavaScript by entering a line of code in a Create Hyperlink dialog box that assigns an attribute to a hyperlink so that the link will return the visitor to the last page he or she visited.

1. Open an existing FrontPage Web or create a new one, and create a new Web page.

2. Enter a line of text that reads "Click here to return to your previous page." Double-click to select the word "here" and click on the Create Hyperlink button in the toolbar.

3. Enter the following code in the Script dialog box, as shown in Figure 3.7.

```
javascript:history.go(-1)
```

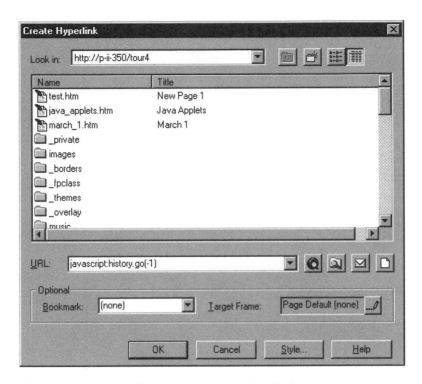

Figure 3.7 *Embedding JavaScript in a hyperlink.*

4. Click on OK to close the dialog box, and test the JavaScript hyperlink in a browser.

Implementing Java in FrontPage Webs

Java applets are handled differently than the JavaScript and VBScripts we just explored. Java applets are organized in separate files, usually with a *.class file name extension, and are saved as part of the Web site.

We'll explore integrating Java applets with FrontPage in more detail in Chapter 11, but for now you should be aware that the basic routine for integrating Java applets is to import the *.class files into your Web.

FrontPage, itself, generates *.class files when you embed a Hover button, one of the Active Elements in FrontPage. These Java applets are stored to the folder _fpclass that is generated when you create a Hover button. Figure 3.8 shows the a folder with *.class files in the FrontPage Explorer.

When you import a Java applet into FrontPage, you can call that applet into a page by selecting Insert, Advanced, Java Applet. The Java Applet

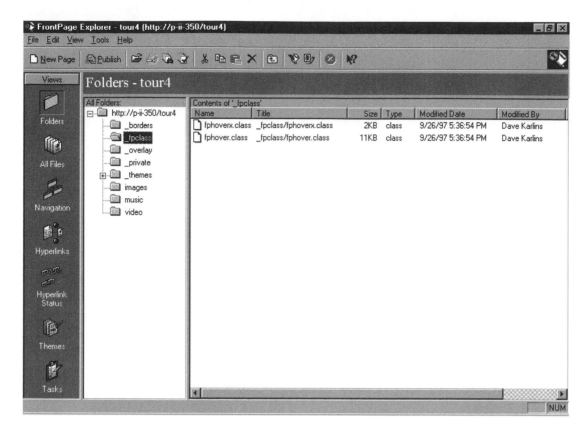

Figure 3.8   *Java applets are saved as files.*

Properties dialog box appears, as shown in Figure 3.9. Enter the filename of the applet in the Applet Source box, and the folder (in your Web site) in which the file is stored in the Applet Base URL box. You can include a message for browsers that do not interpret Java in the Message for Browsers without Java Support.

For more discussion of Java in FrontPage, see Chapter 11.

Assessing the Use of ActiveX Controls

ActiveX controls can be used to display all kinds of media, and also as objects (like buttons) in conjunction with VBScript.

Using ActiveX controls to create interactive Web elements is discussed in Chapter 11. The use of ActiveX controls to present media is explored in Chapter 11.

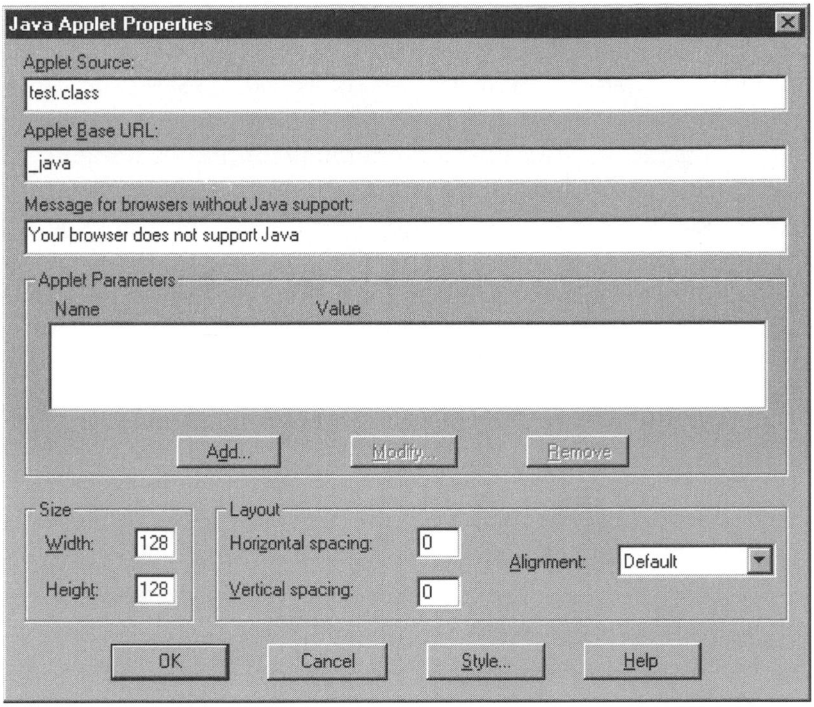

Figure 3.9 *Placing a Java applet.*

Using FrontPage Components

FrontPage's Components and Active Elements provide a set of built-in interactive objects, like Hover buttons, banner ad managers, and hit counters.

Here, I'll just note a few features of components and active elements to situate them in the context of scripting. Most active elements and components rely on VBScript, although Hover buttons, as we've seen, generate Java applets. Some active elements and components require FrontPage server extensions, and are server-side scripts.

Each of the components and active elements is explored in Chapter 5.

MCSD 3.3   Assessing the Use of Server Products

There are two options for implementing FrontPage on a Web server. FrontPage Webs can be published to a server with FrontPage extensions, or to a server without FrontPage extensions. Each alternative is discussed in Chapter 10, where we explore the process of posting FrontPage content to a Web server.

Here, I want to address issues related to implementing FrontPage on a variety of servers. In Chapter 6, "Establishing a Development Environment," I'll address the process of installing FrontPage extensions to a server. But the first step in integrating FrontPage development with an existing server is to know which servers can support FrontPage extensions, and for which servers FrontPage extension files are available.

FrontPage 98 Server Extensions are available for both Windows and Unix based servers, including

- Apache 1.1.3, 1.2.4, 1.2.5
- CERN 3.0
- FrontPage 97 Personal Web Server
- Internet Information Server 2.0 or higher
- Microsoft Personal Web Server (on Windows 95)
- Microsoft Personal Web Server (on Windows 98)
- NCSA1.5.2 (not 1.5a or 1.5.1)
- O'Reilly WebSite and WebSite Pro 1.x and 2.0

You can find a current list of servers for which there are FP extensions available at:

http://officeupdate.microsoft.com/frontpage/wpp/platforms.htm

The following sections provide some comments on implementing FrontPage with different server options.

Using the FrontPage Personal Web Server

The FrontPage Personal Web Server ships with FrontPage 98. It is a development tool capable of testing FrontPage Web sites, including elements that require FrontPage server extension files, like input form management, passwords and image maps.

Limitations of the FrontPage Personal Web Server include the fact that Access Permission settings are not available. However, almost all of the functionality of FrontPage can be tested in the FrontPage Personal Web Server.

The FrontPage PWS runs invisibly (except that it is indicated in the Windows taskbar).

Upgrading to the Microsoft Personal Web Server

Microsoft Personal Web Server (at this writing, version 4.0) ships with IE 4 and higher, and is included with Microsoft Office 2000. Microsoft PWS 4.0

is a more robust version of the FrontPage Personal Web Server, with a more accessible interface, shown in Figure 3.10.

The Microsoft Personal Web Server features something called the Personal Web Manager (shown in Figure 3.10) that allows control over server operation (for example, you can stop the server from running if you wish). It also offers some neat little features for creating virtual directories and logging Website traffic. If you created a Web site using the FrontPage PWS, you can install the Microsoft PWS without disrupting your Web development.

One limitation is that even the new, improved PWS does not allow you to test collecting data input through e-mail.

Microsoft PWS can be used to manage a small corporate intranet when installed on a server. PWS supports Active Server Pages (ASP), so you can also use it to test ASP pages. But the real use of Microsoft PWS, like its ancestor the FrontPage PWS, is for developing sites that will later be published to more powerful servers.

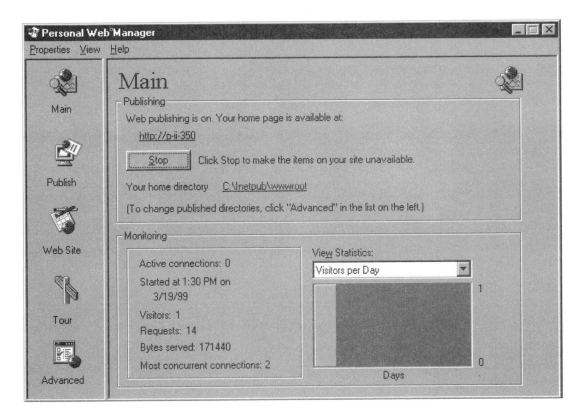

Figure 3.10   *The beefed-up MS Personal Web Server.*

MS PWS comes with a sample root Web, named by default with your computer's system name. This root Web can be replaced with your own FrontPage Web site.

A tutorial on running the Microsoft Personal Web Server is included in *Teach Yourself FrontPage 98 in a Week* by David Karlins with Stephanie Cottrell.

Using Microsoft Internet Information Server

Microsoft Internet Information Server (IIS) is included with Microsoft Windows NT. Unlike the PWS, IIS is capable of handling a full-fledged Web site with multiple visitors on an intranet or on the Internet.

Configuring your own IIS server for the Internet, or an intranet, is beyond the scope of this book and beyond the knowledge you need as a FrontPage expert. Installing and configuring IIS on NT falls within the realm of expertise expected of an NT administrator.

There is an introductory tutorial on installing IIS on NT in *Teach Yourself FrontPage 98* in a Week by David Karlins with Stephanie Cottrell.

There are several advantages to running FrontPage Webs on IIS. You can incorporate firewalls and other security attributes of the NT server installation. And you can assign permissions, and administer who has access to what level of Web access and development. Managing access to Webs is discussed in Chapter 17.

A FrontPage intranet can easily be grafted onto an existing NT networking system. This, again, is the province of the NT administrator, but something you should be aware of in assessing the potential for bringing FrontPage into an NT environment.

Integrating with Netscape Servers

Netscape, while best known for its popular Web browser, makes its money selling Web server software. FrontPage is compatible with Netscape servers if FrontPage extension files are downloaded and installed on a Netscape server.

FrontPage extensions are available for the following Netscape servers:

- Netscape Commerce Server 1.12
- Netscape Communications Server 1.12
- Netscape Enterprise 2.0 and 3.0
- Netscape FastTrack 2.0

Working with Apache Server

Apache servers allow Unix systems to function as Web servers, and Front-Page extensions are available for Apache servers.

Many commercial Apache Web servers have installed FrontPage extensions, and support FrontPage Web sites. These servers (with FrontPage extensions) support all FrontPage features, including themes, counters, and input form management.

One limitation of Unix servers is that they don't reliably support ODBC database features. If your development environment requires ODBC database access, you might consider recommending NT as a better platform to host the site.

Study Break

Identifying the Appropriate Server

Assume that you have been asked to select appropriate servers for a Web development project.

First, identify an appropriate server on which to develop a Web on a local system, before it is shared on an intranet or the Internet.

Then, pick a server that will reliably support a full-featured FrontPage Web that will include ODBC database connections.

Finally, answer the question: Can a full-featured FrontPage intranet be published to a Netscape server?

■ Summary

For many FrontPage 98 users, the built-in and closed environment provided by FrontPage allows them to create FrontPage Webs, while remaining peacefully oblivious to compatibility issues posed by technology like scripting languages, server extensions and database connections.

Some advanced Web features, however, cannot be generated by Front-Page, and require additional scripting. In other scenarios, existing Web elements created using scripts need to be integrated into a new FrontPage Web. For these reasons, FrontPage experts have to be aware of which technologies can be gracefully integrated into FrontPage, and which pose integration problems. JavaScript, VBScript, ActiveX and Java applets can all be plugged into FrontPage Webs.

▲ CHAPTER REVIEW QUESTIONS

1. *Which of the following can help debug scripts? (Select all correct answers.)*
    A. The Script Debugger in the Script dialog box
    B. Error messages in the Preview tab
    C. Error messages in Netscape Navigator
    D. Microsoft SourceSafe
    E. Microsoft Debugger

2. *JavaScript and VBScripts can both coexist in a FrontPage Web.*
    A. True
    B. False

3. *Which of the following are potential sources for JavaScript code? (Select all correct answers.)*
    A. Web sites that provide sample code
    B. Professional coders/
    C. Java applets
    D. VBScript

4. *Java applets are (Select all correct answers.)*
    A. Stored in files
    B. Embedded in HTML code
    C. Copied, or written in the Script dialog box
    D. Dependent on browser compatibility

5. *The FrontPage Personal Web Server is appropriate for which of these uses? (Select all correct answers.)*
    A. Hosting intranet Webs with significant Web traffic
    B. Hosting Internet Webs
    C. Testing FrontPage Webs during development
    D. Hosting FrontPage Webs that will be published to other servers

6. *JavaScripts can be run on a Web server through the FrontPage Script dialog box.*

   A. True

   B. False

7. *One limitation of using VBScripts is that they are not interpreted by Netscape Navigator without a plug-in.*

   A. True

   B. False

8. *Which of the following interactive elements can not be created using the scripts dialog box? (Select all correct answers.)*

   A. Online calculation

   B. Interactive greetings

   C. Java applets

   D. Interactive buttons

9. *Netscape servers cannot provide full functionality for FrontPage Web sites.*

   A. True

   B. False

10. *Some FrontPage components and active elements require FrontPage extensions to function.*

    A. True

    B. False

Designing a Web Site

Professional level FrontPage expertise includes the ability to orchestrate the development of a FrontPage Web in a large-scale and complex environment. In Chapter 4, we'll look at how to implement FrontPage design tools, as well as how to construct an overview for implementing a FrontPage Web. In Chapter 5, we'll do a crash course in constructing user interfaces using FrontPage's design tools, components and active elements. And, in Chapter 6, we'll cover elements of the Web development environment, including integrating with Visual SourceSafe, installing server extensions, and implementing versions of the Personal Web Server.

Developing a Conceptual Design for a Web Site

In this chapter, we will look at material covered in the Developing a Conceptual Design for a Web Site section of Microsoft's Designing and Implementing Web Sites Using FrontPage 98 exam (70-055). Microsoft defines the objectives of this section as: Construct a conceptual design that is based on a variety of scenarios that include:

- Constructing workflow process
- Constructing task sequence
- Satisfying user requirements for interface
- Maintaining a site
- Training

Much of the material in this chapter refers to working in the FrontPage Explorer, particularly in Navigation, Theme, Hyperlinks and Hyperlink Status views. The unifying theme is being prepared to macro-manage Web site development in FrontPage 98.

At the conclusion of this chapter you will be able to:

• Use Task View in the FrontPage Explorer to organize and document Web development

• Design Web structure in Navigation view

• Implement Shared Borders

• Create Navigation Bars

• Assign Themes

• Utilize FrontPage's templates and wizards

• Perform global site editing

• Update hyperlink status

MCSD 4.1   Constructing a Workflow Process

Large Web sites are major projects, like building airports, implementing a training program, or creating a new software application. A recent survey listed Web site manager as the best job in the United States. True or not (whatever happened to point guard in the NBA, or WNBA??), Web managers have tremendous responsibility.

As a FrontPage expert, you are aware of the need to start from a macro plan, and an overview. However, as you interface with clients, be prepared to patiently educate them on the need for this kind of approach. Don't underestimate the need to reorient the client who wants to start talking about designing his or her Web *pages,* before agreeing on an overall structure for a Web site.

FrontPage comes with built-in features that facilitate the process of Web design, implementation and management. FrontPage won't replace your skill at investigating user needs, sizing up a project, and developing a conceptual approach for a Web site. But it will help you organize that process.

In a word, FrontPage's ability to assist in organizing the implementation of a Web project lies in the FrontPage Explorer. The FrontPage 98 Explorer is the control center from which you can macro-manage and document the plan, status and progress of a Web site. In this chapter, we'll explore elements of the FrontPage Explorer, and how they fit into the process of developing and implementing a conceptual design for a Web site. We'll also look at related implementation issues like training.

A friend of mine who does project management seminars emphasizes the importance of pencil sketches on the back of an envelope before you launch your project management software package, the point being that before you dive into a development project you will want to have a clear overview of the basic structure of your project. That is just as applicable to Web implementation. One of the closest things I've found to just such a low-tech environment is Navigation view in the FrontPage Explorer, where you can arrange a navigational hierarchy or flow for your site.

Sketch a Workflow Process for Web Development

Practice what you have learned by sketching out on a sheet of paper the tasks required for the following Web development project.

First, a general navigational structure for the site has to be created.

Along with that, artwork and text content needs to be created and collected. A color scheme for the site must be chosen. Existing Web content must be imported, and new content created. The entire site must then be "put together" in FrontPage.

Using a piece of paper, draw a flow-chart diagramming how this Web site will come together.

The flowchart in Figure 4.1, for example, outlines a basic overview of a Web site in development. Visitors will be presented with three options from the home page, and those three options will in turn provide other limited sets of choices. The "Ordering" page is not linked to the flowchart, because

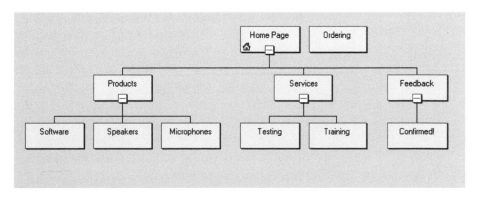

Figure 4.1 *Starting out with a basic plan.*

links to it will be built into every page. This simple structure will be the foundation from which a Web site with hundreds of pages can be generated.

In this case, the basic outline was drawn right in the FrontPage Explorer, although a piece of scratch paper and a pencil provided the rough sketch that preceded it. In section 4.3, I'll explain the process of designing a Web structure in Navigation view in detail.

MCSD 4.2 Defining Task Sequence

Particularly in a large development environment, where hundreds or thousands of Web pages are managed by dozens of developers, designers, programmers, artists and sales managers (to take one possible scenario), maintaining control over assigned and completed tasks is critical. The embarrassing broken links, unfinished pages and unedited Web content that one still finds on many high-profile Web sites is testimony to the need for such task control. And the fact that most high-profile Web sites are increasingly clean of such miscues is testimony to the fact that somebody is managing these sites carefully, and accounting for every assigned task.

FrontPage's Task View is a mini-project manager, allowing you to assign and track tasks. FrontPage itself adds tasks to the Task list when you invoke templates to generate pages. Task View is a critical part of FrontPage when you are in charge of a large project.

Defining and Assigning Tasks

As tasks are assigned in your Web development process, they should be added to the list in Task View. To do that, first create a new Web (or open an existing one). In the FrontPage Explorer, select Tasks from the View bar. If you are defining a new task, click on the New Task button. The New Task dialog box appears, as shown in Figure 4.2.

The New Task dialog box allows you to define the Task Name, the Assign To (person responsible), and to enter a description of the task. You can also select one of the three Priority options: High, Medium or Low. Since the task list can be sorted by any field, (including Priority), it is valuable to enter information for each field, and to make conscious selections in the Priority area.

After you enter a few tasks, you can sort your task list by clicking on any column heading. The Linked To field cannot be entered in the New Task dialog box; the contents are generated when FrontPage creates new Web pages or sites with templates or wizards.

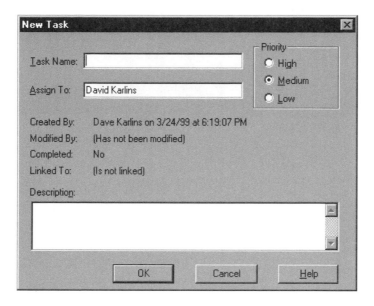

Figure 4.2   *Assigning tasks.*

Automatically Generating Tasks

When you generate sites using FrontPage wizards, the resulting Web site requires much work to complete. For example, the wizards do not generate all the content needed for your pages. FrontPage produces a list of Tasks after you create a site with a wizard, including the task of adding content to each page.

 Tasks created by wizards have the Status, Task, Assign To, Priority, Linked To, Modified Date and Description fields automatically generated by the wizard.

Tasks generated by wizards have the page to which they are attached entered in the Linked To field. Figure 4.3 shows a Task List with Web pages in the Linked To Fields. When you right-click on tasks with Linked To pages, you can select Do Task from the context menu, and immediately open the linked page.

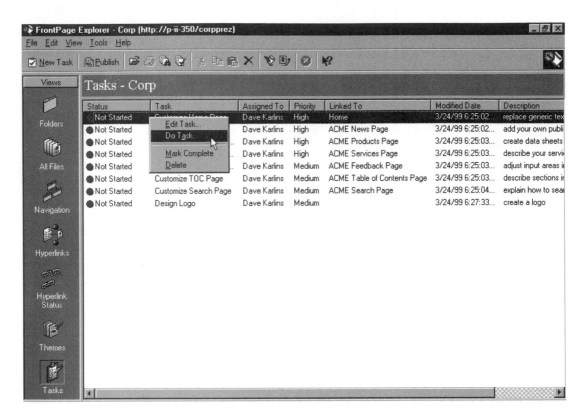

Figure 4.3 *Completing tasks with linked pages.*

Tracking Progress and Task Status

Once you have completed a task, you can mark the task as complete in Task View. To do that, right-click on the task, and select Mark Complete from the context menu, as shown in Figure 4.4.

After you mark a task as completed, the completion date is recorded, and can be displayed by viewing the Task Details dialog box (double-click on a task to view this dialog box). Task View then maintains this record of the completion date for each task, and who the task was completed by.

You can also use Task View to identify unfinished tasks, by clicking at the column heading for the Status column. This sorts tasks by two categories: Completed, and Not Started.

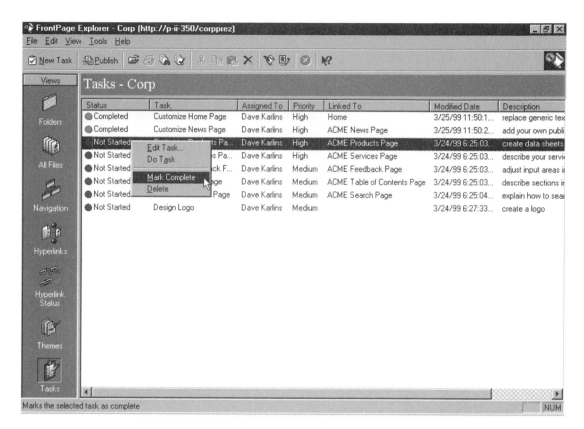

Figure 4.4 *Marking completed pages.*

When you initiate work on a Task through Task View (by right-clicking on a task, and choosing Do Task from the context menu), you will be prompted by the dialog box shown in Figure 4.5 to mark the task as completed.

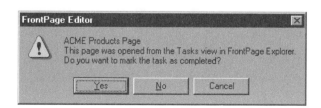

Figure 4.5 *Marking completed pages activated from Task View.*

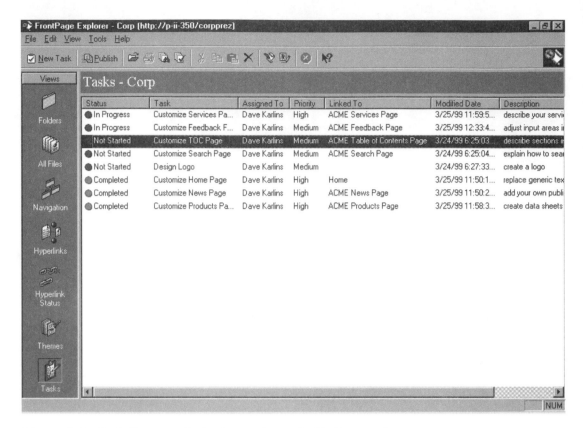

Figure 4.6 *Task View can display incomplete tasks "In Progress."*

The dialog box in Figure 4.5 offers only two options, completed, or not. However, if you select No, the task will be marked "In Progress" in Task View, as shown in Figure 4.6.

After you complete a session and log off a Web site, completed tasks will not be displayed when you reopen the Web. However, you can display completed tasks by right-clicking on a blank area in Task View and choosing Task History from the context menu. Or, you can select View, Task History to display completed tasks.

Assigning and Maintaining a Task List

Practice what you have learned by generating and maintaining a Task list.

First, use the Corporate Presence wizard to generate a Web site. Rather than complete the wizard, select Finish in the first wizard dialog box (we'll explore the wizard itself later in this chapter). FrontPage will generate a Web site, with many pages that need content.

Next, view your Web in Task view. Note the tasks that need completion. Double-click on the first task, and click on the Do Task button in the Task Details dialog box. Make some changes to the Web page, and close and save the page. When prompted, select Yes, mark the page as completed. Open another page from Task View, make some changes, but this time select No when prompted by the dialog box to mark the task as completed.

Finally, double-click on both of the tasks you worked on, and note the information in the Task details dialog box. Sort the Task list by Status, and then by Modified Date.

MCSD 4.3   Creating a User Interface

Many of the chapters in this book discuss implementing various types of Web page content, from hyperlinks to JavaScripts. Here, we will continue our "conceptual and logical design" focus (to quote the Microsoft Skills Matrix).

The three related elements of Web design that we will explore are Web structure, shared borders with navigation bars, and themes. These global elements provide the framework for a Web site. The Web structure defined in Navigation View provides the logic for generated navigation bars. And themes interact with a site by providing global design elements, from typefaces to interactive navigation buttons.

Designing Web Structure in Navigation View

Whether you generate your Web through a wizard or template, or design it from scratch, you can maintain an overview of the site and organize it in Navigation View. The full importance of designing a site through Navigation View will become more clear when we explore navigation bars. The connections between pages you define in Navigation View are the basis for the navigational links created by navigation bars.

To start a Web design in Navigation View, you must start by creating a new FrontPage Web (File, New, FrontPage Web in the FrontPage Explorer). Do you really have to start that way? Yes, if you want to use Navigation View (see box "Navigation View and Imported Webs").

Once you have generated a FrontPage Web from the FrontPage Explorer, you can add Web pages using the New Page button in the FrontPage Explorer toolbar.

You will figure out Navigation View's intuitive method for clicking and dragging pages to new locations in the flowchart. Or, you can refer to a more complete discussion in beginner-intermediate level books like *Teach Yourself FrontPage 98 in a Week* (Chapter 1), or *The FrontPage 98 Bible* (Chapter 3). Here, I'll note some lesser known features of Navigation View:

- The menu option File, Print Navigation View provides a hardcopy of your Web structure for documentation, record keeping and presentations.
- The Rotate button in the toolbar presents your Web structure as a horizontal (instead of vertical) structure, handy for printed output (see Figure 4.7).
- The Size to Fit button in the toolbar toggles between viewing all your Web pages (albeit without being able to read the page titles) and an expanded layout that doesn't fit on the screen.

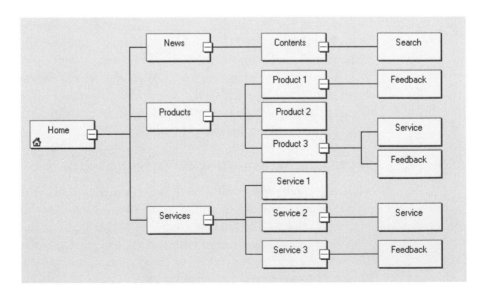

Figure 4.7 *Viewing a site design horizontally.*

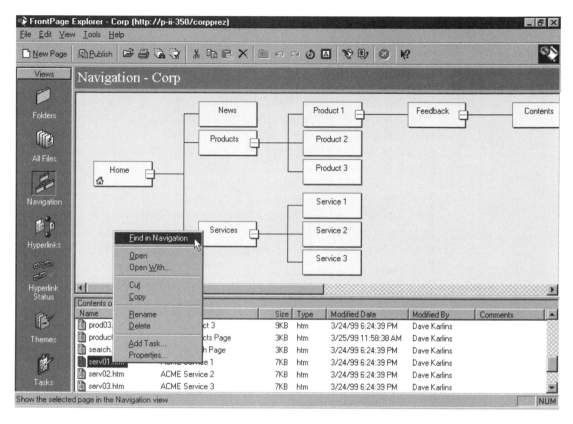

Figure 4.8   *Finding a file in Navigation View.*

- Looking for Web pages that match a file name in Navigation View can be like looking for the proverbial needle in a haystack. The solution: right-click on a file in the files window in Navigation View, and select Find in Navigation from the shortcut menu, as shown in Figure 4.8.
- The easiest way to change a page title (not the *.html file name) is to right-click on a page in Navigation View and select Rename from the context menu (or press F2).
- You can quickly jump from page to page in Navigation View using the tab key.

Navigation View and Imported Webs

One of the questions I hear most frequently from FrontPage developers at my FrontPage Forum (www.ppinet.com) is how do I mesh an existing set of Web pages into Navigation View?

Like many "simple" questions, this one involves educating developers in how FrontPage functions. You can utilize Navigation View only if your Web pages have been *imported into a FrontPage Web*. When I explain this, the objection is often, "but I already have a Web site." The confusion is understandable, given the fact that the distinction between FrontPage "Webs" and "Web sites" is itself confusing.

An essential starting point for solving this problem is an understanding that a FrontPage Web involves much more than a Web site. The FrontPage Web is an organized set of files that allows all the features of FrontPage— from Navigation View to input form data management—to function. In order to take advantage of these features, an existing Web site must be imported into a FrontPage Web.

The basic solution is that no matter how complete or sophisticated an existing Web *site,* it must be imported into a FrontPage Web in order to take advantage of Navigation View and other features of the FrontPage Explorer. The practical solution I usually recommend is to create an empty Web (using the Empty Web template), and then import the elements of the existing Web site into the new FrontPage Web. An alternative to importing a Web into an existing FrontPage Web is to use the Import wizard that appears when you select File, New, FrontPage Web, and select the Import an Existing Web option button in the New FrontPage Web dialog box. This launches a wizard that imports existing Web elements into a FrontPage Web.

Implementing Shared Borders and Navigation Bars

The navigational structure you define in Navigation View provides the logic for navigational links generated site-wide using Navigation bars. Navigation bars are usually, but not necessarily, embedded in shared borders that appear on every page in a FrontPage Web.

In the following sections, we'll explore shared borders and then examine navigation bars.

IMPLEMENTING SHARED BORDERS

Shared borders are simply HTML files that are embedded in the top, bottom, right, or left side of every Web page in a Web site (unless they are disabled on a page-by-page basis).

Since shared borders are Web pages, they can contain anything available in any other Web pages, including hyperlinks, images and text. Since shared borders download only once in a Web site, take that into account when you consider what elements to place on a shared border. A slow-to-download shared border slows down the loading of an initial home page, but after that the contents are already in the visitor's browser.

To define shared borders, select Tools, Shared Borders in the Front-Page Explorer. The Shared Borders dialog box appears, as shown in Figure 4.9. Use the check boxes to assign up to four shared borders. Most designers avoid right shared borders since they can require the use of the horizontal scrollbar in some cases, but theoretically they can be implemented along with top, left, and/or bottom borders.

Experienced Web designers may be asking, "Do shared borders replace frames or embedded pages?" Shared borders are an *alternative* to frames, providing a stable, somewhat interactive (through navigation bars) "frame" for Web pages. Technically speaking, they can be combined with frames, but it's hard to imagine an application of both frames and shared borders that wouldn't be a big mess of frames-within-frames. As for embedded pages, shared borders are embedded pages. They don't preclude the use of other embedded pages, however.

One thing you will want to make part of your development routine is displaying hidden folders, including the one that stores shared border pages. While the folks at Microsoft have elected to hide these files from the unsophisticated user, you want to see them. For one thing, they contain the shared borders files. To display hidden folders, select Tools, Web Settings, and click on the Advanced tab in the FrontPage Web Settings dialog box. In the Options area of the tab, select the Show Documents in Hidden Directories check box, and then OK the dialog box. Hidden folders can now be viewed like other folders in Folders View of the FrontPage Explorer.

Shared borders appear in, and can be edited, directly in the FrontPage Editor. Inexperienced (and somewhat experienced) FrontPage page designers will have to be reminded that *the changes they make to a shared border affect that shared border in **every** page in the Web site.*

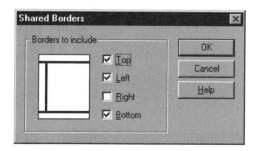

Figure 4.9 *Defining shared borders.*

When a user selects an object, or places his or her insertion point in a shared border, the selected border is marked with a solid line. Unselected shared borders are marked by dotted lines, as shown in Figure 4.10. Expert users may elect to open shared borders directly from the FrontPage Explorer (by double-clicking on them in the _borders folder). Normally, shared borders are edited within an existing page, and the nonexpert user may not be aware that he or she is actually editing a separate HTML page. Editing shared borders is easier that way, but it does not allow you to assign attributes like Page backgrounds, for example, to shared borders.

DEFINING NAVIGATION BARS

Two scenarios, extreme and exaggerated, but useful for understanding Navigation bars:

In scenario one, a Web developer has on staff dozens of graduates of Rhode Island School of Design, each of whom is assigned to carefully hand craft navigational links within various Web pages based on client survey data, focus group interviews, and intuitive sensibilities attained from years of Web design.

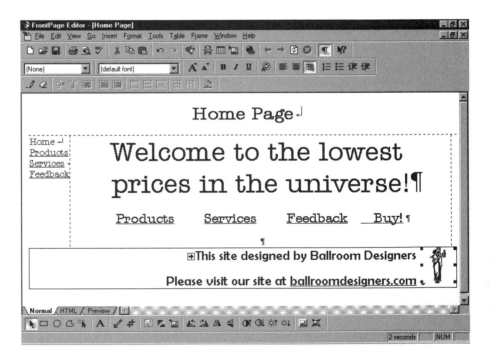

Figure 4.10 *Editing a shared border.*

In scenario two, a Web developer has a limited budget, a huge site to develop quickly, and limited design resources.

Of course, in real life, most situations combine elements of both scenarios, but the point of contrasting these environments is to identify likely candidates for automated navigation bars. Navigation bars generate links on each page in a Web site *based on the logic of the navigational structure defined in Navigation View.* This means that navigation links cannot be tweaked individually for each page.

If a development environment is flexible enough to tolerate these automatically generated links, then Navigation bars can save weeks of time by "deciding" what pages to link to each page. If a client is determined to make page-by-page decisions on links, he or she won't be happy with Navigation bars. Our job is to explain the options, and let the client decide. But I can testify that by relying on Navigation bars, it's possible to constantly and interactively (and automatically!) update navigational links on hundreds, even thousands, of pages almost instantly. That's a compelling argument for this powerful tool.

Does all this mean that generated Navigation bars cannot be tweaked to fine tune links on each page? Yes, it does. The price you pay for automatically generated navigational links is that they are just that—automatically generated. This does not, of course, prevent developers from simply creating direct links within a page itself to any other page. It only means that the links *within a Navigation bar* are automatically generated.

Theory aside, how do you define Navigation bars? The following steps insert Navigation bars in an open Web page (in the FrontPage Editor):

1. Click to place your insertion point where the Navigation bar will be placed. This is usually, but not always, in a shared border.
2. Select Insert, Navigation Bar from the menu.
3. In the Hyperlinks to Include area of the dialog box, choose one of the option buttons to choose a type of logic for assigning links to pages. For more advice on link options, see "What Kind of Navigation Logic?" below.
4. Use the Home Page and Parent Page check boxes to add links to these pages to Navigation bars.
5. In the Orientation and Appearance area, choose either Horizontal (usually used in top or bottom shared borders) or Vertical (usually used with left shared borders). Choose Buttons to generate Theme-based buttons, or Text for button content.
6. Your Navigational bar structure will be illustrated in the grid on the top left of the dialog box, as shown in Figure 4.11. When you are satisfied with your defined links, OK the dialog box.

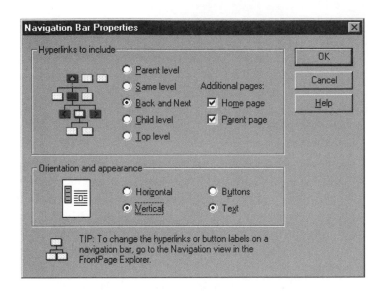

Figure 4.11 *Previewing a navigation bar implementation.*

What Kind of Navigation Logic?

Navigation options boil down to basically two types: hierarchal or lateral. To use FrontPage's family metaphor, hierarchal structures allow links "up" or "down," to parent or child pages. The Parent Level, Child Level and Top Level options in the Navigation Bar Properties dialog box allow for variations of a hierarchal structure. This is the most widely used approach to Web navigation, welcoming a visitor at a Home page, and providing sets of options that take the visitor lower and lower into a flowchart structure.

The second option, a lateral structure, is represented by the Same Level or Back and Next option buttons. This type of Web organization is good for a slideshow, or guided tour approach, where a visitor is offered the option of seeing the "Next" or "Previous" page, on a controlled tour through the site.

While the options in the Navigation Bar Properties dialog box lock you in to one approach or the other, there are other navigation elements you can employ to mitigate the rigidity of these structures:

- The Home Page and Parent Page check boxes in the Navigation Bar Properties dialog box are tremendously helpful, and guarantee links to these pages from any page.

- You can supplement Navigation bar links with a table of contents (Insert, Table of Contents in the FrontPage Editor), or a Search Box (Insert, Active Element, Search Form).

- You can always simply add specific hyperlinks to any page, or add universal hyperlinks directly to a shared border.

Assigning Themes

Themes allow you to instantly and globally assign many design elements to Web pages. Those elements include colors (text, buttons, horizontal lines); graphics like images used for buttons, page background images, bullets images, and horizontal rules; and font styles.

To assign a Theme to an existing FrontPage Web and/or a page:

1. With a Web open, in the FrontPage Explorer, select Themes View in the View bar.
2. Click on Themes in the list on the left side of the window to preview them.
3. With a Theme selected, experiment with the Vivid Colors, Active Graphics and Background Image check boxes. Vivid colors simply adjusts the color scheme, while the Active Graphics option generates interactive navigation buttons.
4. After you select a theme, click on Apply to apply the theme elements to your existing Web site.
5. To disable a theme for an open page in the FrontPage Editor, select Format, Theme. In the Choose Theme dialog box, select one of three options: This Page Does Not Use Themes disables the selected Web theme; Use Theme From Current Web applies the defined theme; and Use Selected Theme allows you to define a new theme for the open page.

Study Break

Designing a Web Structure with Navigation Bars, Shared Borders and Themes

Practice what you have learned by adding shared borders, navigation bars and a theme to a site.

First, open an existing site, or create a new one using the Corporate Presence wizard (you can skip all the steps in the wizard, and just click on Finish in the first dialog box).

Next, assign top and left shared borders to the Web. Delete existing shared border content, and insert navigation bars in each shared border.

Finally, apply a theme, including active graphics. Test the site in your browser.

MCSD 4.4   A Quick Look at Templates and Wizards

FrontPage facilitates Web development with two kinds of templates and wizards—Web templates (and wizards) and page templates.

Templates and wizards can be used to generate "out of the can" Web sites, or can be used to create a basic framework that can be drastically modified by Web developers. Here, we'll quickly identify the features of the main types of templates and wizards in FrontPage.

WEB TEMPLATES AND WIZARDS

The FrontPage MCP/MCSC Exam requires that you be basically familiar with the elements in templates. Using such information might take the form, for example, of knowing that the Discussion Web Wizard can generate a threaded discussion group. Or, that the easiest way to implement a project management Web might be to utilize the built-in Project Web template.

In Chapter 13, we'll return to templates and wizards, and examine them in depth. Here, I'll introduce them with a succinct overview of the features of the FrontPage Web Templates and Wizards:

THE CORPORATE PRESENCE WIZARD

The Corporate Presence Wizard is the most powerful and all-encompassing Web-generating tool in FrontPage. Options in this wizard include:

- A Home Page (a required element)
- A What's New page
- A Products/Services area
- A Table of Contents
- A Feedback Form with confirmation page
- A Search Form

If you take time to experiment with one template, this is the one to work with. It includes most of the elements available in other templates.

THE CUSTOMER SUPPORT WEB

The Customer Support Web template generates a Web site with pages geared to providing customer support and collecting customer feedback. Generated pages include:

- A Home Page (a required element)
- A What's New page
- An FAQ page

- A Bugs (bug report) page
- A Suggestion Form page with confirmation page
- A Download page linked to an FTP site
- A Discussion page that facilitates a threaded discussion group.
- A Search Form

THE DISCUSSION WEB WIZARD

The Discussion Web wizard generates a Web site with an interactive, threadable discussion forum. Visitors post content, which instantly displays (when they refresh their browser window).

The Discussion Web wizard is by far the most accessible way to implement discussion forums in FrontPage. Since the wizard generates a *new* Web, the best way to implement it is to create a discussion forum using this wizard, and then link it to an existing Web.

Figure 4.12 illustrates my discussion Web, generated (and modified from) the Discussion Web Wizard.

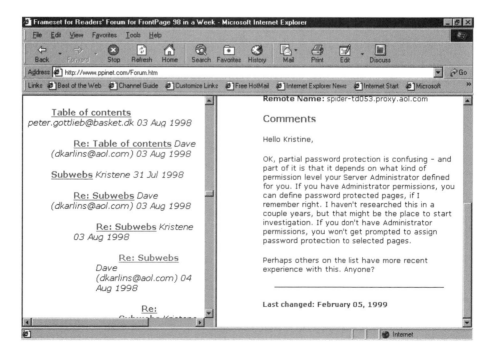

Figure 4.12 *An implemented discussion Web.*

THE EMPTY WEB TEMPLATE

Why bother to use the Empty Web template? Because it creates a *FrontPage Web*, with the necessary server folders to manage FrontPage elements.

Warning

As I've emphasized earlier, and will continue to emphasize, it is necessary to constantly educate developers to the fact that FrontPage's most powerful features are essentially disabled unless development starts with a *FrontPage Web* generated from the FrontPage Explorer. Don't let your developers "skip right to the FrontPage Editor"! Insist that they start with some kind of Web template. This will avoid 50 percent of all FrontPage problems, which are related to not establishing proper server folders when a site is initiated.

THE LEARNING FRONTPAGE TEMPLATE

Not a real FrontPage template, the files here are used for the tutorial that comes with FrontPage 98 on the FrontPage CD. Installing the tutorial is an installation option.

THE PERSONAL WEB TEMPLATE

The Personal Web template provides a nice little template for folks generating a Web site to show off their hobbies and their pets. I use it in training classes to good effect, but it's not a professional site development template.

THE PROJECT WEB TEMPLATE

Project managers—and you know who you are—will find the following project management elements in this template:

- A Home Page
- A Members page with links to project members
- A Schedule page
- A Status page for tracking task status
- An Archive page for completed task data
- A Discussion Forum for project participants
- A Search Form

My theory is that this template was once used by Microsoft software developers. It's specialized, but saves time and has interesting approaches to online project management.

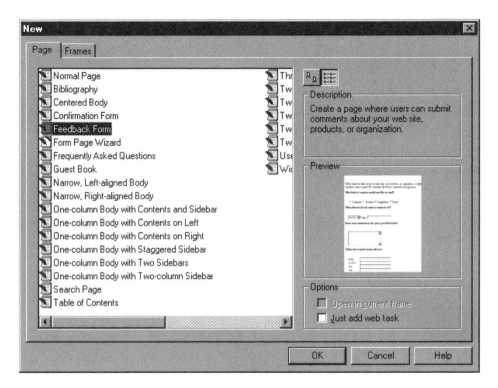

Figure 4.13 *Page template options.*

PAGE TEMPLATES

FrontPage *page* templates and wizards can be used as design guides, but also to generate complex pages. If you are creating an input form or a framed page, you will likely want to adapt a template rather than start from scratch.

To create a new page using a template, select File, New in the Front-Page Editor. The Page tab of the New dialog box is shown in Figure 4.13.

As you click on a template, a preview appears in the Preview area.

Framed page templates are available in the Frames tab of the dialog box. Figure 4.14 shows frame options. For a full discussion of using Frames in FrontPage, see Chapter 7.

To define your own page template, create a page that will be used as a template and select File, Save As from the FrontPage Editor menu. Name the file, and click on the As Template button in the Save As dialog box. The Save As Template dialog box appears, as shown in Figure 4.15. Enter a page title, page name (followed by .htm), and a description, and save the template page.

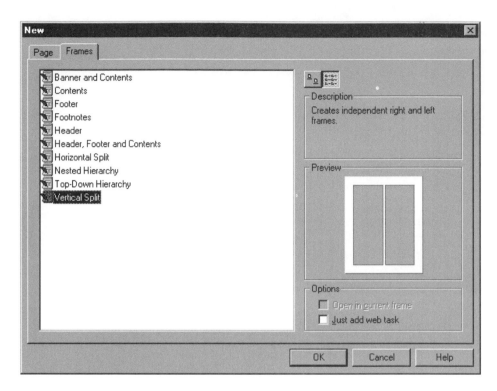

Figure 4.14 *Frame template options.*

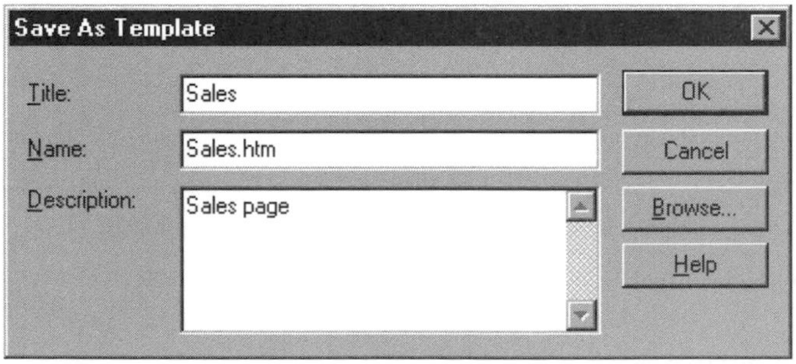

Figure 4.15 *Saving a template.*

Generating a Web with the Customer Support Web Template

Practice what you have learned by generating a new Web, using the Customer Support template.

First, examine the resulting Web site. Test the suggestions input form and the discussion forum by submitting data.

Next, add a new page using the User Registration page template.

Finally, modify and save the new page as a different page template. Experiment with opening a new page using your new template page.

MCSD 4.5 Maintaining a Site

You've already seen how FrontPage facilitates managing a Web site through features like the Task View and Navigation View. FrontPage also has utilities for globally managing and editing site-wide content.

FrontPage allows you to globally edit a Web site, including checking spelling, and implementing a powerful search and replace utility. You can also verify the status of hyperlinks site-wide.

Site-Wide Editing

You can check spelling and employ Find and Replace either in Web pages or Web sites. But the power of using these simple features on a site-wide basis is exponentially more useful than working on a single page. A FrontPage Web manager can quickly ensure that an entire Web site is free of embarrassing spelling errors.

A perhaps even more underrated feature is the ability to globally search and replace within a Web site. A quick change in corporate ownership? No problem, hundreds of Web pages can be updated in moments.

SPELLING

To check spelling for an entire Web site, select Tools, Spelling in the Front-Page Explorer.

To limit the spell check, use Ctrl+Click in Folder view to select pages first, and use the Selected Pages option in the Spelling dialog box to constrain the check. For example, you can sort pages in Folder view by the Modified

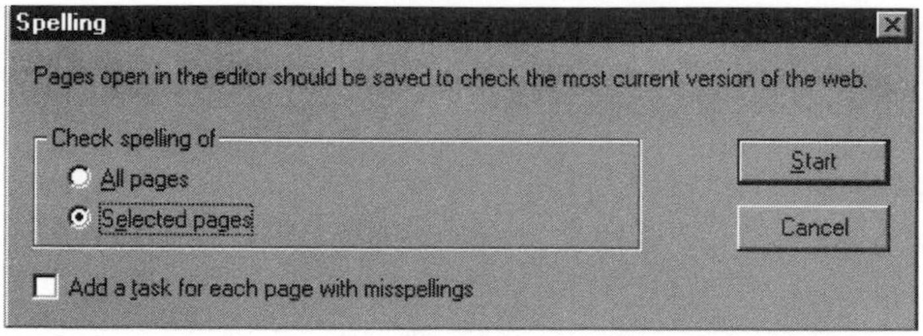

Figure 4.16 *Site-wide spelling options.*

Date field (by clicking on top of that column), and select only recently modified pages.

The Spelling dialog box is shown in Figure 4.16. Use the Add a Task for Each Page with Misspellings check box to add pages that need spelling corrected to the list in Task View.

If you elect to add pages that need spelling corrected to your Task list (a good idea to help manage your time), you can open those pages from Task View. As you do, the spelling checker automatically launches in each page, as shown in Figure 4.17.

FIND AND REPLACE

The Find and Replace features of the FrontPage Explorer are some of the most underrated elements of FrontPage. Can't remember what page included that unfortunate reference to the mega-corporation that recently acquired your start-up? The Find dialog box will track it down. And the Replace dialog box will insert the new corporate name in place of the old.

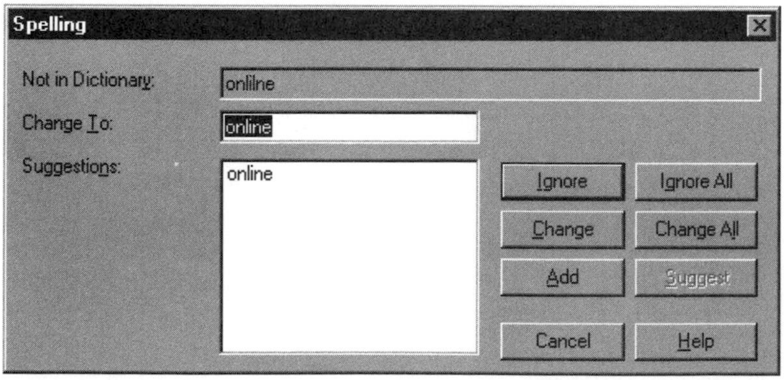

Figure 4.17 *Fixing spelling errors.*

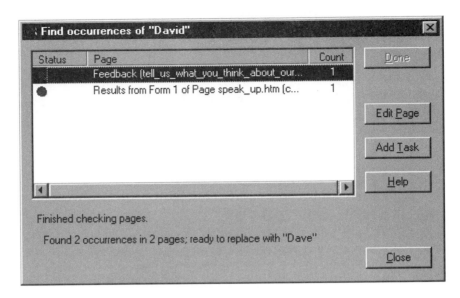

Figure 4.18 *Occurrences of a Search string, ready to be replaced.*

Like the Spelling utility, Find and Replace can be applied to selected pages or an entire site. First, make sure all open pages have been saved. Then select either Find or Replace from the Tools menu in the FrontPage Explorer.

After you employ a Search, a Find Occurances dialog box appears, with a list of pages with your search string. You can open pages from the dialog box by clicking on the Edit Page button, or you can add pages to the Task list by clicking on the Add Task button. A Replace search provides the same dialog box, as shown in Figure 4.18.

You can use the Edit button to open each page in the resulting list. When you do, a traditional Replace dialog box appears, prompting you to replace specific or all occurrences of your text on the page, as shown in Figure 4.19.

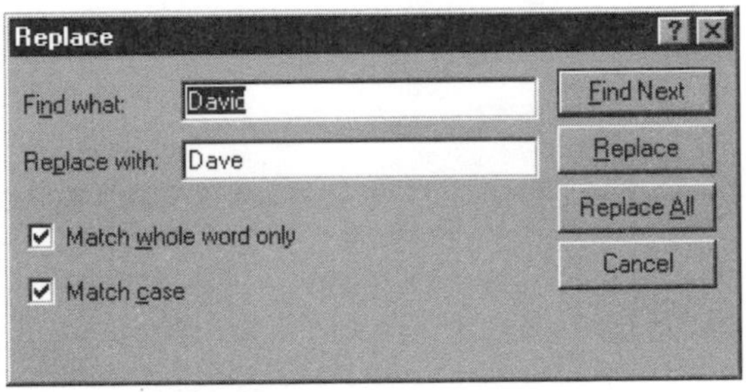

Figure 4.19 *Replacing in a Web page.*

Checking Hyperlink Status

One of the most aggravating errors a visitor can find at your Web site is a bogus hyperlink. Yet these errors are some of the most difficult to identify. Here, again, FrontPage's underrated Explorer provides critical management tools.

You can view all hyperlinks in a FrontPage Web site, and you can also test for broken links.

VIEWING HYPERLINKS

To view all hyperlinks in a Web site, select Hyperlinks view in the FrontPage Explorer. The "+" sign that appears next to Web pages indicates additional links that can be traced.

One problem with tracking down hyperlinks in Hyperlink view is that link display becomes circular if you keep expanding the view. For example, in Figure 4.20, the Feedback and Confirmed pages are linked. So, clicking on either one displays a link to the other, in an endless cycle.

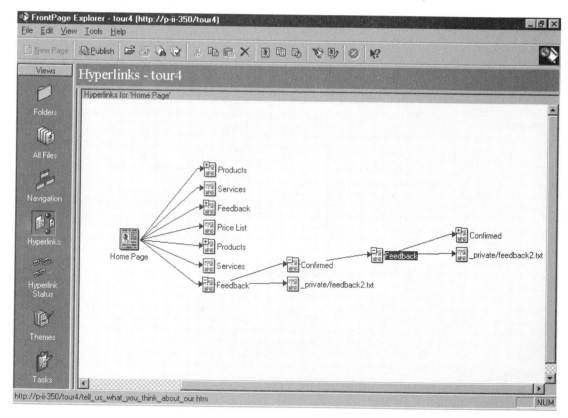

Figure 4.20 *Hyperlink view can become an endless cycle.*

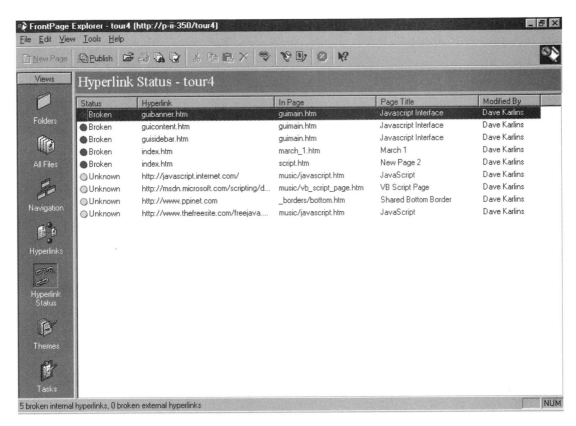

Figure 4.21 *Checking Hyperlink Status.*

Even with its limitations, Hyperlink view allows you to trace hyperlink structure through your site.

UPDATING HYPERLINK STATUS

If you have many links to maintain, you'll want to use Hyperlink Status view. Hyperlink Status view provides a list of links, and their status, as shown in Figure 4.21.

You can have FrontPage test and update your links by selecting Tools, Recalculate Hyperlinks, or Tools, Verify Hyperlinks from the FrontPage Explorer menu. Recalculating hyperlinks updates text indexes produced by search forms in your Web sites. Verifying hyperlinks tests links, both internal and external, and updates the Hyperlink Status view.

Study Break

Defining and Testing Hyperlinks

Practice what you have learned by updating a site's hyperlinks.

First, open an existing site, or create a new one.

Next, add hyperlinks to several off-site locations. If you're stumped for URLs, use www.microsoft.com and www.ppinet.com. Also, add a bad hyperlink (try www.com.com—that was bad last time I tested it).

Finally, save your page. Log onto the Internet and recalculate and verify your hyperlinks.

MCSD 4.6   Training

You should be prepared to recommend training resources. As a FrontPage MCP, you will want to establish a relationship with reliable trainers in your area.

One resource that comes with FrontPage is the interactive tutorial on the FrontPage CD. (The tutorial requires that users have access to the Learning FrontPage Template.)

Other training resources include contracted corporate training centers, including national chains like New Horizons, CompUSA, or local training centers. A quick search using Alta Vista produced dozens of FrontPage trainers in the US and Europe. And, of course, there are plenty of good, available FrontPage books for end users.

■ Summary

In order to really capitalize on the functionality of FrontPage, it is necessary to start from a conceptual overview of your Web site. As opposed to a "page by page" approach to Web development, FrontPage tends to require, and is very supportive of, a "site-wide" approach. Task View in the FrontPage Explorer helps you organize and document Web development as it takes place. The flow-chart layout in Navigation View facilitates designing the way users will interact, not just with individual pages but with a site as a whole.

Other site-wide development tools include Shared Borders, which often host Navigation Bars that provide automatically generated navigational links, and Themes that provide a global look and feel for a site.

FrontPage's templates and wizards can also assist in creating Webs. Finally, after a site is created, FrontPage tools like Spelling, and Search and Replace, allow for global site editing.

▲ CHAPTER REVIEW QUESTIONS

Here are a some practice questions relating to the material covered in the "Developing a Conceptual Design for a Web Site" area of Microsoft's *Designing and Implementing Web Sites Using Microsoft FrontPage 98* exam (70-055).

1. *Which of the following Web management tasks can be accomplished in Navigation View? (Select all correct answers.)*
    A. Changing page titles
    B. Editing shared border content
    C. Adding tasks to the Task list
    D. Recording progress on Tasks
    E. Assigning Themes

2. *Which of the following factors determine generated Navigation Bar links? (Select all correct answers.)*
    A. FrontPage Editor layout
    B. Navigation View layout
    C. Discussion Web entries
    D. Settings in the Navigation Bar Properties dialog box
    E. Page template selection

3. *An easy way to create a Framed page is to use the Personal Web wizard.*
    A. True
    B. False

4. *One way to update an entire Web site is through the Replace feature in the FrontPage Explorer.*
    A. True
    B. False

5. *You can automatically open some Web pages from the Task List generated by the Project Management template.*

   A. True

   B. False

6. *Which of the following allows you to maintain and update hyperlinks? (Select all correct answers.)*

   A. The Hyperlink dialog box

   B. The Hyperlink Update dialog box in Navigation View

   C. Themes view

   D. Hyperlink Status view

   E. The Update Hyperlinks button in the FrontPage Editor

7. *Which of the following factors need to be taken into account in the earliest stages of Web site development? (Select all correct answers.)*

   A. Task assignment

   B. Navigation logic

   C. Shared borders

   D. Input form fields

   E. Hyperlink status

8. *FrontPage allows spell checking in the FrontPage Explorer.*

   A. True

   B. False

9. *You can define a maximum of two shared borders for a Web site.*

   A. True

   B. False

10. *Shared borders are normally hidden from amateur FrontPage users in the FrontPage Explorer.*

    A. True

    B. False

11. *The Navigation Bar appears at the top of every FrontPage Web page.*

    A. True

    B. False

12. *Web wizards sometimes generate which of the following? (Select all correct answers.)*

    A. Input forms

    B. Customized page templates

    C. Hyperlink verification

    D. Task lists

    E. Search and Replace strings

13. *Navigation links can be attached to imported Webs, but only manually in Navigation View.*

    A. True

    B. False

14. *How could you locate a file in Navigation View? (Select all correct answers.)*

    A. A search box

    B. A search engine

    C. Right-click on the File name and select Find in Navigation from the context menu

    D. Select Edit, Search in the FrontPage Explorer

    E. Select Edit, Search in the FrontPage Editor

15. *Navigation View can be used to print out a hard copy of your Web site navigational structure.*

    A. True

    B. False

Designing a User Interface and User Services

In previous chapters we have explored various aspects of defining business, technical and human resource requirements for FrontPage Web sites. You learned to make an assessment of whether, and how, FrontPage can be adapted to various environments.

In this chapter we'll start with basic elements of a user interface, including hyperlinks that provide so much of the dynamic functionality of Web pages. And, we will explore a wide variety of automated elements that can be included in FrontPage Webs. These elements are divided into two categories, Components, and Active Elements. Components and Active Elements are very similar. They allow designers to include objects ranging from search forms to scrolling text marquees in Web pages without doing any programming.

At the conclusion of this chapter you will be able to:

- Develop a conceptual plan for implementing FrontPage's automated Active Elements and Components in a Web site

97

- Understand the basic function of each Active Element and Component
- Address server compatibility issues for each Active Element and Component
- Identify potential browser compatibility issues for Active Elements an*d Components
- Insert Active Elements and Components in Web pages
- Define Active Element and Component properties

MCSD 5.1   Designing a User Interface

The first step in designing a user interface is to investigate the environment for which you are creating a Web site. The point of a user interface is to connect the information provided by the site with visitors to the site.

In Chapter 2, "Analysing Web Requirements," we investigated some of the technical aspects of this dynamic. For example, if visitors to a Web site are using older browsers and not planning to view images, this has to be taken into account in Web design. We also took a quick look at user interface issues like Web navigational structure from a site-wide perspective in section 4.3 of Chapter 4, "Developing a Conceptual Design for a Web Site."

In this chapter, we'll briefly explore some of the human aspects of site design: identifying the message being projected from the Web site, and the requirements of the audience. Another important element of the user interface, input forms, is discussed in Chapter 8, "Creating Input Forms."

The most frequently used tool for allowing visitors to navigate a Web site is links, or, in FrontPage 98 parlance, hyperlinks. In this chapter, we'll also explore some issues in assigning hyperlinks.

Study Break

Explore Navigation-Related Views in the FrontPage Explorer

Practice what you have learned by exploring the views in the FrontPage Explorer that display and control links.

First, create a new FrontPage Web using the Personal Web template.

Next, note the display in Navigation view. This view presents links that will be used to automatically generate Navigation bars.

Finally, click on the Hyperlinks icon in the View bar to see all links to and from pages in the site. The links displayed in Hyperlinks view represent both links generated in Navigation Bars, and any additional hyperlinks that are part of Web page content.

You can delete this Web by selecting File, Delete FrontPage Web from the FrontPage Explorer menu bar.

MCSD 5.2   Identifying Logical Sequence of Flow

Sequence of flow refers to the navigation options provided at a Web site. There are three basic approaches to providing visitor options at a Web site:

1. You can provide sets of options (usually three to five) at each page, guiding a visitor through the site but providing alternatives at each step.
2. You can provide a single, linear navigation option at each page, similar to a slideshow-type presentation, where the visitor's basic options are "Next," or "Back."
3. You can provide a search box or table of contents.

FrontPage 98 allows you to define global navigational strategies using Navigation Bars. Navigation Bars were introduced in Chapter 4, and are discussed in detail in Chapter 7, "Creating User Interfaces."

Navigation Options

The types of navigation options you provide depends on the material presented at the site, and the types of visitors. If you are overseeing the development of a Web site that will provide access to 1500 different technical papers, a hierarchal, flowchart-style set of navigation buttons would be annoying and cumbersome. The best navigational tools would probably be a list of the articles, perhaps generated by FrontPage's table of contents component, or a search box. Figure 5.1 shows a no-nonsense home page with a list of article links and a search box.

On the other hand, if you are creating a Web site to present a corporate image, it might well be more appropriate to guide visitors through the Web site by presenting three to five options at each page, and providing links up and down a flowchart, using parent/child page links. This type of navigational strategy is best implemented with Navigation Bars, which are explained in detail in Chapter 7. Figure 5.2 shows a Web site generated by FrontPage's Corporate Presence wizard, offering visitors a small number of navigation options.

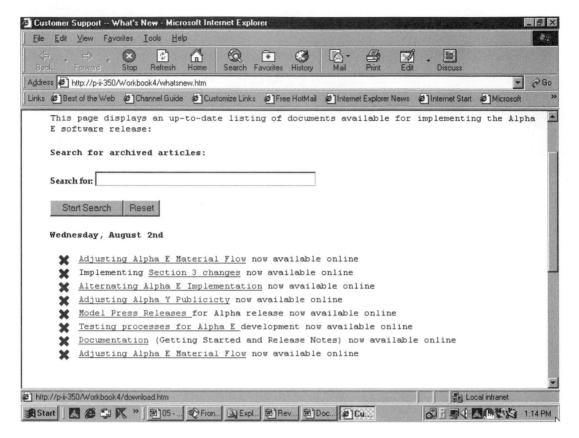

Figure 5.1 *The navigational structure of this no-frills Web page is appropriate for visitors searching through a long list of articles.*

From the perspective of a visitor, there is not necessarily a distinction between an external and internal link. That is, you can define links to pages outside your site, or within your site, and in either case, the visitor clicks on a linked text or image and activates the link.

Study Break

Designing Three Types of Navigational Flow

This Study Break requires only a scratch pad and a pencil. Use it to sharpen your understanding of developing a logical flow for a Web site.

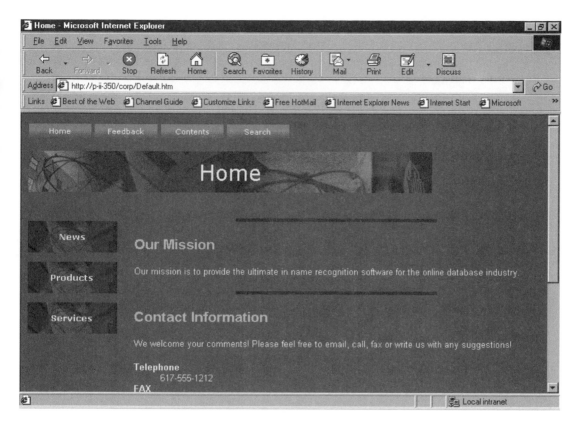

Figure 5.2 *Sometimes it is appropriate to narrowly define navigation options for visitors.*

1. Sketch out a navigational flow for a Web site that contains 11 white papers on product design. The basic "flow" of the site should look something like a spider's Web, with each of the white papers linking back to the home page.

2. Sketch a navigational flow for a Web site that provides links to corporate products, services, and support. Each of these three areas of the Web will have links to other pages.

3. Finally, sketch the navigational flow for a site that provides a guided tour of a company's product line, with "Previous" and "Next" options at each page.

Figure 5.3 shows sketches for each of these scenarios.

Defining Hyperlinks

The main tool for allowing visitors to navigate within and out of a Web site is links. FrontPage 98 uses the term hyperlinks synonymously with links, and here I'll just refer to them as links for short.

Providing well placed, intuitive, and useful links is one of the most important aspects of Web design. Some considerations in what kinds of links to provide, and how many, were discussed briefly in the section "Navigation Options," earlier in this chapter. The art of laying out a Web site, and strategies for providing navigation options, are beyond the scope of this book and not in and of themselves essential for the FrontPage MCP test. As a FrontPage expert, you can rely on templates that provide built-in link strategies, or draw on the expertise of books, design firms, and consultants who specialize in design strategies. However, you should be prepared to advise them as to design issues. (Conceptual and logical design is one of the test elements.)

While you don't need to be an expert in the psychology of link navigational structures, you do need to understand the technical aspects of links and how FrontPage defines them. If you're not familiar with how links are defined in FrontPage 98, introductory level books have extensive discussions of that process. For a basic introduction to hyperlink strategies and techniques, see Chapter 6, "Defining Hyperlinks," in *Teach Yourself FrontPage 98 in a Week*, or the section "Working with Hyperlinks" in *The FrontPage 98 Bible*, pages 34–36.

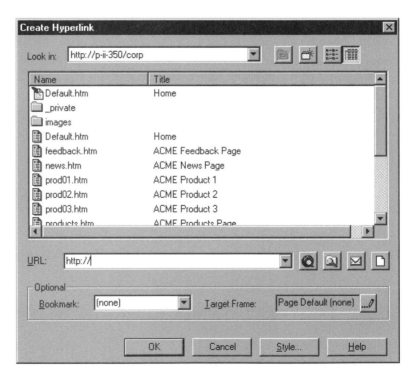

Figure 5.3   *Three site flow options.*

Here, we'll briefly review the basic process. To define a link in FrontPage 98:

1. Select either text, an image, or use one of the hotspot tools in the Picture toolbar to select a part of an image in the FrontPage Editor.
2. Click on the Create or Edit Hyperlink button in the FrontPage Editor Standard toolbar. The Create Hyperlink dialog box opens.
    Note: If you use one of the hotspot tools to select part of an image, the Create Hyperlink dialog box opens automatically.
3. Enter a URL in the URL box, or select one of the pages in the FrontPage Web in the list in the dialog box.
    Note: You can include a bookmark if your link is targeted at a specific bookmark within a Web page. Then click on OK in the Create Hyperlink dialog box. The selected text or image appears in the FrontPage Editor as a link.

When you define links, aside from selecting a target, you can elect to make your link relative or absolute, and you can control the way the linked page is displayed. Those options are discussed next.

Relative and Absolute Links

A relative link is a link within a Web. For example, the URL in the Create Hyperlink dialog box in Figure 5.4 is simply "news.htm." That is not a full URL. It assumes that the link is within the existing URL Web structure.

When you select link targets from within an open FrontPage 98 Web, those links are defined as relative links. They do not require that a visitor's browser reopen the current Web.

On the other hand, if you are defining links to a site external to your own Web site, it is necessary to include the entire URL.

Defining Target Frames

When visitors follow an external link, they leave the Web site. Of course they can use the Back button in their browser to return to your Web site, but sometimes there are reasons to maintain more of a connection with the original site. For example, a site might provide links to related Web sites, but not want to lose all connection with a visitor.

There are two basic options for keeping your Web site in a visitor's browser window while he or she explores a link out of your site. One is to display the target page with a frame in your Web site. This strategy is discussed in Chapter 7 (section 7.3) of this book, in the section on Frames.

The other strategy is to define a link that opens in another browser window, so that your Web site remains in the visitor's original browser window.

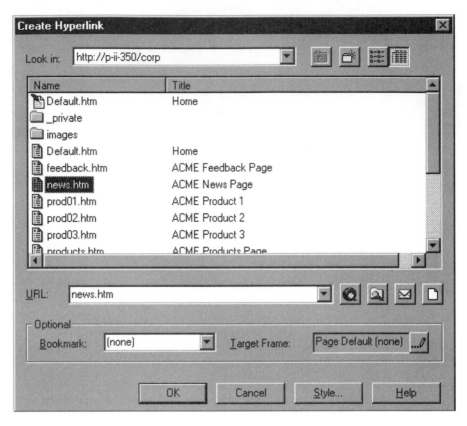

Figure 5.4 *Relative links, within a Web, do not require a full URL.*

To define a link in a new browser window:

1. Define the target URL for a link in the URL box of the Create Hyperlink dialog box.
2. Click on the Change Target Frame button in the lower right of the Create Hyperlink dialog box. The Target Frame dialog box opens.
3. Select New Window in the Common Targets list in the Target Frame dialog box, as shown in Figure 5.5. Then OK the dialog boxes.

5.3 MCSD   Using FrontPage Components

FrontPage Components embed powerful and interactive elements in Web pages. As a FrontPage MCP, you should have a basic overview of what each component does, and also how they fit into an overall plan for a Web site.

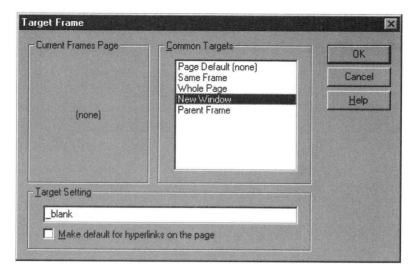

Figure 5.5 *Defining a new window target for a hyperlink.*

For example, you'll need to know that when your client wants a Search box placed in a Web page, his or her Web site must be published to a server with FrontPage server extensions, or it will not work.

It will be helpful if you have experience working with each of these Components, and there is no substitute for spending some time experimenting with each of them. Here, I'll review what those Components are, and help you organize your understanding in a way that will get you through this section of the exam.

The FrontPage MCP exam does not require that you know anything about writing Java applets or Active X code. But you will be asked questions relating to the process of integrating an existing chunk of Java or Active X code into a Web page. We'll review that process in this chapter as well.

To prepare for the FrontPage MCP test, don't worry about memorizing every detail of every Component. Remember the points I made in the introduction to this book. Microsoft is looking for folks to "climb under the hood" of FrontPage. They want you to be able to analyze and repair major breakdowns, and make strategic decisions about Web site development.

MCSD

The FrontPage MCSD exam includes questions about how to implement different Components. You will need to know what different Components do, and under what circumstances.

To help you answer all questions in this section of the exam, keep these two properties in mind:

- Components let you use pre-programmed elements that normally would require a scripting language like Java or Active X to create.
- Most FrontPage Components work only if the Web is published to a Web server with FrontPage extensions.

Keeping these two properties clearly in mind will help you answer several of the questions in the exam.

How Components Work

All components are inserted in the FrontPage Editor. They are activated when a browser interprets HTML tags that are generated by FrontPage when a user inserts a component from the menu. The HTML code calls a component in the same way that HTML tags refer to a graphic, a sound file, or a Java applet. You can customize how Components are activated by editing HTML attributes in the Component tag. Figure 5.6 shows an example of the HTML used to point to a Component.

When a browser opens a Web page containing an embedded Component, the server activates the appropriate Component, enabling it to perform its magic before the page is sent. Components are closely tied to the operation of the server. No special additions are required at the user's end. A Netscape browser will display Components as well as Microsoft's browser.

Note

The Component comment is embedded using a variant on a standard comment tag. This "hijacking" of HTML's comment tag is part of the reason that FrontPage does not support standard HTML comments.

FrontPage Components and FrontPage Extensions

Most Components require program modules that actually reside in the Web server. These files are included in the FrontPage extension files that can be attached to servers. Without these extensions, most Components won't work. You will be asked, in various ways in the exam, how to handle Web sites that use Components. To answer correctly, it is important to remember that most Components work only on FrontPage-enabled Web servers.

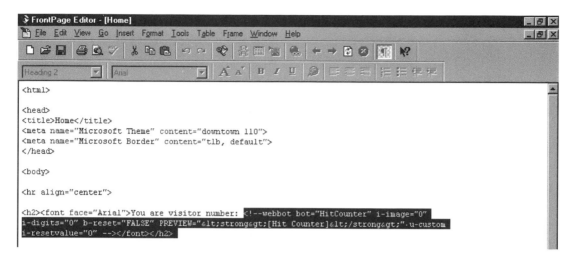

Figure 5.6   *Components use WebBot HTML tags.*

You should also be prepared to answer questions relating to a scenario where a client is developing Web sites using a server that does not have FrontPage extensions. In most cases, that client should avoid using Front-Page 98 Components.

Throughout this book, I'll note situations where various FrontPage elements require FrontPage Components. In some cases, I will identify workarounds or alternatives for sites published to non-FrontPage servers. For example, in Chapter 10 we'll examine form data management options for sites published to servers without FrontPage extensions.

Surveying the Properties of FrontPage Components

While an overview of how Components work is important, you will also need a basic understanding of what each Component does to answer questions in the exam. You won't be asked about every Component, but you will be asked about some of them. You can use Table 5.1 as a guide to remembering the function of each Component.

You will not need detailed knowledge of how each Component works to pass the exam, but you can't pass this section of the test without a general understanding of what each Component does.

There is no substitute for experience with FrontPage Components. You will have to walk through each one on your own, and experiment with it. Here, I'll briefly identify each Component available in FrontPage. Remember, the exam itself is not open book, so I'm afraid you won't be able to pin this up on the computer when you take the test! But here's a handy cheat sheet for a last minute review:

Table 5.1 *Component Definitions*

Component	What it does
Comment	Places text that displays in the FrontPage Editor, but not in a browser.
Confirmation Field	Special Components that display data from input forms to create customized confirmation pages.
Hit Counter	Tracks the number of visits to a page.
Include Page	Embeds a page within a page.
Insert HTML	Allows you to insert HTML code.
Page Banner	Creates a page title display.
Scheduled Image	Embeds an image for a set time period.
Scheduled Include Page	Embeds a page for a specified time period.
Substitution	Embeds embedded code fields that reflect field data defined in the Parameters tab of the Web Settings dialog box.

EMBEDDING COMMENTS

Comments are used by developers to leave reminders and notes for page development. A comment can be used to coordinate between different developers. For example, the developer responsible for page text can leave a note for the developer responsible for page design that the text is available, and how to find it.

Comments are inserted into a Web page in the FrontPage Editor. To insert a comment:

1. Click to set the insertion point in an open Web page in the FrontPage Editor.
2. Select Insert, FrontPage Component. The Insert FrontPage Component dialog box opens, as shown in Figure 5.7.
3. Click on Comment in the list of components in the dialog box. Then, click on OK. The Comment dialog box opens, as shown in Figure 5.8.
4. Enter comment text, then click on OK in the Comment dialog box. The comment appears in the FrontPage Editor.

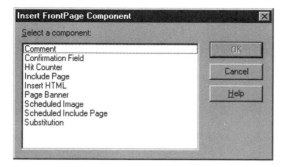

Figure 5.7 *Components are selected from the Insert FrontPage Component dialog box.*

When you move your cursor over a comment in the FrontPage Editor, a robot icon appears indicating that this is not regular page text, but a FrontPage Component, as shown in Figure 5.9.

Comment text can be formatted directly in the FrontPage Editor. To edit the text, you can reopen the Comment dialog box by double-clicking on the comment.

While comments are not visible in browsers, they can be revealed if a visitor views a Web page's source code. Since browsers enable visitors to view source code, avoid placing confidential or indiscreet information in comments.

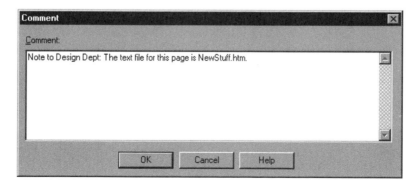

Figure 5.8 *Comments are defined in the Comment dialog box.*

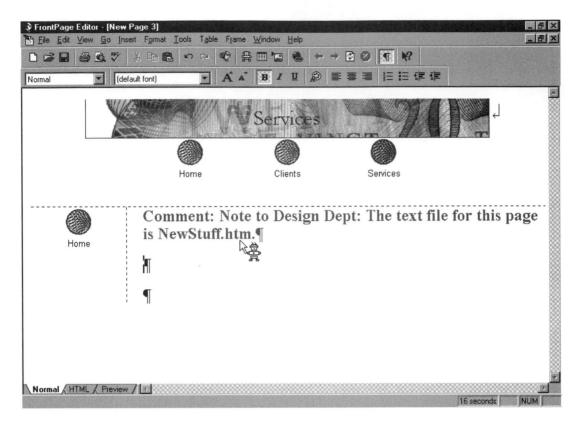

Figure 5.9 *Comment text is revealed as a FrontPage Component by the robot icon that appears when you move your cursor on top of a comment.*

USING CONFIRMATION FIELDS

Confirmation Fields are FrontPage Components that display data from input forms to create customized confirmation pages. If you are not familiar on at least a basic level with how FrontPage 98 generates input forms, it may be helpful to study a basic introduction to FrontPage input forms, such as Chapter 11 of *Teach Yourself FrontPage 98 in a Week*, or Chapter 11 of *The FrontPage 98 Bible*.

A Quick Overview of How Input Forms Work in FrontPage

Data input forms can be inserted into any Web page in the FrontPage editor. These input forms collect data through a set of input form fields. Each input form must have at least one input field, and a submit (and usually a reset) button.

Web servers that have FrontPage extensions installed can process this data without any additional scripting at the server or in the Web page. The data is saved at the server in a file. FrontPage allows you to define the file format to which you will send input data.

When you create an input form with FrontPage 98, a confirmation page is automatically generated. This confirmation page appears in a browser window after a visitor submits form data. Confirmation pages echo the field name for input forms, and then display the information the visitor entered. Figure 5.10 shows a confirmation form automatically generated from FrontPage 98.

The confirmation pages automatically generated by FrontPage may well be satisfactory for many Web sites. However, if a developer needs to define custom conformation pages, these pages can be designed from scratch by using the Confirmation Field Component.

If you are using custom confirmation fields, you will first create a custom confirmation page for an input form. To create a custom confirmation page:

1. Create and save a new page that will serve as the confirmation page for an input form.
2. Open the Web page with the input form in the FrontPage Editor.
3. Right-click in a defined input form and select Form Properties from the context menu.
4. Click on the Options button in the Form Properties dialog box. The Options for Saving Results of a Form dialog box appears. Click on the Confirmation Page tab.
5. In the URL of Confirmation Page (Optional) box, enter the URL for the confirmation page you created in step 1.
6. Click OK twice to return to the FrontPage Editor.

With the steps above, you have created a (so far blank) confirmation page for an input form, and you have defined that new (blank) page as the confirmation page for visitors after they enter data into a form.

With the confirmation page thus defined, you are now ready to place confirmation fields manually. To do that:

1. On a piece of paper (or use copy and paste to a create a list in a word processor), write the exact name of each field in the input form. Field names are revealed by double-clicking on a form field in the FrontPage Editor.
2. Open the confirmation page in the FrontPage 98 Editor.
3. Enter a text label for the field, for example, "You told us your name is:"
4. Select Insert, FrontPage Component.
5. Double-click on Confirmation Field in the list of FrontPage Components. The Confirmation Field Properties dialog box appears.

6. Enter (or copy) the exact name of the field for which you want to display user input, as shown in Figure 5.11. Then click OK.
7. The field name displays in brackets in the page. The field name can be formatted in the FrontPage Editor.

After you define confirmation fields, you can test them by publishing your Web page to a Web server with FrontPage 98 extensions, and entering data into the input form. After you submit the form, your confirmation page with custom defined confirmation fields will appear. Figure 5.12 shows a custom designed confirmation page, with displaying confirmation fields.

ADDING HIT COUNTERS

Hit counters count and display the number of visits to a page. FrontPage's Hit Counter Component places a hit counter in a Web page. To insert a hit counter:

1. Open the Web page in which the hit counter is to be inserted in the FrontPage Editor.
2. Select Insert, FrontPage Component.
3. Double-click on Hit Counter in the list of FrontPage Components. The Hit Counter Properties dialog box appears, as shown in Figure 5.13.
4. Select one of the six options buttons to select a style for the hit counter.
5. Use the Reset Counter check box to define a starting number for the counter (the default is zero).
6. Use the Fixed Number of Digits check box to define the number of digits that display (the default is the minimum number of digits needed to display the total number of hits).
7. Click OK to insert the hit counter.

USING INCLUDE PAGES

Included pages are pages that are embedded within a Web page. Included pages can be used as a tool for maintaining and updating large Web sites. For example, if a sales site for a large corporation included a price list on 773 different pages, that information could be embedded in those pages as an included page. When prices changed, a single Web page could be edited in the FrontPage Editor (instead of 773!), and the changes would appear in each page in which the price list page was embedded.

The first step in embedding an included page is to create and save that page in the FrontPage Editor.

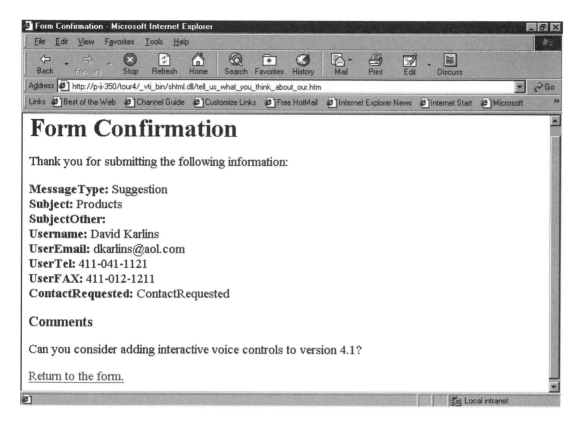

Figure 5.10   *FrontPage automatically generates confirmation pages for input forms.*

To include a page in another page:

1. Open the page in which the embedded page will be included.
2. Click to place your insertion point and select Insert, FrontPage Component.
3. Double-click on Include Page in the list of FrontPage Components. The Include Page Component Properties dialog box appears.
4. In the Page URL to Include box, enter the URL of the embedded page, or use the Browse button to locate the page.
5. Click on OK. The included page appears right in the FrontPage Editor. However, the included page must be opened separately in the FrontPage Editor to change its contents.

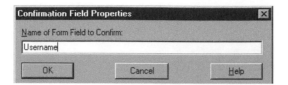

Figure 5.11 *The Confirmation Field Properties dialog box assigns fields to display.*

INSERTING HTML

There are two ways to enter HyperText Markup Language (HTML) code directly into a Web page in FrontPage 98. You can use the HTML tab in the FrontPage Editor to work with a text editor to write code. Or, you can use the Insert HTML Component. The difference between these two approaches is that HTML code entered in the HTML tab is translated and displayed in

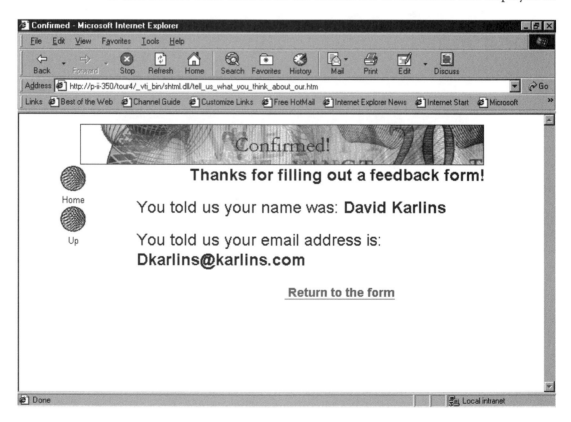

Figure 5.12 *Confirmation fields in a custom defined confirmation page.*

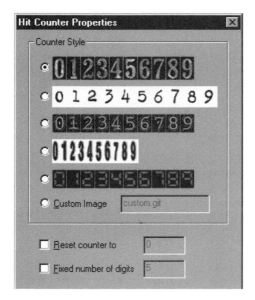

Figure 5.13 *Defining a Hit Counter.*

the FrontPage Editor, while code entered as an HTML component is not displayed in the FrontPage Editor. HTML code entered as an HTML component is interpreted and displayed in a browser, but not the FrontPage Editor.

To insert an HTML component:

1. In the FrontPage Editor, select Insert, FrontPage Component.
2. Double-click on Insert HTML in the list of Components. The HTML Markup dialog box appears, as shown in Figure 5.14.
3. Enter HTML code in the HTML Markup dialog box, and then click on OK.

The code you enter as a component displays as an icon (shown in Figure 5.15). It will be translated and displayed when viewed in a browser.

CREATING PAGE BANNERS

Page banners display the page title. If you apply a theme to a Web page, page banners are automatically generated.

To insert a page banner:

1. Open a Web page in the FrontPage Editor, and select Insert, FrontPage Component.

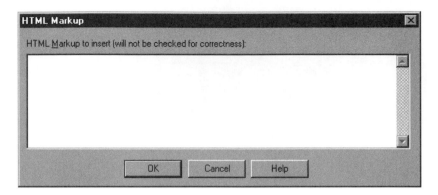

Figure 5.14 *You can enter HTML code in the HTML Markup dialog box.*

2. Double-click on Page Banner in the list of FrontPage Components. The FrontPage Banner Properties dialog box appears, as shown in Figure 5.16.
3. Select either the Image or Text option buttons. If a theme is assigned to a page, an image will be generated using the page title text. If you select text, the banner will display just text.
4. Click OK to insert the banner.

SCHEDULED IMAGES AND SCHEDULED INCLUDE PAGES

The Scheduled Image and Scheduled Include Page Components work something like Included Page Components. The difference is that these embedded files appear only for a set time period. When you insert either of these Components, you will be prompted to provide a starting date and time, and an ending date and time. The scheduled page or image will display only during this defined time period.

Figure 5.15 *The component icon.*

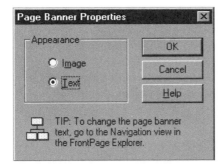

Figure 5.16 *Inserting a Page Banner.*

You can also define an optional additional URL for a page that will display before and after the defined image or page. The Scheduled Include Page Component Properties dialog box is shown in Figure 5.17.

SUBSTITUTION

The Substitution Component embeds defined fields in a page. You can use it to instantly update pages with code values that are defined in the Parameters

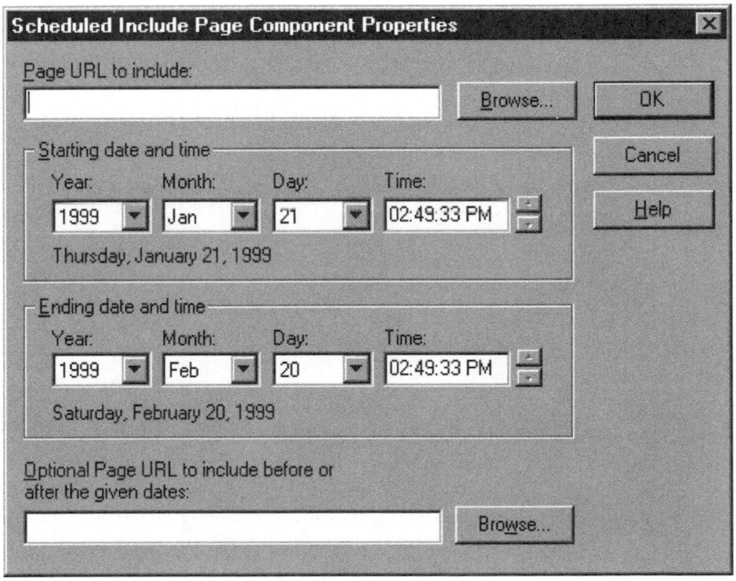

Figure 5.17 *Images or Web pages can be scheduled to appear within pages during defined time periods.*

tab of the Web Settings dialog box in the FrontPage Explorer. FrontPage automatically defines four variables that can be inserted into any page. Those variable fields are:

- Author: the author who created the Web page.
- Modified by: The author who last modified the page.
- Description: A defined description of the Web page.
- Page URL: The location of the page in the FrontPage Web.

You can define custom substitution fields for a Web site in the FrontPage Explorer. To define substitution fields:

1. In the FrontPage Explorer, select Tools, Web Settings. Click on the Parameters tab of the FrontPage Web Settings dialog box.
2. Click on the Add button, and enter a substitution field name in the Name field of the Add Name and Value dialog box.
3. Enter a Value to be displayed when the substitution field is inserted, as shown in Figure 5.18. Then click OK.
4. Use the Add button to define additional substitution fields, then click on OK in the FrontPage Web Settings dialog box.

Once you have defined substitution fields, you can place them or either of the four default substitution fields in a Web page. To insert a substitution field:

1. Open a Web page in the FrontPage Editor, and select Insert, FrontPage Component.
2. Double-click on Substitution in the list of FrontPage Components. The Substitution Component Properties dialog box appears
3. Select a substitution field from the Name drop-down list, as shown in Figure 5.19. Click on OK to insert the value of the selected field.

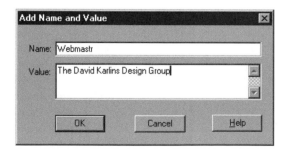

Figure 5.18 *Defining custom substitution fields.*

Figure 5.19 *Substitution fields can be inserted into Web pages.*

Inserting Timestamps

Timestamps work like Components, although they are a separate menu option. When you insert a Timestamp, you create a "timestamp" HotBot code in HTML

You may be asked a question that requires you to know whether Date and Time elements require FrontPage extensions. The answer is Yes, they do.

To insert a timestamp:

1. In the FrontPage Editor, select Insert, Timestamp. The Timestamp Properties dialog box appears, as shown in Figure 5.20.
2. In the dialog box, click on the Date This Page Was Last Edited options button to display the date you last changed a page. Select the Date This Page Was Last Automatically Updated to display when the page was automatically updated (for example, with a change in a substitution field).
3. Select a format from the Date Format drop down list. If you wish to display the time as well, choose a format from the Time Format dropdown list. Then, click on OK.

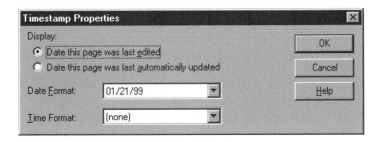

Figure 5.20 *Defining a Timestamp.*

You won't be asked detailed questions about the customizable detail for each Component. But you do need to be prepared to identify which Component solves which problem in page design. For example, you might be asked how a page can be embedded within another page for a set period of time, and you would need to know that the Scheduled Include Page component will do that task.

Sometimes it is difficult for a developer to know if an object on a page is a FrontPage Component (or a Timestamp). For example, there is no way to know, just from looking at the page, that the table in Figure 5.21 is an Include Page component. The indication that an object is a FrontPage Component is the little robot icon that appears when you move your cursor over the object in the FrontPage Editor.

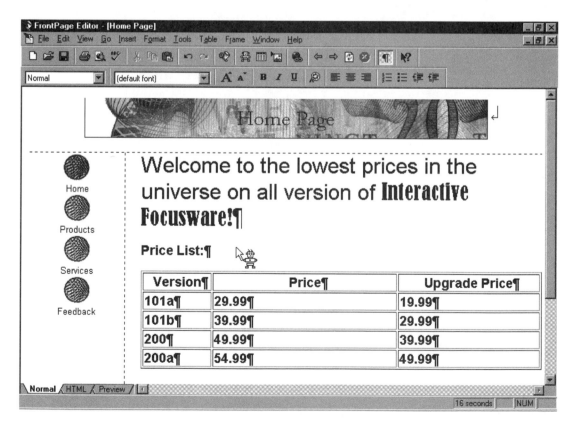

Figure 5.21   *Robot icons identify FrontPage Components.*

Study Break

Inserting FrontPage Components into a Web Page

First, create a new Web using the Personal Web template. Open the home page for the Web in the FrontPage Editor, and insert a comment reminding yourself to add content to this page

Next, create a new page with a price list. Include that page in all the existing pages in the Web site. Open and change the price list. Save the changed page, and note changes in the other Web pages.

Finally, create a new page using the Feedback Form template. Create another new page that will function as the confirmation page for the feedback form. Design the custom confirmation page so that it echoes the data input into the UserName, UserEmail, and UserTel fields in the input form, like the one shown in Figure 5.22.

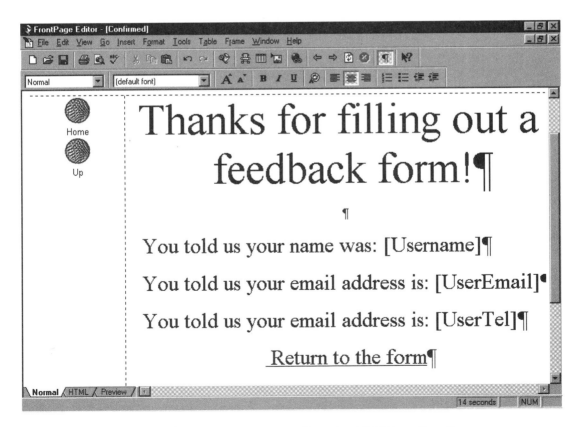

Figure 5.22 *Custom confirmation pages use Confirmation Field FrontPage Components.*

| MCSD 5.4 | **Including Active Elements** |

Active Elements include a wide assortment of mini-programs that do everything from display glowing navigation buttons to providing a search box. As a FrontPage Microsoft Certified Professional, you should have a basic overview of what these elements add to a Web site, and how they work. A quick overview of the Active Elements is available in Table 5.2.

Table 5.2 *Active Element Definitions*

Active Element	What it does
Hover Button	Generates buttons that can be used for navigation. These buttons alternate the display of different effects and/or images.
Banner Ad Manager	Generates a banner that rotates different images.
Marquee	Displays text that scrolls across the page.
Search Form	Creates a search box for the Web site.
Hit Counter	Generates a display of the number of visits to a page. Exactly the same as the Hit Counter Component.
Video	Inserts an *.avi format.

Active Elements and Browser Compatibility

Question: Are the objects generated by Active Elements interpreted by all browsers?

Answer: Yes ... and no.

Two of the Active Elements, Hover buttons and the Banner Ad Manager, generate Java applets. Pages with Hover buttons or Banner Ads require Java enabled browsers to display. Every version of Netscape Navigator and Internet Explorer version 3 and higher meets those requirements.

Other page objects generated by Active Elements are not as widely browser-friendly. Scrolling text marquees are activated by HTML code that is not interpreted by older versions, or Netscape 4.5.

Another compatibility issue arises when you include *.avi format video files using the Video Active Element menu option. Current versions of Netscape (through version 4.5) do not interpret *.avi video files, while IE 3 and higher does.

The remaining Active Elements generate code that is interpreted by current generation browsers.

Creating Hover Buttons

Hover buttons react when a visitor's mouse cursor hovers over them in a browser. Hover buttons can react by changing color, or shade, or displaying other effects like glowing, reverse colors, or bevels. The main functionality of Hover buttons is that they are fun, and add colorful interactivity to a Web page.

To define a Hover button:

1. In the FrontPage Editor, with a page open, select Insert, Active Elements, Hover Button. The Hover Button dialog box appears, as shown in Figure 5.23.
2. In the Button text box, enter text to display on the button.
3. If you wish to assign a hyperlink to your Hover button, use the Browse button next to the Link to box to locate a target link.
4. Use the remaining boxes in the dialog box to define effects to apply to the button. The effects will become active when a visitor moves his or her mouse cursor over the button.
5. The Custom button in the Hover Button dialog box opens up the Custom dialog box, shown in Figure 5.24. You can define sounds or images to display in a Hover button, in addition to the available list of effects. Finally, click on the OK button to generate the Hover button.

Hover buttons are created by generating Java code. Because of that, they are compatible with any browser that interprets Java. You can see the Java code in HTML view in the FrontPage Editor, as shown in Figure 5.25.

Using the Banner Ad Manager

The Banner Ad Manager creates an object that alternates the display of different images. The name comes from the fact that many Web sites include a banner at the top or bottom of the page that rotates a number of different

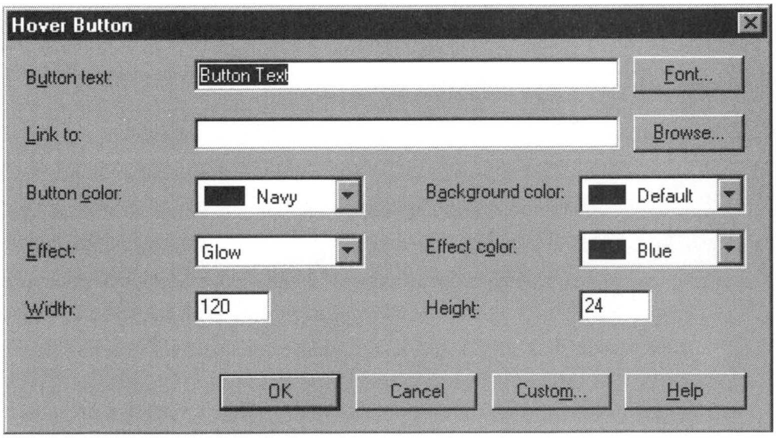

Figure 5.23 *Defining a Hover button.*

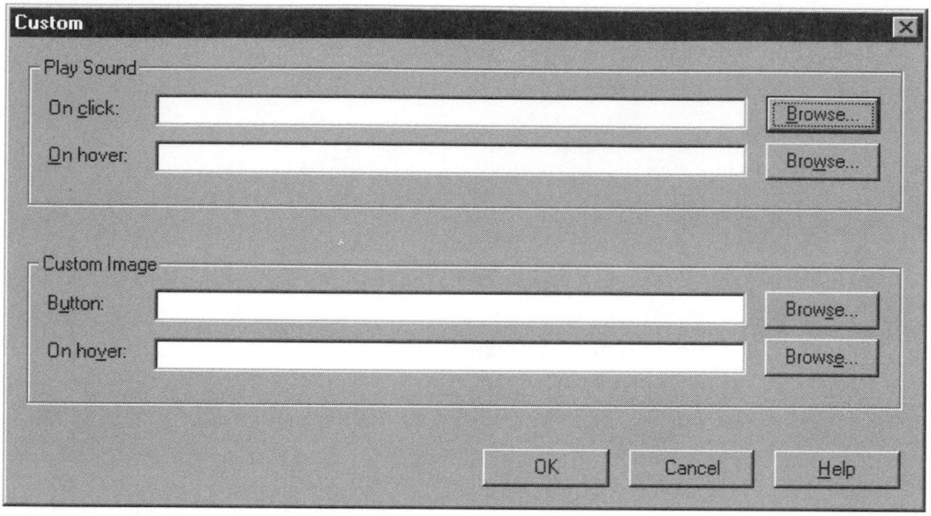

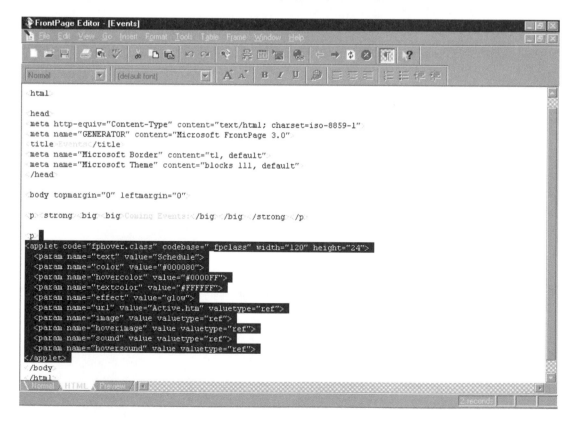

Figure 5.24 *Defining special image and sound effects for a Hover button.*

Figure 5.25 *Hover buttons are Java applets.*

advertisements. However, Banner Ads can be any group of images, not necessarily advertisements.

To define a Banner Ad:

1. In the FrontPage Editor, with a page open, select Insert, Active Elements, Banner Ad Manager. The Banner Ad Manager dialog box appears, as shown in Figure 5.26.
2. Use the Add button to add images to the list of Images to Display.
3. Use the pull-down list and box in the Transition area of the dialog box to define a type of transition from one image to the next.
4. Use the Browse button next to the Link To box to select an (optional) link target for the Banner Ad. Finally, click OK to add the banner to the page.

Links from Banner Ads are limited a single target, which means you cannot use them to provide different links to each image displayed in the banner. In other words, no matter how many images are in the banner, they must all link to the same target.

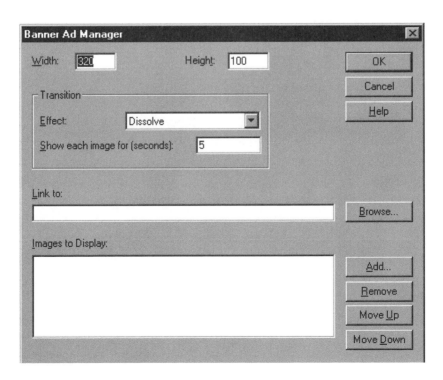

Figure 5.26 *The Banner Ad Manager dialog box.*

Defining a Text Marquee

Scrolling marquees move text across, or back and forth in a browser window. You can scroll, slide, or alternate text, from right to left, or left to right.

- Scrolling moves text back and forth across the screen.
- Sliding moves text into view from one side of the marquee, and then locks it in place once the entire text is displayed.
- Alternating bounces text back and forth across the screen like a ping pong ball.

Marquees are among the least compatible of Microsoft FrontPage objects. Marquee text, when viewed in Netscape, doesn't move. It does display, but it just appears like normal text. Marquees are visible in IE starting with version 2.

To define a marquee:

1. In the FrontPage Editor, with a page open, select Insert, Active Elements, Marquee. The Marquee Properties dialog box appears, as shown in Figure 5.27.
2. Enter text to display in the Text box of the dialog box.
3. Use the remaining option buttons and boxes to define the marquee display. Then click on OK.
4. You can preview the marquee effect in Preview tab of the FrontPage Editor, or in Internet Explorer.

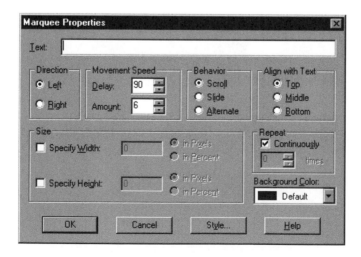

Figure 5.27 *Defining Marquee Properties.*

Creating a Search Form

Search forms allow visitors to locate pages in a Web site based on matching criteria. Search forms are particularly useful in Web sites with large numbers of pages, where visitors will want to locate data directly, rather than being guided by navigational links.

To insert a search box:

1. In the FrontPage Editor, select Insert, Active Elements, Search Form. The Search Form Properties dialog box appears.
2. Use the Search Form Properties tab to define the size of the search field, and the labels for the submit and reset buttons.
3. In the Search Results tab, you can restrict the search to a defined Web folder by entering that folder in the Word List to Search box.
4. The Score, File Date and File Size check boxes define the information that is displayed with search results.
5. After you define your search form, click on OK.

The three check boxes in the Search Results tab of the Search Form Properties dialog box control how results are displayed. Figure 5.28 shows all three search result options displayed.

- Score is the closeness of match.
- File date is the date the page was last changed.
- File size is the size of the Web page.

How Does FrontPage "Score" Results?

The system used to score search matches in FrontPage is undocumented. Just how is the match "score" calculated? A bit of experimenting reveals the basic method behind score assignments.

Figure 5.28 shows the results with three Web pages displayed that match a search criteria. The highest score went to a page with text that matched the search criteria. This is the most weighted element in determining a search "score." The middle score went to a page where the page title matched the search criteria. Page titles are the second most important element in assigning a page score. The lowest score went to the page that simply had a link that matched the criteria. Pages with links that match search criteria are the least important element in defining a search box "score."

You can hide pages from search engines by placing them in folders that begin with an underscore. By default, a folder called, for example, _private, is not available to FrontPage Search forms.

The more sophisticated templates and wizards generate, or can generate, Search Forms. Search Forms are optional elements in Webs options in

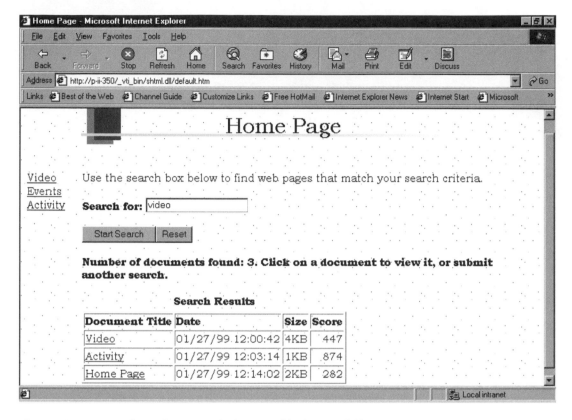

Figure 5.28 *Search results can include score, file date, and file size.*

the Corporate Presence wizard and the Discussion Web wizard. The Front-Page Customer Support Web and Project Web templates create pages with Search Forms.

Inserting a Hit Counter

The Hit Counter Active Element is exactly the same thing as the Hit Counter component. Perhaps the interface will be streamlined in future versions of FrontPage. For a full discussion of Hit Counters, see the section "Adding Hit Counters" in this chapter.

Including Video Files

To insert a video:

1. In the FrontPage Editor, with a page open, select Insert, Active Elements, Video. The Video dialog box appears.
2. In the Video dialog box, select a video file in your Web (to import a video file, use the Import dialog box, explained in the section "Importing Existing Web Sites" in Chapter 2).
3. Click on OK in the dialog box. The video is embedded in the Web page. The first frame of the video displays in the FrontPage Editor.
4. Right-click on a video object in the FrontPage Editor, and select Image Properties to define display attributes for the video. The Video tab in the Image Properties dialog box allows you to define how a video displays.

There are other video formats that can be inserted into FrontPage Web pages using the Insert, File command. These video formats (like MPEG) are available to visitors with browsers that have plug-in programs that play these files.

Study Break

Inserting a Search Form, a Marquee, a Hit Counter, and a Hover Button in a Web Page

First, open an existing Web (or create a new one using the Personal Web template). Open a page in the FrontPage Editor, and insert a marquee that displays a message welcoming visitors to your Web page. Use yellow as the background color for your marquee.

Next, add three Hover buttons. Use the same effects and colors for each button, but use them as separate links to three different Web pages.

Finally, create a Search Form that displays Score and File Date for matching pages. If possible, test your page in both Internet Explorer and Netscape Navigator. (All elements will function in IE 3 and higher, and the Search Form and Hover buttons will work, but the scrolling text marquee will not display in Netscape Navigator 4.5.)

■ Summary

In this chapter, we quickly looked at one of the most basic dynamic elements of a user interface—hyperlinks. Hyperlinks (or links—same thing) transform text or images into transport points to other locations on the Web.

Most of this chapter was devoted to a survey of FrontPage's Components and Active Elements. We looked at each Active Element and Component and explored how these add interactivity to Web pages.

Many Active Elements and Components create server compatibility issues for Web sites, and we noted these. For example, the Java applets required for Hover buttons cannot be interpreted by IE version 2. And, Netscape Navigator 4.5 does not recognize the scrolling text marquees generated by FrontPage's Marquee component.

▲ CHAPTER REVIEW QUESTIONS

Here are some practice questions relating to the material covered in the "Designing User Interface and User Services" area of Microsoft's Designing and Implementing Web Sites Using Microsoft FrontPage 98 exam (70-055).

1. *FrontPage Search Forms generate lists of pages that match search criteria by including which of these elements? (Select all correct answers.)*
   A. Matching page titles
   B. Matching comment text
   C. Matching navigational links
   D. Matching field names
   E. Matching page text

2. *Which of the following are important factors in defining navigation strategies for a Web site? (Select all correct answers.)*
   A. Bandwidth
   B. Site content
   C. Encryption strategies
   D. FrontPage extension files
   E. The intended audience

3. *Browser compatibility is an issue when using FrontPage Components.*
   A. True
   B. False

4. *Hover button Active Components are Java applets.*
   A. True
   B. False

5. *Banner Ad Manager Active Elements are ActiveX scripts.*
   A. True
   B. False

6. *Which of the following are techniques for directly entering HTML code in the FrontPage Editor? (Select all correct answers.)*
   A. Entering HTML in the HTML tab
   B. Entering HTML in the Preview tab
   C. Entering HTML in an HTML Component dialog box
   D. Entering HTML in a Code dialog box
   E. Entering HTML as an Include Page Component.

7. *Some FrontPage Active Elements work only if FrontPage Web Sites are published to:*
   A. Microsoft Internet Information Server version II or higher
   B. Servers with FrontPage Extensions
   C. Unix servers
   D. Apache servers
   E. Web servers that support sufficient bandwidth

8. *Confirmation fields test the validity of hyperlinks.*
   A. True
   B. False

9. *Comment text can be viewed in most Web browsers using options to view source code.*
   A. True
   B. False

10. *Most FrontPage Active Elements require an advanced level of scripting skill to add to Web sites.*
    A. True
    B. False

11. *Confirmation fields are required for custom-designed confirmation pages.*
    A. True
    B. False

12. *Which of the following Components or Active Elements might be useful for embedding changeable data in dozens of Web pages in a Web site? (Select all correct answers.)*
    A. Substitution Components
    B. Scheduled Include Page Components
    C. Search Form Components
    D. Hover buttons
    E. Marquees

13. *Hover buttons are interpreted only in Internet Explorer.*
    A. True
    B. False

14. *Which of the following templates or wizards include options for search forms? (Select all correct answers.)*
    A. The Corporate Presence wizard
    B. The Personal Web template
    C. The Discussion Web wizard
    D. The FrontPage Customer Support Web Template
    E. The Project Web template

15. *FrontPage Page Banner Components display: (Select all correct answers.)*
    A. alternative images
    B. page titles
    C. page file names
    D. embedded Java applets
    E. scheduled images

Establishing a Development Environment

Installing FrontPage is more complex than in-
stalling Microsoft Office applications like Excel or
Word. It involves selecting, installing, and config-
uring a Web server on which to test and publish
FrontPage Webs. And it involves integrating
FrontPage with existing development tools.

In this chapter, we'll explore the process of installing FrontPage, setting up and configuring
FrontPage servers, and installing server extensions
that are essential to many important FrontPage
features.

At the conclusion of this chapter you will be able to:

- Understand the role of server extensions in
  FrontPage Web development

- Install FrontPage 98

- Install FrontPage 98 Server Extensions

- Install and use the Personal Web Server

- Understand how FrontPage 98 can be integrated with Visual SourceSafe

133

FrontPage 98 and FrontPage Server Extensions

Installing FrontPage 98 is a bit more complex and challenging than installing other types of application software. The challenge comes from integrating the three essential components of FrontPage 98. Two of those components make up the FrontPage program itself, and they are the FrontPage Explorer and the FrontPage Editor. The third element in the equation is a Web server. Without a Web server, FrontPage is a severely truncated program.

As a certified professional, you will need to understand, explain, and implement policies that adhere to the vital connection between FrontPage, and FrontPage server extensions. For example, without a connection to a FrontPage-friendly Web server, your clients will have a much more difficult time implementing input forms, and find it impossible to utilize many of the helpful FrontPage Components and Active Elements explored in Chapter 5.

In this section, I'll discuss conceptually how FrontPage's interdependent components work together, and then I'll get under the hood and explore the nuts and bolts of making the connections between all the required elements of FrontPage.

FrontPage Server Extension files circumvent and replace the need to write custom CGI code to handle processes like handling input form data or handing image map input. They are the keys that unlock much of the power of FrontPage.

Just how dysfunctional are FrontPage Webs when they are published to a server without FrontPage extensions? Throughout this book, as we investigate and explore various elements of FrontPage 98, you'll see notes that this or that feature requires that a site be published to a server with FrontPage extensions in order to work. Here, I'll review the FrontPage components and elements that don't work if a site is published to a non-FrontPage server. Many of these features can be enabled on servers without FrontPage extensions, but only with special programming at the server, and/or special arrangements with the server administrator.

Actually, Microsoft has gone to significant lengths to make sure that FrontPage can be used to develop Webs for non-FrontPage servers. The marketing strategy seems to be one of presenting a product that works with or without a FrontPage-friendly Web site. For example, FrontPage 98-generated input forms can be processed by servers without FrontPage extensions, but only if those servers have their own CGI coding to handle data, and only if the FrontPage-generated Web is custom-configured to mesh with those CGI scripts. Figure 6.1 shows an input form being configured for a server that does not have FrontPage extensions.

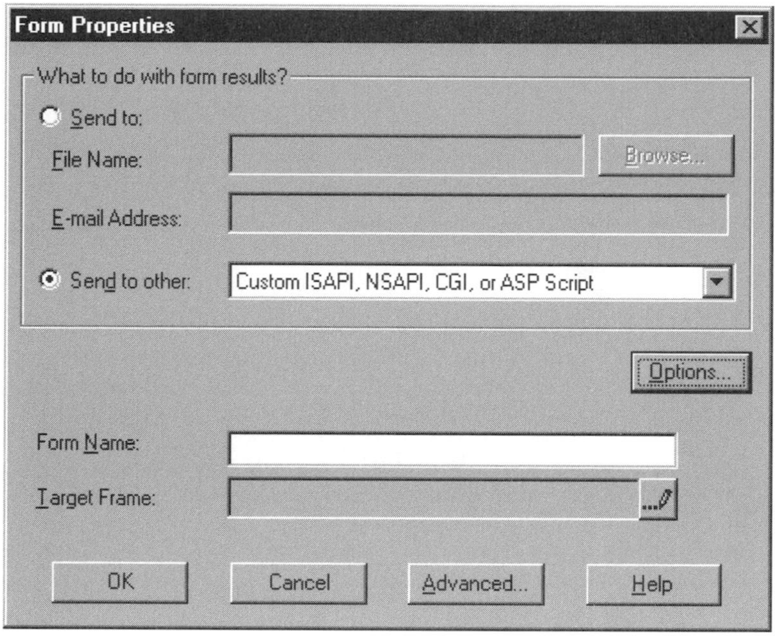

Figure 6.1   *Configuring input form processing for a non-FrontPage Web server.*

Similarly, FrontPage-created image maps can be processed by non-FrontPage Web servers, but only if these servers are specially configured to work with other image map standards. I'll address these specific issues when we look at the particular FrontPage feature (like image maps or input form processing). But the following is a list of key FrontPage features that require FrontPage extensions to work without any special arrangements with a Web server administrator:

- Discussion forums
- Hit counters
- Image maps
- Input form processing
- Registration
- Remote authoring
- Search boxes

If you are planning on implementing any of the features in the list, that is a significant argument for finding a Web server with FrontPage extensions to host your Web site, or installing FrontPage extensions on your Web server.

There are two basic options for publishing a FrontPage Web site to a server with FrontPage extensions: Contract with one of the hundreds of commercial Web site providers who support FrontPage, or install FrontPage server extensions on your own Web server. An extensive list of providers who support FrontPage is found at:

http://microsoft.saltmine.com/frontpage/wpp/list/

A typical offering for FrontPage-enabled Web hosting is illustrated in Figure 6.2. Of course, as the ads say, "prices may vary," but you can get a general picture of the price range for FrontPage Web hosting from the folks at Akorn.net.

Later in this chapter I'll explain the process of installing FrontPage server extensions on a Web server.

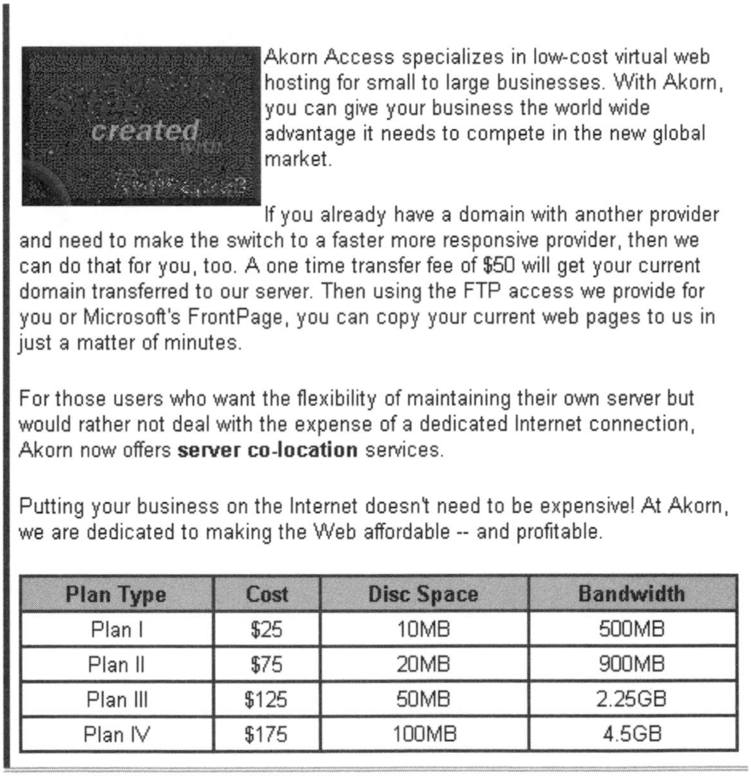

Akorn Access specializes in low-cost virtual web hosting for small to large businesses. With Akorn, you can give your business the world wide advantage it needs to compete in the new global market.

If you already have a domain with another provider and need to make the switch to a faster more responsive provider, then we can do that for you, too. A one time transfer fee of $50 will get your current domain transferred to our server. Then using the FTP access we provide for you or Microsoft's FrontPage, you can copy your current web pages to us in just a matter of minutes.

For those users who want the flexibility of maintaining their own server but would rather not deal with the expense of a dedicated Internet connection, Akorn now offers **server co-location** services.

Putting your business on the Internet doesn't need to be expensive! At Akorn, we are dedicated to making the Web affordable -- and profitable.

Plan Type	Cost	Disc Space	Bandwidth
Plan I	$25	10MB	500MB
Plan II	$75	20MB	900MB
Plan III	$125	50MB	2.25GB
Plan IV	$175	100MB	4.5GB

Figure 6.2 *Hosting options from a commercial FrontPage-friendly Web site provider.*

Installing FrontPage 98

During the installation process you will encounter three substantial decisions:

- Should you install Internet Explorer?
- Should you install Microsoft Image Composer 1.5?
- Should you install the Personal Web Server?

These options are displayed in the Install splash screen, as shown in Figure 6.3.

Before walking you through the process of installing FrontPage, it will be helpful to provide an overview on these three components of FrontPage 98 so you can provide informed advice on which elements to install under different situations.

Should You Install Internet Explorer?

There is no substitute for testing FrontPage Web sites during the development process, using the two globally dominant Web browsers—Internet Explorer and Netscape Navigator. FrontPage's Preview mode does allow you to preview some site features that are not functional in the FrontPage Editor, but a complete test of a Web site requires frequent previewing in a browser.

Figure 6.3 *Three options for Installing FrontPage 98.*

For example, input form processing cannot be tested in Preview mode; testing input form data handling requires a browser.

For some not-so-mysterious reason, Microsoft has chosen not to include Netscape Navigator with FrontPage. But Microsoft has been kind enough to bundle Internet Explorer with FrontPage. Since browsers are updated frequently, and have been updated since FrontPage 98, you may well want to get the latest version of IE from Microsoft's Web site (www.microsoft.com) or install it from your Windows or Office CD.

Should You Install Image Composer?

Microsoft Image Composer (version 1.5) is bundled with FrontPage 98, and is one of the installation options presented when you install FrontPage. Even the folks at Microsoft don't seem to quite appreciate what they have in

Figure 6.4 *Microsoft Image Composer 1.5.*

Image Composer. It's fast, powerful, and free when you buy FrontPage. You won't see ads for Image Composer during half time at the superbowl, but it is a professional level Web graphics tool that comes with FrontPage.

Unlike more prestigious graphics tools like PhotoShop, PhotoPaint or CorelDRAW, Image Composer is dedicated to creating graphics for Web sites. It is the default graphics editor for FrontPage 98, and launches (if installed), when a developer double-clicks on an image in the FrontPage Editor.

Because Image Composer is not directly addressed in the MCP/MCSD exam, we won't explore it in depth here. But you should be aware that this program is part of the installation options, and that it launches when you double-click on a picture in the FrontPage Editor, or on an image file in The FrontPage Explorer.

Since Image Composer is not the focus of questions in the exam, I'll leave our discussion of it to the brief description above, and a quick look at the interface in Figure 6.4. I'll also touch on Image Composer in Chapter 12, when we discuss Web graphics.

For complete exploration of Microsoft Image Composer, see *Wild Web Graphics with Microsoft Image Composer* (Que Books). You can also find tutorials on Image Composer at www.ppinet.com.

Study Break

Changing Default Graphics Editor

While I'm one of the world's biggest proponents of Image Composer, I will concede that you are going to encounter environments where the developers would rather assign their own favorite graphics program as the default image editor.

You can define a different image editing program as the default graphics editor in the FrontPage Explorer.

1. Select Tools, Options and click on the Configure Editors tab.

2. Select the gif image type and click on Modify.

Figure 6.5 shows Paint Brush being configured as a default Web graphics editor for gif images. This process can be repeated for jpeg and other file formats.

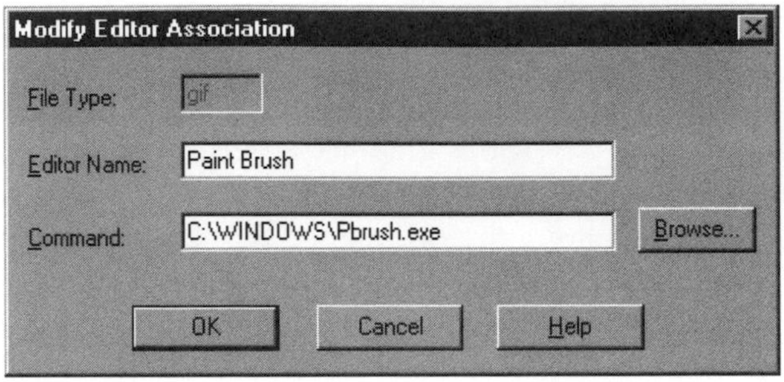

Figure 6.5 *Reconfiguring the default image editor.*

Installing FrontPage 98

After you select Install FrontPage 98 from the Install splash screen, the familiar Microsoft install interface appears. You'll be prompted to exit all programs (you should, to make installation more reliable).

You'll need to agree to adhere to the Microsoft FrontPage license agreement, and you'll need to provide the CD key that is on the back of your CD case. Don't lose the case! You'll need it each time you reinstall FrontPage, or when you need to add or remove components.

You'll also need to select a folder in which to install FrontPage. Like other Microsoft Office applications, tampering with the default installation folders creates an ongoing challenge to find files, and if possible it's best to accept the default folder, C:\Program Files\Microsoft FrontPage. The folder structure and executable program files for installed FrontPage are shown in Figure 6.6.

If you select the Custom (as opposed to the Typical) option button in the Setup Type dialog box, you can use the check boxes in the Select Components dialog box to include the Server Extensions Resource Kit and the Server Extensions Administration Forms in your installation, as shown in Figure 6.7.

The Server Extensions Resource Kit (SERK) provides information on installing FrontPage extensions on various servers. The most recent version of this information (at this writing SERK version 1.4) is available from Microsoft at: http://officeupdate.microsoft.com/frontpage/wpp/

The SERK also explains how to use the associated Server Extensions Administration Forms, HTML forms that facilitate remote administration of server extensions. Updated versions of these forms are available online as well, currently at:

http://officeupdate.microsoft.com/frontpage/wpp/SERK/default.htm

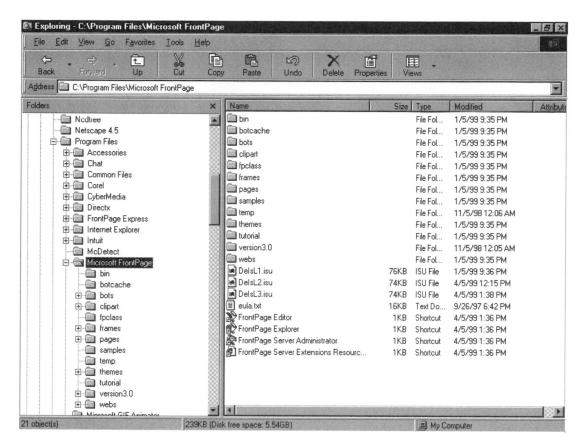

Figure 6.6   *The FrontPage program folder structure.*

Other check boxes allow you to install the FrontPage Personal Web Server or additional clip art. The clip art decision simply depends on how much clip art your development team will require.

FRONTPAGE PERSONAL WEB SERVER?

Normally, it is not necessary or desirable to select the FrontPage PWS check box during installation. The Server administration programs are small, and you can install them in case you need them later.

The FrontPage Personal Web Server presents a confusing installation issue. The distinction between the FrontPage Personal Web Server, and various versions of the Microsoft Personal Web Server is one of the more confusing and undocumented components of FrontPage. In brief, the FrontPage PWS is a stripped-down version of the Microsoft PWS, and there is no reason

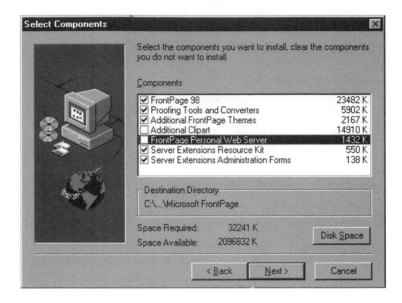

Figure 6.7 *Installing the Server Extensions Resource Kit and Server Extensions Administration Forms.*

to install it if you can install Microsoft PWS instead. Microsoft PWS is included on the FrontPage CD, and is also available (version 4) with Office 2000 or Internet Explorer 5.

The only real reason to know what the FrontPage PWS is, is in case you are asked about it on the exam, or you run into an environment where it is installed in stone, so to speak, and you have to work with it. The FrontPage PWS does not have handy features (like the ability to stop it from running without exiting) that are included with its younger and bigger brother. However, FrontPage PWS can be used to test FrontPage Web sites. The FrontPage PWS can only be maximized (or minimized), it has no options.

After you complete the installation wizard, the dialog box in Figure 6.8 indicates that you have completed installing FrontPage, and you can launch the FrontPage Explorer.

RUNNING THE TCP TEST

TCP stands for Transmission Control Protocol, and IP stands for Internet Protocol. IP defines the format used to transfer data across the Internet. TCP routes Internet data to its destination correctly. TCP/IP refers to both these functions, and together they enable FrontPage to interface with Web servers.

High on the list of support questions I field at my Web site and in on-site consulting is failure to connect FrontPage to a Web server. A whole

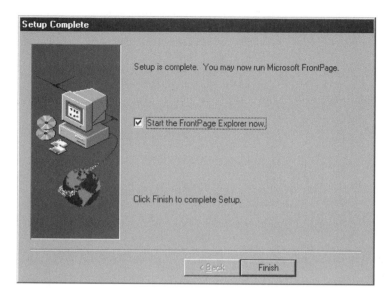

Figure 6.8 *Installation complete.*

range of server-integration issues can be identified and resolved by running the underrated TCP/IP test that comes with FrontPage.

One way to find the program is to use the Windows Find key to search for the program Tcptest.exe on your computer. Depending on what versions of Windows and Office you have, this program may be located in different directories, but a search for Tcptest.exe will reveal it.

When you double-click on the program file, the FrontPage TCP/IP test window appears, as shown in Figure 6.9. If your system does not "pass" the test, you will be prompted with a wizard that will alter your system configuration to allow for FrontPage Web development.

Figure 6.10 shows the TCP/IP test window after a successful test.

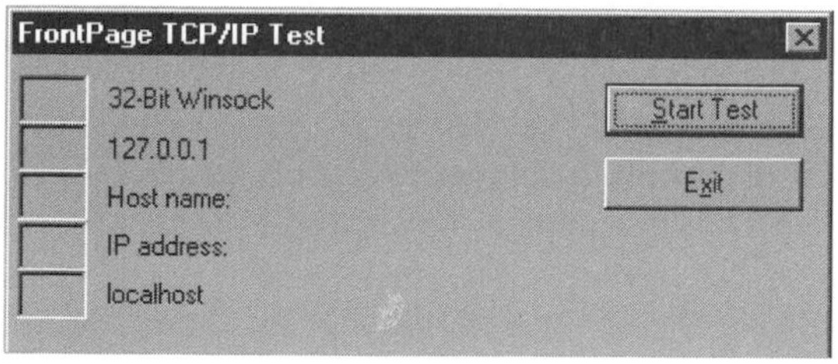

Figure 6.9 *Initiating the TCP/IP test.*

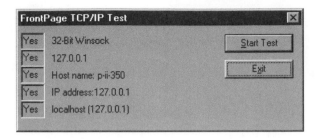

Figure 6.10 *A successful TCP/IP test.*

Study Break

Performing the TCP/IP Test on Your System

The TCP/IP test identifies whether your system is ready to be used for FrontPage Web development. Try it:

1. First, locate the file Tcptest.exe. Default installation places the file in this folder: C: \Program Files \Microsoft FrontPage \bin.

2. Run the test. Note the results.

3. If any of the required elements for FrontPage Web development are not present, you will be prompted with a dialog box allowing you to fix them.

MCSD 6.2   Installing FrontPage 98 Server Extensions

FrontPage Server Extensions may well represent the single most universal challenge to implementing Web development with FrontPage 98. To be a bit too crude, you can basically assume that FrontPage Web sites will not work well unless they are published to Web servers that have special files called FrontPage Extensions installed.

FrontPage Server Extensions can be installed on these servers:

- Microsoft Internet Information Server (IIS)
- Microsoft Personal Web Server (Microsoft PWS)
- FrontPage Personal Web Server (FrontPage PWS)
- Netscape Communicator
- Netscape Commerce
- Netscape Enterprise

- Netscape Fastrack
- WebSite

Normally, Microsoft Server software (including FrontPage PWS, the Microsoft PWS and IIS) has FrontPage extensions installed by default. However, sometimes you will want to reinstall FrontPage extensions to these servers (for example, to upgrade to a new version of extensions).

To install FrontPage server extensions on your system:

1. Locate the program that launches the FrontPage Server Administrator on your system. This might be either fp98swin.exe or fpsrvwin.exe on your system, depending on your operating system. Use the most recent version of either of these files in your system. They are installed by default in the following folder:
C:\Program Files\Microsoft FrontPage\version3.0\bin

You can run them by double-clicking on the file name in the Windows Explorer. If you followed the installation advice earlier in this chapter, the FrontPage Server Administration files were included in your custom installation. If not, use the FrontPage CD to install Server Administration files. Run your FrontPage Server Administrator program. When it launches, it will look like the window in Figure 6.11.

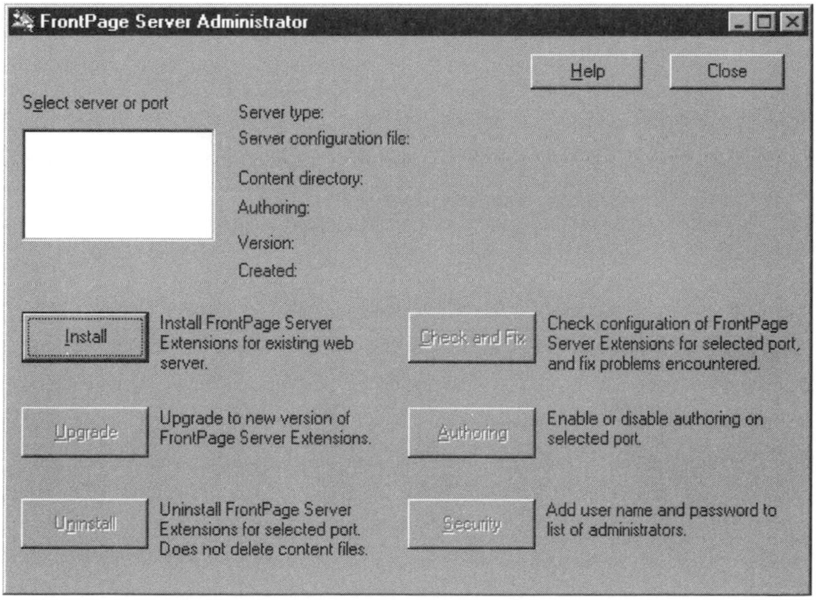

Figure 6.11   *The FrontPage 98 Server Administrator.*

2. Click on the Install button, and select the type of server to which you are installing FrontPage 98 extensions from the Server Type drop-down menu. Servers that you have installed on your system will be available in this drop-down menu. Then, OK the Configure Server Type dialog box.
3. After you select a Server, the Confirmation dialog box shown in Figure 6.12 documents the server type, the server port, and the document root folder for your server.
4. After you identify the server to which you are installing FrontPage extensions, you may be prompted to enter an administrator name. The information you are prompted for will vary depending on the server. After you provide all the information required by the particular server to which you are installing FrontPage extensions, FrontPage extension files will be copied to your server. Once FrontPage extension files are installed, the Upgrade, Uninstall, Check and Fix, Authoring and Security buttons in the Server Administrator dialog box become active, as shown in Figure 6.12.

Ports and Servers in FrontPage 98

Server administration involves installing and maintaining FrontPage server extensions on assigned servers and ports. Servers provide Web content and interface with a Web client that interprets and interacts with the content on the server. You can install one, two, even three (or theoretically

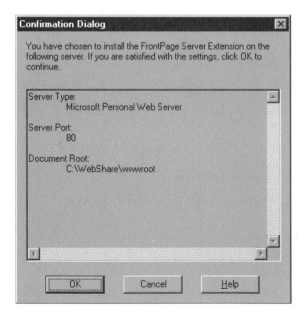

Figure 6.12 *Server extensions have been installed.*

more) servers on your computer. For example, you could install the frugal FrontPage Personal Web Server to test your FrontPage Web, the slightly more robust Microsoft Personal Web Server for a small, interoffice intranet, and Microsoft Internet Information Server to use your NT server as a full-fledged Internet access server.

When you install servers, FrontPage will associate that server with a port. Every server must be associated with a port to connect to clients on the Internet, or on an intranet. The default port for installing a first server is 80, and the FrontPage assigns the second server to 8080 by default. If you install more than one server on your system, you must associate a different port with each server.

By allowing you to install a full-fledged server with FrontPage extensions on even a stand-alone desktop or laptop, FrontPage enables you to test your Web site in a real-world Web environment before transferring the files to an Internet or intranet-connected server.

Upgrading Server Extensions

One troubleshooting challenge that you will encounter periodically is resolving server extension conflicts between different installed servers. For example, when an upgrade comes out for FrontPage 2000, you will want to upgrade the FrontPage extension files on your servers to support whatever new features in FrontPage require updated server files.

To upgrade installed FrontPage Server Extensions for a selected server and port, click on the Upgrade button in the FrontPage Server Administrator. The root Web and any sub-Webs will be upgraded to the latest version of the Server Extensions on the server machine.

Uninstalling Server Extensions

The Uninstall button in the FrontPage Server Administrator removes FrontPage extensions from the selected port.

When you uninstall server extension files, FrontPage will not tamper with your defined Web sites. So, your HTML, GIF and other Web content files will not be uninstalled. Nor will your server software itself be uninstalled. However, your server will function without FrontPage extensions, and will not support many important FrontPage features.

Administering Server Security

You can use the Security button in the FrontPage Server Administrator to add a user name and password to the list of administrators for the selected port.

In Figure 6.13, I'm adding myself as an administrator.

The Authoring button in the FrontPage Server Administrator allows you to enable or disallow authoring on the Web you are administering. Dis-

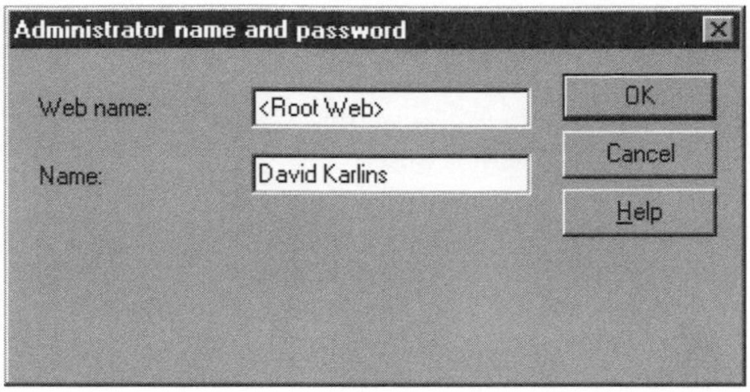

Figure 6.13 *Adding an administrator.*

able authoring if you do not want to allow anyone to edit the contents of a Web site.

The Check button in the FrontPage Server Administrator fixes missing FrontPage directories and files that are required for FrontPage to access a server. If you are using Microsoft Internet Information Server or the Microsoft Personal Web Servers, the Fix button also displays a dialog box with an option to tighten security. If you select the Yes option button, FrontPage assigns the maximum security settings to folders and files in your Webs.

Study Break

Identifying and Checking Servers on Your System

In this exercise you will use the FrontPage Server Administrator to identify existing servers.

First, locate the FrontPage Server Administrator program.

Next, run the FrontPage Server Administrator program. Click on the Install button in the FrontPage Server Administrator window, and click on the Server Type drop-down menu in the Configure Server Type dialog box. The list reveals servers installed on your system (if any). After viewing the list, click on Cancel.

Click on the Check and Fix button in the FrontPage Server Administrator. If prompted to change your security settings, select No. Examine the report generated by the Check and Fix button.

Finally, close the FrontPage Server Administrator window.

MCSD 6.3 Installing the FrontPage Personal Web Server or the Microsoft Personal Web Server

The FrontPage Personal Web Server is shipped with FrontPage, and can be installed if you select the Custom installation option and select the Front-Page Personal Web Server check box. The Microsoft Personal Web Server ships with Windows 98 and FrontPage 98. It can be installed from the PWS folder in FrontPage 98.

If users check the FrontPage Personal Web Server check box during installation, they will automatically install the FP PWS, with FrontPage Extensions.

The folder includes an HTML page (E:\PWS\Upgrade\enu\Upgrade.htm, if your CD is in drive E) that provides helpful discussion of the differences between FrontPage PWS and Microsoft PWS, beyond what I've explained here. It also explains how to tell which server you have installed, and how to run both on your system. That last option (running both MS PWS and FP PWS) is one that should be attempted only by system administrators who enjoy creating non-essential system conflicts. As I've indicated before, the Microsoft Personal Web Server is simply better, and it is hard to imagine an environment that would call for installing both the MS PWS and FP PWS. But you may confront such a situation, and it will be necessary to recognize it.

The FP PWS is indicated by the window tray button in Figure 6.14.

The Microsoft Personal Web Server is indicated by the tray button in Figure 6.15.

The PWS folder on the FrontPage CD has five folders for different language setup programs for the Microsoft Personal Web Server. The PWS\enu folder holds the file pwssetup.exe. Double-click on that file to install the Microsoft Personal Web Server.

Figure 6.14 *This tray button indicates FrontPage Personal Web Server is installed.*

Figure 6.15   *This tray button indicates Microsoft Personal Web Server is installed.*

Using Microsoft Personal Web Server

Microsoft Personal Web server is essentially a stripped-down version of Internet Information Server. By installing it and using it (instead of the FrontPage Personal Web Server), you can enable many Web administration tools not available in the FP PWS. For example, MS Personal Web Server allows you to restrict access to users or groups, and to assign password encryption for your site.

At this writing, the MS PWS was available as part of IE 5, and can be downloaded from: http://www.microsoft.com/windows/ie/download/windows.htm

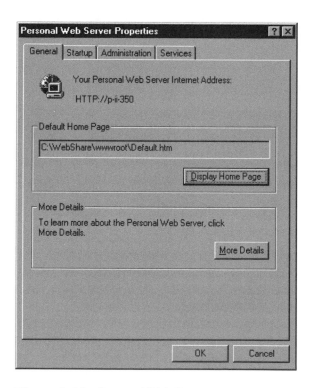

Figure 6.16   *Personal Web Server properties.*

You can activate the Personal Web Server Properties box by double-clicking on the icon in the Windows tray. The General tab displays the default server home page, as shown in Figure 6.16.

The Startup tab of the Personal Web Server Properties dialog box has Start and Stop buttons that allow you to start or stop the Web server. It also includes option buttons that start the PWS on startup of your system, and show the server icon in the taskbar.

The real power of Microsoft PWS is activated by the Administration button in the Administration tab. This launches Administration Web page interface. That Web page includes a link to Local User Administration, shown in Figure 6.17.

Finally, the Services tab allows you to enable or stop HTML and/or FTP transmission to and from your Web server.

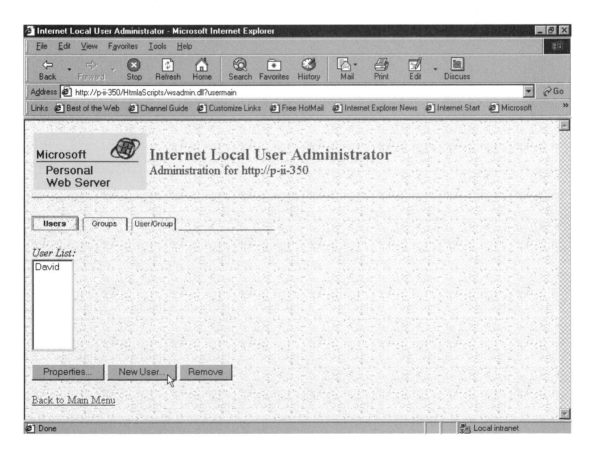

Figure 6.17 *Adding users in the Internet Local User Administrator.*

Study Break

Stopping and Restarting Your Server

You may want to stop your Web server from running. For example, installing some software (or hardware) requires that a Web server be stopped.

First, identify your server.

Next, double-click on the icon for your server in the System Tray to open the Server Window. Stop the server.

Finally, restart the server.

MCSD 6.4   Integrating with Visual SourceSafe

Microsoft wants FrontPage experts to be familiar with integrating FrontPage development with Visual SourceSafe. Visual SourceSafe can be used by developers of large and complex Web sites to manage versions of files. Files are "checked out" of SourceSafe for editing, and backup versions are stored. SourceSafe, then, keeps a log of changes to files.

All this can be used to track FrontPage Web site files as well. Visual SourceSafe can create a map of the HTML files in your Web site, and manage revisions.

The Visual SourceSafe interface looks something like the FrontPage Explorer, and lists and manages access to files.

While Visual SourceSafe protects files from unauthorized access *within* a development environment, it does not play the same role as Firewall software in protecting your files from *outside* intrusion.

This basic overview of what Visual SourceSafe does should get you through the SourceSafe questions in the exam, and allow you to explain to managers of SourceSafe environments how they can integrate FrontPage into their file management systems. For more information on SourceSafe, see:

- *Special Edition Using HTML 4,* Que, Chapter 38 "Managing and Staging Files"
- *Special Edition Using InterDev,* Chapter 22
- The SourceSafe Web site at http://msdn.microsoft.com/ssafe/

Study Break

Reading up on Visual SourceSafe

> Visual SourceSafe is a completely different program than FrontPage. But Microsoft wants us to be aware that in development environments where it is in use, it can also be used to monitor and supervise access to Web files.
>
> Read up a bit on how Visual SourceSafe works so that you are familiar with the basic concept and terminology. To do that, visit: http://www.microsoft.com/products/prodref/223_ov.htm.
>
> This site provides a very clear, basic overview of how SourceSafe works.

■ Summary

Installing FrontPage 98 involves installing not just FrontPage, but also selecting, installing, and configuring a Web server, without which you cannot publish or test FrontPage Webs.

FrontPage comes with two servers, the FrontPage Personal Web Server, and the Microsoft Personal Web Server. The Microsoft PWS is a much more robust, full-featured server that allows you to perform administrative tasks like assigning user permission and passwords.

FrontPage extension files enable Web servers to support essential FrontPage features like easy-to-use image maps and self-defining form handling. These extension files can be installed on a variety of servers.

▲ CHAPTER REVIEW QUESTIONS

Here are a some practice questions relating to the material covered in the "Establishing a Development Environment" area of Microsoft's *Designing and Implementing Web Sites Using Microsoft FrontPage 98* exam (70-055).

1. *FrontPage is shipped with which of the following Web browsers? (Select all correct answers.)*

   A. Netscape Navigator

   B. Netscape Communicator

   C. Internet Explorer

   D. AOL's proprietary browser

2. *Which of the following types of Web servers can have FrontPage extensions installed to them? (Select all correct answers.)*

    A. FrontPage Personal Web Server

    B. Microsoft Personal Web Server

    C. Microsoft Internet Information Server

    D. Netscape Commerce Server

    E. Netscape Communicator

3. *By default, the first server defined as Port 80.*

    A. True

    B. False

4. *Server extensions frequently need to be upgraded when FrontPage 98 is installed.*

    A. True

    B. False

5. *Visual SourceSafe provides much of the same functionality as firewall protection software.*

    A. True

    B. False

6. *Which of the following are options for installing FrontPage 98? (Select all correct answers.)*

    A. You can elect to install the FrontPage Editor.

    B. You can elect to install the FrontPage Personal Web Server.

    C. You can elect to install the Microsoft Personal Web Server.

    D. You can elect to install Microsoft PhotoDraw.

    E. You can elect to install Internet Explorer.

7. *Many key FrontPage components work only when FrontPage Web sites are published to (Select all correct answers):*

    A. Microsoft Internet Information Server version II or higher

    B. Servers with FrontPage Extensions

    C. Unix servers

    D. Apache servers

    E. Web servers that support sufficient bandwidth

8. *Visual SourceSafe is of little use if you are managing a small Web site with just one developer.*

   A. True

   B. False

9. *The Microsoft Personal Web Server provides significantly more functionality than the FrontPage Personal Web Server.*

   A. True

   B. False

10. *If two servers are installed on the same system, the second server often uses Port 8080.*

    A. True

    B. False

11. *FrontPage server extensions eliminate the need for much CGI programming.*

    A. True

    B. False

12. *Which of the following elements of a FrontPage Web site require FrontPage server extensions? (Select all correct answers.)*

    A. Discussion forums

    B. Hit counters

    C. Search forms

    D. Hover buttons

    E. Image maps

13. *FrontPage can be used only to develop sites for servers with FrontPage extensions.*

    A. True

    B. False

14. *Which of the following will help trouble-shoot server errors? (Select all correct answers.)*

    A. The TCP/IP test

    B. The Server Administrator

    C. The FrontPage Editor

    D. FrontPage Server Extensions

    E. Internet Explorer

15. *Visual SourceSafe protects against which of the following dangers? (Select all correct answers.)*

    A. Unauthorized entry into a Web site

    B. Deleting crucial Web site files

    C. Unauthorized editing of Web pages

    D. Viruses

    E. Undocumented changes to Web pages

Creating User Services

FrontPage's array of built-in user services includes navigational systems, frames, and shared borders. We'll explore all of these in Chapter 7. Chapters 8, 9, and 10 are devoted to a detailed examination of creating input forms utilizing FrontPage's automated validation scripts, and managing input form results.

Creating User Interfaces

Here's a quick, one-question quiz: What do Shared Borders, Navigation Bars and framed pages have in common? If you guessed that they are different ways to implement navigation strategies, you've got a good grasp of the options Front-Page provides for orchestrating Web site browsing. If not, no problem. We'll connect these somewhat disparate elements of page design in this chapter, and you'll emerge with an understanding of the skills you need to make these features available to the FrontPage developers you assist with Web development.

159

In earlier chapters, particularly Chapter 5, "Designing a User Interface and User Services," we explored navigation strategies from the perspective of identifying and defining logical flow systems. We compared scenarios where, for example, visitors are looking for one of several thousand technical white papers at a Web site, with a situation where the Web site is presenting a carefully orchestrated sequence of Web pages to introduce a corporate image. These different scenarios require different strategies for placing navigation links. But regardless of what kind of flow between pages is defined for a Web site, there are some universal elements that facilitate visitors getting around.

The most universal element of facilitating Web site navigation is the placement of easy-to-find links which visitors can use to chart a course around (or out of) the site. In this chapter, you'll see how navigation bars, shared borders and frames provide alternatives for managing site navigation.

At the conclusion of this chapter you will be able to:

- Create shared borders for a Web site
- Understand how shared borders are saved and edited
- Configure shared borders
- Describe the role and functioning of navigation bars
- Alter the default titles assigned to navigation bars
- Create framed pages
- Define alternate page content for browsers without frame capability
- Define and troubleshoot frame page links

Defining Shared Borders

Shared borders can be placed on the right, left, top, or bottom border of Web pages, or any combination of those locations. Frequently, pages will be designed with shared borders on the top and left side of the page, and will include a page title (on top) and navigation links (on the left side). However, pages can have as many as four shared borders. Four borders on a page can present a somewhat cluttered look, but technically it is possible. Figure 7.1 shows a Web page with four shared borders in the FrontPage Editor. In the FrontPage Editor, the shared borders are delineated by dotted lines, but when the page is viewed in a browser, those lines are not visible.

Shared borders are *shared* in that there can be only one set of shared borders for an entire Web site. That means that if you define a top border for a Web page, that top border applies to every Web page in your Web site.

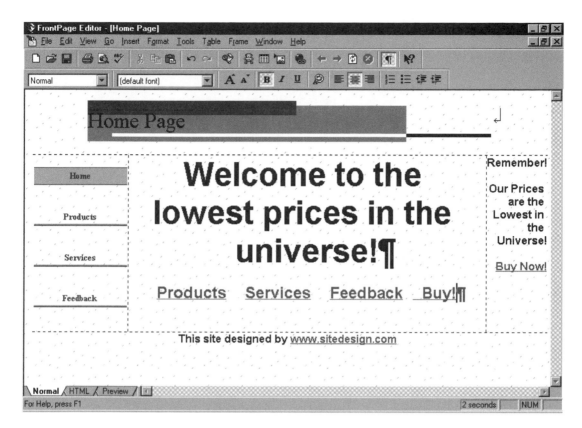

Figure 7.1   *Pages can include as many as four shared borders.*

You can turn off shared borders on selected pages. But you cannot define a different shared top border for different pages.

Does this mean that if you define four shared borders for a Web site each page must display all four of those shared borders? No, it does not. You can elect to display, or not display any of a site's shared borders on any Web page.

A frequent support question from FrontPage designers is: Why can't I change a shared border for just a single page? The answer is that shared borders are just that—*shared*. Elements that should appear on only one page should not be placed in shared borders. When a shared border is edited *in any page*, the changes are saved to the shared border and affect every page to which that shared border is assigned.

MCSD 7.1   Configuring Shared Borders

In Chapter 4, "Developing a Conceptual Design for a Web Site," we explored shared borders in the context of global Web design strategies. Here, I'll assume you're familiar with the use of shared borders as navigation aids, and their relationship with structures defined in Navigation View.

In this section, we'll look more closely at how shared borders are defined and edited both for an entire Web and for specific Web pages. Shared borders can be created or modified in either the FrontPage Editor or the FrontPage Explorer. And shared borders (unlike the more rigid Navigation Bars we discussed in Chapter 4) can be modified for individual pages. When you generate shared borders in the FrontPage Editor, you can both define global shared borders, and elect whether or not to display some, all, or none of those borders in the open page.

To generate shared borders for a Web site in the FrontPage Explorer, follow these steps:

1. Select Tools, Shared Borders. The Shared Borders dialog box appears as shown in Figure 7.2.
2. Use the check boxes to include up to four shared borders. The small preview screen on the left side of the dialog box illustrates the borders as you assign them.
3. After you assign shared borders, click on OK.

The options for defining shared borders in the FrontPage Editor are more flexible, and confusing. You can both generate new shared borders in the FrontPage Editor (just like we did in the set of steps above), or you can elect to display or hide those shared borders on the particular page you have open.

To generate shared borders for a Web site in the FrontPage Editor, follow these steps:

1. Select Tools, Shared Borders. The Page Borders dialog box appears as shown in Figure 7.3.
2. Select the Use Web Default option button to apply the default Web page border settings (the ones we defined in the earlier set of steps). Or, select the Set for This Page Only options button to display selected borders on the open page.

Note   While there is an option for defining shared borders for "This Page Only," that option button is a little deceptive. You can elect to display or hide shared borders for the open page, but you cannot define a *separate* shared border or set of shared borders for the selected page.

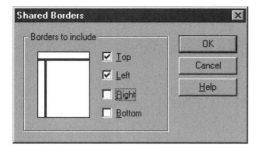

Figure 7.2 *Defining shared borders in the FrontPage Explorer.*

3. If you chose the second option in step 2, you can use the check boxes to include up to four shared borders for the selected page.
4. After you assign shared borders, click on OK.

Editing Shared Borders

After you define shared borders, they appear on Web pages in the FrontPage Editor demarcated by dotted lines. When you first generate a shared border, comment text appears in the shared border advising you to add some content. Again, that content will be assigned to a shared border, that is, embedded in any page in which you elect to display a shared border.

Shared borders are actually distinct Web pages kept in a hidden folder. When changes are made to a shared border in any Web page, and that page is then saved, the changes are applied to the hidden page file. That is why you will see a dialog box like the one in figure 7.4 when a page is saved.

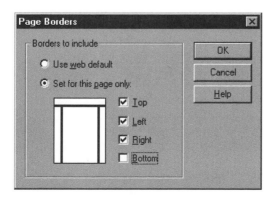

Figure 7.3 *Including shared borders in a specific page.*

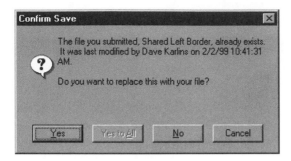

Figure 7.4 *Shared borders are distinct HTML Web pages, and are updated when Web pages are saved.*

Shared borders can have any content that any other page can have. You can insert text, graphics, even multimedia objects. However, shared borders are most frequently associated with navigation links. You can insert your own navigation links in a shared border (Home Page, external links, and so on). Or, you can combine shared borders with FrontPage's navigation bar elements to automatically include links to selected pages within a site. We'll explore navigation bars in the next section of this chapter.

Shared Borders and Frames

At this point in our discussion, experienced Web designers may be saying to themselves, "Hmmm, don't shared borders provide some of the same functionality that frames do?" We'll dig into that relationship at the end of this chapter, when we explore frames, but here it's worth noting that yes, there is quite a bit of overlap between the role played by framed pages and the role of shared borders.

Both frames and shared borders literally *frame* a page, and both often include navigation content. For this reason, it is rare that a site designer will want to employ both frames and shared borders.

From an aesthetic standpoint, pages surrounded by both frames and shared borders would be extremely cluttered. And from a function standpoint, both frames and shared borders provide an opportunity to include constant page elements that interact with changing page elements.

Which is better? That's a judgment call. Shared borders are less complex, less obtrusive, and more widely recognized, but they aren't as powerful or flexible as frames.

Exploring Hidden Folders

As mentioned earlier, shared borders are actually distinct HTML Web pages that are saved as part of the Web site. These files are saved in a hidden folder called _borders. The folder is generated automatically by FrontPage when shared borders are defined. And the files within it are automatically changed when border properties are changed.

Shared border files are named top.htm, bottom.htm, left.htm and right.htm. It is possible to open these files directly in the FrontPage Editor, and change them.

If you want to delete existing shared border files, you can delete them yourself in the hidden folder.

To view hidden file folders:

1. Select Tools, Web Settings from the FrontPage Explorer menu, and click on the Advanced tab in the FrontPage Web Settings dialog box.
2. Select the Show Documents in Hidden Directories check box, as shown in Figure 7.5.
3. Click on OK in the dialog box. The hidden folders appear in the Front-Page Editor, as shown in Figure 7.6.

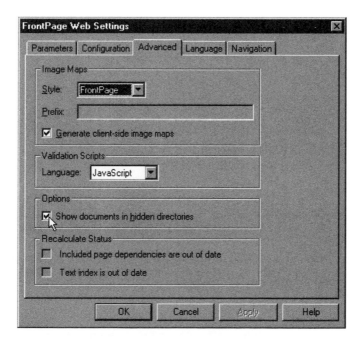

Figure 7.5 *Revealing hidden folders.*

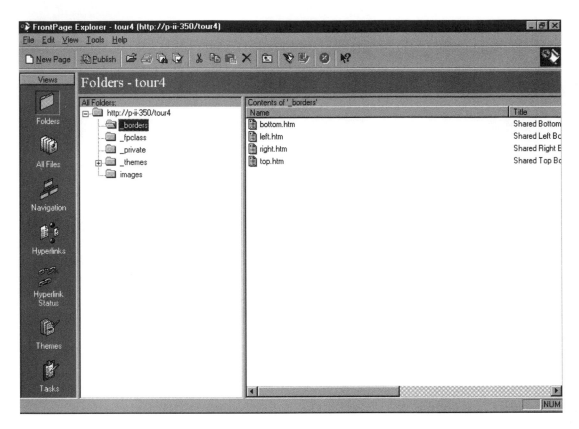

Figure 7.6 *Hidden folders, revealed.*

The _borders folder will have up to four html (*.htm) files. These are Web pages that can be opened and edited. In addition, if you embed image files or other files in shared borders, those files will display in the _borders folder as well.

> **Note** Other hidden folders include the _fpclass folder that holds Java applets, and the _themes folder that holds files used for themes. The _overlay folder contains image files for graphics associated with navigation buttons and page banners generated by themes.

There are some advantages to editing shared border pages by themselves, as opposed to editing them in another page in which they are embedded. For example, when you open an embedded shared border page, you can edit page properties like background color.

You'll find more discussion of shared borders in:

- Chapter 19 of *Teach Yourself FrontPage 98 in a Week*
- Chapter 8 of *The FrontPage 98 Bible*
- Chapter 7 of *Special Edition Using FrontPage 98*

Study Break

Assigning a Background Color to a Shared Border

To reinforce your understanding of shared borders, define a background color for a shared border.

1. Open an existing Web site, or create a new Web site using the Personal Web template.

2. Open a Web page, and from within it, define a shared border on the left side of the page. Save the page in which you created the shared border.

3. View hidden files in the FrontPage Explorer, and identify the folder with shared borders.

4. Open the shared border *.htm file in the FrontPage Explorer and assign a yellow page background. Close the shared border *.htm page. Select View, Refresh in the FrontPage Explorer, and examine changes to your shared border as it appears embedded in the original Web page.

Inserting Navigation Bars

Navigation bars are FrontPage's system for automatically inserting a logical selection of links in a page. The logic for this system of links is defined for the entire site. In this way, navigation bars have something in common with shared borders: they are *global*. You don't need to include a navigation bar on every page, but every navigation bar you place in your Web site will employ the same logic to generate a set of links for the page.

The logic for generating links in navigation bars is based on the structure of a Web site as defined in Navigation View in the FrontPage Explorer. Web navigation can be between parent and child pages, or between pages on the same hierarchal level. For example, in the Web site displayed in Figure 7.7, the home page has three child pages (Products, Services and Feedback). Those three child pages are on the same flowchart level. So, if you elected to generate links to child pages in your navigation links, the home page would automatically include links to the three child pages below it in the Navigation View flowchart. If you assigned same-level links, the Products, Services and Feedback pages would all be linked to each other.

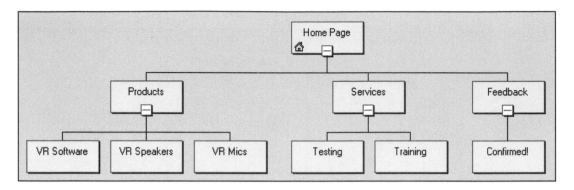

Figure 7.7 *Navigation bars are generated based on the structure defined in navigation links.*

Tips for Navigation Bars

- If there are no navigation links defined in Navigation View, no navigation links will be generated in a navigation bar.
- The Buttons option in the Navigation Bar Properties dialog box will generate graphical buttons only if a theme is applied to the page. (Themes can be assigned in Themes View in the FrontPage Explorer).
- The Home Page and Parent Page check boxes include the home page and parent page (using the family tree analogy in Navigation View). Most of the time, visitors will appreciate links to a home page in a Web site.
- Navigation bars are typically placed in shared borders. Placing navigation bars in shared borders includes them in each page in which the shared border displays.

MCSD 7.2 Altering Default Titles for Navigation Bars

Navigation bars are a powerful and sometimes confusing tool. The first question you will hear as a FrontPage Web site administrator is, "How can I change the navigation bar on this page?" You will need to educate the developers you work with to understand that navigation bars are different than custom links placed on a specific page. They are, instead, a system of generating links that is applied to an entire Web site, and cannot be customized for each page.

Links that are not generated in navigation bars can still be placed on specific pages in a Web site, or even all pages in a Web site. Remind developers that they can compensate for links not provided by navigation bars using simple hyperlinks. If a Web site needs a link from page A to page B, you can simply insert that link in the page itself.

You can also place hyperlinks to a selected URL on every page of a Web site by adding them to shared borders. Keep in mind, however, that links placed in a shared border appear in all pages in which the shared border is displayed.

 To edit a navigation bar, right-click on the bar and select Edit FrontPage Component Properties from the context menu. The Navigation Bar Properties dialog box reappears.

Once developers grasp the way navigation bars are defined and generated, the next two most frequently asked questions about navigation bars are:

- How can I change the titles for navigation bars?
- How can I change the labels generated for the home page, the next page, the previous page, or the parent page?

We will explore the solution to these two problems in the following sections.

Altering Navigation Bar Titles

When new pages are added to a Web site in Navigation View, FrontPage 98 assigns non-descriptive titles like "New Page 13." When navigation bars are generated, it is those page titles that display as links. That might work well for a numerology Web site, but for most Web sites, these page titles need to be a bit more creative and descriptive.

You can change page titles in Navigation View. To do that:

1. In the FrontPage 98 Explorer, select Navigation View.
2. Right-click on a page in the Navigation View flowchart, and select Rename from the context menu, as shown in Figure 7.9
3. Enter a new page title in the flowchart box for the page, and click outside the page. Page titles in navigation bars will be automatically updated to reflect new page titles.

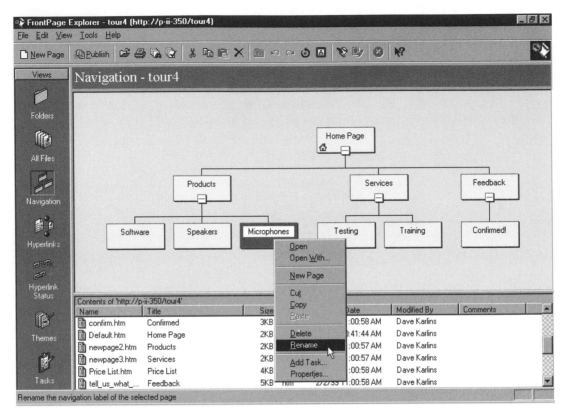

Figure 7.9 *Changing page titles in Navigation View defines link titles generated by navigation bars.*

Defining Navigation Labels

Some generated navigation links in navigation bars come with titles like, "Home," "Up," "Back," "Next." Home, obviously, provides a link to the home page. "Up" is a link one step up the flowchart defined in Navigation View. "Back" is not the same as the Back button in a Web browser. This "Back" link is determined by the page to the left of the current page in Navigation View. Similarly, the "Next" page is defined as the page to the right of the current page in navigation View.

The labels Home, Back, Up and Next can be changed. For example, "Back" can be changed to "Show Previous Page." Or the label assigned to a home page can be changed from "Home" to "Home Page," or "Return to Our Home Page."

A Back and Next navigation bar strategy creates navigational links that work like a slideshow, with visitors being prompted to see the "next" or "previous" page in a series.

To change navigation bar labels:

1. In the FrontPage Explorer, select Tools, Web Settings. The FrontPage Web Settings dialog box appears.
2. Click on the Navigation tab.
3. Click in any of the four boxes to enter a new name for a navigation label, as shown in Figure 7.10.
4. Click on Apply to implement the new label. You can view changes in the FrontPage Editor, or by previewing Web pages in a browser.
5. Click on OK.

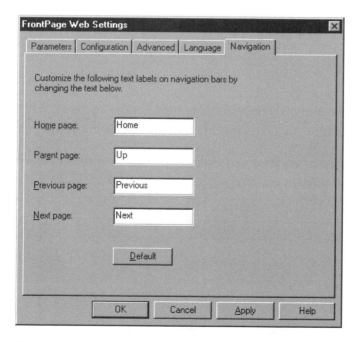

Figure 7.10 *Navigation bar labels can be changed.*

Study Break

Creating Shared Borders with Navigation Bars

To reinforce your understanding of shared borders and navigation bars, define both for a Web site.

1. Create a new Web site using the Personal Web template.

2. Define shared borders for the top and bottom of each page in the new Web site. The template automatically inserts navigation bars in the top shared border.

3. In the home page, create a link to the Interests page (using the Create or Edit Hyperlink button). Then, insert a navigation bar in the bottom shared border using a Back and Next link strategy, and including links to the Home and Parent page, as shown in Figure 7.11.

4. Change the navigation label for the previous page from "Back" to "Previous." Test your site in a browser, and experiment with the generated links. Your navigation bar labels will reflect the labels you defined in step 3, as shown in Figure 7.12.

MCSD 7.3 **Creating and Using Framed Pages**

Framed pages are another way to provide a navigation environment for visitors to your site. Framed pages (called framesets) frequently combine a stable page (often to the left, sometimes at the top or bottom of a larger page),

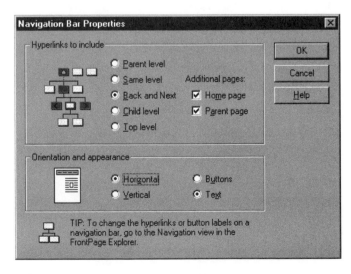

Figure 7.11 *Defining a Back and Next link structure for a navigation bar.*

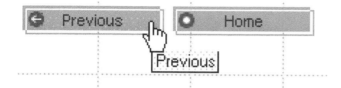

Figure 7.12 *Navigation labels are displayed in generated navigation bars.*

and a linked page, the content of which is determined by links selected in the stable page. For example, a two-window frame can provide a useful way to help visitors navigate your Web site.

Figure 7.13 shows a two-page frameset I use for my FrontPage Forum (at www.ppinet.com). The frame on the left lists all articles submitted to the discussion forum, while the frame on the right displays individual articles.

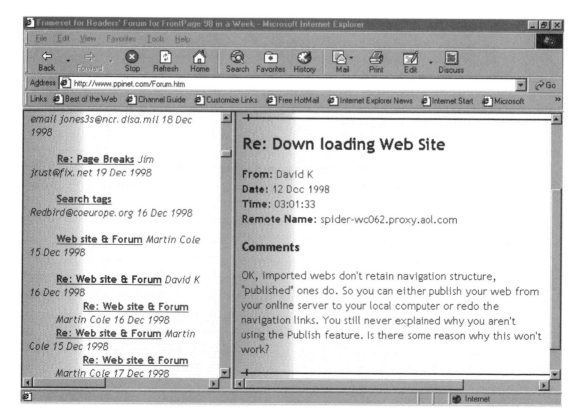

Figure 7.13 *A two-frame frameset.*

Visitors click on an article title in the right window, and the article displays in the left window.

The downside of organizing Web pages into framesets is that they can easily degenerate into a cluttered-looking Web site. There may be aesthetic arguments for three-and four-page framesets, but most designers restrict their frame layouts to two pages when they use frames. Since shared borders and framesets provide similar functionality, you will usually want to avoid combining them.

To Frame . . . Or Not to Frame?

Frames are perhaps the most controversial element of Web page design. On the positive side, frames can be a useful navigational technique, with one frame providing a "table of contents" that displays pages in an adjoining frame. Another framing technique is to use frames to provide more content in a browser window, somewhat analogous to TV displays that allow rabid sports fans to watch two games at once on their TV monitor.

The negative side of frames is that they tend to create cluttered and confusing displays. This problem is, of course, exacerbated when framesets include more than two pages.

The debate over frames among the Web page design community is strongly tilted against the use of frames, with most designers aspiring to clean, even sparse page presentation. In part, the criticism directed at frames is a result of badly-implemented frames. A recent visit to the Web Pages that Suck Web site showed badly-defined frames listed as the #1 design mistake.

Even opponents of frames acknowledge that some content almost demands framesets, like discussion forums that list articles in one frame, and display article content in a connected frame.

For helpful discussion of Web design issues, including the use of framesets, visit the Web Pages that Suck Web site at www.Webpagesthatsuck.com. The site is a project of the authors who wrote the book, *Web Pages that Suck.*

Frames separate a Web browser's screen into distinct, independent HTML pages. Each frame in a frameset can be scrolled independently. You can scroll in one frame, while leaving another frame on the same page unchanged.

Framesets are composed of at least three HTML files. Each page within a frameset (and to have a frameset you need a minimum of two embedded pages) has its own HTML file. Plus, an additional HTML file organizes the embedded Web pages.

Defining Framesets in the FrontPage Editor

Framesets are generated in FrontPage by employing one of ten Frame templates in the FrontPage Editor. Developers start with one of these templates, and then modify it to conform to their particular needs.

To create a frameset, follow these steps:

1. In the FrontPage Editor, select File, New and click on the Frames tab in the New dialog box. The five frameset templates are listed, as shown in Figure 7.14.

> If you already have a page open that you wish to convert into a frameset, you can select Frame, New Frames Page from the FrontPage Editor menu. This is a alternate way to access the list of Frame templates.

2. As you click on framesets in the list on the left side of the dialog box, the frameset is previewed (and described) on the right side of the dialog box.
3. After you choose a frameset template, click on OK in the Frames tab of the New dialog box. After you generate a frameset, the FrontPage Editor looks like the setup in Figure 7.15, with five tabs instead of the usual three. You are now ready to define pages in each frame.
4. Each of the pages in the frame must be created individually. You can either design the page within the Frameset, or embed an existing page. If you want to create a new page, click on the New Page button in the

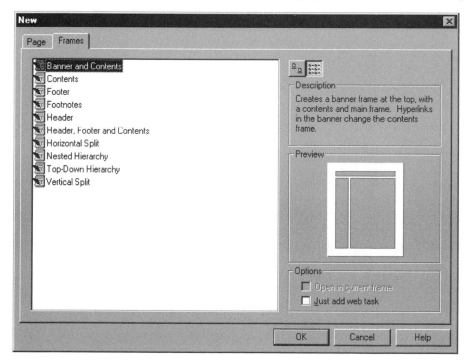

Figure 7.14 *FrontPage provides ten templates to begin frameset design.*

In addition to the three tabs normally available in the FrontPage Editor (Normal, HTML, and Preview), Framesets display a No Frames tab and a Frames Page HTML tab. The No Frames tab displays a page that will appear when the frameset is visited by a browser that does not support frames. The Frames Page HTML page allows you to view or edit the HTML code for the page that contains the embedded frames.

frame. To assign an existing page to the frame, click on the Set Initial Page button. Or, you can assign an existing page to a frame. To assign an existing page, click the Set Initial Page button in a frame window, and select a page to insert into the frame.

The Set Initial Page button defines a page from which visitors will select navigation links to other pages that display within the frame. In designing a frameset, you generally designate one page as an initial page, and other pages as target pages that are displayed when visitors select links in the initial page.

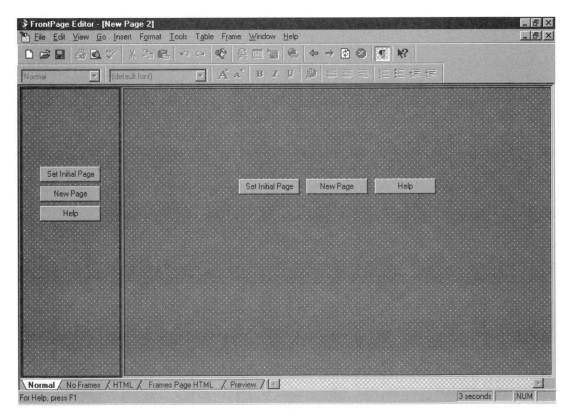

Figure 7.15   *Framesets are composed in the FrontPage Editor.*

5. To save a frameset, select File, Save from the menu. This saves the selected page within your frame. (Selected pages are outlined in blue in the Front-Page Editor.) When the Save As dialog box opens, you will see a window on the right side of the dialog box that indicates which page you are saving. After you save a page within a frame, you will then be prompted to save the frameset that contains the page, as shown in Figure 7.16

The Frames Page HTML tab displays the HTML code for the page that controls the frame itself. Figure 7.17 shows this tab. The HTML code in this tab defines the structure of the frame and the included Web pages.

MCSD 7.4 Alternatives for Browsers that Do Not Recognize Frames

As a FrontPage MCP, part of your mission is to anticipate every possible thing that can go wrong with implementing FrontPage Web sites. One of those danger areas is browser compatibility. As time flies by, and Netscape and Microsoft pass out millions of copies of their latest browsers, the issue of frames compatibility is receding, but still present. In short, unless the Web site you are developing is for a captive intranet audience, where everyone has the latest version of IE or Netscape, you will want to provide alternatives for

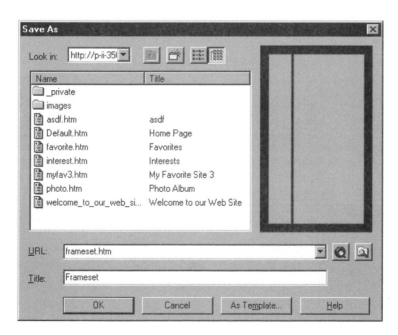

Figure 7.16 *Saving a frameset involves saving both individual Web pages and the frameset HTML file that defines the structure of the frame.*

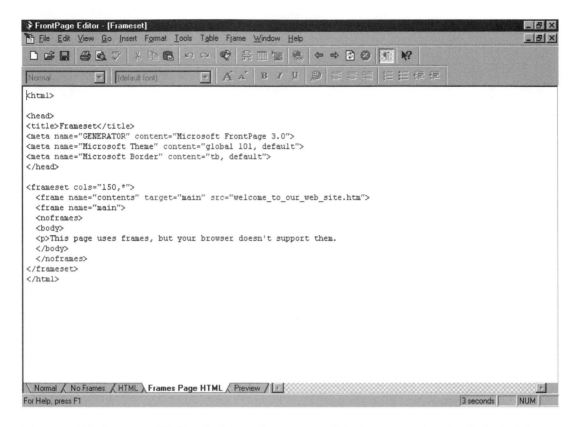

Figure 7.17 *Frameset HTML code defines the structure of the frame and identifies the included pages.*

visitors who come to your Web site with browsers that do not interpret frames. On the "frameless" list of browsers is version 2 of Internet Explorer, along with AOL version 1, and Netscape Navigator version 1.

When you create frames in the FrontPage Editor, you will see five tabs. The additional tabs are the No Frames tab and the Frames Page HTML tab. The No Frames tab, shown in Figure 7.18, previews the way your page will look when visitors see your site using a browser that does not interpret frames.

There is no need to deprive frameless visitors of the entire content in your frameset. You can create an alternate page that displays in browsers that don't recognize frames. FrontPage automatically generates such a page, but the rather unfriendly default No Frames page just tells visitors that they can't see the page in their browser. The No Frames page can be edited, just like any other Web page in the FrontPage Editor.

Sites designed to accommodate frameless browsers should provide alternate content in the No Frames page. If your site absolutely requires

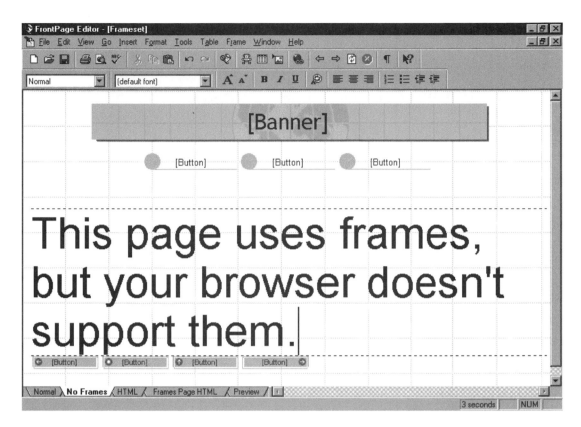

Figure 7.18 *The No Frames page displays when a frameset page is visited by an older browser that does not interpret frames.*

frames to function (for example, a discussion list), you might provide a link for visitors to download the current version of Internet Explorer or Netscape Navigator. At this writing, those links are:

Internet Explorer: http://www.microsoft.com/windows/ie/

Netscape Navigator: http://www.netscape.com/comprod/mirror/ client_download.html

Defining Frame Properties

Frame properties define how each page within a frameset will display in a browser. For example, you can decide how much of the browser window to allot to a selected page within a frameset. You can also decide whether or not to display a separate scrollbar for a selected frame page.

Frame properties include:

- The size that each page will display at within the frameset
- The spacing and borders between windows in the frame
- Whether to display scrollbars in each window of the frame
- Whether or not to let visitors resize frame windows in their own browser

To define properties for a selected frame:

1. With your frameset open in the FrontPage Editor, and a frame selected, choose Frame, Frame Properties.
2. Define column width and row height in pixels or as a percentage of the entire frame.

You might find it easier, though, to resize widths by dragging on the window dividers in the FrontPage Editor. Figure 7.19 shows width being adjusted that way.

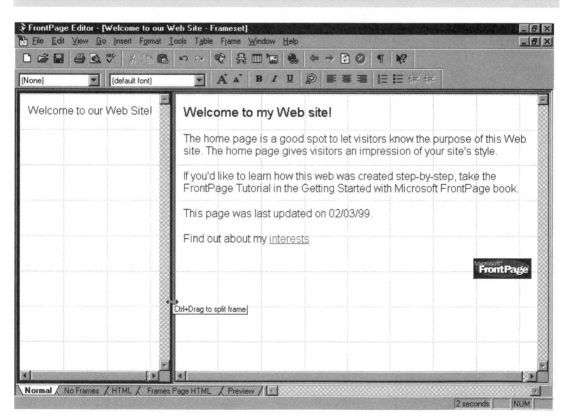

Figure 7.19 *Defining frame page size.*

3. Use the Name area of the Frame Properties dialog box to change the name of the frame.

4. Use the Options area of the Frame Properties dialog box to define how a frame will be displayed. Click on the Resizable in Browser button to provide visitors the option to resize the different windows within a frame. Use the Show Scrollbars drop-down menu to show scrollbars in the Frame If Needed, Never, or Always. The Margins spin boxes define the width of the margin, or buffer space, within a selected window of a frame. Margins are defined in pixels. You can change the page that will load in the frame by using the Browse button to choose a new initial page.

5. When you have defined frame properties for the selected frame, click on OK in the dialog box.

Coordinating Frames and Links

Hyperlinks provide a special challenge when they are placed in framed pages. As a FrontPage MCP, you need to understand how links work within frames. That understanding will help you coordinate site design, and also troubleshoot frame page links that produce unwanted results, like frame sets appearing within framesets appearing within framesets to produce a messy maze for visitors.

To illustrate the kinds of pitfalls that arise when frames are combined with links, we'll conduct a quick troubleshooting experiment. Figure 7.20 shows a simple, two-page frameset as viewed in a browser. When a visitor selects a link in the frame on the left, the target of that link opens in the frame on the right. This is intuitive and allows the frame on the left to function as a stable navigational tool for the Web site.

Now, to illustrate a typical frame/link problem, Figure 7.21 shows what happens if the link in the frame on the left opened the target page in the *same frame*.

When a visitor selects a link in a framed page, several things can happen. Those options can be categorized as three possible results:

• The page the visitor selects can be displayed in the same frame from which the hyperlink was clicked.

• The page the visitor selects can be displayed in a target frame connected to the initial frame, while the initial frame remains unchanged.

• The page the visitor selects can be displayed in a full window, with no frames involved.

When you generate a frameset using a template, FrontPage assigns a frame in which to display linked page. For example, if you use the Contents

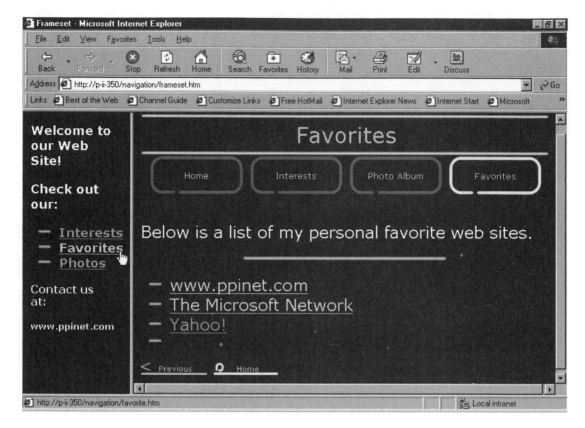

Figure 7.20 *When a visitor clicks on linked text in the left-side frame, the target of the link displays in the frame on the right.*

template to define a frameset, hyperlinks in the left-hand window display target pages in the right side of the frame. Other templates assign other target link frames.

Why would you want to assign different target properties to different hyperlinks within a frame? One frequent scenario is that some hyperlinks are to internal pages within your Web site, and you will want to display them in a target frame, while other links lead to pages outside your Web site that you wish to display full-screen, without frames.

You can examine or change the target for a single hyperlink, or for all hyperlinks within a frame.

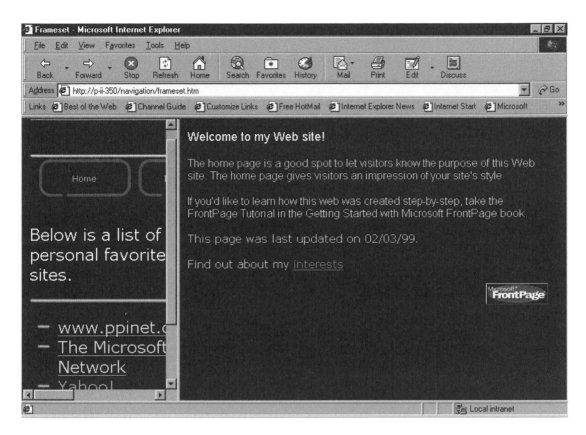

Figure 7.21   *Ouch! A frequent troubleshooting challenge occurs when a frame link opens the target page in the wrong frame.*

To define frame hyperlink targets:

1. With your frameset open in the FrontPage Editor, click on a hyperlink and select Edit, Hyperlink Properties. The Hyperlink Properties dialog box appears.
2. Click the Change Target Frame button (a screen tip identifies it—it is next to the Target Frame area). The Target Frame dialog box opens.
3. Use the Current Frames Page graphic on the left side of the dialog box to select a target within the frameset, as shown in Figure 7.22. Other options include Whole Page (which displays the target link without a frameset) or New Window (which opens a new browser window displaying the linked page). Use the Make Default for Hyperlinks on the Page check box to assign your linked target frame definition to all links within the frame.

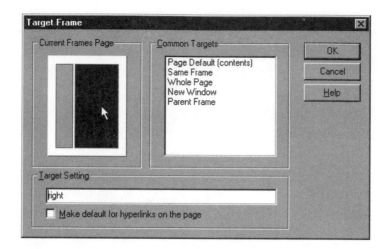

Figure 7.22 *Defining a target frame link.*

4. Then click on OK twice to apply the target properties to the link.

Additional background on Framesets is available in the following resources:

The FrontPage 98 Bible, Chapter 8.
Teach Yourself FrontPage 98 in a Week, Chapter 21.
Special Edition Using FrontPage 98, Chapter 9.

Study Break

Creating Framed Pages with Links

Reinforce your understanding of framed pages and links by creating a two page frameset with a variety of link targets.

1. Use the Personal Web template to create a new Web site. Use the Header template to create a new frameset. Embed the default.htm (Home Page) on the bottom of the frameset, and use the top frame to create a new page with links to the Home, Interests, Photo Album, and Favorites pages.

2. Resize the boundary between the frame windows so that the top frame is just the right size to display the page links, as shown in Figure 7.23.

3. Create a "No Frames" page that displays links so that visitors can download current browsers that support frames.

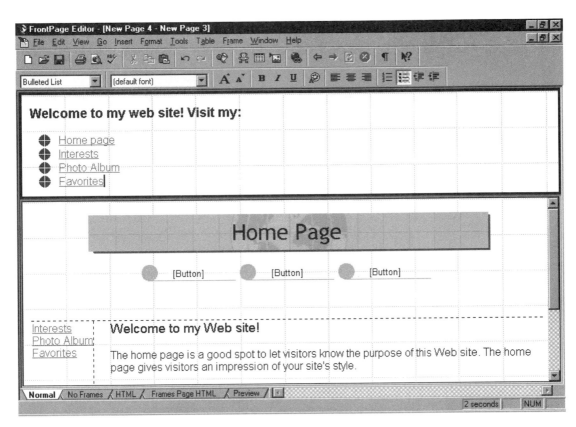

Figure 7.23 *In this frameset, the top frame serves as a stable navigational page with links that display pages in the bottom frame.*

4. Test your frameset and links in a browser. Then, change the hyperlink targets so that one of the links opens the target page in a whole page, and a second link opens the target window in a New window. Save your page, refresh your browser display, and test these links again in your browser.

■ Summary

Shared borders, navigation bars and framed pages are all options for navigation strategies. Shared borders and frames share the ability to provide a consistent "framing" navigational structure for a Web.

Shared borders are a more subtle, and more universally recognized option for providing such a framed structure for pages. Frames are not recognized by older browsers. And they present a significant design challenge based on the fact that browser windows are small to start with, and dividing them into frames leaves even less room to display Web content. However, frames are the most powerful and flexible tool available for providing page navigation options.

Frames also present a particular challenge when defining hyperlinks. Unless the target of a link is specifically and correctly defined, a visitor can find him-or herself trapped in a maze of frames. For all these reasons, frames require thorough testing using as many browsers as possible, and every link in a framed page needs to be carefully tested in a browser.

▲ CHAPTER REVIEW QUESTIONS

1. *If you are advising developers of a Web site using frames, you might well encourage them to do which of the following? (Select all correct answers.)*
   - A. Include webBots that exclude browsers that do not recognize frames
   - B. Use alternate "No Frames" content pages
   - C. Add links to the Microsoft and Netscape Web sites so visitors can upgrade browsers if their browser does not recognize frames
   - D. Use Microsoft SourceSafe controls to prevent incompatible frame pages
   - E. Avoiding the combination of frames and shared borders

2. *How many shared borders can be defined for a Web page? (Select all correct answers.)*
   - A. 1
   - B. 2
   - C. 4
   - D. 7
   - E. There is no limit on the number of shared borders assigned to a Web page

3. *Shared borders are demarcated in a browser by... (Select all correct answers.)*
   - A. blue lines
   - B. dotted lines
   - C. gray shading
   - D. Shared borders are not necessarily demarcated in a browser

4. *Shared borders are (Select all correct answers.)*

    A. Web pages

    B. saved in the _borders folder

    C. generated by navigation bars

    D. dependant on Web page relationships defined in navigation view

5. *Which of the following are potential challenges when framesets are used in a Web site?*

    A. Some browsers don't interpret frames

    B. Hyperlink targets can open links in the wrong frame

    C. Design challenges

    D. Alternate pages should be defined

6. *A Web designer has inserted navigation bars in a Web page, but no links appear. Which of the following could be preventing navigation links from being generated? (Select all correct answers.)*

    A. A Theme has been assigned to the page

    B. There are no links in the page that match the criteria defined for navigation bars

    C. No shared borders were defined

    D. No navigation structure was defined in Navigation View

    E. Page titles were not assigned in Navigation View

7. *The text generated in Navigation bars is defined in Navigation View.*

    A. True

    B. False

8. *How can you change the labels generated for the Next and Previous pages in navigation bars? (Select all correct answers.)*

    A. Embed the navigation bar in a shared border

    B. Edit the settings in Navigation Bar Properties dialog box

    C. Edit Web Settings in the FrontPage Explorer

    D. Edit navigational flow in Navigation View

9. *Shared borders can include hyperlinks and text, but not navigation bars.*

    A. True

    B. False

10. *Which of the following types of files can be found in hidden directories? (Select all correct answers.)*

    A. Shared border pages

    B. Navigation View files

    C. Java applets

    D. Files used in Themes

    E. Help files

Creating Input Forms

Input forms provide some intriguing challenges for a FrontPage Expert. You will need to understand how to create forms, how to combine them with validation scripts, and how to handle the data entered in forms. I'll break these three aspects of form design into three chapters, and begin here with form design, focusing on form fields.

In this chapter, I'll start with the basic element of an input form, the input form field. Every input form is made up of at least one input form field. Since there are several types of fields, and they all have their own "laws," understanding each of them is necessary in order to effectively collect visitor input.

At the conclusion of this chapter you will be able to:

- Understand the relationship between input forms and input form fields.
- Understanding the role of each type of input form field.
- Define properties for each of the five types of input form fields.
- Collect data via hidden form fields.
- Apply labels to fields, and understand browser compatibility issues related to labels.
- Embed images in forms.

MCSD 8.1   Setting Form Properties

Before diving in to form field definitions, it will be useful to briefly outline how FrontPage handles form input. An overview of this process will help you navigate through the MCSD/MCP exam, and the ability to explain and plan different types of form management will be essential in your role in supervising the implementation of FrontPage Web sites.

FrontPage 98 can collect input data in forms without the need for server-side scripts. Until the advent of FrontPage, collecting data though input forms required meshing the Web site with Common Gateway Interface (CGI) scripts on the Web site server. These server-side scripts managed the process of saving input data to the Web site. By managing this process through FrontPage extension files installed on a server, FrontPage allows designers to collect input data without worrying about connecting to CGI scripts. All of this supposes that the Web site is published to a server with FrontPage extensions installed.

When we return to a detailed exploration of form properties in chapter 10, we'll look at how form data can be sent to a variety of targets, including email, text files and HTML pages.

Three Steps in Collecting Input Form Data

1. Creating data input forms.

2. Validating user input by using form field validation scripts.

3. Managing form input data.

Input forms are comprised of fields that collect data. Validation scripts test that data before it is submitted to a server. The final step in the process requires defining target files and file formats for the data, and specifying how the data will be managed at the Web server.

By default, FrontPage form field data is saved to files in a _Private directory generated by FrontPage for each Web site to hold input data. These files can be opened in your default text editor from the server (including the Personal Web Server) by double-clicking on them in the FrontPage Explorer.

Explore Form Properties

Practice what you have learned by exploring the form properties for a generated form.

First, create a new FrontPage Web using the Customer Support Web templete.

Next, open the generated Suggestions page in Navigation view in the FrontPage Explorer.

Right-click inside the form (defined by dashed lines) in the Suggestions page and choose Form Properties from the shortcut menu. Note the file to which input will be saved. By default, input to this form is saved to an html (*.htm) file. We'll explore more Form properties in chapter 10, but for now you have noted that every input form is linked to a target page to which input data is posted.

You can leave thsi page open in the FrontPage Editor, as we will return to it in the next Study Break.

In this chapter, we'll start to explore this process with the creation of data input forms. In chapter 9, we'll dig into the process of validating user input with field validation scripts. And then, in chapter 10, we'll cover the process of collecting user input, including taking a look at alternatives when a site is published to a Web server without FrontPage extensions.

MCSD 8.2   Adding Fields to Data Forms

Defining input forms is an art. For example, I recently took on a project where I had to translate dozens of survey forms from a sales organization into Web input forms. Aside from the technical writing aspect of the job, it was necessary to make decisions as to how to structure the data collection process into specific input form fields. Questions like "How large is the client's sales force?" could be translated into a one-line text box that collected only numbers, or a set of radio (option) buttons that provided choices like "1–25," "26–100," "100–1000," etc. In many ways, this process is very similar to designing a database.

While it takes experience to design input forms that effectively collect exactly the information needed for a Web site, the starting point is an understanding of what each Input Form Field does, what its limitations are, and what properties can be assigned to it.

There are five types of input fields:

- Radio button
- Check box
- Drop-down menu
- One-line text box
- Scrolling text box

Each type of input field is useful for collecting different types of data. For example, if you want to provide a list of software version options, and you want to allow visitors to select only one of those options, a set of radio buttons can restrict a visitor to a single choice. On the other hand, if you are collecting customer feedback, a scrolling text box allows visitors to submit paragraphs of text, if necessary. Figure 8.1 shows an input form with each of the five types of input form fields.

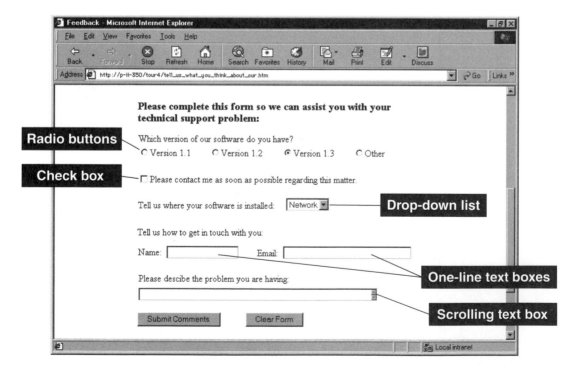

Figure 8.1 *Each of the five types of form fields provides a different way to collect visitor input.*

Input form fields and input forms go hand in hand. Form fields (or fields, for short) collect specific bits of information. That information is processed by an input form. The form properties determine whether the data will be saved to a Web server as a text file or an HTML file, and how the Web site will interact with a server. In Chapter 10, we will explore this process in detail. For the purposes of defining input fields, it is necessary here only to be aware that input fields must be embedded in an input form.

Explore Form Field Types

Practice what you have learned by exploring various form field types included in the input form on the Suggestions page generated by the Customer Support Web template.

First, open the FrontPage Web generated in the last Study Break. If you closed that Web, generate a new Web using the Discussion Web using the Customer Support Web template.

Next, view (or open) the Suggestions page in the FrontPage Editor.

Double-click on the Category drop-down menu in the FrontPage Editor. The drop-down Menu Properties dialog box opens, revealing the properties of this input form field. For now, simply note the options—we'll return to them later in this chapter.

Close the drop-down Menu Properties dialog box by clicking on Cancel, and double-click on the other form fields in the form. Identify the types of form fields being used.

Finally, you can delete this Web by slecting File, Exit (don't save any changes you might have made) in the FrontPage Editor, and then selecting File, Delete FrontPage Web in the FrontPage Explorer.

Input forms are generated automatically when you insert any element from the Form Field submenu. In addition to the five types of input fields, the following other form elements are found in the Insert, Form Field submenu:

- Push Buttons
- Form Field Images
- Labels

Inserting any form field, or a Push Button, Form Field Image, or Label, will generate a form. The form will be indicated in the FrontPage Editor by a dashed line, as shown in Figure 8.2.

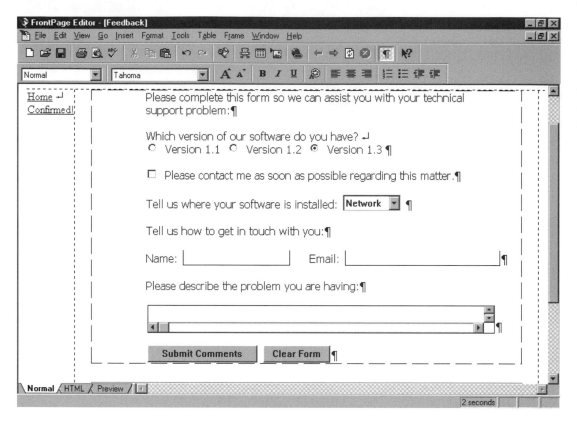

Figure 8.2 *Form fields are indicated in the FrontPage Editor by dashed lines.*

When organizing form fields into forms, keep in mind that each form collects data into a separate record. So, for example, if you are collecting visitor comments and customer orders in the same page of a Web site, you will almost certainly want to collect that information in two separate forms. The results of the visitor comments might be saved to an HTML Web page, while the results of the order form would be probably be sent to the server in delimited text format and imported into a database.

To review the relationship between forms and form fields:

- Every form field must be placed within a form in order for the data submitted to be saved to a server.

- Forms are indicated in Web pages by dashed lines.

- Multiple input forms can be placed in FrontPage Web pages.

- Whenever you place a form field element in a Web page in the Front-Page Editor, a form is automatically generated (unless you insert the field in an existing form).

Now that you have an overview of how forms and form fields work, it is necessary to examine the different types of input fields. Each of the five fields plays a unique role in collecting data.

MCSD 8.3   Setting Field Properties

Field properties depend on the type of input being collected. To take one example, the properties that can be defined for a set of radio buttons include setting a tab order for users who move from one radio button to another using the tab key. Radio button properties also involve selecting a default selection. For example, if your set of radio buttons asks visitors to rank your Web site on a scale ranging from "This Site Is Great" to "This Site Stinks," you might well elect to make "This Site Is Great" the default option, while "This Site Stinks" might well be last radio button a visitor will select using the tab key (just a little marketing suggestion).

Other types of fields provide other types of options. For example, drop-down menus can force a visitor to select one option from a list, or allow multiple selections. Text boxes can accept text, numbers, or both. You can also define certain types of fields as required fields, meaning that a visitor must fill in that field before he or she can submit the form (useful where information like a credit card number is required input).

Knowing the properties available for each type of field will help you design input forms that collect exactly the type of data required for your Web application. In the following sections, we'll examine the properties available for each type of field.

Using Radio (Option) Buttons

Radio buttons get their name from the car radio metaphor, where you press one of the buttons to select a station. Also referred to as option buttons, radio buttons are normally used to provide a set of options where a visitor can and must select one, and only one, option from a group of options. For example, if an order form requires a form of payment, a designer might offer radio buttons for one of several versions of a software application, as shown in Figure 8.3.

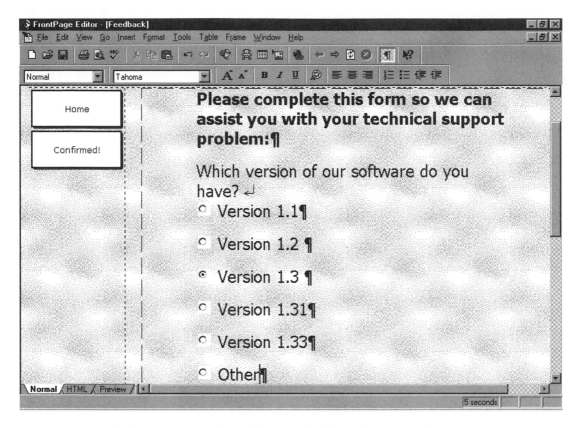

Figure 8.3 *Radio buttons are used to collect a single choice from a set of options.*

The group of buttons that are grouped together to provide a set of options are (intuitively) called a group. Visitors will be allowed to select only one option from a group. You may include multiple groups of radio buttons in a form.

To insert a radio button:

1. Click to set your insertion point in an open Web page in the FrontPage Editor.
2. Select Insert, Form Field, Radio button from the menu bar.
3. Double-click on the radio button to open the Radio Button Properties dialog box.
4. Edit the Group name (optional) in the Group Name box. The Group Name is shared by all radio buttons in a group.

Because each radio button in a group must have the same group name, experienced FrontPage developers start with one radio button, copy it, and then modify the copies to provide additional options.

5. Assign a value in the Value box (like "Visa" for example) for the radio button. Every radio button has a distinct, unique value.
6. Choose an initial state using the Selected or Not Selected option buttons in the dialog box. Only one button in a group may be initially selected.
7. Set tab order by entering a value in the Tab Order box. Tab order defines the sequence by which a visitor moves through a form using his or her Tab key. After you define radio button properties, OK the dialog box.

Assigning tab order is explored in detail in Chapter 2. The Radio Button Properties dialog box also allows you to define validation scripts. Validation scripts are discussed in detail in Chapter 9. The dialog box also includes a Style button. Assigning styles and Cascading Style Sheets are explored in Chapter 13, "Using Style Sheets and Templates."

Providing Check Boxes

Check boxes can be either selected or not selected. They are not defined in groups in the same way that radio buttons are. So, for example, if you want to provide a set of options and allow a visitor to select all, some, or none of them, check boxes are the appropriate input form field type.

Figure 8.4 shows a set of check boxes in an input form. Visitors can select any combination of topics for which they want to receive information.

To insert a check box:

1. Click to set your insertion point in an open Web page in the FrontPage Editor.
2. Select Insert, Form Field, check box from the menu bar.
3. Double-click on the check box to open the Check Box Button Properties dialog box.
4. Enter a field name for the check box in the Name box.
5. Set an initial state for the check box.

Form designers have to apply some sales psychology to determine whether or not the initial setting should be checked or unchecked. Setting the default at checked means you are more likely to have visitors "select" that check box, but it may be the case that they simply accepted the default without thinking about it.

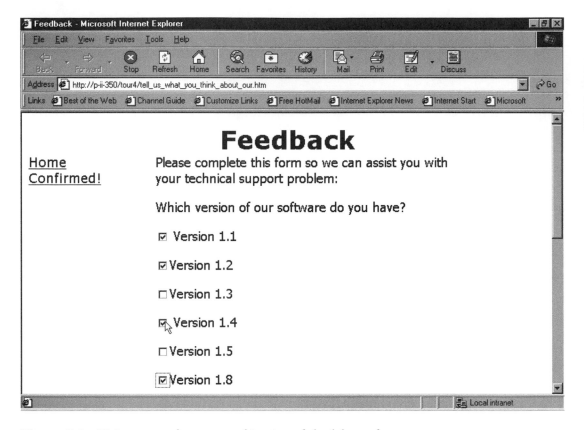

Figure 8.4 *Visitors can select any combination of check boxes from a set.*

6. Accept the default value for a check box ("ON"), or change it. Since check boxes are either checked or not checked, a simple value like "ON," or "Yes" is appropriate. A completed Check Box Properties dialog box, with a Name ("Contact?") and a value ("Yes") is shown in Figure 8.5.

7. Set tab order by entering a value in the Tab Order box. Tab order defines the sequence by which a visitor moves through a form using his or her Tab key. After you define check box properties, OK the dialog box.

Defining Drop-down Menus

The function of drop-down menus (sometimes called drop-down lists) is similar to that of radio buttons, in that they are usually used to provide visitors

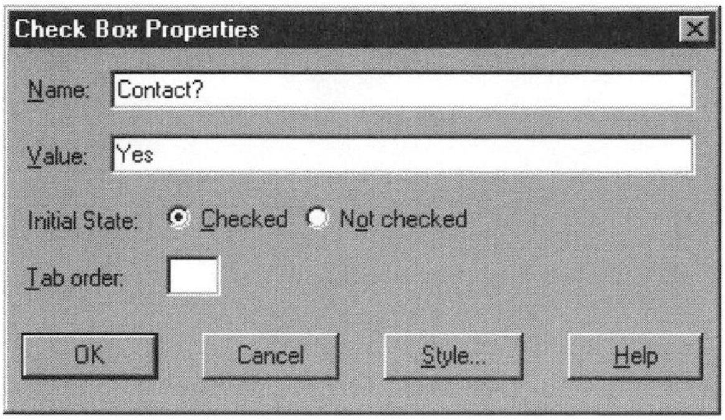

Figure 8.5 *Defining a check box.*

with a way to select a single option from a set of options. Therefore, the main difference between drop-down menus and sets of option buttons is mainly one of design. Drop-down menus do not display all options until a visitor clicks on the down-arrow, and only the first option is immediately displayed.

Drop-down menus, however, are more flexible than sets of radio buttons. It is possible to define a drop-down list that accepts multiple options. In that way, a drop-down menu can function like a set of check boxes, in that a visitor can select some or all options (you can even include a "none of the above" option in a drop-down list). Figure 8.6 displays a drop-down menu that permits more than one selection. This type of list requires that the visitor use the Ctrl key as he or she clicks on additional options to add them to the list of selected items. Multiple-selection drop-down menus are technically possible, but most visitors will find mulitple-option drop-down menus confusing. Users generally expect to pick one option from a drop-down menu.

To insert a drop-down menu:

1. Click to set your insertion point in an open Web page in the FrontPage Editor.
2. Select Insert, Form Field, Drop-down Menu from the menu bar.
3. Double-click on the Drop-down Menu to open the Drop-down Menu Properties dialog box.
4. Enter a field name for the menu in the Name box.
5. Use the Add button to add new choices to the menu. The Add Choice dialog box appears. By default, the value of the menu option is the same as the Choice. To define a different value for a choice, use the Specify

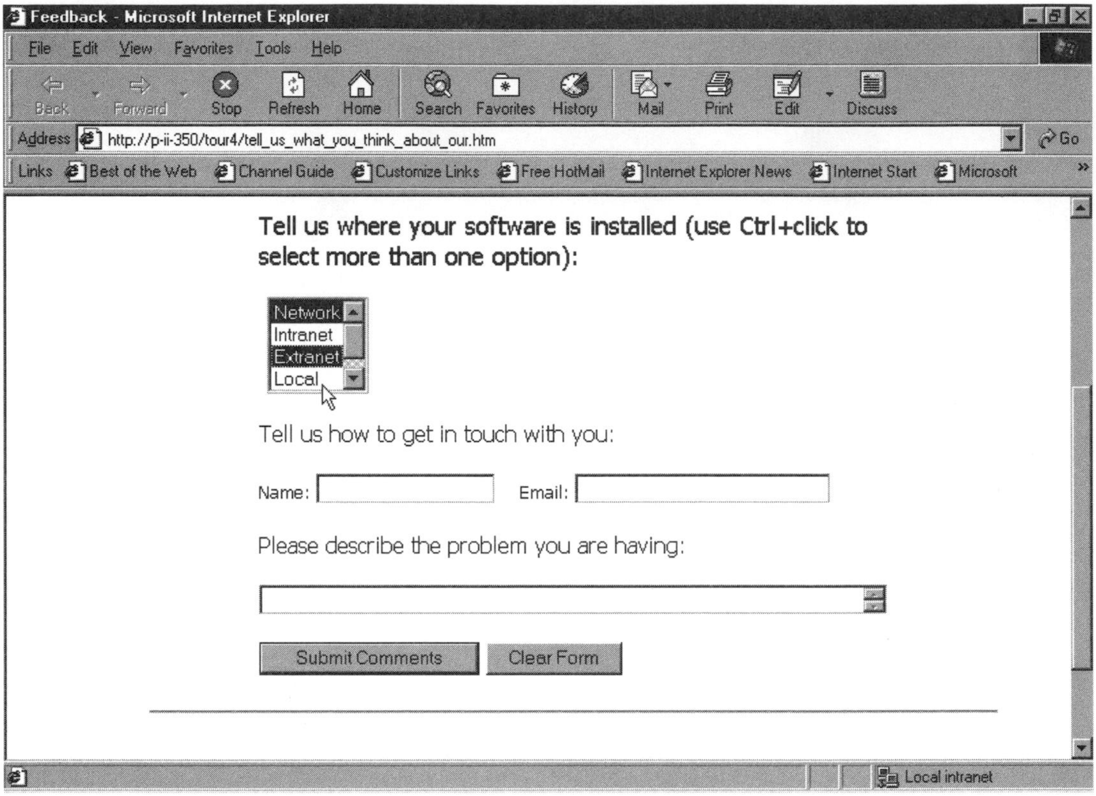

Figure 8.6 *It is technically possible to create drop-down menus that accept more than one option.*

Value check box in the Add Choice dialog box. You might do this, for example, if there were marketing reasons to display one label as the choice in the menu, and another value for internal record keeping. A menu choice with a different displayed choice name and value is shown in Figure 8.7.

6. Set an initial state in the Initial State area of the dialog box. If you allow multiple selections, you can have more than one option selected by default. After defining each choice, OK the Add Choice dialog box. Repeat this process to define as many options as necessary.

7. You can define the height of the drop-down list in the Height field in the Drop-down Menu Properties dialog box. However, you can also do this by clicking and dragging on sizing handles in the FrontPage Editor.

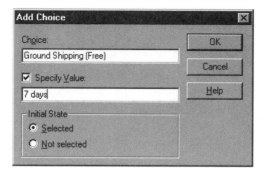

Figure 8.7 *You can display one choice name for visitors, and use another value for internal record keeping.*

8. The Modify, Remove, Move Up and Move Down buttons allow you to change your menu choices. The Allow Multiple Selections radio buttons determine whether or not your drop-down menu will accept more than one choice.

9. Set tab order by entering a value in the Tab Order box. Tab order defines the sequence by which a visitor moves through a form using his or her Tab key. After you define drop-down menu properties, OK the dialog box.

Placing One-line Text Boxes

The three methods of collecting input that we have explored to this point (radio buttons, check boxes and drop-down menus) all permit visitors to select from pre-defined options. That's a good thing if you want visitors to tell you which credit card to use, or whether or not you should contact them. Other types of input, ranging from e-mail address and phone numbers to complaints and comments, require more flexible input fields. You can collect text and numbers in either a one-line, or a scrolling text box.

One-line text boxes collect only one line of text. That line can be up to 999 characters long. It is often very helpful to combine one-line text boxes with validation scripts that, for example, ensure that a Social Security number or phone number contains the right number of digits, and numbers, not letters. Validation can also be used to define the number of characters that will be accepted in a one-line text box.

To insert a one-line text box:

Validation for all input form field types is covered in detail in chapter 9 of this book.

1. Click to set your insertion point in an open Web page in the FrontPage Editor.
2. Select Insert, Form Field, One-line Text Box from the menu bar.
3. Double-click on the inserted text box to open the Text Box Properties dialog box.
4. Enter a field name for the menu in the Name box.
5. Assign default input by entering text in the Initial Value box. Default input is not commonly used for text boxes.
6. Define text box width in characters by entering a value in the Width in Characters box.
7. The Yes option button in the Password Field area allows you to display visitor input as asterisks instead of the actual entered text.
8. After you define one-line text box options, click on OK.

Defining a one-line text box as a password field only protects data from being viewed "over the shoulder" of the person entering that information by displaying asterisks on a computer screen. Password-type input fields do not encrypt data during transmission.

Inserting Scrolling Text Boxes

Scrolling text boxes are similar to one-line text boxes except that:

- Scrolling text boxes are not limited to 999 characters.
- Scrolling text boxes not limited to one line of text.
- Scrolling text boxes cannot be defined as password fields (displaying asterisks instead of entered data).

Scrolling text boxes are the most unrestricted form field, and are used for collecting information like comments. While default data is allowed in scrolling text boxes, it is rarely used. Figure 8.8 shows a scrolling text box in the FrontPage Editor.

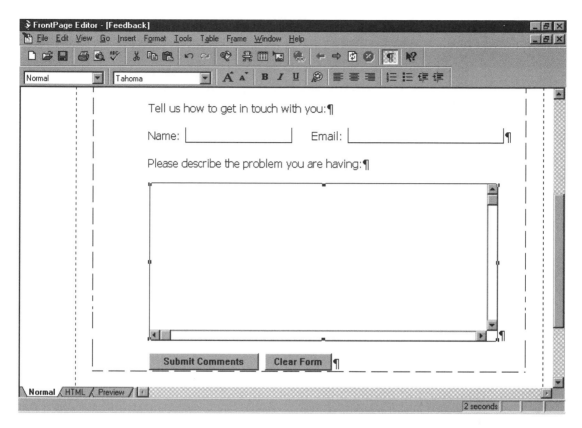

Figure 8.8 *Scrolling text boxes are not limited to one line of text.*

The size of a scrolling text box does not restrict the amount of data that can be entered. Once a visitor enters more data than will fit in the displayed box, the vertical scrollbar attached to the box becomes active.

The process for setting properties for scrolling text boxes is very similar to defining properties for one-line text boxes.

Adding Push Buttons to a Form

In order to submit forms to a server, the form must include a submit button. By default, when you add any form field to a page, a form is created that includes a submit and a reset button. The submit button sends the information in the form fields from the visitor's browser to your Web server. The reset button clears the contents of the form. Reset buttons are optional, but

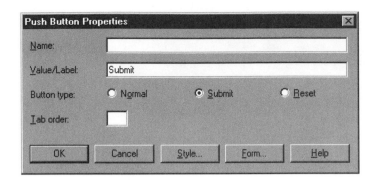

Figure 8.9 *Defining push button properties.*

convenient for visitors who want to erase the contents of an entire form. Submit buttons are mandatory for a functioning form.

You can edit the default settings for submit and reset buttons by double-clicking on either of them. Doing this opens the Push Button Properties dialog box, shown in Figure 8.9.

Field names are useful for most input form fields. For example, when a site administrator reviews records, it will be helpful to have a field name like "contact" next to input information like "Yes." Without the field name, the data would be hard to interpret and use. However, there is no such need for a push button field name. The Name field can be left blank in the Push Button Properties dialog box.

For a full exploration of using Normal buttons to define scripts in Frontpage, see Chapter 15 of *The FrontPage Bible.*

The Value/Label field in the dialog box defines the label that will be displayed on the button. The Submit and Reset option buttons define the type of button. The Normal option is not used for input forms, but to define buttons that launch scripts.

Creating an Input Form

Practice what you have learned by creating an input form in a Web page.

First, create a new Web using the Personal Web template, or open an existing Web site and create a new page. (Click on the New icon in the FrontPage Editor toolbar.) Be sure you start by creating a new Web or opening one in the FrontPage Editor as forms will not work if you do not have a FrontPage Web open. Also, be sure to have the FrontPage Personal Web Server running, or log onto another Web server.

Next, begin creating a form by inserting a one-line text box. Enter a label for the one-line text box saying "Name." Name the text box "Name" as well. Add a second text box collecting visitor's email address. Add a set of radio buttons providing the following options: urgent, important, not urgent. Add a check box as well, giving visitors the option of being contacted, or not. Your form should look something like the one in Figure 8.10.

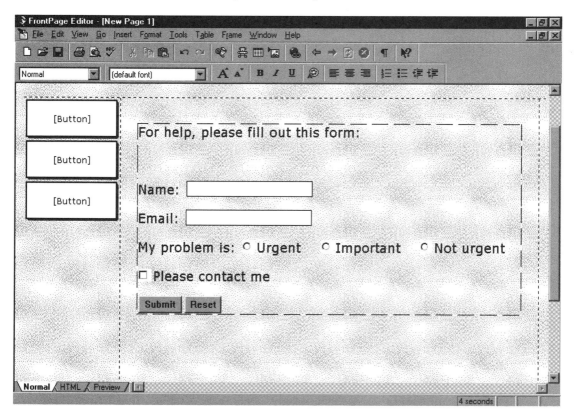

Figure 8.10 *This form includes a set of radio buttons and a check box.*

Troubleshoot your form: Each field should have an appropriate field name and value. All three radio buttons should have the same group name, but different values. Delete the default Name for both submit buttons in the Properties dialog box; this data is not necessary to collect.

Finally, test your input form by saving your page and previewing the form in your Web browser. Input some selected data, clicking on the submit button to send the data to the server. View the data in your text editor (probably Notepad in Windows) by viewing the contents of the _Private folder in the FrontPage Explorer (double-click on the file). You may need to refresh your FrontPage Explorer view to see the data file. Don't delete this Web. You'll use it in the next Study Break.

Embedding Images in Forms

So far, we've explored the five types of form fields that can be utilized in input forms. There are other elements that can be included in input forms as well, including images, labels and hidden fields.

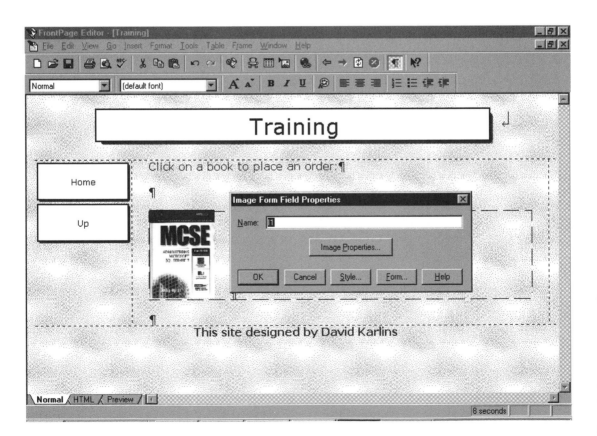

Figure 8.11   *Images can function as push buttons to activate scripts.*

Images can be inserted into forms as push buttons, and linked to scripts. They function much like normal push buttons in that their attributes are dependent on scripts. These images can have their image properties defined just like any other picture. Figure 8.11 shows an image form field, with the Image Form Field Properties dialog box open.

Images that are inserted into forms as input form fields can have all the normal image attributes like size, file type, and border defined by clicking on the Image Properties button in the Image Form Field Properties dialog box.

Scripting is discussed in Chapter 3, "Defining the Technical Architecture for a FrontPage 98 Web Site," of this book.

Applying Labels to Fields

Labels link text to a radio button or check box, allowing a visitor to click on the associated text to select the radio button or check box. Labels are of significant help to visitors who are trying to make selections, and have difficulty clicking exactly on a small radio button or check box. Figure 8.12 zooms in on a visitor selecting a radio button in Internet Explorer 5 by clicking on the associated label text.

The downside to labels is that older versions of Internet Explorer, and even the most recent versions of Netscape Navigator (4.5 at this writing) do not recognize labels. There's no particular danger, however, to including labels in your input forms. If visitors to a Web site arrive with browsers that don't recognize form field labels, they can simply select radio buttons and check boxes the old-fashioned way, by clicking on the circle or square.

To assign a label to a check box or radio button:

1. Enter text to the right or left of a check box or radio button that you will associate with the form field as a label.
2. Click and drag to select both the text and the check box or radio button.
3. Select Insert, Form Field, Label. A dotted line will appear around both the form field and the text label in the FrontPage Editor.

Which version of our software do you have?
○ Version 1.1 ⊙ Version 1.2 ○ Version 1.3

Figure 8.12 *Labels make it easier for visitors to select radio buttons or text boxes—as long as they are using Internet Explorer version 4 or higher.*

Adding Hidden Fields

In addition to the data you collect in defined form fields, you can also collect additional form field data that is automatically collected by the Web server. Those additional (hidden) fields are:

- Time
- Date
- Remote Computer Name
- User Name
- Browser Type

The Time and Date fields tell you the time and date that the form was submitted. The Remote Computer Name tells you the server from which your site was contacted. This information is sometimes useful in that it can identify the country or city from which you were visited. User Name reveals the name of the user accessing the page if he or she has registered that name with a server. Finally, the Browser Type field tells you the type and version of browser used to visit your page.

All these fields can be added to the data collected when a form is submitted. To add hidden fields to input data:

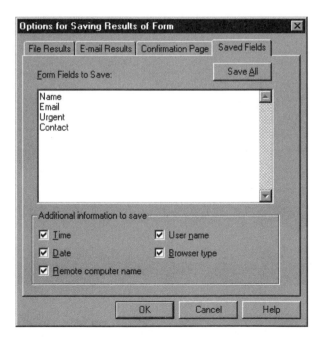

Figure 8.13 *Collecting hidden data from visitors.*

1. Right-click inside an input form and select Form Properties from the context menu.
2. In the Form Properties dialog box, click on the Options button. The Options for Saving Results of a Form dialog box appears.
3. Click on the Saved Fields tab.
4. Use the check boxes in the Saved Fields tab to choose which hidden fields to save, as shown in Figure 8.13. Then, OK the dialog boxes.

Study Break

Adding Labels and Hidden Fields to an Input Form

Practice what you have learned by adding labels and hidden fields to the input form you created in the previous Study Break.

First, convert the text and radio buttons, and the text and check box to labels.

Next, change the input form properties to collect these hidden fields from visitors: Date, Time and Browser Type.

Finally, test your input form by re-saving your page, and previewing the form in your Web browser. If you have both Netscape Navigator and Internet Explorer installed, use them both to test your form, and note compatibility issues regarding labels. Submit a couple of new records, and view the contents of the _Private folder in the FrontPage Explorer to which your data was saved. Note the hidden fields included among the collected data.

■ Summary

In this chapter we began the process of looking in depth at how FrontPage input forms collect data. Here, we examined in some detail the five types of input form fields, and how they work. Each of these fields has a unique set of properties that can be used to fine-tune the type of data collected by the field.

You also learned how input forms can be used to collect hidden data, hidden in the sense that the visitor does not consciously or actively enter that data. Hidden data includes information like the time and date that data was entered, and the visitor's browser type. Finally, we looked at FrontPage data field labels. These labels make it easier for visitors to select check boxes and radio buttons, but they do not function in Netscape Navigator.

▲ CHAPTER REVIEW QUESTIONS

Here are some practice questions relating to the material covered in the "Create Data Input Forms" area of Microsoft's *Designing and Implementing Web Sites using Microsoft FrontPage 98* exam (70-055).

1. *Drop-down menus allow which of the following input options? (Select all correct answers.)*
   A. Only one selection
   B. Multiple selections
   C. 999 characters of input text
   D. Only numbers and letters
   E. Numbers, letters and symbols

2. *Which of the following are browser-sensitive form objects? (Select all correct answers.)*
   A. Check boxes
   B. Radio buttons
   C. Labels
   D. Submit buttons

3. *You can find out what browser visitors are using by collecting hidden field data.*
   A. True
   B. False

4. *One-line text boxes can collect unlimited input.*
   A. True
   B. False

5. *Groups of radio buttons must have the same group name.*
   A. True
   B. False

6. *Which types of form fields are appropriate for collecting up to 3000 characters of input data? (Select all correct answers.)*
    A. Check boxes
    B. Labels
    C. One-line text boxes
    D. Scrolling text boxes
    E. Hidden fields

7. *Password-type fields are appropriate for which types of form field input? (Select all correct answers.)*
    A. Sensitive information that should be hidden from someone observing data input
    B. Data that requires a password-protected server
    C. Data that is being sent to a password-protected server
    D. One-line text boxes
    E. Check boxes

8. *Password-type fields provide moderate-level encryption protection.*
    A. True
    B. False

9. *Form fields require a form to function.*
    A. True
    B. False

10. *Labels make form fields convenient for visitors, but are very browser sensitive.*
    A. True
    B. False

11. *Setting aside security issues, radio buttons are one viable form for collecting credit card numbers.*
    A. True
    B. False

12. *Which form field type or types are appropriate when you want to force users to select just one of several options? (Select all correct answers.)*

    A. One-line input boxes

    B. Radio buttons

    C. Drop-down menus

    D. Labels

    E. Scrolling input boxes

13. *By default, input data is collected in the _private folder in a Web site.*

    A. True

    B. False

14. *Which of the following are hidden field options? (Select all correct answers).*

    A. Server name

    B. Date

    C. ISP type

    D. Browser type

    E. Social Security Number

15. *Which of the following are appropriate uses for scrolling text boxes? (Select all correct answers.)*

    A. Collecting large amounts of text

    B. Collecting password fields displaying asterisks

    C. Providing sets of mutually exclusive options

    D. Providing sets of non-mutually exclusive options

    E. Collecting image files

Validating User Input

The FrontPage MCSD/MCP test puts special emphasis on a conceptual and technical understanding of collecting and processing data in input forms. I suspect this is because Microsoft would like us all to understand, and stretch the limits of FrontPage as a tool for connecting to online databases. Meshing FrontPage 98 with data management allows companies and organizations to squeeze a tremendous amount of value from FrontPage, and use it to create Web sites that without FrontPage would require significant coding.

Client-Side Scripts and Validation Fields

The challenge all this presents to you as a FrontPage MCP or MCSD is that you need to have quite a detailed understanding of how FrontPage can collect and manage data. In the previous chapter you explored the process of creating input form fields, and began to look at how FrontPage generates input forms that manage the data for input form fields. You learned that FrontPage can collect data input without using server-side scripts because it relies on FrontPage extension files in the Web server in which a site resides. In the next chapter, we'll examine in detail the various options for defining how input forms manage data.

In this chapter we'll explore validation scripts. Validation tests user input before the data is sent to a Web server. For example, if the designer of an input form wants to require that the "Name," "Email" and "Credit Card" form fields be filled in correctly before data is submitted to a server, he or she can attach validation scripts to those fields that test the data before it is sent to the server. If the data in those fields is not supplied by the visitor, or if it is not correctly formatted (for example, if there are not enough numbers in the credit card number), the data can be rejected even before it is submitted to the server and the visitor will be advised to correct the information.

At the conclusion of this chapter you will be able to:

- Understand how client-side scripts valid data before it is submitted to a Web server.
- Assign required status to input fields.
- Validate to restrict input to selected input types (like text or numbers).
- Validate to test input for length (like requiring ten digits for a phone number).
- Validate input data to test for value constraints (like requiring a credit card expiration date greater than the current date).

MCSD 9.1   Validating Input Using Form Field Validation Scripts

Client-side validation scripts can be applied quickly to test data, even before it is submitted to a Web server. Submitting data to a Web server is going to take a while, depending on the speed of a client's modem and other factors. However, client-side validation scripts test data instantly using JavaScript or VBScript.

Data that is submitted in an input form can be validated either at the server or right in the Web browser. Validation through a Web browser is referred to as client-side validation scripting.

The advantages of client-side validation scripts include the fact that they do not require the same kind of advanced coding required for server-side validation, and the fact that they are faster. Client-side validation scripts are faster because the user's input is tested right in the Web browser, even before the data is submitted to the server. This is possible because browsers are able to interpret and test the validation scripts generated by FrontPage.

FrontPage generates client-side validation scripts without requiring any programming by the developer. These validation scripts operate independently of the server connection, provided that the user's browser interprets the JavaScript generated by FrontPage.

Browser compatibility issues for validation scripts are discussed in the next section of this chapter.

Following is a a quick experiment you can perform to experience client-side validation scripting. It requires the following:

- A FrontPage Web with an input form that has a one-line text box (refer to Chapter 8, "Creating Input Forms," for instructions on how to do this).
- A connection to a Web server–The FrontPage Personal Web Server or Internet Information Server 4.0 will work well for this experiment.

Personal Web Server version 4.0 is a significant improvement in reliability over the version of the Personal Web Server that shipped with Front-Page 98. It is available with Internet Explorer version 5.0.

If you have a Web open, and a connection to a Web server, you're ready for this experiment that will help expose how client-side validation scripting works:

1. Connect to a Web server. The Personal Web Server will work well for this experiment.
2. Open an existing Web site (or create a new one), and in the FrontPage Editor create an input form with at least one one-line text box form field. If you saved the input form you used in the first or second Study Break in Chapter 8, that will work fine.
3. Double-click on a one-line text box to open the Text Box Properties dialog box.

4. Click on the Validate button in the dialog box.
5. In the Data Length area of the dialog box, click to select the Required check box.
6. Click on OK in both dialog boxes to return to the FrontPage Editor.
7. Save your Web page, and preview it in a browser. Attempt to submit the form with data entered in the one-line text box to which you attached the "Required" validation script. The data should be submitted to the server.
8. In your Web browser, click on Back to return to the input form. Attempt to submit the form with the required field left blank. You will see a dialog box informing you that you need to enter a value for the field, as shown in Figure 9.1.
9. Now that you have tested your validation script in a browser, with your Web server connected, disconnect your server. If you are using the Personal Web Server, click on the Stop button in the Personal Web Manager. Figure 9.2 shows the stop button in Personal Web Server version 4.0. Alternately, if you are logged on to an Internet or intranet server, you can log off to break your connection to the server.
10. With your server off, test your input form again. If you attempt to submit a correctly filled out input form, your browser will be unable to connect to a server, and you will see an error message something like the one in Figure 9.3.
11. Use the Back button on your browser to return to your input form, and delete all data from the required input field. Attempt to submit the input form page again. The script that detects validation errors still works, even without a server connection.

If you wish to regain your connection to a Web server, don't forget to restore your server connection. If you are using the Personal Web Server to experiment with FrontPage Web sites, double-click on the Personal Web Server icon in your Windows tray and click on the Start button. Or, reconnect to your intranet or Internet server.

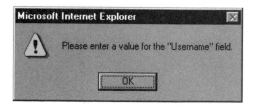

Figure 9.1 *Validation scripts provide instructions to visitors who attempt to enter forms with incorrect or missing data.*

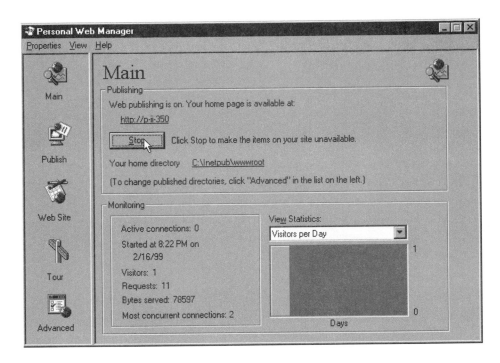

Figure 9.2 *Turning off a server connection will allow you to test validation scripts without a server.*

The point of this little hands-on experiment was to reinforce the concept of client-side validation scripts. They work before, or even *without* a connection to a Web server. Of course, data cannot be submitted to a Web server without a connection between a browser and a Web server, but validation scripts can still work without that linkage.

How FrontPage Generates Validation Scripts

Before we examine in detail the different types of validation rules that can be assigned to various input form field types, it will be helpful to understand how FrontPage generates validation scripts.

FrontPage 98 can generate validation scripts using either JavaScript or VBScript. The default setting is JavaScript. JavaScript is compatible with Netscape Navigator versions 2.0 and higher, and Internet Explorer versions 3.0 and higher. VBScript, on the other hand, is compatible only with versions 3.0 and higher of Internet Explorer. Therefore, if a Web site is being designed for visitors using both Netscape and IE, you should advise the developers to generate JavaScript validation scripts. There is no particular reason to recommend switching validation scripts to IE unless an organization has an internal policy of doing all Web site scripting in IE. That would maintain a

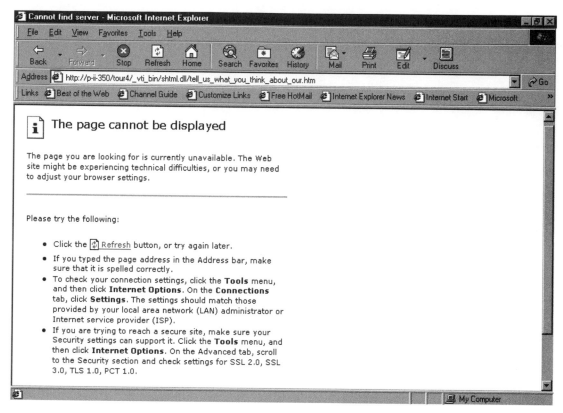

Figure 9.3 *You cannot submit an input form without a server connection.*

uniform development environment, but restrict validation scripts to working only with visitors using IE. Such an environment would exist only for an intranet Web site accessible only to internal users using recent versions of IE.

To define the scripting language for validation scripts, follow these steps:

1. Open (or create) the Web for which you are defining validation scripting language.
2. In the FrontPage Explorer, select Tools, Web Settings, and click on the Advanced tab in the FrontPage Web Settings dialog box.
3. In the Validation area of the Advanced tab, use the Language drop-down menu to select VBScript, JavaScript, or None, as shown in Figure 9.4.

Note

Validation scripting languages are defined separately for each Web site.

4. After selecting a scripting language, click on OK. If you changed validation scripting languages, you will see the dialog box shown in Figure 9.5. Click on Yes in that dialog box to recalculate your existing validation scripts.

Study Break

Changing Validation Scripting Language

Practice what you have learned creating a validation script, examining the scripting code, and changing the script language.

First, create or open a Web site, and create or open a page with a one-line input form field in an input form.

Next, assign a "Required" validation property to the validation form. Test the input form in a browser without entering a value in the field. Test the form again with the validation requirement met. View the generated validation script in the HTML tab in the FrontPage Editor.

Finally, change the scripting language for validation scripts to VBScript, and note the changes in the HTML code in the FrontPage Editor.

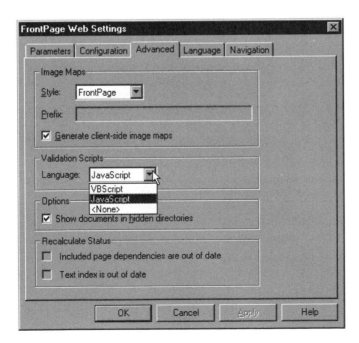

Figure 9.4 *You can choose either JavaScript or VBScript for validation scripts.*

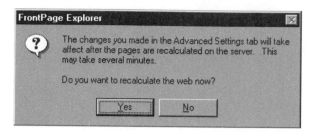

Figure 9.5 *Validation scripts can be recalculated to use a different scripting language.*

MCSD 9.2 Defining Required Fields

In the first part of this chapter we focused on the technical aspects of client-side validation scripts. It is important that you have at least a basic conceptual understanding of how validation scripts work in order to determine if validation testing is possible in a Web site.

The other side of managing form field validation requires you to switch from your role as technical advisor to your role as site manager, designer, and even site psychologist in order to advise developers on when, and how, to require form field validation.

Validation can take two basic forms:

- Validation can test to make sure that required form fields have been filled in.
- Validation can test to make sure that the data in a field is of the appropriate type.

In many cases, it will be appropriate to designate *all* input form fields as required fields. For example, in a customer technical support form, you might need *all* the form fields filled out in order to correctly identify and respond to a visitor's problem. Without an e-mail address to respond to, a description of the problem, etc., the form will not be of much use. Similarly, if you are designing an input form to take orders for a product or services, or to register visitors for seminars or events, you might well need all the form fields filled out in order to process the request.

On the other hand, some form fields might be optional. For example, if you are providing a set of check boxes, you would, by definition, not require that any particular check box be selected. If you are providing a set of options that require the visitor select at least one of them, use radio buttons instead of check boxes. In other words:

- Check boxes cannot be defined as required fields.
- A *group* of radio buttons can be defined as a required fields, and visitors will be forced to select *one* option from the set of radio buttons before submitting the form.

Drop-down menus and text boxes can also be defined as required fields.

Defining Required Radio Buttons

No one particular radio button can be defined as a required field. After all, the point of a group of radio buttons is to allow a user to choose one option from a set of options. However, you *can* force visitors to choose one option from a group of radio buttons.

Sometimes it is not necessary to require a user to choose from a set of radio buttons. Groups of radio buttons often have a default selection. In that case, users are forced to either accept the default option or make another choice. In that way, radio buttons have a built-in required element to them. Assigning a required validation property to a group of radio buttons is really necessary only when none of the radio buttons is a default selection.

To define a group of radio buttons as a required field:

1. Double-click on any one of a group of radio buttons to open the Radio Button Properties dialog box.
2. Click on the Validate button to open the Radio Button Validation dialog box.
3. Select the Data Required check box.
4. In the Display Name box, enter a name that will be used in validation warning messages to identify the field. For example, if you are requiring visitors to choose one version number for their software, you could define the Display Name as "version number." Figure 9.6 shows the results of attempting to submit a form without choosing from a set of required radio buttons.
5. After you define the validation properties, click on OK in the Radio Button Validation dialog box, and click on OK in the Radio Button Properties dialog box.

Defining Required Drop-Down Menus

Requiring that visitors make a selection from a drop-down menu is similar to requiring that visitors choose one option from a set of radio buttons. Since drop-down menus have a default selection (the first item in the menu), by default a visitor has to select at least one option from the list.

Figure 9.6 *You can define the name for a set of option buttons.*

One example of where a requirement validation becomes relevant is when you use the first option in a drop-down menu to define the drop-down menu. For example, in Figure 9.7, the first menu item is "Pick one." You can force visitors to select a menu item *other than the first item* through a requirement validation.

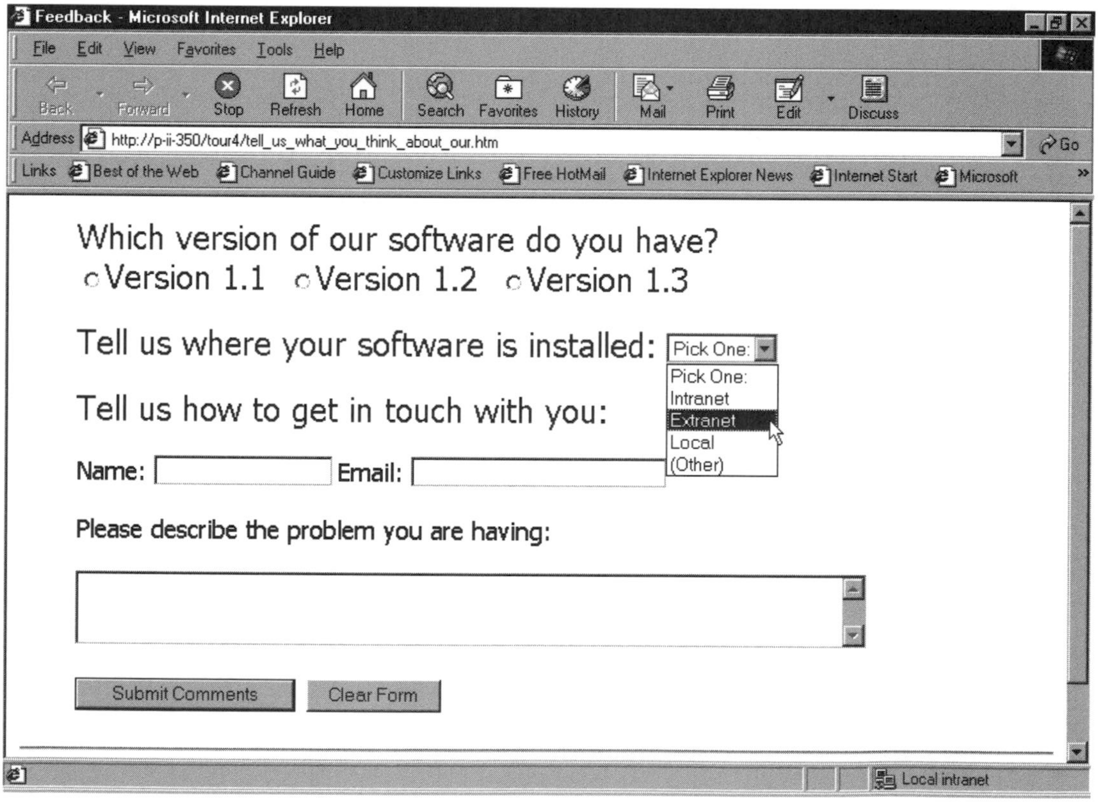

Figure 9.7 *Sometimes you want to require that users select a menu item other than the first item in a drop-down menu.*

To define a drop-down menu as a required field and force visitors to select an option other than the first item in the list:

1. Double-click on a drop-down menu to open the Drop-Down Menu Properties dialog box.
2. Click on the Validate button to open the Drop-Down Menu Validation dialog box.
3. Select the Data Required check box.
4. In the Display Name box, enter a name that will be used in validation warning messages to identify the field. For example, if you are requiring that visitors choose an installation location for their software, you could define the Display Name as "Where Is Your Software Installed" as shown in Figure 9.8.
5. To force visitors to select an option other than the first item in the drop-down menu, click on the Disallow First Item check box. Then click on OK twice to close both dialog boxes.

Defining Required Text Boxes

You can define either a one-line text box or a scrolling text box as a required field. For example, if your input form includes form fields for a credit card number, a user name, an e-mail address, or a phone number, you might decide that these fields must be filled in before the form will be accepted.

To define a one-line or scrolling text box as a required field:

1. Double-click on any text box to open the Text Box Properties dialog box.
2. Click on the Validate button to open the Text Box Validation dialog box.
3. Select the Required check box.
4. In the Display Name box, enter a name that will be used in validation warning messages to identify the field.
5. Click on OK twice to close both dialog boxes.

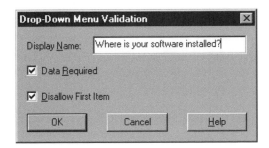

Figure 9.8 *Defining a required drop-down menu.*

Defining Required Form Fields

Practice what you have learned by making form fields required.

First, open a Web and select File, New in the FrontPage Editor to open a new Web page. From the Page tab in the New dialog box, double-click on Feedback Form to generate a new page with an input form.

Next, change the radio button group so that none of the radio buttons are selected by default. Make the group of radio buttons a required field, and assign a Display Name of "Type of Comment." Make all the rest of the fields in the form required, except for the fax number and the check box. Define Display Names to each of the fields.

Finally, test your required fields by attempting to submit your form with various fields left blank. Figure 9.9 shows an example of the kinds of dialog boxes that will appear, prompting users to complete required fields. Save the page to use in the next Study Break.

MCSD 9.3   Assigning Validation Properties

Validation properties are a powerful way to ensure that data entered in text boxes conforms to required sets of rules. For example, if you collect a zip code or postal code, you can define a set number of digits. If you collect a credit card number, you can ensure that users don't enter letters when numbers are required.

Validation properties are only relevant to text boxes. Other than requiring that one of a group of radio buttons, or that at least one item in a drop-down menu is selected, validation rules aren't applicable to check boxes, radio buttons, or drop-down menus. For those form field types, the designer builds in validation by providing a set of options.

While, technically, validation rules can be assigned to scrolling text boxes, in practice that is rarely done. Scrolling text boxes by definition pro-

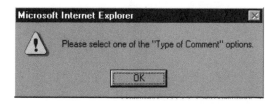

Figure 9.9 *A user has not filled out a required field.*

vide unlimited space for entering text, and are usually used for free-form entries like comments or suggestions, not for collecting data like Social Security numbers or e-mail addresses. Therefore, we will focus on defining validation rules for one-line text boxes, but keep in mind that technically these same validation settings can be assigned to scrolling text boxes.

To define validation rules for a one-line (or scrolling) text box:

1. Double-click on any text box to open the properties dialog box.
2. Click on the Validate button to open the validation dialog box.
3. Define validation rules (see descriptions below).
4. Click on OK to close both dialog boxes.

The following sections have descriptions of the types of validation properties that can be applied to text boxes.

Defining Data Types

The four options in the Data Type drop-down menu allow you to define how you want to restrict input in the text box. The options are:

- No Constraints
- Text
- Integer
- Number

If you elect to place no constraints on a field, any character will be accepted. The Integer constraint requires that fields have whole numbers (1, 2, 3 ... 99999, etc.) entered, while the Number validation rule allows numbers with decimal places (like 1.4).

The Text validation data type allows you the most control over user input. You might apply a Text validation rule to a form field that is collecting visitors' names, for example. Other fields that might use a Text constraint include City, State, and even Address.

Note Applying a Text constraint does not mean that the field cannot accept numbers. Text fields can be defined to accept numbers, letters, and selected symbols.

If you assign a text constraint, you can then use the four check boxes in the Text Format area of the Text Box Validation dialog box to set further rules for what kind of text will be accepted. The options for text validation are:

- Letters allows letters A–Z. Symbols and non-English language characters are not allowed.
- Digits allows numbers.
- Whitespace allows spaces or tabs. If you are applying validation rules to a scrolling text box, the Whitespace option allows carriage returns and forced line breaks (Ctrl+Enter).
- Other allows you to define additional characters. For example, if you are collecting e-mail addresses, you might allow letters, digits and the "@" symbol, as shown in Figure 9.10.

If you assign an Integer or Number data type, you can further define the format for numeric data the field will accept in the Numeric Format section of the Text Box Validation dialog box. The Grouping options allow you to accept numeric values separated by commas (like 12,500), or by decimal places (like 12.500). The Decimal options allow you to define which decimal separator you wish to allow for Numbers (either a period or a comma).

Defining Data Length Constraints

The Min Length and Max Length fields in the Data Length area of the Text Box Validation dialog box allow you to specify the minimum (Min Length) and maximum (Max Length) number of characters you will accept in a text box.

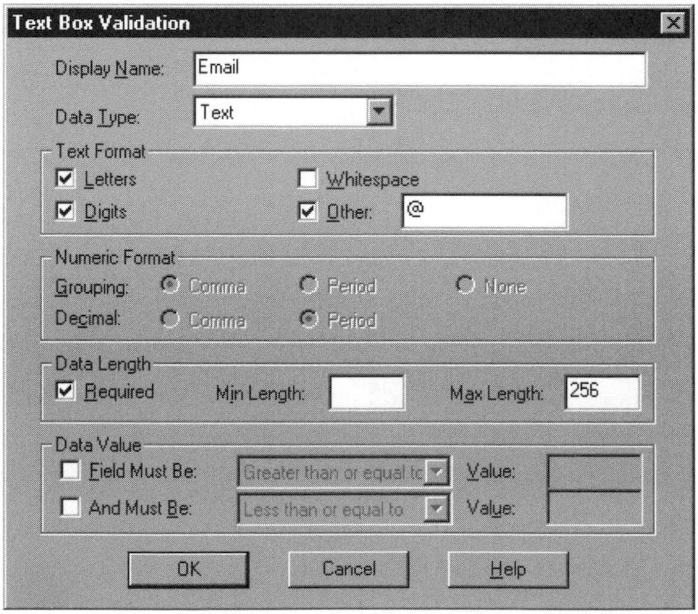

Figure 9.10 *Defining validation rules for e-mail addresses.*

You can assign the same value to the Min Length and Max Length field to constrain input to a set number of digits. For example, a phone number, credit card number, Social Security number, or year field can all be constricted to a set number of digits. This ensures that visitors are entering valid information, and helps catch data entry errors.

Minimum and maximum length can be used to constrain input, even if you don't apply other validation rules.

Defining Data Value Constraints

Data value constraints can be applied to any type of data. You can apply either one or two data value constraints. Each constraint can use the following operators:

- Less than
- Greater than
- Less than or equal to
- Greater than or equal to
- Equal to
- Not equal to

Each data value constraint combines an operator from the list above with a value. So, for example, if you are collecting an expiration date for a credit card, the first value could be constrained to be greater than or equal to the current year, while the second value could be constrained to being less than the year 2020, for example.

Study Break

Applying Validation Constraints to a Text Box

Practice what you have learned by making form fields required.

If you created and saved an input page in the previous Study Break, use that form. If not, open a Web and select File, New in the FrontPage Editor to open a new Web page. From the Page tab in the New dialog box, double-click on Feedback Form to generate a new page with an input form.

Next, change the Name field so that only letters and white space are accepted. Assign a minimum length of 4 characters to the Name field. Allow only numbers, letters, the "@" symbol, and a period to be accepted in the email field. For the Tel field, require 12 digits and allow numbers, white space, parentheses and the - symbol.

Finally, test your validated fields by attempting to submit your form with an email address that has a character other than those permitted (like an exclamation point), a name field with a number in it, and a phone number that is only 7 digits. Figure 9.11 shows an example of the kind of dialog boxes that will appear, prompting users to correct their entry if it violates validation rules.

■ Summary

Validation scripts test the data that is entered into a form field to see if it meets defined criteria. This criteria can include the length of input, the value of input, or a field can be defined simply as "require." If visitors attempt to submit data that does not match the defined validation criteria, that data will be rejected and the visitor will see a message explaining how to correctly complete the form before submitting it.

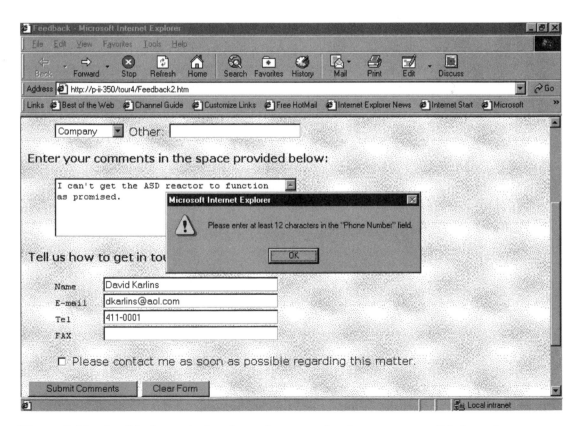

Figure 9.11 *A validation script has detected an entry that does not meet validation rules.*

Validation scripts test data before the data is sent to a Web server. This makes validation scripts work quickly, as the visitor does not need to wait for his or her data to reach the Web server to have it tested.

▲ CHAPTER REVIEW QUESTIONS

Here are some practice questions relating to the material covered in the "Validation Scripts" area of Microsoft's *Designing and Implementing Web Sites Using Microsoft FrontPage 98* exam (70-055).

1. *Which of the following validation options can be applied to radio buttons? (Select all correct answers.)*

    A. A radio button can be a required field

    B. A group of radio buttons can be a required field

    C. Radio buttons can have validation scripts attached to them

    D. Radio buttons can be validated for data type

2. *Text box fields can be defined to validate for which of the following? (Select all correct answers.)*

    A. Letters

    B. Numbers

    C. White space

    D. Non-letter or number characters like the @ symbol

3. *Values can have validation scripts attached that check to see if a number is greater than 0.*

    A. True

    B. False

4. *Drop-down menus can have validation scripts attached that check to see if a number is greater than 0.*

    A. True

    B. False

5. *FrontPage automatically generates server-side validation scripts.*

    A. True

    B. False

6. *Which types of form fields allow validation scripts that check to see if a required field has been filled out in a form? (Select all correct answers.)*

    A. Check boxes

    B. Labels

    C. One-line text boxes

    D. Scrolling text boxes

    E. Hidden fields

7. *Validation scripts require which of the following to work? (Select all correct answers.)*

    A. A compatible browser

    B. FrontPage 98 extension files on the Web server

    C. SSL encryption

    D. One-line text boxes

    E. The ability to handwrite JavaScript code

8. *FrontPage generates validation scripts by default in JavaScript, but you can change that so FrontPage generates validation scripts in VBScript.*

    A. True

    B. False

9. *Check boxes can be defined as required fields.*

    A. True

    B. False

10. *A Text data type would work well for validating e-mail addresses.*

    A. True

    B. False

11. *Number data types can be formatted to accept either a period or a comma to demarcate decimal places.*

    A. True

    B. False

12. *If you were creating a validation for a form field that was collecting zip codes, which of the following validation constraints might be useful? (Select all correct answers.)*

    A. Data value constraints

    B. Data length constraints

    C. Grouping constraints

    D. Integer data type constraints

    E. Required constraints

13. *VBScripts are not as universally compatible with Web browsers as JavaScripts.*

    A. True

    B. False

14. *Where do you assign required constraints to form fields? (Select all correct answers.)*

    A. At the server

    B. In the Validation dialog box for that type of field

    C. In the browser

    D. In the Web settings dialog box in the FrontPage Explorer

15. *Where do you change the default scripting language for validation scripts? (Select all correct answers.)*

    A. Internet Explorer

    B. Netscape Navigator

    C. In the Web settings dialog box in the FrontPage Explorer

    D. In the Form Field Properties dialog box

    E. In the Form Properties dialog box

Processing User Input

Perhaps the single most powerful element in FrontPage 98 is the ability to manage form input data without the need for server-side scripting. Before the advent of FrontPage, it was necessary to link input forms to customized scripts, or programs that resided on a Web server. FrontPage eliminates the need for these server scripts by handling the process of managing form data through FrontPage extension program files.

If you are overseeing the development of a Web site that collects data through input forms, you will need to recognize and deal with two possible scenarios:

- You are responsible for the development of a Web site with input forms that is being published to a server with FrontPage extensions.

- You are responsible for the development of a Web site with input forms that is being published to a Web site that does not have FrontPage extensions.

233

In this chapter, we will focus on how to manage form input in sites that are published to servers with FrontPage extensions. In the real world, this is a major reason why an organization will choose FrontPage as their Web development platform—so that they can take advantage of FrontPage's ability to collect input data. At the same time, as a FrontPage expert, it will be necessary for you to recognize and work with clients who for various reasons want to develop their site content in FrontPage, but elect to publish their sites to non-FrontPage-friendly servers.

In this chapter, we'll complete our exploration of how FrontPage manages input data. At the conclusion of this chapter you will be able to:

- Understand how FrontPage Webs process input data.
- Send input data to an e-mail address.
- Send input data to a text file.
- Send input data to an HTML page.
- Display input data results in framed pages.
- Manage input data when a Web is published to a server without Front-Page extensions.

Managing Form Data

FrontPage automates the process of collecting input data. In many ways, this process is analogous to the way FrontPage generates HTML code: Users can design extremely complex Web sites that in reality are in HTML, yet the user does not even need to be aware that FrontPage is generated in HTML as they design Web pages. In a similar way, FrontPage will collect input data and save it to various file formats without the user even being aware that program files on the Web server are handling the data.

The caveat, of course, is that this only works if a Web site is published to a server with FrontPage extensions. The FrontPage Personal Web Server, Microsoft Personal Web Server (shipped with Internet Explorer), and Internet Information Server (shipped with Windows NT) all provide these FrontPage extension files. FrontPage extension files exist for one of three types of targets:

- An e-mail address
- A text file
- A Web page

Each of these types of targets has its own advantages and disadvantages. You don't have to limit input data to one target. You can send the information that visitors enter into your forms to one, two, or all three of the targets.

Collecting form input as e-mail allows you to receive data input as it is submitted. The limitation of getting form input as e-mail is that the data is not stored in a file, and it cannot be organized in any kind of database or document. Figure 10.1 shows an e-mail message containing input form data.

Using More Than One Type of Target for Data

You can combine different targets for data. For example, you can set up data collection so that you receive both an e-mail copy of input form data and that same data is saved to a text file for use as a database.

I use a combination of e-mail and text form targets to collect input to my Web site. Input from visitors who ask questions or make suggestions ends up in my e-mail, but also goes into a database that helps me track the quantity and type of input I get at my site.

A Web page can also be the target for input data. This is used for bulletin boards and guest books, where you want visitors to be able to access and read the data that is fed into your site through forms. Figure 10.2 shows the results of an input form viewed with a Web browser.

Finally, form data can be saved to text files, from which it can be integrated into mailing lists, databases and spreadsheets. Figure 10.3 shows an input data record being examined in form view in Microsoft Excel. Here, I'm using Excel's ability to display individual records in Form view.

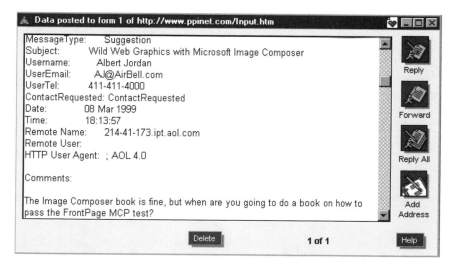

Figure 10.1 *Collecting form data as e-mail instantly delivers input.*

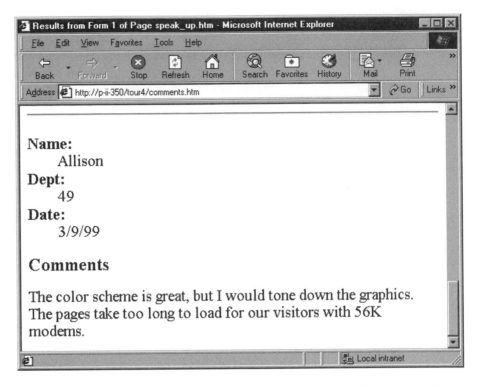

Figure 10.2 *Input data can be posted directly to a Web page that is accessible to visitors to your site.*

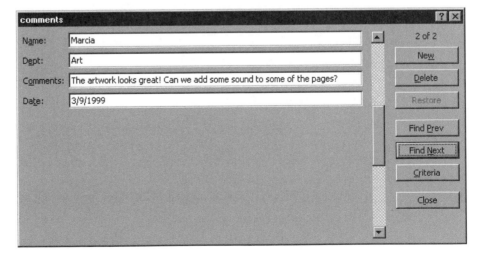

Figure 10.3 *Viewing input data in Excel.*

MCSD 10.1   ## Sending Form Results by E-mail

Collecting input data through e-mail provides instant notification when a visitor submits an input form at your Web site. For example, if you are taking orders through an input form, e-mail results will notify you immediately when an order is placed.

To send input collected in a form to an e-mail address, follow these steps:

1. Create an input form (see Chapter 8, "Creating Input Forms," for a full discussion of defining input forms).
2. Right-click in the form and select Form Properties from the context menu.
3. Select the "Send to" radio button.
4. Enter the target e-mail address in the E-mail Address area of the Form Properties dialog box. You may enter more than one target e-mail address by separating addresses with semicolons (;).
5. If you want your form input to go only to an e-mail address (and not to a file), delete the default file in the File Name field of the Form Properties dialog box as shown in Figure 10.4.
6. Click on the OK button in the Form Properties dialog box.

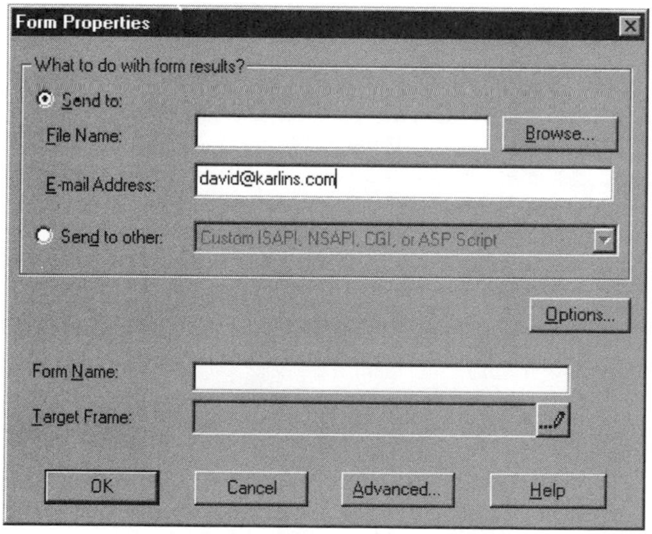

Figure 10.4   Directing input data to an e-mail address target.

You can control the format of the e-mailed data. The e-mail data can come to you as formatted text, unformatted text, or as HTML. You can elect to display or hide field names. You can also define a subject line and reply-to line in the e-mail you receive.

To define the format of e-mail data:

1. Right-click in your form and choose Form Properties from the options menu.
2. Click the Options button in the Form Properties dialog box.
3. Click the E-Mail Results tab in the Options for Saving Results of Form dialog box.
4. You can choose alternate formatting for your message from the E-Mail Format drop-down menu.
5. After you define the E-mail results, click on OK twice to close the dialog boxes. Figure 10.5 shows e-mail results being defined as formatted text.

You can also define a subject line for e-mail form data. For example, you might want to assign a subject line of "Order" for e-mail input forms used collect online orders, or "Feedback" for a form that is collecting feedback on your Web site.

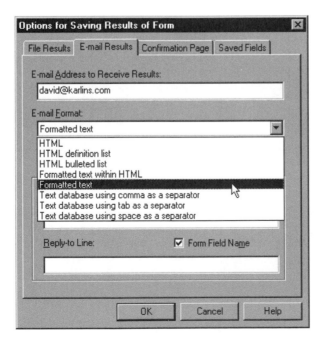

Figure 10.5 *Data targeted to e-mail forms is usually defined as formatted text.*

To define subject lines for input form data sent to an e-mail target:

1. Right-click in your form and choose Form Properties from the options menu.
2. Click the Options button in the Form Properties dialog box, and select the E-mail results tab.
3. Select the Include Field Names check box if you want the input to appear with a field name in your e-mail.
4. In the Subject Line field, enter the message that you want to display in your e-mail subject line when you get input form results sent to you, as shown in Figure 10.6. If you don't enter anything in the Subject Line field, input data form results are sent to you in an e-mail message with a subject line of "Form Results."
5. You can assign the results of an input form field to display in the subject line of e-mail input messages. To do this, click the Form Field Name check box and then enter the form field name in the Subject Line area. For example, if you have a "Contact Me" field, you can display the results of that field in your e-mail subject line.

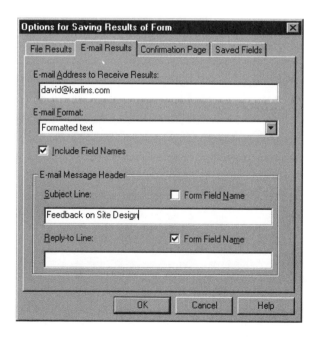

Figure 10.6 *Defining an e-mail subject line for input form data.*

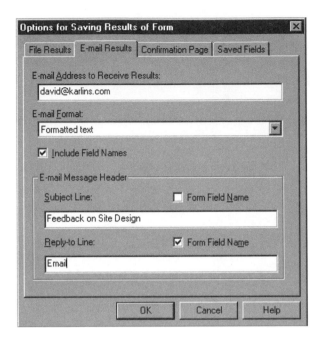

Figure 10.7   *Defining a default respond-to field for e-mail-targeted input data.*

6. The Reply-to Line area field in the dialog box allows you to define the Reply-to line in e-mail using a field in your input form. For example, if your input form has a field called "E-mail" that is used to collect e-mail addresses from visitors submitting the form, then you could use the Reply-to Line box to enter "E-mail," as shown in Figure 10.7.

7. Once you define all the options for receiving input via e-mail, click the OK button in the Options for Saving Results of Form dialog. Then click OK again to close the Form Properties dialog box.

Some servers with FrontPage extensions do not handle e-mail results for input forms. The FrontPage Personal Web Server will not support e-mail results. If you attempt to define an input form with an e-mail address as the data target, and your server does not support e-mail input, you'll see the warning message in Figure 10.8. However, you can develop a Web site that sends input data to e-mail addresses using the FrontPage Personal Web Server, and then later publish that site to a server that does support e-mail targets for input forms.

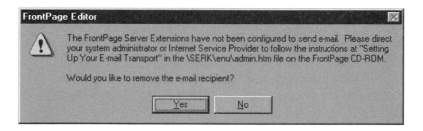

Figure 10.8 *Some servers do not support e-mail results for input forms.*

Collecting Form Results as E-mail

Practice what you have learned by defining an input form that collects feedback from visitors, and directs that input to your e-mail address.

You can generate an input form quickly by using the Guest book template in the New dialog box (select File, New in the FrontPage Editor).

Next, change the target for the input data from a file to an e-mail address. Remove the default target for the data.

If your server supports e-mail form data, test your data target by submitting input data, and reading the results in your e-mail program.

MCSD 10.2   Sending Form Results to a File

You have two options for collecting form data in files. You can collect the form data in HTML files, or you can collect it in text files. If data input is for public consumption, and you wish to share it at your Web site, you can simply dump that data into a Web site and allow visitors to see their own comments. The second option is to collect data in text formats destined for the corporate database, your organization's mailing list, or a spreadsheet where data can be crunched.

Actually, there is a third option for collecting data in a file. You can send data to both an HTML Web page and to a text file. But normally, as the FrontPage data collection guru, you will assist your developers in deciding which of the two formats is more appropriate for their data.

Sending Input Form Data to HTML Pages

If you are simply creating an input form that will collect comments from visitors and post them to a page where they can be viewed, you can save time by using the guest book template. This template creates an input form that sends data to a Web page called Guestlog.htm.

If you want to create your own input form, or if you want to redirect input data from one of the other input form templates to a Web page, you can do that by defining an HTML page as the target for input data.

To send input form data to a Web page:

1. Right-click in an input form and select Form Properties from the options menu.
2. Enter an existing HTML page in your Web site in the File Name area or use the Browse button to pick one. Or, enter a new filename for a page that you will create to display input. If you do define a new Web page, the filename must end in .HTM or .HTML. If you enter a new filename, a new HTML page is created to display input form results.
3. Click the Options button and click the File Results tab. Then, choose HTML, HTML Definition List, HTML Bulleted List or Formatted Text Within HTML from the File Format drop-down menu. These four options provide slightly different ways of displaying data in HTML (see box below for a discussion of each option).
4. Click the OK button in the Options for Saving Results of Form dialog box. Then click on OK in the Form Properties dialog box.

There are four options for displaying data in an HTML page. While the differences are not dramatic, they do provide distinctive ways to display input data in a Web page. The four choices are:

- HTML—displays text in the default text format for your Web site.
- HTML definition list—displays outdented field names, and indented field data, as shown in Figure 10.9.
- HTML bulleted list—displays field names, followed by field data as bullet lists (see Figure 10.10).
- Formatted text within HTML—displays HTML with non-standard format elements like extra white spaces between words, and tab spaces.

If you want visitors to be able to access the input form data that was sent to a Web page, you will want to include a link to the Web page somewhere in your site. Typically, either the input form page or the confirmation page has a link that says something like "To read other visitors" comments, click here."

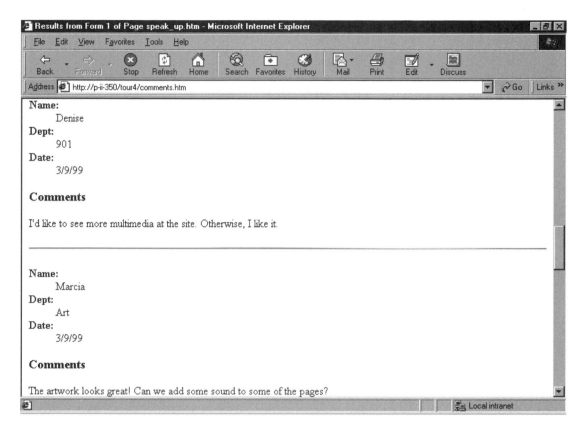

Figure 10.9 *Displaying input data in a Web page using HTML Definition List formatting.*

Private Web Pages for Input Data

What if you want to collect input data in a Web page (for example suggestions, comments, complaints), but you don't want that Web page available to the public? You can make an HTML data-target unavailable to the general public by saving it in the _Private folder at your Web site. A typical _Private folder and its contents are shown in Figure 10.11.

FrontPage creates a _Private folder when your Web site is initially generated in the FrontPage Explorer. Normally files in the _Private folder are not identified when visitors use search boxes at your site, and they do not appear in generated navigation links. However, these files are not protected from visitors who know the URL and go there directly.

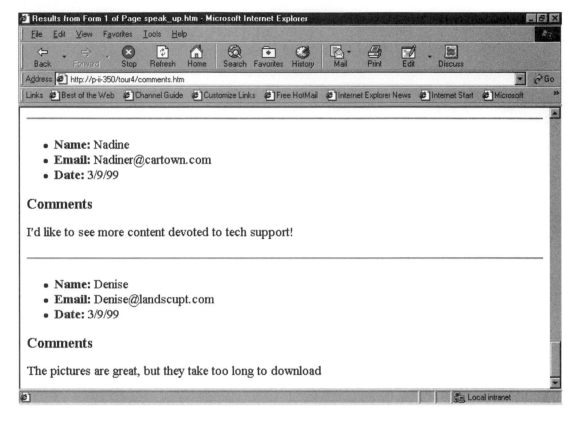

Figure 10.10 *Displaying input data in a Web page using HTML Bullet List formatting.*

Collecting Data in an HTML Page

Practice what you have learned by sending form data to a Web page where it can be shared by visitors to a Web site.

Start by creating a new Web page using the guest book template. Add additional input fields to collect the name and e-mail address of a visitor.

Next, define the target of the form as a file called "Comments.htm". Format the data as HTML Definition List, and include the Date hidden field. Then, place a link in the input form page to the Comments.htm page.

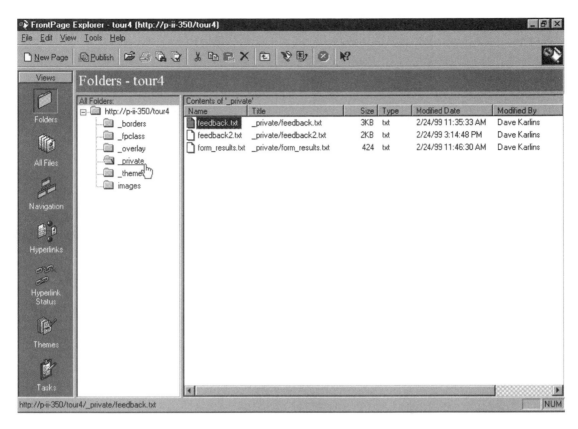

Figure 10.11 *Form input data can be stored in the _Private folder to hide it from search box result lists and navigation links.*

Finally, test your input form by previewing the form in your browser, and entering several comments. View the HTML page in your browser, and follow your link to the Comments.htm page to view input data.

Sending Data to Text Files

The most powerful format for collecting data is the ubiquitous text file. Data saved to text files is available in the site's Web server. You can open these text files using software applications like spreadsheets, word processors, database programs, project management applications, and contact management software.

As with other input data, if you are collecting data in text file format for internal use, you should place the target file in the _Private folder that FrontPage 98 creates in your Web site.

To send input data from a form to a text file:

1. Right-click anywhere in a data input form and select Form Properties from the options menu.
2. Click on the Send To radio button in the Form Properties dialog box.
3. Enter a filename or browse to an existing file. You can configure your target files to automatically launch an associated application file from the FrontPage 98 Explorer by assigning an associated file name extension to the file. For example, if you wish top open a text file in Excel, use a filename extension of .XLS.
4. You can further control the appearance and format of form input saved to a text file. Your options include separating fields with commas, tabs, or spaces. To define the type of separation between fields, click the Options button in the Form Properties dialog box and select the File Results tab in the dialog box. Assigning associated applications is discussed a little later in this section.
5. Use the File Format drop-down menu in the File Results tab of the Options for Saving Results of Form dialog box to select a text delimiting format.

Figure 10.12 *Saving form input as text with fields separated by tabs.*

Most database, word processing, and database files can import text files where fields are separated by either commas or tabs. Figure 10.12 shows tabs being selected as the divider between fields in the results file.

6. After you define your text format, OK both dialog boxes.

You can open text files on your Web server using applications on your local system. One way to do this is to launch the application, then navigate in the File Open menu to find your Web server file. The easier way is to attach an associated file name to the text file, and then launch the application simply by double-clicking on the file name in Folders view of the FrontPage Explorer.

Applications are launched depending on what application is associated with a file name extension. To add or edit the default extension associations, select Tools, Options in the FrontPage Explorer. Use the Add button to add new file name extensions and associated programs. For example, in Figure 10.13, I'm adding the *.db file name extension to the list of associated extensions, and defining Microsoft Access as the program that will launch when a user double-clicks on a file with a *.db file name extension.

Study Break

Saving Input Data to an Excel File

Practice what you have learned by collecting data and saving it to an Excel spreadsheet file.

Start by opening the Web page you used in the last Study Break, or by creating a new Web page using the Guest book template. Add an additional one-line text box to collect a numeric rating for the Web site, something like the one shown in Figure 10.14. If you are ambitious, adventurous, and want to experiment (and if you're preparing for the FrontPage MCP/MCSD test those qualities will help), add a validation rule restricting input to integers from 1–10 (review Chapter 9, "Validating User Input," for help with validation rules).

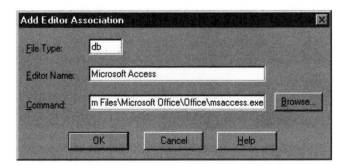

Figure 10.13   *Associating a file name extension with an application.*

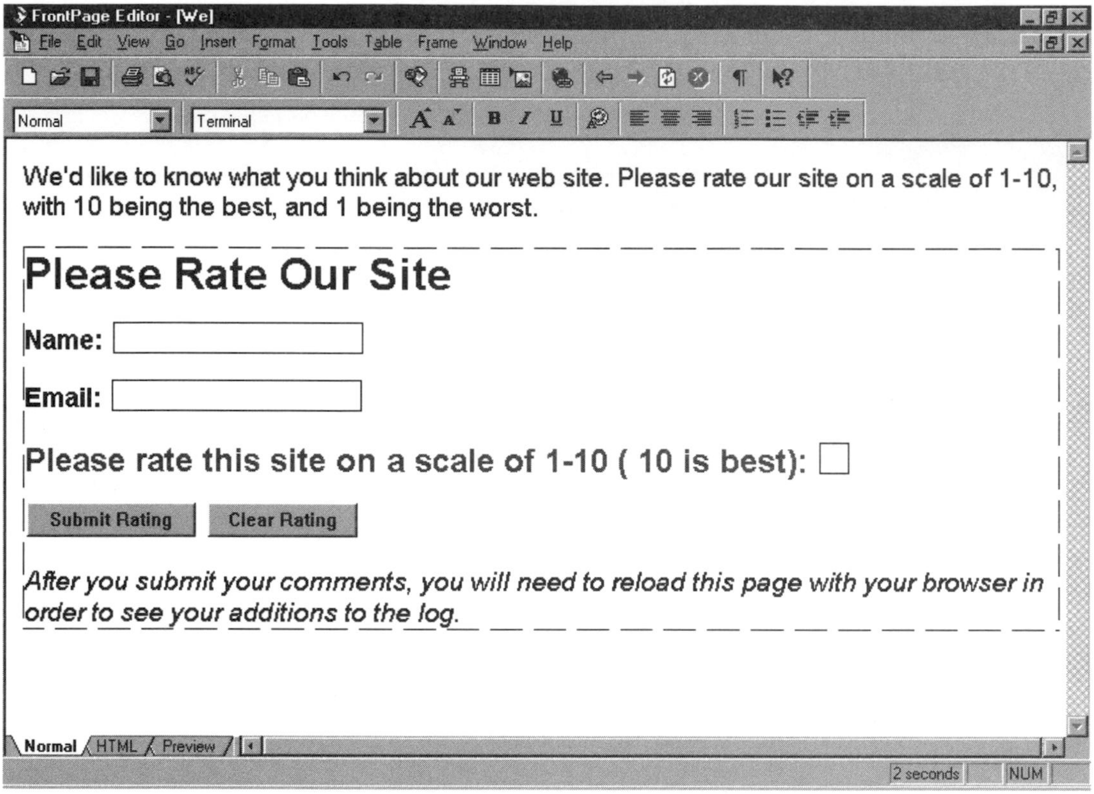
FrontPage Editor - [We]
File Edit View Go Insert Format Tools Table Frame Window Help
Normal
Terminal
We'd like to know what you think about our web site. Please rate our site on a scale of 1-10, with 10 being the best, and 1 being the worst.
Please Rate Our Site
Name:
Email:
Please rate this site on a scale of 1-10 (10 is best):
Submit Rating
Clear Rating
After you submit your comments, you will need to reload this page with your browser in order to see your additions to the log.
Normal
HTML
Preview
2 seconds
NUM

Figure 10.14 *Collecting data for crunching in a spreadsheet.*

Next, define the target of the form as a file called "Rating.xls". Format the data as a Text Database Using Tab as a Separator, and include the Date hidden field. Finally, test your input form by previewing the form in your browser, and entering several rating values. Open the file in Excel, if you have Excel installed, and examine the data in spreadsheet form. Figure 10.15 shows some ratings figures being crunched in Excel.

MCSD 10.3 Displaying Form Results in a Frame

In Chapter 7, "Creating User Interfaces," you explored the process of defining framed pages for Web sites. Framesets (pages that encompass more than one unique Web page) can be used in combination with input forms to create an interactive Web site.

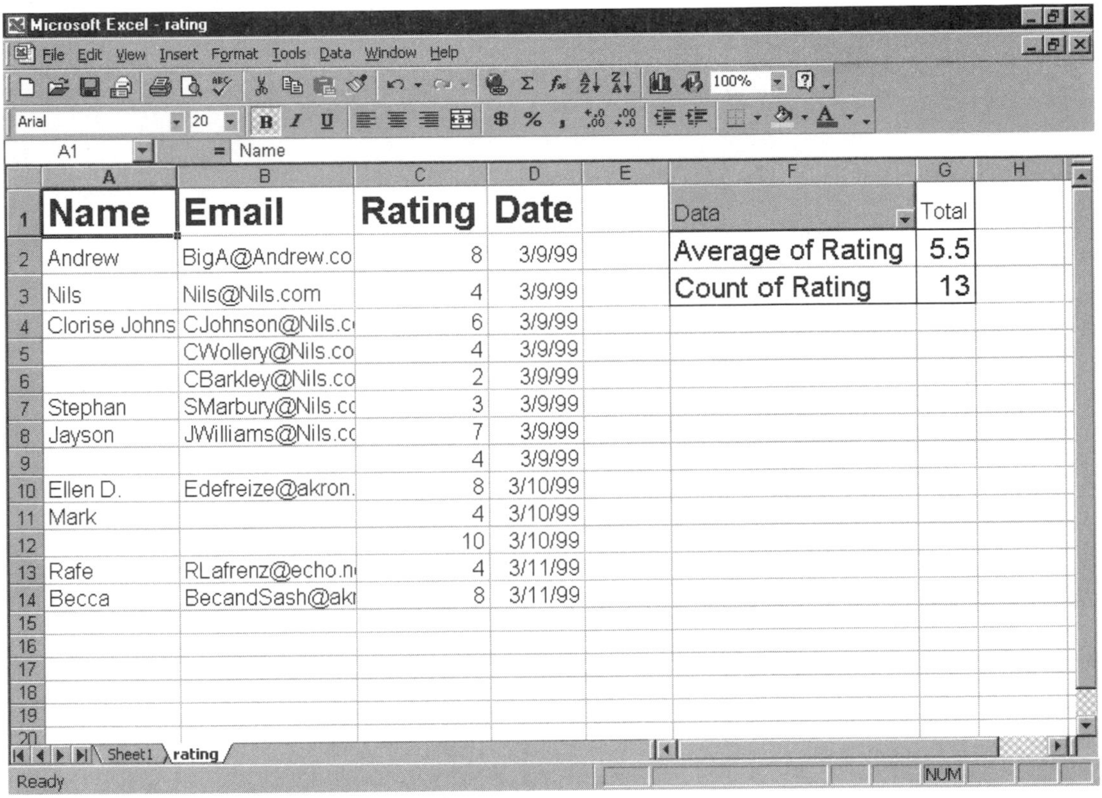

Figure 10.15 *Crunching input data in Excel.*

By combining input forms with framed pages, visitors can enter form data and view results at the same time. This creates a level of interactivity that is more immediate than even a Guest book-type page that we explored earlier in this chapter. Figure 10.16 shows a framed Web page that displays both the input form and the results page at the same time.

To create a frameset that includes both an input form and a results page is not significantly different than creating any frames page. However, displaying form results in a page is a specific topic on the exam, and also a particular challenge you may encounter as a FrontPage expert. Therefore, it is worthwhile to walk through the specific process of putting together a page that displays form results in a frame.

To create a frameset that displays both an input form and form results:

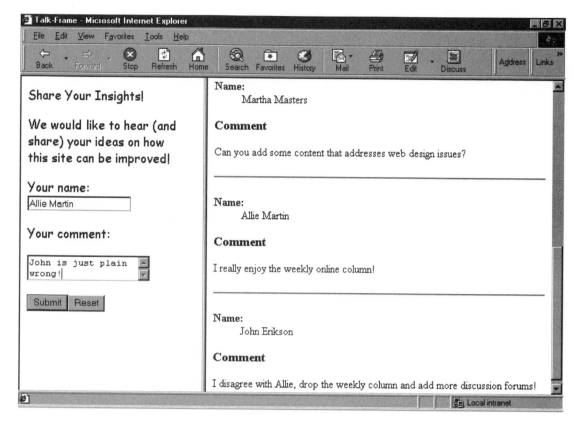

Figure 10.16 *Combining input forms and results pages in a frameset increases the immediacy of interactive forms.*

1. With a FrontPage Web open, in the FrontPage Editor select File, New and select the Frames tab in the New dialog box.
2. Choose any of the frame template options. Click OK to create the page. For the example demonstrated in Figure 10.16, I used the Vertical Split template.
3. In one of the generated frame pages, create a page that will display the results of the input form. Save that page.
4. In another of the generated frame pages, click on the New Page button and create a page with an input form. Define the target page for the input data as the results page you just saved in another frame within your frameset. Define the File Format (in the File Results tab of the Options for Saving Results of Form dialog box) as one of the HTML format

options. Figure 10.17 shows a target HTML page being defined. After you define the target page, OK both dialog boxes.

While the set of steps above creates a basic, interactive frameset with an input form and a results page, FrontPage is also capable of generating more complex discussion forums that include search boxes, tables of contents, and threaded discussions (where visitors can reply to specific postings, rather than simply post their contribution at the end of the list).

The complex interactive discussion forum described above is generated using the Discussion Forum wizard in the FrontPage Explorer.

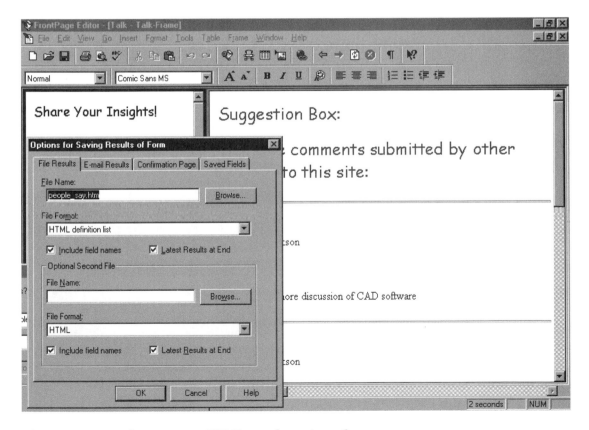

Figure 10.17 *Defining a target HTML page for an input form.*

Study Break

Displaying Form Results in a Frame

Practice what you have learned by creating a frameset with both an input form and a results page.

First, open a FrontPage Web and create a new frames page with a two-frame layout.

Next, create a results page with a title on top, something along the lines of "Here is some feedback from visitors to our site." Save this page. Then, in the remaining frame, create a new page that has an input form. Direct the results of the input form to the first page you created and saved in the frameset, and save input results as HTML Definition List. You can use the input form in Figure 10.16 as a model.

Finally, test your frames page by saving it and viewing it in a browser. Enter some data in the input form and post it. Refresh the frames page, and view the posted data in one frame and the input form in the other.

MCSD 10.4 Managing Form Data Without FrontPage Extensions

While managing form data without FrontPage server extensions is not a specific topic area of the MCP/MCSD exam, issues related to non-Front-Page servers are sprinkled through the exam under the general topic of defining technical architecture, and they intersect with form data management questions.

One of the main selling points of FrontPage 98 is its ability to manage input form data without the need for server-side scripts. In an ideal world, an organization that elects to develop a Web site using FrontPage will install FrontPage server extension files, or contract with a Web site provider who has FrontPage server extensions installed.

Sometimes, that will not be the case. Instead, an organization might elect to develop a Web site using FrontPage, but *not* install FrontPage server extensions and instead rely on other types of server-side scripts to process form input. In that case, Microsoft wants you, as a Microsoft Certified Professional, to be able to plug a FrontPage Web site into a server that handles form input with server-side CGI, NSAPI or ISAPI scripts.

Isn't that kind of like pounding a round peg into a square hole? Yes, it is. And typically, organizations who elect to do their development in Front-Page will take advantage of the easy-to-use and powerful form data management features that come with FrontPage server extensions. But some won't, and someone has to be there to manage that situation. That someone is you, the FrontPage guru.

Just because you are a FrontPage guru, however, doesn't mean that you are a guru at writing the complex, server-side code needed to manage form data without FrontPage extensions. What you should be prepared for is to identify those situations where such connections are appropriate, and make the connection in FrontPage (not at a server) so that input data can be processed through server-side scripts.

Form Handling Options

FrontPage offers the option of sending form input to a server to be processed with ISAPI, NSAPI or CGI scripts, or by ASP code. In Chapter 2, "Analyzing Web Requirements," we examined the role of ASP (Active Server Pages) code. Here, we'll look briefly at who uses ISAPI, NSAPI and CGI scripts to process input data, and how to connect FrontPage input forms to these servers.

CGI (Common Gateway Interface) scripts are the most frequently used code for managing form input in non-FrontPage servers.

ISAPI (Internet Server Application Programming Interface) and Netscape's NSAPI (Netscape Server Application Programming Interface) are competing programming standards that can be used on Web servers. ISAPI and NSAPI scripts function similarly to CGI applications. CGI scripts can be written for many server platforms, including Apache, Unix, Windows NT, Apple and other platforms. And, CGI scripts can be written in many programming languages, including C and Perl. ISAPI scripts can be run only on Microsoft platforms. FrontPage extensions are, in fact, ISAPI programs.

Connecting Form Handling to Server Scripts

If you are going to use a CGI, ISAPI, NSPAI or ASP server-side script to process form input, you can define that connection in the Form Properties dialog box. Open that dialog box by right-clicking in an input form and selecting Form Properties from the context menu.

In the Form Properties dialog box, select the Send to Other options button, and then click on Options to define the form handling script. The Options for Custom Form Handler dialog box appears, as shown in Figure 10.18.

The Options for Form Handler dialog box asks you to provide an Action, a Method, and an Encoding type. The short answer to what to enter in these three boxes is that this information is provided by the server administrator, depending on the application used to process form data. That appli-

Figure 10.18 *Defining a form handler for a non-FrontPage server.*

cation will have its own unique, direct URL, and you will need that URL in order to define your form processing connection.

- In the *Action* box, you enter the URL of the form handler script. This URL will be supplied to you by the server administrator. The URL will look something like http://www.myserver.com/cgi-bin/myscript.cgi.

- In the *Method* box, you select either the POST or GET method for sending data to the server. The GET method appends form data to the URL, and is clumsier and less frequently used than the POST method. The POST method handles data transfer in a way that is more efficient, faster, and less visible to clients. Most of the time, you will use the POST method, but this will be determined by the server administrator.

- You can leave the *Encoding Type* box blank, unless your server administrator requires a non-standard encoding method.

The Options for Custom Form Handler also has a Style button. Theoretically, this button allows you to define text attributes like spacing, alignment, and fonts that are not available in HTML tabs. Successfully assigning these inline styles to form data, however, is dependent on whether or not the server script will recognize these attributes, as well as whether a browser will recognize them.

For more information on the world of form-processing scripts, you can check out the following resources:

- *Web Forms and CGIs: Making Web Pages Interactive* by Chris Savage and Linda Lee is a discussion paper available at http://www.nlc-bnc.ca/pubs/netnotes/notes19.htm. While a bit dated, this paper provides a clear overview of how CGI scripts function in relation to input forms.

- *Using Netscape Communicator 4* by Mark R. Brown has a useful discussion of CGI scripting in Chapter 26.

- If you are operating in an environment that includes Macintosh servers, Stewart Buskirk's *Web Server Construction Kit for Macintosh* walks you through the process of integrating with CGI scripts in detail in Chapter 7, and provides a very coherent overview of CGI scripts in general.

■ Summary

FrontPage Webs that are published to servers with FrontPage extension files can collect data and send it to a server without the need for additional server-side scripting. This ability to manage data input without server-side scripts is one of the most powerful features of FrontPage. Input data can be directed to any combination of an e-mail address, a text file, or an HTML page.

Where a FrontPage Web is published to a server without FrontPage extensions, you can use FrontPage's form handling options to direct input data to CGI scripts at the server.

▲ CHAPTER REVIEW QUESTIONS

Here are some practice questions relating to the material covered in the "Processing User Input" area of Microsoft's *Designing and Implementing Web Sites Using Microsoft FrontPage 98* exam (70-055).

1. *Which of the following is a useful strategy for collecting input data that will not be easily accessible to visitors to a Web site? (Select all correct answers.)*
   - A. Collect input data through e-mail
   - B. Provide a URL link to a Web page displaying form results
   - C. Attach validation scripts to the input form
   - D. Save the data to a file in the _Private folder
   - E. Save the data to a text file

2. *Which of the following is a useful strategy for making input data available to visitors? (Select all correct answers.)*
   - A. Collect the input data through e-mail
   - B. Save the data in a _Private folder
   - C. Save the data as a formatted HTML file
   - D. Remember to assign an *.htm or *html file name extension to the target file
   - E. Remember to assign password protection to the file

3. *Every input form in a Web page has its own unique form handling properties.*
   A. True
   B. False

4. *A single page can have no more than one input form.*
   A. True
   B. False

5. *If a server has FrontPage extensions installed, you can always use that server to process form data as e-mail.*
   A. True
   B. False

6. *You can collect form data in which of the following formats? (Select all correct answers.)*
   A. Web pages
   B. Scrolling text boxes
   C. FrontPage extension scripts
   D. Text files
   E. E-mail

7. *FrontPage input forms require which of the following to work without server-side scripting? (Select all correct answers.)*
   A. Internet Explorer 4.0 or higher
   B. FrontPage 98 extension files on the Web server
   C. SSL encryption
   D. Embedded HTML coding
   E. JavaScript coding

8. *FrontPage can manage data with client-side scripts if FrontPage extension files are installed.*
   A. True
   B. False

9. *You can collect the same input data from a single form as both e-mail messages and an HTML bulleted list.*
   A. True
   B. False

10. *You can display input data and an input form side-by-side by using a frameset.*

    A. True

    B. False

11. *A good way to collect input data for a guest book-type Web page is an HTML Definition list.*

    A. True

    B. False

12. *If you are using server-side CGI scripts to manage input data on a server without FrontPage extensions, which of the following do you need? (Select all correct answers.)*

    A. The URL of the form handling script at the server

    B. An encoding type, if the server using a non-standard encoding method

    C. An ISAPI script installed on the Web server

    D. A CGI script installed on the Web server

    E. An e-mail address for the CGI script

13. *You can always test form management for input forms collecting data as text files using the Microsoft Personal Web Server with FrontPage Extensions.*

    A. True

    B. False

14. *You can always test form management for input forms collecting data as e-mail using the Microsoft Personal Web Server with FrontPage Extensions.*

    A. True

    B. False

15. *Which of the following are good ways to collect input data destined for an Excel spreadsheet? (Select all correct answers.)*

    A. HTML Definition List

    B. HTML Bulleted List

    C. Text using a comma as a separator

    D. Text using a tab as a seperator

    E. e-mail

Adding Advanced User Services

In addition to advanced Web objects that are built in to FrontPage, the FrontPage Exam requires an understanding of how to integrate elements from non-FrontPage sources into FrontPage Webs. In Chapter 11, I'll walk though the process of incorporating both ActiveX controls and Java applets, and we'll discuss the complex world of Dynamic HTML and how it operates within FrontPage. In Chapter 12 we'll look at how tables, graphics, and animation can be used as design tools, and in Chapter 13 we'll examine how FrontPage works with styles and how to attach external style sheet files.

Incorporating Java Applets, ActiveX, and DHTML

Java, ActiveX and Dynamic HyperText Markup Language (DHTML) are all technologies for implementing client-side interactivity on a Web page. All three programming approaches allow your visitors to see animation or interact with your Web page without waiting for messages to be transmitted to and from a Web server.

The FrontPage MCSD/MCP exam does not test your skills, or lack of them, as a Java, ActiveX or DHTML developer. What is expected of you is a basic understanding of what these technologies do, and how they plug into FrontPage 98.

At the conclusion of this chapter you will be able to:

- Understand how Java, ActiveX and DHTML fit into Web development.
- Integrate Java applets into a FrontPage Web.
- Include ActiveX components in a FrontPage Web.
- Implement FrontPage 98's built-in DHTML-based components.
- Integrate DHTML applications into a FrontPage Web Site.
- Identify potential compatibility conflicts with Java, ActiveX, and DHTML components in FrontPage Webs.

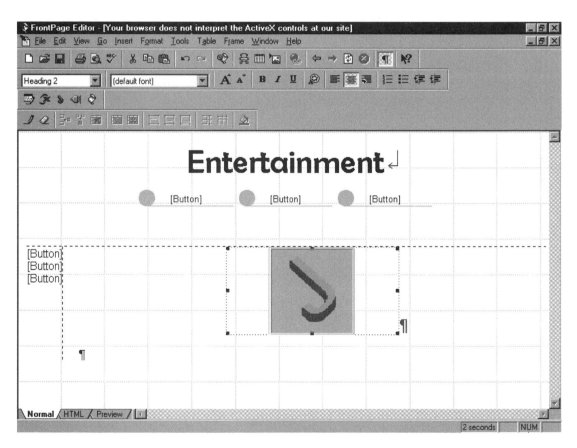

Figure 11.1 *A Java applet embedded in the FrontPage Editor.*

Compatibility Issues

FrontPage 98 makes it easy to plug Java applets, ActiveX components, and DHTML into Web pages. In that sense, FrontPage 98 is fully compatible with all three. ActiveX, being a child of Microsoft, is somewhat more Front-Page friendly than Java. When you embed a Java applet, all you see in the FrontPage Editor Normal tab is the big "J" icon, shown in Figure 11.1.

You can, however, preview Java applets in the Preview tab of the Front-Page Editor. ActiveX components actually display in the FrontPage Editor, although you'll see them more clearly with the Preview tab.

Java, ActiveX, and DHTML present major browser compatibility issues for users, and these need to be taken into account when implementing these technologies. Older versions of browsers do not interpret Java, but IE version 3 and later, and Netscape Navigator version 2 and later, do. One overriding compatibility issue is that ActiveX controls are not interpreted by Netscape Navigator as of version 4.5. As a result, the best you can do is to provide a message to visitors that they are missing out on an ActiveX control, as shown in Figure 11.2

DHTML is a somewhat more nebulous concept, and there are competing versions of it. Many of the DHTML effects created in FrontPage are not recognized by Netscape Navigator.

MCSD 11.1   Embedding Java Applets

As a FrontPage expert, you won't be expected to be a Java programmer, but you should understand the basic way Java applets are created, and how they can be integrated into FrontPage. In Chapter 3, "Defining the Technical Architecture for a FrontPage 98 Web Site," we explored the process of embedding JavaScrips and VBScripts into Web pages. These scripts could simply be copied into the Script dialog box, and embedded in a FrontPage Web page. Java Applets are more complex, and, correspondingly, potentially more powerful. Java Applets often call other files when they are executed, so they are usually saved in Web folders along with the image files and other files required to run them.

Java Applets are not editable in the same way that scripts are. Before Java applets are embedded in Web sites, they are compiled. Compiled Java applets have a *.class file name extension, and since they are compiled they cannot be edited with a text editor like JavaScripts or VBScripts.

If you are going to be working with Java Applets, you may want to display the Advanced toolbar (in the FrontPage Editor, select View, Advanced

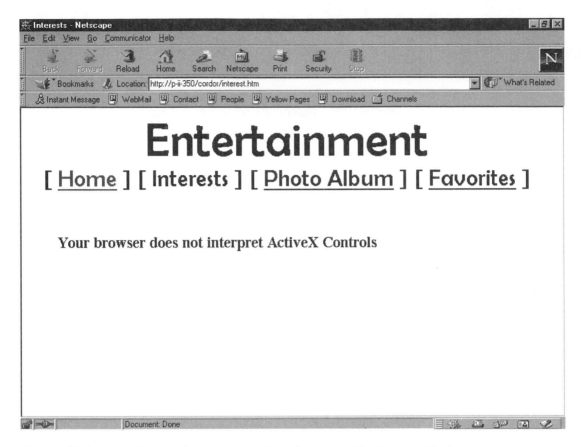

Figure 11.2 *ActiveX controls aren't much fun when viewed in Netscape Navigator.*

Toolbar from the menu bar). The Insert Java Applet button in that toolbar substitutes for selecting Insert, Advanced, Java Applet from the menu bar.

The following steps outline the process of embedding a Java applet into a Web page.

1. Import the folder with your Java applet files into an existing FrontPage Web. To do this, select File, Import in the FrontPage Explorer (with a Web open), and click on the Add Folder button in the Import File to FrontPage Web dialog box. Navigate to the folder that has the files for the Java applet, and double-click on the folder to add it to the import list. Then, click on OK to copy the folder and its contents into your FrontPage Web.

2. With the content files required for your Java applet imported into your FrontPage Web, open a Web page in the FrontPage Editor into which you will embed the Java applet.

3. In the FrontPage Editor, click to set your insertion point where you will insert the Java applet, and select Insert, Advanced, Java Applet. The Java Applet Properties dialog box appears, as shown in Figure 11.3.

4. In the Applet Source box, enter the file name for your applet.

5. In the Applet Base URL box, enter the folder in your Web that holds the applet files. This is necessary only if the applet is not in the Web root directory.

6. In the Message for Browsers without Java Support, enter a message that will display. This can be something like "Your browser does not support Java applets displayed on this page."

7. Applet Parameters are supplied by the Java coder. If the Java applet comes with instructions to add parameters, use the Add button in the dialog box to enter these parameters. When you do, the Set Attribute Value dialog box appears, as shown in Figure 11.4. Enter an attribute Name, and use the Specify value check box to enter a value in the Value field. Then click on OK to close the dialog box.

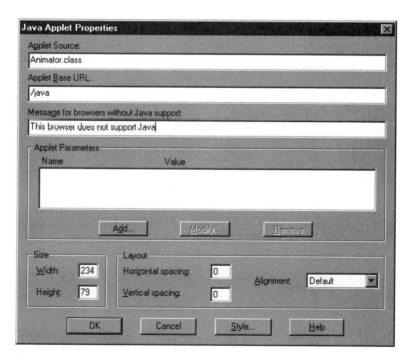

Figure 11.3 *The Java Applet Properties dialog box.*

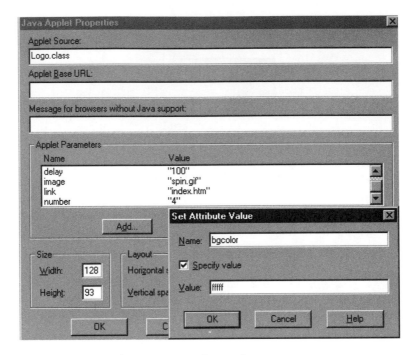

Figure 11.4 *Defining Java Applet attributes.*

8. Click on OK when you have finished defining your applet properties.
9. You can resize the display frame for the Java applet by clicking and dragging on the size handles around the Java icon in the FrontPage Editor.
10. After saving the page in which the applet is embedded, you can preview the applet in the Preview tab of the FrontPage Editor.

Study Break

Embedding a Java Applet

Practice what you have learned by downloading an existing Java applet and its associated files, importing the files into a FrontPage Web, and testing the applet. You can find some simple Java applets and their associated files at http://java.sun.com. Experiment with the Logo sample, or another one of the downloadable Java samples available from the Sun Java Web site.

Download one of the compiled Java applets (like Logo), and its associated image files. Note the parameters for the Logo file listed at the Web site. After you download the files (they will be zipped), unzip them into a folder and import that folder into an open FrontPage Web.

Enjoy this Java Applet9

Figure 11.5 *Defining Applet parameters.*

Use the Java Applet Properties dialog box to define the Java applet, and the parameters that were listed at the Web site for the applet. The parameters for the Logo file are shown in Figure 11.5.

After you configure your applet, you can test it in the Preview tab of the FrontPage Editor. The Logo applet found at the Java Sun site is demonstrated in Figure 11.6.

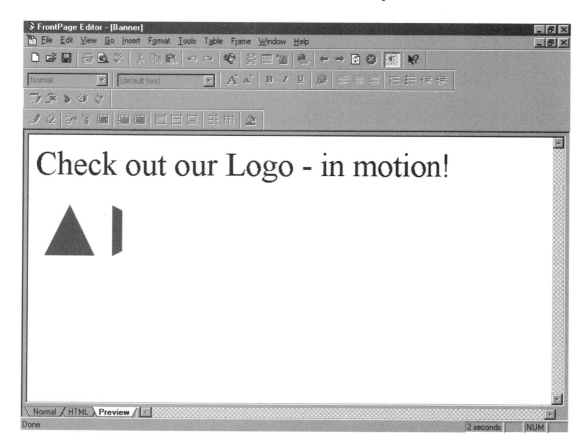

Figure 11.6 *Testing an applet in the Preview tab.*

For a complete overview of integrating Java into FrontPage 98, see *The FrontPage 98 Bible* by David Elderbrock with Paul Bodensiek, Chapter 16.

Embed a few Java applets, and you'll run into situations where they don't work. Of course, the first question to ask is whether or not the applet you were provided really works. Assuming it does, you will want to make sure you have been supplied with all the parameters required to make the applet work, and that you have correctly defined them. If Java applets are not found when you test your page in a browser, check to see that you entered a correct and complete path to the Java applet. Finally, remember that not all browsers interpret Java applets.

Study Break

Java Troubleshooting Tips

Walk through these troubleshooting steps with an embedded Java applet:

First, make sure you have been supplied all the required parameters by the Java programmer, and that you have entered them correctly in the Applet Parameters area of the Java Applet Properties dialog box.

Next, make sure that you have entered a path to the folder with the applet, if necessary, in the Applet Base URL area of the Java Applet Properties dialog box.

Make sure that the browser on which you are testing the applet supports Java.

Finally, make sure that all files called by the applet (for example, image files) are in the same folder as the applet, or that you have included full paths to the files in the parameters list.

MCSD 11.2   Incorporating ActiveX Controls

Like Java, ActiveX is a programming language that can be interpreted by Web browsers. Unlike Java, however, ActiveX controls are interpreted at this time *only* by Internet Explorer version 3 and higher. This makes ActiveX a development platform suited only to environments (such as an intranet) where every visitor is using Internet Explorer.

With that considerable limitation, ActiveX is a powerful tool for developing client-side animation and interactivity in Web sites. In Chapter 12, "Incorporating Tables, Graphics, Animation, and Media," we will explore the role of ActiveX components in presenting media files. There, you'll learn how ActiveX can function like an on-line VCR, providing controls to allow the visitor to activate and have power over how media files are exhibited in his or her browser. Here, we'll look at the programming side of ActiveX, where controls are integrated with configurations that provide animation or interactivity.

Since ActiveX is the development platform promoted by Microsoft, it's no surprise that Microsoft FrontPage provides substantial development tools for ActiveX. As a way of getting some hands-on experience with ActiveX, we'll walk through a quick implementation to display animated text. Ready? Fire up FrontPage, and follow these steps for a quick micro-tutorial on implementing ActiveX in a FrontPage Web page:

1. Open a FrontPage Web, and open a page in the FrontPage Editor.
2. Click to place your insertion point, and select Insert, Advanced, ActiveX Control from the menu.
3. From the Pick a Control drop-down menu, select Label Object, as shown in Figure 11.7.
4. Click on the Properties button in the dialog box to display the Properties window. The Properties window has two parts—the interactive graphical window that displays to the left, and the grid on the right in Figure 11.8.
5. Select the Caption field in the Properties grid, and type "Welcome to Our Web Site" in the Apply line at the top of the Property window.

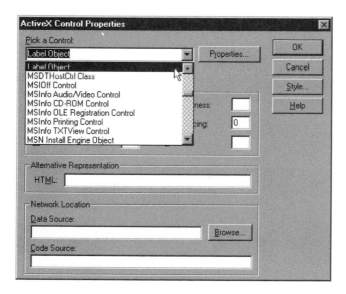

Figure 11.7 *Selecting an ActiveX control.*

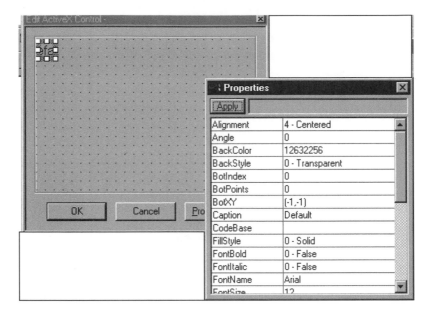

Figure 11.8 *Two different ActiveX Properties windows.*

Then, click on Apply to define the text to be displayed, as shown in Figure 11.9.

6. In the Angle field, enter 15 and click on Apply. This determines an angle for text rotation.

Figure 11.9 *Entering a caption for an ActiveX control.*

7. Click and drag in the Edit ActiveX Control window to resize the control until the text fits, as shown in Figure 11.10.

8. You can experiment with additional properties, like Font Size, Font-Bold and FontItalic.

9. After you experiment with additional properties, click on OK to return to the (first) ActiveX Control Properties window.

Now that you've got a bit of ActiveX programming under your belt, we can take a look at how to configure the way ActiveX components are displayed. This is controlled in the ActiveX Control Properties dialog box:

- The Name box allows you to assign a name to a control. Additional ActiveX programming can incorporate these control names into programs.

- The Layout area allows you to define the alignment, border thickness, horizontal and vertical spacing, width and height of the control.

- The HTML box in the Alternative Representation area allows you to enter text to display for browsers that do not interpret ActiveX.

- The Data Source field in the dialog box allows you to enter a URL for a file that has parameters for the control, if they were provided by the developer.

- The Code Source field allows you to identify a URL for an ActiveX control if that particular control is not supported by Internet Explorer.

Figure 11.10 *Resizing an ActiveX Control window.*

Defining an ActiveX Control

Practice what you have learned by creating an ActiveX control, and formatting its display on a page.

1. First, create an ActiveX Label control that displays the word "Tilt" at a 30-degree angle.

2. Next, add a 2-pixel outline around the control, and center it.

Define an alternate HTML page for browsers that do not recognize ActiveX. If possible, test your page in both IE and Netscape.

MCSD 11.3   Applying Transitions and Other DHTML Effects

Dynamic HTML (DHTML) is generally defined as the process of combining JavaScript or ActiveX with style sheets to create client-side animation and interactivity. Examples of DHTML include outlines that collapse or expand, or objects that fly around on a Web page.

There are serious compatibility problems in implementing DHTML that you should be aware of. They include:

- Netscape Navigator and MSIE have different object models for how "layers" are positioned and manipulated, so you have to code for both NS Navigator and MSIE.

- You have to trap for MSIE 4.0+ and NS 4.0+ (if you are doing cross-browser code) and serve out one set of DHTML pages for those browsers and another set of pages for non-DHTML browsers. This means that most designers only use DHTML for menus, entry or "flash" pages—or for special features (such as a drag and drop objects).

- Although there are a number of excellent Websites (and books) providing code and examples, they tend to use different coding techniques, which can be very confusing. A quick survey of about 13 DHTML books at a local megastore revealed some brilliant code, but only a seasoned JavaScript programmer would know how to use much of it. One problem is that the Netscape Object model (first out of the blocks) is a lot cruder than the Microsoft model (which is pretty similar to the model they use for Visual Basic and Access programming). This means that to really know what you're doing you have to know both object models. Not a fun process—especially since the Microsoft model makes so much more sense and since Netscape is committed to using it in future browsers.

- FrontPage 98 has its own built-in support for some of this DHTML coding, although some of it, such as the animation effects, works only in MSIE.

In short, folks in a dedicated intranet situation can go wild using DHTML. But out there in the wild world of the Internet, DHTML elements are likely to provoke browser compatibility problems.

Study Break

DHTML FAQs

Q: Why do some DHTML objects work in IE and not Netscape?

A: Microsoft's version of DHTML uses a positioning model not supported by Netscape Navigator.

Q: What's the relationship between presenting media using plug-ins or ActiveX components, and using DHTML?

A: Most developers consider DHTML a replacement for plug-ins that show static text and images, or simple animations. The assumption is that if you are just transmitting text code, the download and display times are much faster without plug-ins. However, DHTML doesn't include providing audio and video; it is strictly in-page interactivity.

Q: Are FrontPage-generated transitions like collapsible outlines and animated objects recognized by Netscape Navigator 4.5?

A: Nope.

Generating Animated Text and Images

One property of DHTML is the ability to attach animation to selected text or images. You can easily generate animated text in the FrontPage Editor. Simply select Text, and choose Format, Animation, and select an animation effect from the fly-out menu, as shown in Figure 11.11.

Testing animation effects in the Preview tab of the FrontPage Editor requires that you have IE 4.0 or higher installed on your system. Even with IE 4 or higher installed, I've encountered difficulties (bugs) in testing DHTML in the Preview tab, and often have to resort to previewing a page in my browser to test the effects. In Figure 11.12, I'm testing the Drop In By Word anima-

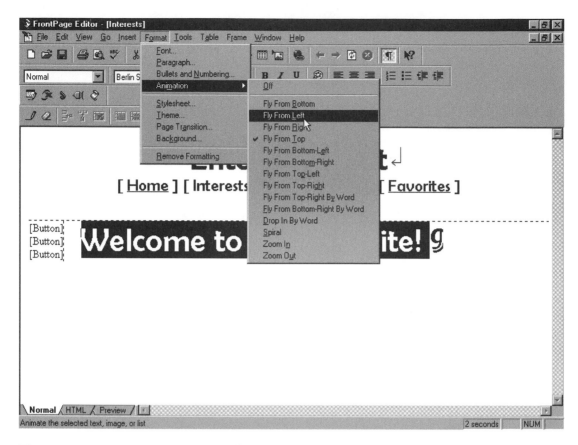

Figure 11.11 *Assigning animation effects to text.*

tion effect in IE 5. Of course, the effect is more fun in a browser than in a static figure, but you can see the word "our" moving into place in the figure.

Animation effects can be applied to images the same way. First, select the image, then choose Format, Animation and experiment with the animation options.

I didn't expect animated text and images to function in Netscape Navigator, but when I tested a variety of animation effects in Netscape 4.5, I found that they not only didn't work, but they created some unpleasant effects, like widening the browser window to several screen widths (requiring lots of horizontal scrolling to see the whole page). The bad results of applying the Spiral animation effect to an image and viewing the page in Navigator are displayed in Figure 11.13.

Figure 11.12 *The word "our" is moving into place in an animation.*

Formatting Page Transitions

FrontPage 98 also uses DHTML to generate a variety of page transitions. Page transitions are applied to an entire page. You choose one by selecting Format, Page Transition from the menu bar with a page open in the FrontPage Editor.

The Page Transitions dialog box is shown in Figure 11.14. Transitions can take effect when a visitor enters or exits a page. The Site Enter and Site Exit options apply the transition only when a page is visited as the first page in a site. In other words, these options prevent the transition from displaying if a visitor comes to the page from another page within your Web site.

The Page Transitions dialog box also includes a list of transition effects. The duration of these effects is (roughly) defined by the number of

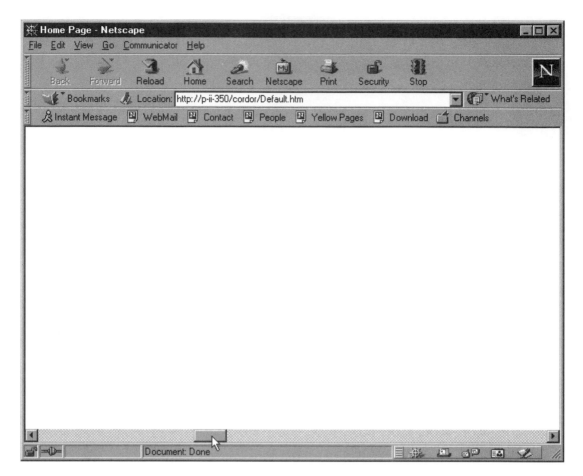

Figure 11.13 *What happened to my page? Applying an animation effect to a graphic caused Netscape Navigator 4.5 to multiply the width of my page by about ten, requiring lots of horizontal scrolling to see the page.*

seconds you enter in the Durations box. Of course duration is affected by download time.

Page transitions are not recognized by Netscape Navigator 4.5, or earlier versions.

Creating Collapsible Outlines

Collapsible outlines are a DHTML feature that allow visitors with Internet Explorer 4 or higher to collapse or expand outlines. Figure 11.15 shows an outline in the process of being expanded in Internet Explorer.

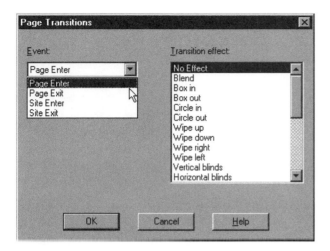

Figure 11.14 *Page transition options.*

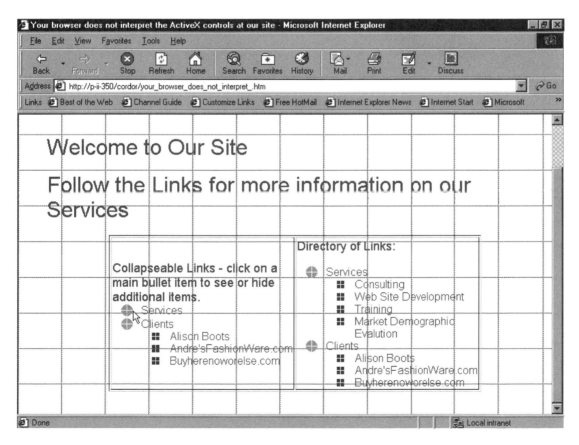

Figure 11.15 *A collapsible outline viewed in Internet Explorer 5.*

To create a collapsible outline, follow these steps:

1. In the FrontPage Editor, begin a numbered list or a bullet list by clicking on the Numbered List or Bulleted List buttons in the Formatting toolbar.
2. Enter (type) first level text, and press Enter. A new numbered or bulleted line is begun.
3. Click on the Increase Indent button in the Formatting toolbar twice to make the current item a sublevel. These sublevels will be displayed or hidden when the list is viewed in IE.
4. Continue to create your list, clicking the Decrease Indent button in the Formatting toolbar twice to return to first level headings.
5. You can use the same procedure we just explored to created additional levels of indenting. After you complete your list, select the first item in your list and right-click. From the context menu, select List Properties. The List Properties dialog box appears.
6. Select the Enable Collapsible Outlines check box in the List Properties dialog box, as shown in Figure 11.16. Click on OK in the dialog box.

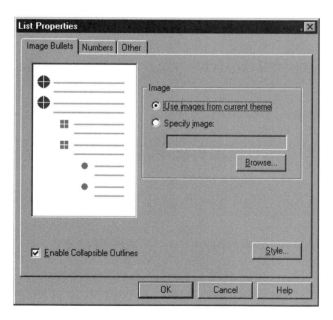

Figure 11.16 *Enabling Collapsible Outlines.*

Attaching DHTML Effects to Text and a Graphic, and Testing
the Effect in Browsers

Practice what you have learned by assigning DHTML effects to text, and to a page, and by creating
a collapsible outline.

First, open a FrontPage Web and then open a page in the FrontPage Editor. Select some text on
the page, and choose Format, Animation—and then choose an effect from the fly-out menu.

Next, assign a page transition to your page.

Finally, create an outline with sublevels. Make the outline collapsible.

Test your DHTML loaded page in IE and Netscape Navigator and note the contrasting results.

■ Summary

Java, ActiveX, and Dynamic HyperText Markup Language (DHTML) allow
you to include client-side animation or interactivity on Web pages. Plugging
in Java applets, ActiveX components and DHTML is the easy part in Front-
Page 98. Assuming you've been provided with a Java applet, FrontPage
provides a dialog box that allows you to enter all the parameters that will
make the applet work. ActiveX is even easier to implement, as FrontPage
provides an interactive Property dialog that lets you define ActiveX components, or plug in someone else's

FrontPage generates its own DHTML elements—animated text and
graphics, page transitions, and collapsible outlines.

The hard part of using Java, ActiveX, and DHTML is that they all cre-
ate browser compatibility problems. Older browsers do not interpret Java.
ActiveX controls are not interpreted by Netscape Navigator as of version 4.5.
And DHTML effects generated by FrontPage are not recognized by
Netscape.

▲ CHAPTER REVIEW QUESTIONS

Here are some practice questions relating to the material covered in the "Incorporating Java Applets, ActiveX and DHTML" area of Microsoft's *Designing and Implementing Web Sites Using Microsoft FrontPage 98* exam (70-055).

1. *Which of the following elements of a FrontPage Web site might present compatibility problems when the site is viewed in Netscape Navigator 4 or higher? (Select all correct answers.)*
   - **A.** Java applets
   - **B.** JavaScripts
   - **C.** Dyanmic HTML
   - **D.** ActiveX
   - **E.** Interlaced GIFs

2. *Which of the following are true of Java applets? (Select all correct answers.)*
   - **A.** They are represented by a "J" icon in the FrontPage Editor
   - **B.** They present compatibility issues in IE 4 and higher
   - **C.** They may require parameters from a developer
   - **D.** They require FrontPage Server Extensions
   - **E.** They can be used to provide client-side animation

3. *DHTML presents major compatibility problems because Netscape Navigator and Internet Explorer use different positioning models.*
   - **A.** True
   - **B.** False

4. *Collapsible outlines cannot be interpreted by Netscape Navigator 4.*
   - **A.** True
   - **B.** False

5. *Java *.class files can be edited in the Java Properties dialog box.*
   - **A.** True
   - **B.** False

6. *Which of the following can be generated directly in the FrontPage Editor? (Select all correct answers.)*
   - **A.** Java applets
   - **B.** Java *.class files
   - **C.** JavaScript based DHTML
   - **D.** DHTML page transitions
   - **E.** ActiveX controls

7. *FrontPage generates Page Transitions as (Select all correct answers):*
   A. Server-side scripts
   B. Client-side JavaScript
   C. Client-side Java
   D. Server-side VBScript
   E. Objects that are interpreted only by MSIE and not Netscape Navigator

8. *Java applets present less browser compatibility problems than ActiveX controls.*
   A. True
   B. False

9. *FrontPage will generate DHTML for collapsible outlines.*
   A. True
   B. False

10. *Java applets can be tested in the Preview tab of the FrontPage Editor.*
    A. True
    B. False

11. *If a Java applet is not working when you test it in IE4, there is a good chance that the problem is browser incompatibility.*
    A. True
    B. False

12. *Developers who attach animation to images should be warned of which of the following problems? (Select all correct answers.)*
    A. Animation can be applied only to text, not images
    B. FrontPage Animation effects are not interpreted by IE version 3
    C. Animation can be assigned only to pages, not images
    D. DHTML Animation requires a Java-friendly browser
    E. FrontPage Animation effects are not interpreted by Netscape Navigator version 3

13. *If an ActiveX component does not work when you test it in Netscape Navigator 4, there is a good chance that the problem is browser incompatibility.*
    A. True
    B. False

14. *Which of the following will help trouble-shoot Java applet errors? (Select all correct answers.)*

    A. Check for missing parameters

    B. Check for browser compatibility

    C. Check to make sure you have entered a complete path for the applet folder

    D. Check to make sure you have entered a complete path for the alternate display folder

    E. Check to make sure that all images are in the same folder as the *.class file

15. *Which events can trigger FrontPage-generated Page transitions? (Select all correct answers.)*

    A. When a page is refreshed

    B. When a page is reloaded

    C. When a page is exited

    D. When a page is scrolled

    E. When a page is saved

Incorporating Tables, Graphics, Animation, and Media

Tables, graphics, and media can all be used as elements in presenting Web content in FrontPage Web sites. As a FrontPage expert, you won't be expected to master the aesthetics of graphics or the art of creating sound and video content. But you will be expected to advise and orchestrate the process of integrating graphic content and media into a Web site.

In this chapter we'll cover key elements of graphical page layout and design including tables, embedding graphic images, and presenting animated images, sound, and video. At the conclusion of this chapter you will be able to:

- Use tables as a design tool for column layout and object placement.
- Embed graphic images in Web pages.
- Manage graphic image file issues like file type, transparency, interlacing and location.
- Create image maps from images.
- Assign text labels to images.
- Format and edit images in FrontPage.
- Assign images as page backgrounds.
- Create animated graphic images.
- Deliver sound and video files in FrontPage Web pages.

MCSD 12.1   Including Tables in FrontPage Web Pages

Tables have two functions in Web page design. They are used to present columns and rows of data, and they are used as a page design tool.

When tables are used to display columns and rows of data, they function much like tables in word processor programs or spreadsheets. However, unlike tables in Excel (or even Word), there are no calculations tools available for tables in FrontPage 98. When calculation is required in a table, the best solution is to do the math in Excel (or another spreadsheet), and copy the table into FrontPage. In this chapter, we'll briefly explore using tables to present columns and rows of data.

The most powerful use of tables is as a page design tool. While HTML 4 does allow for the placement of floating objects on a Web page, these tools are not directly accessible through FrontPage, and are in the "growing pains" stage. In short, tables remain the tool of choice for placing objects on a page.

Tables can be used to design complex page layouts by using cells as a substitute for the role frames play in a desktop publishing program. By embedding tables within table cells, you create a tremendous amount of design potential. For example, you can create columns for a newspaper-style display by using a table to create columns. Figure 12.1 shows a Web page in the FrontPage Editor, revealing the table underlying the page design. Page design with tables keeps professional Web designers working long into the night, and is a challenging art.

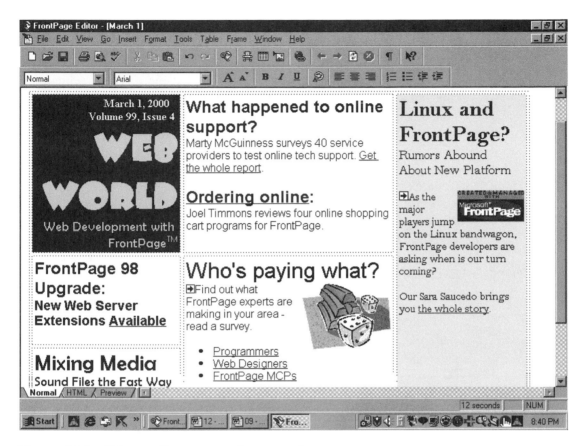

Figure 12.1 *Using a table to create column page layout.*

Most modern browsers interpret tables, but not all. If you expect visitors using older versions of Web browsers, you should avoid table designs that require the visitor's browser to interpret all table attributes. Neither version 1 of AOL's browser, nor Internet Explorer version 1 display tables.

Every FrontPage expert need not be a page design artiste, but you should be prepared to troubleshoot the often confusing formatting issues that arise when tables are used as layout tools.

Note What about enhanced HTML for placing objects? Each month brings a new innovation in some form of enhanced HTML that promises complete control over object placement on Web pages. However, these cutting edge HTML standards are by definition not going to be recognized by most browsers. It's still the case that for the vast majority of Web design, tables are the main tool for placing objects on a Web page.

Using Tables to Present Data

You can design and enter data in tables right in FrontPage. However, if your development environment includes people who use Microsoft Office, you will want to make contributors to your Web site aware that they can simply copy and paste spreadsheet cells from Excel or another spreadsheet into FrontPage. Figure 12.2 shows cells simply being dragged from an Excel window into the FrontPage Editor. Word tables can be copied and pasted into FrontPage as well.

If your development environment includes people using spreadsheet programs like Microsoft Excel, those files can be inserted directly into a Web page using the Insert, File menu command.

Be aware that when Excel files are inserted into a FrontPage Web page, they do not retain all formatting attributes. They do retain some formatting—boldface will be consistent between the original Excel file and the HTML version of the table in FrontPage. Other formatting that translates well includes font color, italics and font type.

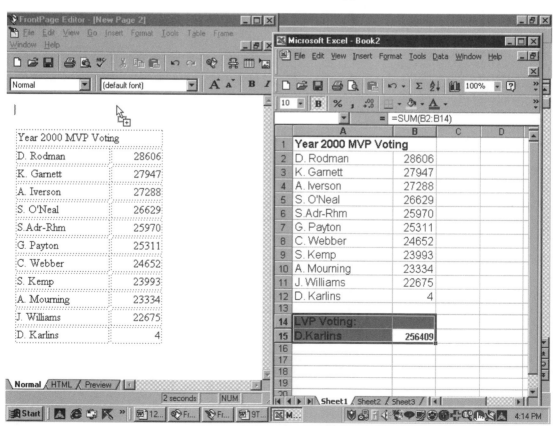

Figure 12.2 *You can copy cells from spreadsheet programs right into FrontPage as tables.*

How does FrontPage handle Excel worksheets that have data on more than one tab? The data on each tab gets consolidated into a single Web page.

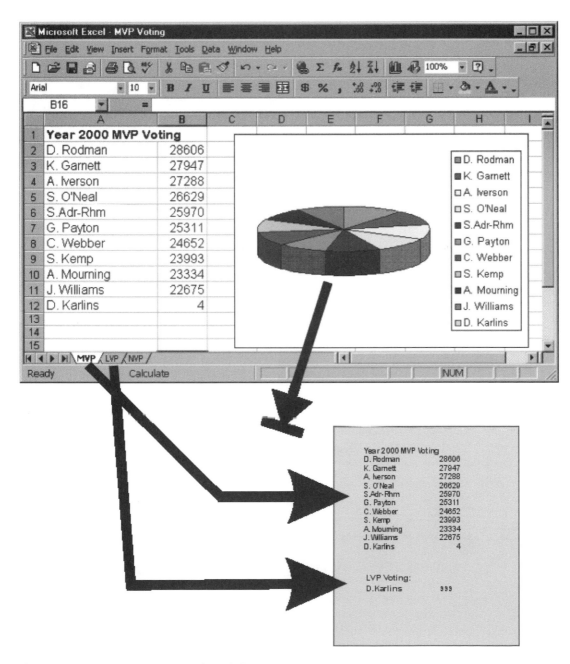

Figure 12.3   *Importing an Excel worksheet.*

1. Figure 12.3 illustrates what happens when you insert an Excel worksheet into a FrontPage Web page: Each tab in the worksheet is added to the same page in the Web page.
2. Charts do not import.

Tables as Design Tools

Tables play a major role in Web page design. Without using tables, HTML code provides little control over horizontal and vertical spacing. You cannot fine-tune line spacing or create vertical columns of text or images.

When you turn off border display, tables act as invisible frames holding objects, including blocks of text and graphics. They can even store media players. Individual cells can be formatted to produce an effect similar to frames in a printed-page design program.

Tip

If you are a Web page designer, or work with one, you have some introduction to the role of tables as a design tool. For more discussion of table layout techniques, see the following resources: *Designing Web Graphics* by Linda Weinman (New Riders), Chapter 13; *Teach Yourself FrontPage 98 in a Week* by David Karlins (Sams), Chapter 5; *FrontPage 98 for Dummies* by Asha Dornfest (IDG), Chapter 9.

Creating Tables

You can define tables two ways—digitally or graphically. If you or your page designer are more inclined towards a graphical approach, the Tables toolbar allows you to literally draw a table on your Web page. Or, you can define initial table settings digitally with the Insert Table dialog box. Figure 12.4 shows the Insert Table dialog box used to define a table.

As an alternative to defining a table by entering rows and columns in a dialog box, you can simply draw the table on the page. The Draw Table drawing tool allows you to draw a table and table cells right on your Web page. Figure 12.5 shows a table being drawn with the Draw Table tool. We'll explore both techniques here.

DEFINING TABLES WITH THE INSERT TABLE DIALOG BOX

When you select Table, Insert Table or click the Insert Table button in the FrontPage Editor Standard toolbar, the Insert Table dialog box appears. You need to click to place your insertion point in the FrontPage Editor *before* you insert a table using the dialog box. The dialog box allows you to define the initial settings for the table:

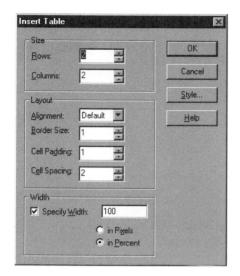

Figure 12.4 *Defining columns and rows using the Insert Table dialog box.*

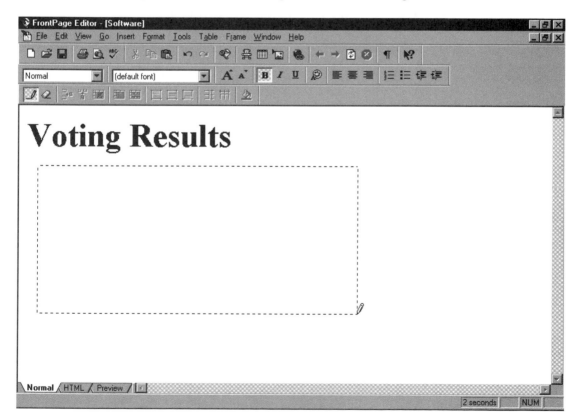

Figure 12.5 *Designing a table with the Draw Table tool.*

The Rows and Columns spin boxes define the number of rows or columns in the table.

The Alignment drop-down menu allows you to position your table within a Web page. Older Web browsers interpret instructions to align a table on the left or right side of a page. In addition, Netscape Navigator 4.5 and IE 5 will support centered tables.

The Border Size box defines the width of the border *around a table* in pixels. Cell borders are formatted separately, and will be explored a bit later in this chapter. If you define a width of zero, there will be no built-in spacing between the table and surrounding text and other elements.

The Cell Padding box defines the space between the contents of each cell in the table, and the border of the table. Cell padding, like border size, is defined in pixels.

Cell Spacing differs from cell padding in that spacing is the space between cells, rather than between cell contents and the border of the cell.

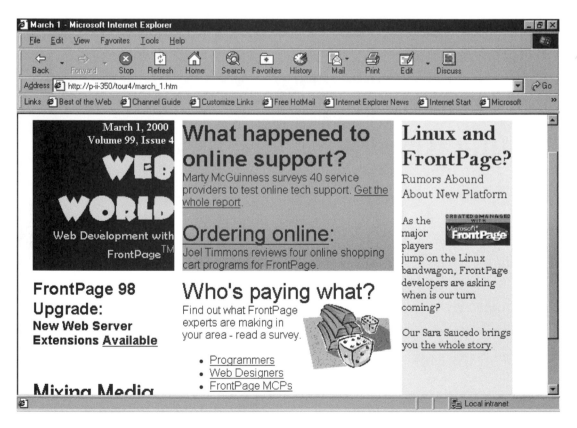

Figure 12.6 *Lots of spacing between cells, but no padding.*

Sometimes it doesn't matter whether space between cells is defined via cell padding or cell spacing. If the cell contents are text, and no border or cell background is applied, the effects of spacing and padding are similar. Figure 12.6 shows a table with 12-pixel spacing as viewed in a Web browser.

In the page layout displayed in Figure 12.6, the wide spacing creates odd gridlines between cells, and the lack of cell padding causes cell contents to awkwardly bump against the edge of the cell.

Figure 12.7 shows the same table displayed in Figure 12.6, but this time with 12-point *padding* within cells, and *no spacing* between cells. In this case, the large padding and zero spacing creates a more appropriate display in the browsers.

You can specify the width of a table either in pixels or percentages. So-phisticated Web designers spend hours debating the relative merits of defining table size each way. If you define a table in percent, you can be certain that the table will fill that percentage of a browser window, regardless of the

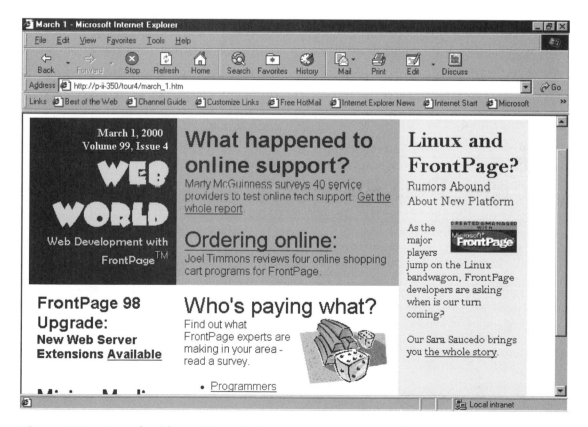

Figure 12.7 *Lots of padding within cells, but no spacing between cells.*

monitor resolution setting or browser window size. If you define table width at 50%, that table will fill half the visitor's browser window.

If you define table width in pixels, you can control the absolute size of the table, regardless of the size of a visitor's browser window. A table defined at 660 pixels wide might require a visitor with a VGA monitor to use the horizontal scrollbar to view the entire table.

DRAWING TABLES

The Draw Table tool is particularly useful when designing tables for page layout. Select Table, Draw Table, and use the pencil-like drawing tool to draw an outline of your table.

You can continue to use the Draw Table tool to divide your table into cells, as shown in Figure 12.8.

You can also draw tables using the Insert Table tool, as shown in Figure 12.9. All the Insert Table tool allows you to do is define the number of rows

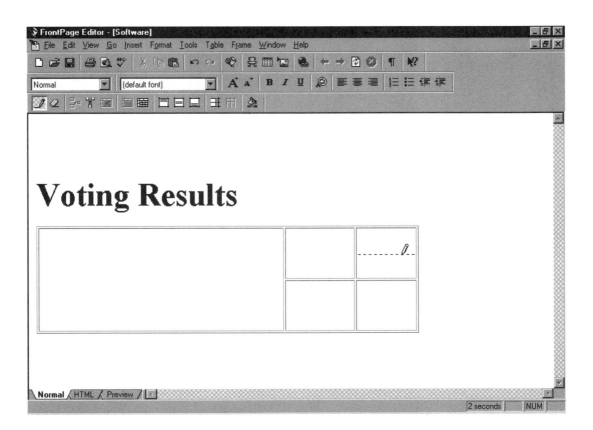

Figure 12.8 *Drawing cells.*

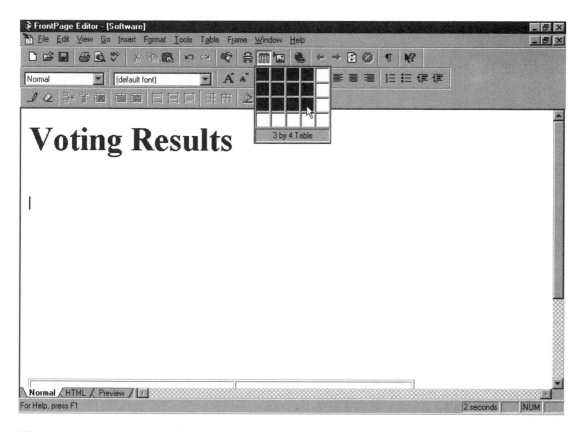

Figure 12.9   *Inserting a table with four columns and three rows.*

and columns. But sometimes that's all you need. If you are planning to insert text or graphics in a table, you can simply let FrontPage resize your table for you.

CONVERTING TEXT TO TABLES

The final option for creating tables is to convert existing text to tables. FrontPage can convert blocks of text to a table using commas, tabs, or other characters as field separators, which get translated into column dividers when the text is converted to a table.

To convert text to a table:

1. Enter (or copy or import) text, with commas, tabs, or another character as a divider between data fields. This character will be used to divide the data into columns when it is converted into a table.

2. Click and drag to select all the text.
3. Select Table, Convert Text to Table. The Convert Text to Table dialog box appears, as shown in Figure 12.10.
4. Select an option in the Separate Text At area, and OK the dialog box to transform the text into a table.

As a FrontPage MCP, be prepared for a frantic call from a page designer who has placed a table on the top of a page, and cannot insert text or objects above that table. If you get stuck with a table at the top of your Web site, you can add some content above the table by clicking the HTML tab and placing at least one character (any letter will do) above the code that starts **<table**. You can always return to the page in Normal view, and change the inserted character into some other object.

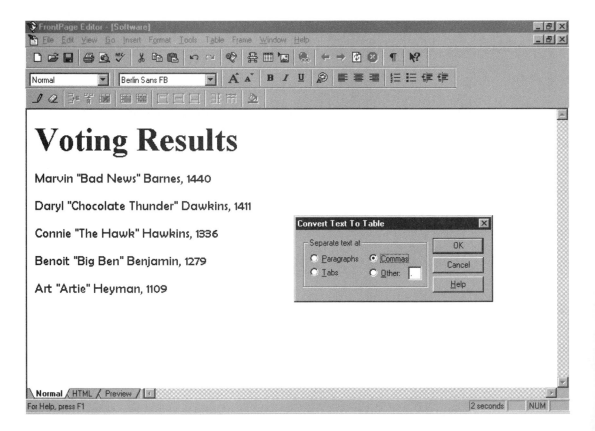

Figure 12.10 *Converting text to a table.*

Defining Tables

Practice what you have learned about creating tables.

First, with a Web page open, insert a 3-column by 4-row table at the top of the page. Add a line of text above the newly inserted table.

Next, draw a table inside one of the cells in your new table.

Finally, enter three rows of text with names and numbers (like "Dave, 100"). Convert that text to a table.

Setting Table Properties

You can define table properties for any existing table in the Table Properties dialog box. Simply right-click in a table, and select Table Properties from the context menu to open the dialog box, shown in Figure 12.11. Table properties include Alignment, Background colors, Borders and Size. We explored these properties in the previous section on defining tables.

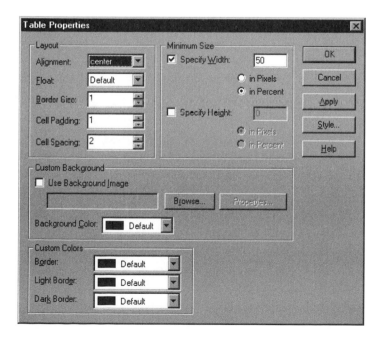

Figure 12.11   *Defining table properties.*

Float allows you to choose whether you want text to flow to the right of the table or to the left of the table. This feature applies if the table is less than the full width of the page. The default setting will keep text from flowing around a table

The Use Background Image checkbox allows you to assign any graphic image to a table. You can also assign background images to specific cells. Table color affects an entire table. Assigning background colors to tables is an effective design tool, but also one of the most dangerous. Since cell backgrounds are not interpreted by all browsers, you should avoid using dark cell backgrounds with light colored text. If a browser does not recognize the background color, the text will be unreadable.

The drop-down lists in the Custom Color area of the Table Properties dialog box allow you to define borders and border shadows. Of course, you can apply border shadows only if you have defined a border width of one pixel or greater.

You can define table height by clicking the Specify Height checkbox in the Table Properties dialog box. Table height is normally generated by the number of rows in your table and the size of your text fonts and images and is not constrained by any value you assign here.

Assigning Table Captions

Caption text is grouped with a table. Define caption text by clicking in a table and choosing Table, Insert Caption from the menu bar. Then type a caption. You can format caption text size and font style just as you do any other text.

Caption text is attached to a table. When you move a table or change the float properties, the caption text "sticks to" the table, and adopts the properties assigned to the table. So, for example, if a table needs a title (like "Table 1: 1999 Sales), you can attach that text to the table as a caption.

Caption text is included in the HTML definition of a table, and uses the `<caption ... </caption>` HTML tags, as shown in Figure 12.12.

Managing Rows and Columns

You can change column width simply by clicking and dragging on the dividing line between columns. Figure 12.13 shows column size being manipulated.

FrontPage 98 also has a feature to equalize column width. To equalize the width of table columns, first select the columns in your table that you want made even, then choose Table, Distribute Columns Evenly from the menu bar. This feature works only if you have not manually assigned the cell width.

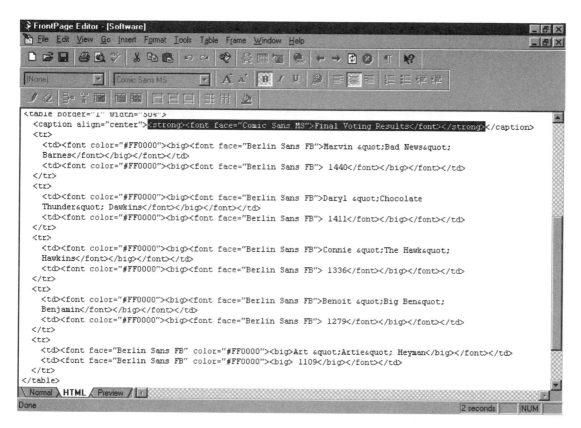

Figure 12.12 *HTML code for caption text.*

You can also assign the same height to selected rows. If you have more than one row in a table and the rows are uneven, first select multiple rows, then select Table, Distribute Rows Evenly from the menu bar.

You can add cells to a table simply by adding new table content. To do that, select the last cell in the table and press the Tab key on your keyboard. You can also define new rows and columns using the menu bar.

To add a new row or column to a table:

1. Select a cell contiguous to where the new row or column should go.
2. Select Table, Insert Rows or Columns from the menu bar.
3. Select the Columns or Rows radio button.

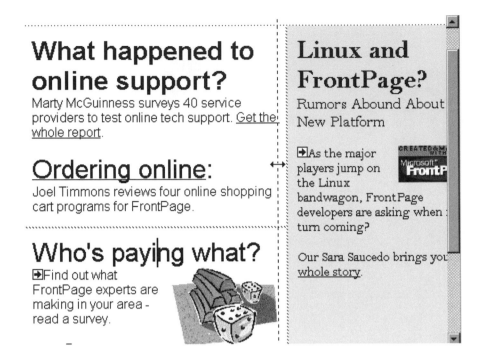

Figure 12.13 *Changing column width.*

4. Assign a number of rows or columns in the Number of spin box, and choose the Right of Selection, Left of Selection, Above Selection, or Below Selection radio buttons to define where the new columns or rows will go. Then OK the dialog box. Figure 12.14 shows two columns being inserted to the right of the selected cell.

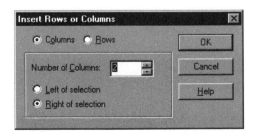

Figure 12.14 *Inserting columns.*

DEFINING CELL PROPERTIES

Cell-specific formatting attributes that can be used in page design include horizontal and vertical alignment, text wrap attributes, size, background image, background color and border colors.

Cell properties are defined in the Cell Properties dialog box. To access that dialog box, right-click in a cell and choose Cell Properties from the context menu. The Cell Properties dialog box is shown in Figure 12.15.

The Horizontal Alignment drop-down list allows you to define the alignment of the contents of a cell to the left, right, or center of the cell. You should be aware that the results of these settings are somewhat unpredictable and unreliable. They tend to conflict with the alignment tools in the FrontPage Editor Format toolbar.

The default Horizontal Alignment option aligns the cell contents based on the preceding cell. The horizontal alignment options generally duplicate paragraph alignment attributes that can be assigned using the Right, Center, and Left align tools in the Format toolbar. In general, those paragraph alignment tools are more reliable than defining horizontal alignment in the Cell Properties dialog box.

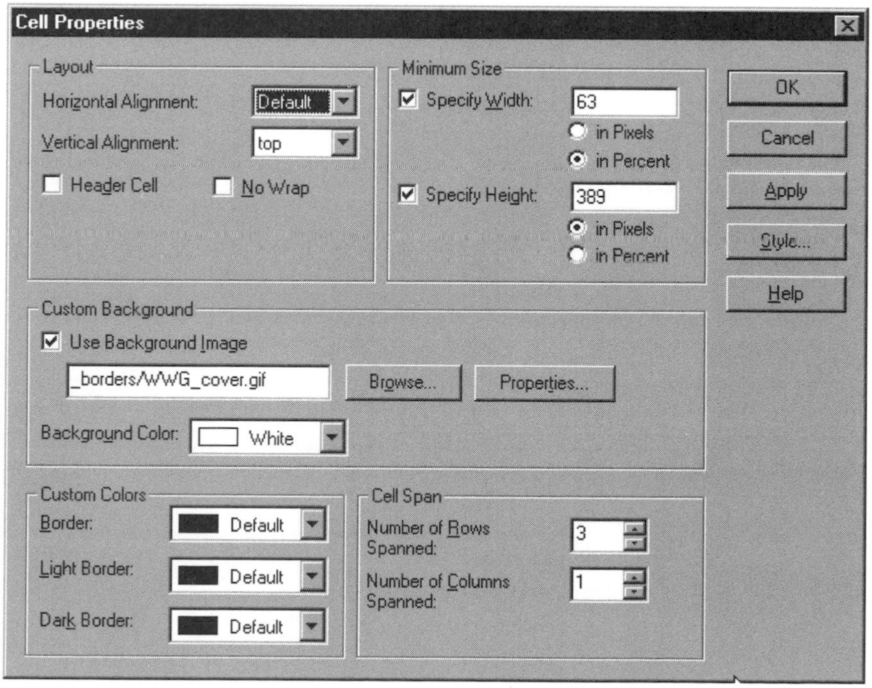

Figure 12.15 *Defining cell properties.*

Vertical alignment options are:

- Default—aligns vertically to the position of the cell when it was created.
- Top—aligns the cell contents even with the top of the cell.
- Baseline—aligns cell contents along the bottom of any text with the bottom of the largest text in a cell. This is used when you have more than one font size in a single cell.
- Bottom—This aligns cell contents with the bottom of the cell.

Within the Cell Properties dialog box you'll find the Header cell check box. This check box assigns boldface type to text in the cell. Can't you do that just by formatting text? Yes, you can. The Header check box harks back to earlier eras, when this HTML tag was necessary for table formatting.

You can also select the No Wrap check box in the Cell Properties dialog box. When you turn off table text wrap, you automatically expand the width of the cell by adding more text on a line.

The drop-down boxes in the Custom Background area of the Cell Properties dialog box are used to assign formatting to selected cells. These attributes can be used to assign different background images or colors to cells, as shown in Figure 12.16.

In the Cell Properties or Table Properties dialog boxes, the style button opens a Style dialog box. The Style dialog box allows you to define format that is not standard HTML. These attributes are known as inline styles, and are not globally recognized by browsers.

Design Techniques with Tables

Placing tables within cells and merging cells are two techniques for stretching the design capabilities of tables. You can use tables to organize vertical and horizontal spacing in your Web site. One technique is to use row height as a spacing control for text.

TABLES IN CELLS

Embedding tables within cells allows detailed control over white space and positioning of Web page objects. When you place a table inside a cell, you

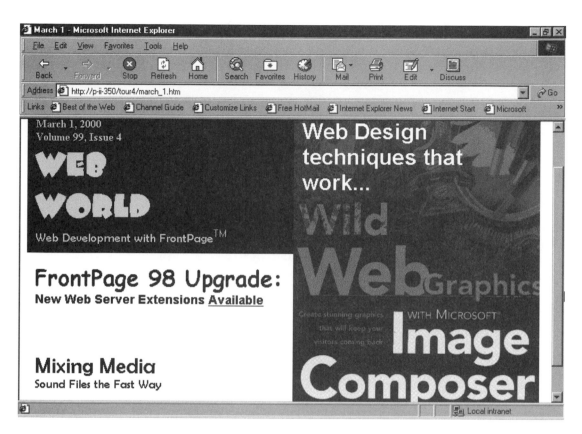

Figure 12.16 *Using an image as a cell background.*

can create blocks of white space that are normally difficult to achieve in Web page layout. The technique of embedding tables within tables is sometimes used by designers to place images precisely on a page. Figure 12.17 shows a table being placed inside a cell.

When you embed tables within tables, it can be confusing to assign cell properties. Alignment, color background, and other attributes should not conflict. For example, if you implant a table within a cell and use different vertical alignment for the embedded cells than you have in the larger cell, the alignment results are going to be unpredictable. Sometimes you need to combine these cell properties to create desired layout effects. If so, expect to do plenty of troubleshooting and not a little detective work to track down the origin of that one cell property that a designer wants to use, or remove.

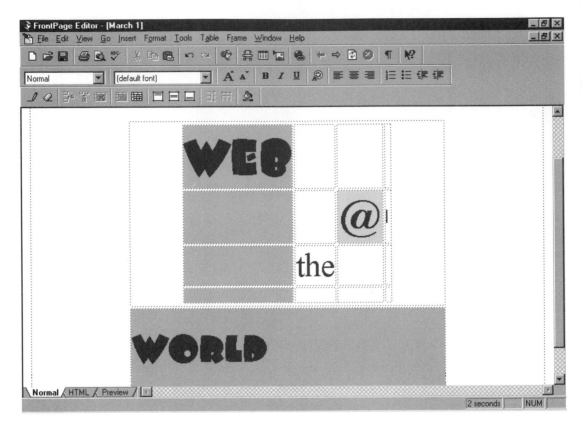

Figure 12.17   *Inserting a table in a cell.*

MERGING CELLS

Another technique for creating the illusion of floating table objects is merging cells. To merge cells:

1. Click and drag to select the neighboring cells.
2. Select Table, Merge Cells, or right-click and select Merge Cells from the Context menu, as shown in Figure 12.18.

Study Break

Formatting Tables

Practice what you have learned about formatting tables.

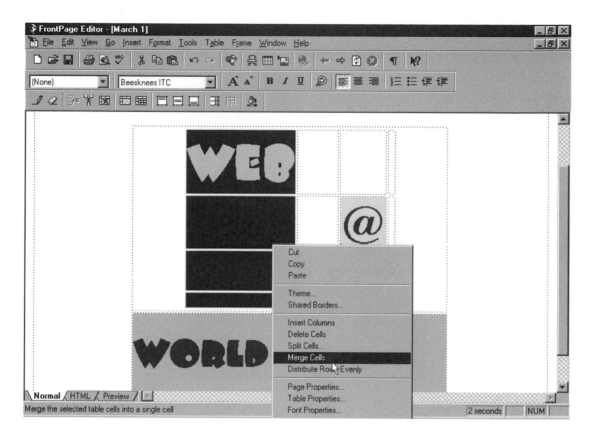

Figure 12.18 *Merging cells.*

First, with a Web page open, insert a 3-column by 1-row table at the top of the page. Assign a different background color to each cell.

Define a border size of zero for all cells in the table. Then, define cell padding of 6 and cell spacing of 0. Drag on the bottom border of the table to increase the height, so that the table is approximately shaped in a square.

Finally, use the Draw Table tool in the Table toolbar and divide one of the columns into three rows. Assign new colors to each cell in the divided column, as well as to the undivided columns, so that your table looks something like the one in Figure 12.19.

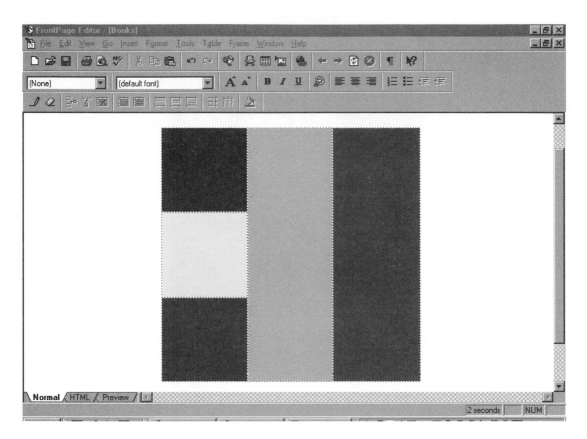

Figure 12.19   *A formatted table.*

MCSD 12.2   Using Graphics in FrontPage Web Pages

As a FrontPage expert, your role in relation to graphics and illustrations is analogous to that of an art gallery director. You don't need to be an artist, but you do need to know how to present artistic elements.

Once your graphic designer has cooked up an illustration, photograph, logo, or sitemap graphic, that image must be prepared for presentation on the Web. Overall, FrontPage handles that process smoothly, while providing the Web designer many options for how to display images. Here, we'll look under the hood at how that process works so that you can troubleshoot image problems, and we'll explore the variety of options for displaying images.

Copying Images into FrontPage Web Sites

The simplest way to place an image in FrontPage is to copy it into the Front-Page Editor. Any image that can be copied to the Windows clipboard can be copied into an open Web page in the FrontPage Editor. *Any* image? Even from vector-based formats like CorelDRAW or Adobe Illustrator? Yes, any image can be copied into FrontPage. The caveat is that those images will be converted automatically into either GIF or JPEG format bitmap graphics when they are saved as part of the Web page.

Other options for inserting images into FrontPage include:

- Inserting an image file into a Web page
- Scanning a photo or other illustration directly into FrontPage
- Using clip art

In general, if you can see an image on your monitor you can copy it into FrontPage. However, there are limitations to that technique. Some illustrations do not copy, or do not copy well through the clipboard into FrontPage. I've run into problems, in particular, with vector based images. Some images copy, but lose quality when copied into FrontPage through the clipboard. And some images will be provided for a Web site in file form.

Importing Image Files

You can insert graphic files directly into FrontPage from the following formats:

- GIF and JPEG (*.gif, *.jpg) are the two generally recognized Web-compatible graphic formats. The section "Saving Images in Web Compatible Formats" later in this chapter explores the differences between these file formats in more detail.
- Bitmap (*.bmp) is among the most universally recognized formats for saving images. If a designer comes to you and asks "Can you handle my Dream 3D images?," your answer can always be, "Can you save those to a bitmap format for me?"
- Portable Network Graphics (*.png) PNG is a standard similar to GIF. For a time, Microsoft was promoting it as an alternative to GIF mainly because of copyright issues. PNG has not been adopted as a standard for Web graphics like JPEG and GIF at this point.
- TIFF (*.tif), or Tagged Image File Format, is widely used for scanned images and has the advantage of being a format to which most Macintosh graphics programs can save files.

- Windows Metafile (*.wmf) Similar to the BMP bitmap format in that many Windows applications can save to this format. It often does a better job of handling artwork than *.bmp files.
- SUN Raster (*.ras) A format for saving bitmap images that allows each pixel to be defined for color, brightness, and intensity.
- PostScript (*.eps) is another widely available format for saving both images and text.
- PCX (*.pcx) is a bitmap file type developed for the old PC Paintbrush program and retained as a generic file format.
- Targa (*.tga) is a file format that originated with the Truevision graphics adaptor. This format was developed for images acquired via video production equipment.

While you don't need to know how to create images in these file formats, you should be generally aware of the kinds of sources from which you will be getting graphics. If you're working closely with graphic designers who are creating illustrations, you may want to dive a bit deeper into the world of Web graphics. Following is a quick study version of the different graphic image formats supported by FrontPage 98.

Different file formats handle images differently. A TIFF image, for example, might well be forty times as large as a PNG file. As for quality, it is necessary to experiment with different graphic design programs to find formats that import well into FrontPage. In Figure 12.20, I experimented by saving a CorelDRAW vector-based image (that cannot be displayed in a Web site) to EPS, TIFF, PNG, and PCX formats. On my monitor (and ultimately in a Web browser), the EPS image looks a bit sharper and handled the outline around the logo better than the other formats. And the other formats required more resizing than the EPS file. And, when I tried to copy the image through the clipboard, I got text instead of a graphic! The point is you may have to encourage your graphic designers to provide more than one file option for illustrations.

Note the four-sided border (with the star extending beyond the border) in the EPS file, compared to the left border only on the PNG, TIFF, and PCX images.

There are two options for inserting an image file into a FrontPage Web page. You can insert an image file directly into a page open in the FrontPage Editor, and later save it to your FrontPage Web. Or, you can import the file into a FrontPage Web, and then insert it into the page.

To insert a file directly into a page from your local drive:

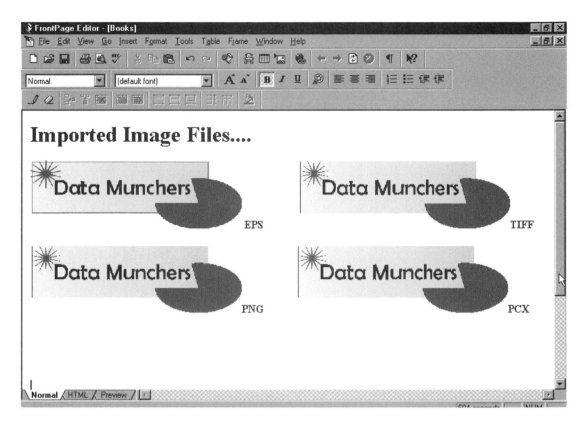

Figure 12.20 *Image borders for this logo are handled differently depending on the type of file format.*

1. With your Web and Web page open, click to place an insertion point in the FrontPage Editor.
2. Select Insert, Image.
3. Click on the Select a File on Your Computer button in the Image dialog box, as shown in Figure 12.21.
4. Use the Select File dialog box to navigate to the image on your computer.
5. Select the image file and OK the dialog box to insert the image.

At this point, you have placed an image in the Web page, but have not saved that embedded image file to your FrontPage Web. We'll explore that process separately, since it applies to all images imported into your page, or altered there, regardless of whether they are copied, imported, scanned or edited in the FrontPage Editor.

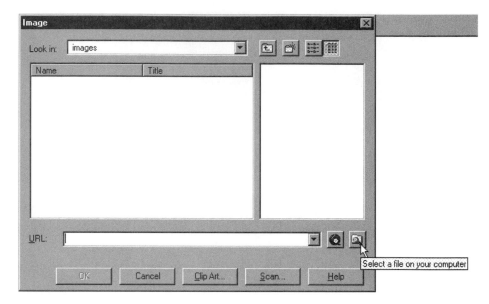

Figure 12.21 *Inserting an image from your computer.*

To import an image into your FrontPage Web, and then place it on a page:

1. With your Web open, in the FrontPage Explorer select File, Import.
2. Click on the Add File button in the Import File to FrontPage Web dialog box.
3. Select a file (or files, using Shift+click) in the Add File to Import List, as shown in Figure 12.22, and click on Open to add the files to your import list.
4. Click on OK in the Import File to FrontPage Web dialog box to add the files to your Web.

The imported files can now be inserted directly into a page in the FrontPage Editor using the Insert, Image file command.

Scanning Images into FrontPage

Images can also be scanned directly into FrontPage, or inserted right from a digital camera. If you are administering a creative environment where developers want to bring scanned illustrations or digital camera images directly into FrontPage, the easiest solution is to connect them to a TWAIN compliant scanner. TWAIN complaint scanners and cameras conform to Windows 95/98 plug and play standards.

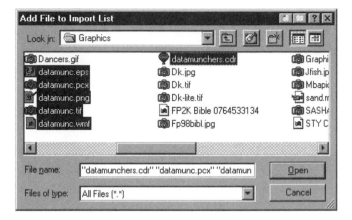

Figure 12.22 *Importing image files into a Web.*

To scan an image or insert a digital camera image directly into a Web page:

1. With your FrontPage Web open, and your page open in the FrontPage Editor, select Insert, Image.
2. Click on the Scan button in the Image dialog box.
3. If you have not previously defined the source for your image (a scanner or a digital camera), click on the Source button and choose the image source from the Select Source dialog box. After you select a source, click on the Acquire button. A dialog box from your scanner or camera will appear, something like the one shown in Figure 12.23.

Figure 12.23 *Acquiring an image from a scanner.*

4. Define the image to scan or import from your camera, and scan or import the image (the specific dialog box buttons will depend on your image source).

After you scan an image or insert a digital camera image, OK the Image dialog box to place the picture on the page.

Saving Images in Web-Compatible Formats

If you copy an image into a Web page, insert clip art, import an image from a scanner or digital camera, that image must be saved to the FrontPage Web. As soon as you save the page in which the image is embedded, the Save Embedded Files dialog box appears, as shown in Figure 12.24.

Unless you have defined an imported image such as a JPEG file (see Defining Image Properties later this chapter), your embedded image will be saved automatically to the GIF file format.

GIF images have the advantage of allowing interlacing (gradually fading in images that take a long time to download) and transparency (a single color can be made transparent, allowing an image to appear to be placed directly on the Web page background).

JPEG images have the advantage of managing complex colors better by providing a more sophisticated system for mixing color pixels to create colors not supported by Web browsers.

The general rule is to use JPEG format for photos and other illustrations where the original has hundreds of colors or more, and GIF format for other images. Again, unless you specifically define an image as a JPEG file in the Image Properties dialog box, images are automatically converted from

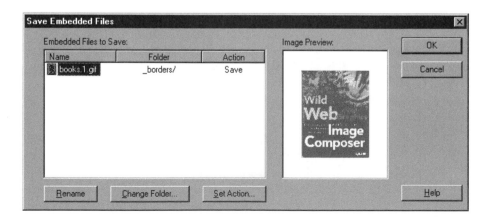

Figure 12.24 *Saving an embedded image as a file.*

their original format to GIF when they are saved to the Web through the Save Embedded Files dialog box.

The Save Embedded Files dialog box also allows you to use the Rename button to assign a name to the file other than the default name. You can also use the Change Folder button to assign the image to a folder other than the default folder.

The Set Action button in the dialog box opens the Set Action dialog box, shown in Figure 12.25. If an image has already been saved, or if there is an existing file with the same name that is assigned to the embedded image, you will have three options in the Set Action dialog box. You can overwrite an existing image file with the same name as the file you are saving, or discard changes you made to the image and reinsert the existing file. The final option (Don't Save), saves the Web page without saving the embedded image.

If you have imported an image into a FrontPage Web before placing it in your Web page, that image is already saved to the Web and you will not be prompted with the Save Embedded Files dialog box unless you have edited the image in the FrontPage Editor.

Editing Images in FrontPage

FrontPage is not an image editing program, but it does come with a small but useful array of image editing tools right in the FrontPage Editor.

The Image toolbar that opens when an image is selected offers tools for assigning hotspots, transparency (in GIF images), and editing image appearance and file size.

ASSIGNING HOT SPOTS

The Rectangle, Circle, and Polygon tools in the Image Toolbar allow you to draw hotspots in an image that function as hyperlinks.

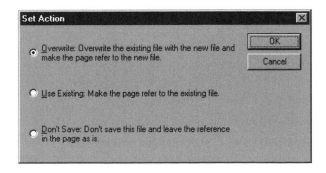

Figure 12.25   *Three options for resaving embedded files.*

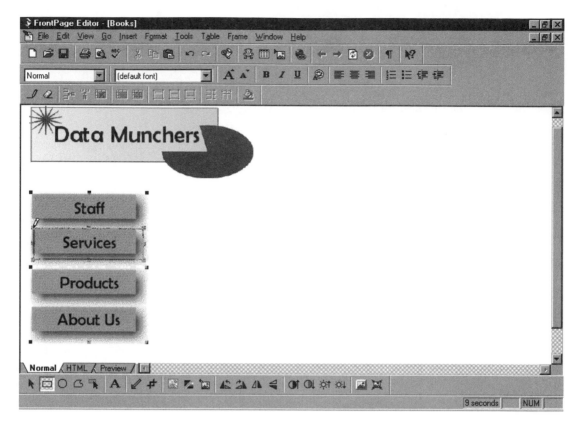

Figure 12.26 *Outlining an image map hotspot.*

To assign a hotspot, select one of the three shape tools and click and drag to outline a section of your image, as shown in Figure 12.26.

As soon as you release your mouse button, the Create Hyperlink dialog box opens, and you can define the target for the link.

Once you define hotspots, the Select tool allows you to select them and the Highlight tool highlights hotspots. These tools make it easy to identify, select, and if necessary, edit or delete hotspots.

The image maps generated by FrontPage 98 are client-side image maps. The data that processes the links is stored in the Web page itself. These image maps can function only if the Web is published to a server with FrontPage 98 extensions. FrontPage server extensions enable the client-side image maps generated in FrontPage to work.

If you need to publish your site to a non-FrontPage server, and you want to include server-side image maps, FrontPage 98 allows you to assign NCSA, CERN, or Netscape server-side image maps in the FrontPage Explorer.

To define an alternate image map standard in the FrontPage Explorer, select Tools, Web Settings, and click on the Advanced tab in the FrontPage Web Settings dialog box. Use the Image Maps Style drop-down menu to define an alternate Image Map style, as shown in Figure 12.27.

If you select a non-FrontPage style for image maps, you will be prompted to enter a location for the image map script in the Prefix box in the FrontPage Web Settings dialog box.

Assigning Transparency

To make a single color in an image transparent, first select the image. Then select the Transparency tool in the Image toolbar, and click on the color in the image you wish to make transparent. Typically this will be a white background, as shown in Figure 12.28.

After you assign transparency to an embedded image, you will be prompted to resave the altered image when you save your Web page. If you assign transparency to an image that has been saved as a JPEG image, you will be prompted to change the image type to a GIF image, since JPEG images do not support transparency.

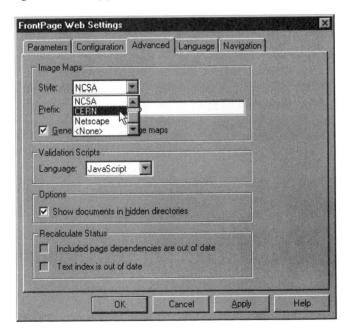

Figure 12.27 *Defining image map style for non-FrontPage, enabled servers.*

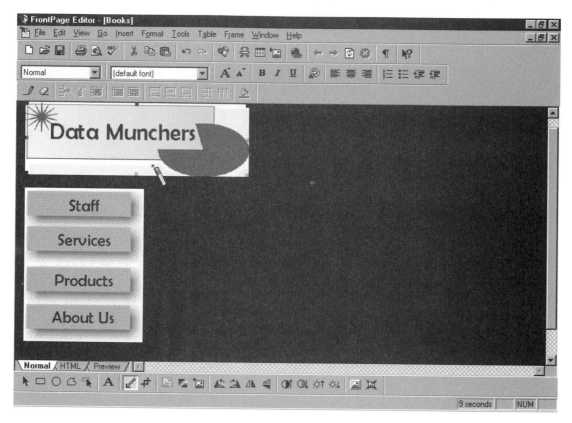

Figure 12.28 *Assigning transparency.*

ASSIGNING TEXT LABELS

You can place text boxes on top of images using the Text tool in the Image toolbar. To insert text on an image, select the image, and then click on the Text tool. A text box will appear with eight sizing handles. Use those handles to resize the text box. Use the Select tool in the Image toolbar to select the text box and move it within the image.

You can assign text formatting to a selected Text Label from the Formatting toolbar, just as you would format selected text in your Web page, except that formatting can only be applied to an entire Text label. Figure 12.29 shows a text label with color being assigned to the font.

CROPPING IMAGES

The Crop tool displays eight small cropping handles on a selected image. You can click and drag on any of the corner or side cropping handles to re-

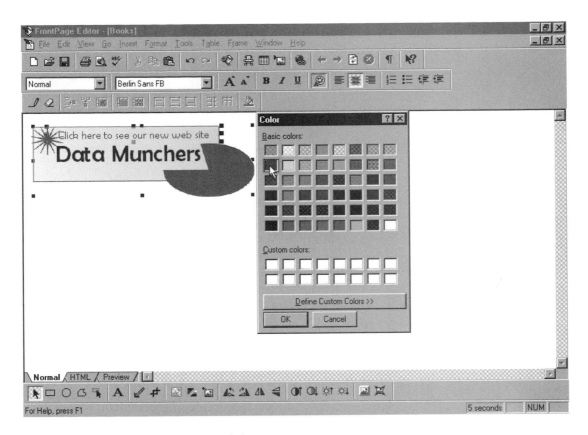

Figure 12.29 *Formatting a Text Label.*

define the shape of an image. Cropping is different than resizing an image in that it acts like a pair of scissors, and cuts away sections of the image.

Clicking on the Cropping tool a second time cuts the image to the size defined by the crop handles.

FORMATTING IMAGES

Most of the remaining tools in the Image toolbar actually change the appearance of an image. Table 12.1 describes the effects of these tools.

The Resample tool in the Image toolbar can radically improve page download time. If, for example, you resize an image by reducing the size by 50%, you can resample that image so that fewer pixels are saved as part of the image file. The smaller file size will result in faster page loading. However, once you resample an image and resave the embedded image with a page, you cannot restore the missing pixels if you later decide to enlarge the image.

Table 12.1 *Formatting Image Tools*

Tool	Effect	How it looks
Original	(unchanged image)	
Washout	Applies a lightening, watercolor effect	
Black and White	Converts image to black and white	
Restore	Returns the image to its saved version	
Rotate Left, Rotate Right, Reverse, Flip	Rotates 90% or mirrors horizontally or vertically (Reverse shown)	
More Contrast, Less Contrast	Sharpens or dulls image (more contrast shown)	
More Brightness, Less Brightness	Adds or lessens intensity (more brightness shown)	
Bevel	Adds a 3-D frame around the image	

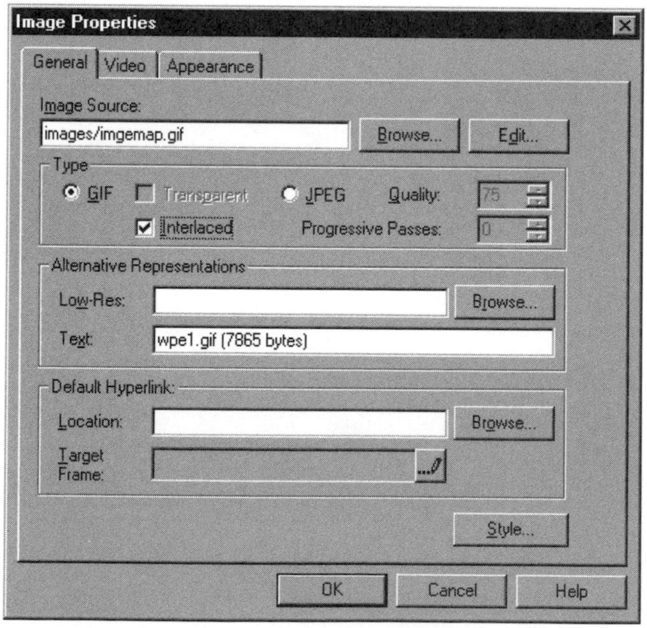

Figure 12.30 *Setting image properties.*

Defining Image Properties

The Image Properties dialog box allows you to define the image file type, alternative text and graphic representations, hyperlink properties, alignment, spacing, border thickness, and size. All these properties can be assigned from within FrontPage.

The Image Properties dialog box is accessed by right-clicking on any image, and selecting Image Properties from the context menu. The Image Properties dialog box is shown in Figure 12.30.

The image properties you can control in the Image Properties dialog box are divided between the General and the Appearance tab. A third tab defines video properties and will be discussed later in this chapter.

Image properties are listed in Table 12.2.

Table 12.2 *Image Properties*

Property	Tab	What It Does
Image Source	General	Defines the image file to be displayed.
Type	General	Defines the file type, GIF (with or without interlacing and transparency) or JPEG (and JPEG quality).
Low-Res		Defines an alternate smaller image displayed in some browsers while the image is loading in a browser.
Text		Defines text that displays in imageless Web browsers, and also text that displays when a cursor is pointed at an image in modern browsers.
Default Hyperlink		Defines a hyperlink activated by clicking on the image.
Target Frame		Defines a frame in which to display a link—used only in framesets.
Alignment		Defines location for images. Left and Right alignment flow text around an image.
Border Thickness		Defines the width of a border around the image in pixels. The default for images that function as links is one pixel, but you can change it to zero to display no border.
Vertical and Horizontal Spacing		These spin boxes define the buffer around an image in pixels.
Size		The spin boxes and option buttons in this area define the size of an image in pixels or percent of the browser window size. The Keep Aspect Ratio check box forces resizing to conform to the original shape and proportions of the image.

Figure 12.31 illustrates a few image properties. The text, displayed when the cursor points to the image, is defined in the Text box in the General tab. The left alignment of the image (allow text to flow to the right) was defined in the Alignment drop-down menu in the Appearance tab. The border was removed from the image in the Border Thickness spin box in the Appearance tab.

Using Images for Web Page Backgrounds

Images can be assigned as backgrounds for Web pages in the Page Properties dialog box. Normally, background images are tiled—small images are placed side-by-side like tiling on a floor to create a background that fills an entire Web page.

Tiling images allows the page to load faster, as only a small image needs to be downloaded. Creating tiled images for page backgrounds is an art in its own right, but that's a job for your project's design team. Figure 12.32 shows a background image being created in Microsoft Image Composer. This

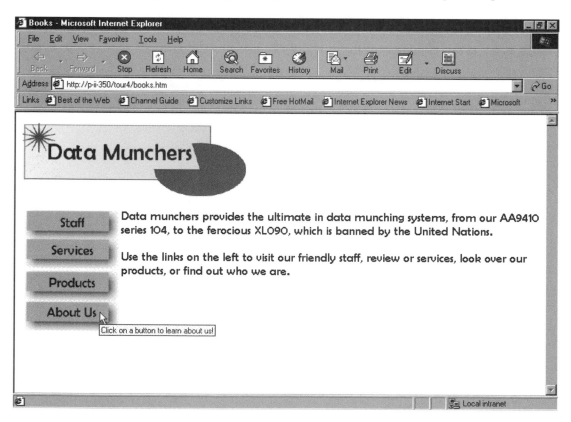

Figure 12.31 *A left-aligned image with alternate text and no border.*

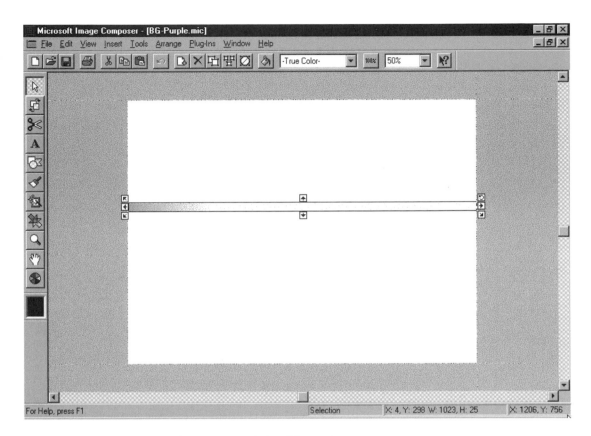

Figure 12.32 *Background images are tiled to fill a Web page.*

image will be tiled vertically to fill a page. You can jump ahead to Figure 12.33 to see how this image will look as a Web page background.

FrontPage also provides a set of clip art images that can be applied to page backgrounds.

To assign a file as a page background:

1. With your FrontPage Web open, and your page open in the FrontPage Editor, select File, Page Properties.
2. Click on the Background tab.
3. Click on the Background Image check box. Then click on the Browse button to open the Select Background Image dialog box. Use a file in your Web site, or use the Select a File on Your Computer button to navigate to an image file on your computer. Or, click on the Clip Art button to use one of the background images that comes with FrontPage 98.

Note A frequent troubleshooting question for FrontPage professionals: "Why can't I access the background tab of the Page Properties dialog box?" The answer is that a theme has been assigned to a page. Remove the Theme (Format, Theme in FrontPage Editor), and you can assign a background of your own choosing.

4. Use the Watermark check box to freeze the location of a background image. This technique tends to place a distracting image behind your page content, but on rare occasions it can be effective. Watermark background images are sometimes large files that are not tiled. After you apply a background image to a page, you can save that image as an embedded file when you save your Web page.

Figure 12.33 shows a Web page with a background image tiled vertically to fill the browser window.

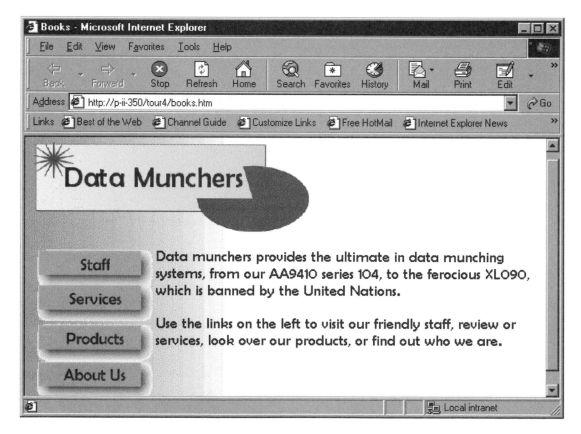

Figure 12.33 *A background image tiled to fill a Web page.*

The expanding universe of Web graphics is itself a giant field of endeavor. Some useful resources are:

- *Web Graphics Sourcebook* by Ed Tittel, Susan Price and James Michael Steward (Wiley)—a comprehensive but concise guide to the science of Web graphics.
- *<designing Web graphics.2>* by Lynda Weinman (New Riders) is a respected overview of the aesthetics of Web graphic design.
- *PhotoShop Web Magic* by Ted Schulman, Renée LeWinter and Tom Emmanuelides (Hayden) focuses on techniques for creating PhotoShop images for the Web.
- *Creating Great Web Graphics* by Laurie McCanna (MIS) is full of recipes for graphics that will work in Web sites.
- *Wild Web Graphics with Microsoft Image Composer* by David Karlins (Que) covers the graphic design program bundled with FrontPage 98. Image Composer resources can be found at www.ppinet.com.

Study Break

Formatting an Image

Practice what you have learned about editing the properties of an image using the Image toolbar.

First, with a Web page open, insert a piece of clip art. A cartoon will do fine for this experiment.

Next, select the cartoon to activate the Image toolbar.

Use the Transparency tool in the Image toolbar to make one color in your image (the background color) transparent.

Experiment with the Brightness and Contrast tools to increase both brightness and contrast.

Finally, save your page, and with it the embedded image file.

MCSD 12.3 Animating Graphics

One of the biggest challenges I face when I consult with Web developers is explaining the limitations of Web sites in conveying media via Web sites. The constraining fact of life for most Web site/browser environments is that even with the latest streaming technology, animated video clips will simply take too long to download for most visitors to tolerate. There are, of course, exceptions to that situation, which I'll discuss in section 12.4 of this book, Delivering Media. But there is one solution for creating animations that is within the grasp of even a modest Web server and a visitor with a 56K modem, and that is animated GIF images.

Animated GIFs are actually a collection of several images that have been saved to a single GIF file. The way the GIF file format handles multiple images is to store only necessary data for each image. So, if 90% of the contents of one frame in an animated GIF are the same as the previous frame, the file size is increased only by about 10% when the second frame is added to the animation.

You can insert an animated GIF file just as you would any image file. The FrontPage Editor will display animation in the Preview tab, or you can view the animation in your browser.

If visitors' browsers do not support animated GIFs, the image will display only the first frame of the animation.

FrontPage itself is not capable of creating animated GIFs. However, FrontPage 98 ships with an invaluable tool called GIF Animator, which can be used to create animated GIFs.

Following is a quick tutorial on generating animated GIFs using GIF Animator. You can use it to introduce yourself to the process of creating animated GIFs.

1. Insert a series of images in FrontPage that will be used for the different "frames" of your animated image. A quick, easy way to do this is to take one image, copy it, and apply different effects to individual copies of the image.
2. Launch Microsoft GIF Animator (found under Programs, Microsoft Image Composer in your task bar), and size the GIF Animator and Image Composer windows so you can see both of them on your screen.
3. Drag your images, one at a time, into the frames in GIF Animator, as shown in Figure 12.34.
4. After you have placed separate images in Frames in GIF Animator, click on the Animation tab in the GIF Animator, and click the Looping check box. Select a number of times for your animation sequence to repeat in the Repeat Count spin box, or click the Repeat Forever check box. You can let your animation run continuously by checking the Repeat Forever check box.
5. Switch to the Image tab in the GIF Animator and click on the Select All tool in the toolbar at the top of the GIF Animator so that the Image settings apply to all your frames. Start with a setting of 24 in the Duration spin box.
6. Try different transitions in the Undraw Method drop-down list.

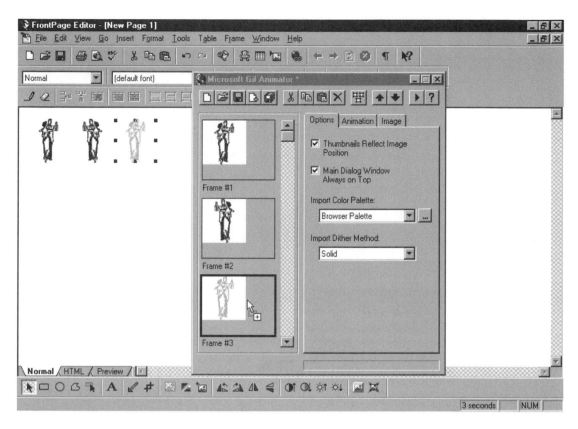

Figure 12.34 *Creating an animated GIF.*

7. Use the Select All button, and in the Image tab assign a transparent background to all selected frames.
8. Click on the Preview button in the GIF Animator toolbar to preview your animated GIF image. Then close the Preview window.
9. Save your animated GIF as a file, and embed the animated GIF file into your Web page.

Study Break

Inserting an Animation

Start by placing a cartoon image from the Clip Art selection on a FrontPage Web page in an open Web.

Next, copy that image and paste it onto the page, creating a duplicate copy of the cartoon.

Use the Reverse tool in the Image toolbar to flip the copy of the cartoon horizontally. When prompted, select No, you do not want to apply Reverse to both copies of your image.

With the two images on your page, save your page. Each image will be saved as a separate embedded file.

With your two images ready to animate, launch Microsoft GIF Animator, and copy the two images into GIF Animator frames. In the Animation tab of Microsoft Gif Animator, select first the Looping, then the Repeat Forever check boxes. In the Image tab of Microsoft GIF Animator assign a duration of 25 to both frames.

Finally, save the animated GIF file and embed it in your Web page. Test the animation by viewing it in Preview tab. Save and close your Web page.

MCSD 12.4   Delivering Media

The world of media delivery is:

a. The most exciting dynamic thing happening on the Web.
b. One of the most challenging, cutting edge and frustrating elements of Web design.

The answer is a combination of both a and b. If your FrontPage Web development responsibilities involve adding multimedia to Web sites, you're going to have a lot of fun and a lot of headaches.

Media delivery challenges over a FrontPage Web site can be understood and resolved by breaking the problem down to two elements:

• The media file type
• The media delivery type

Figure 12.35 illustrates the use of several media file types, and different media delivery options. The Web page in this figure includes a QuickTime Movie (MOV) file, an AVI video file, a MIDI (MID) sound file, and a Real Audio (RA) file. The QuickTime Movie file is displayed in a QuickTime plug-in. The AVI video file is presented both as an inline video and as an ActiveX control. The MIDI music file is displayed as a plug-in. And the Real Audio file can be run online using an ActiveX control.

Media file types include audio files in Real Audio, WAV files, and MIDI music files, or video files like QuickTime movies, or AVI video.

Figure 12.35 *Several types of media files, plus several ways to deliver media, are shown here.*

Options for presenting these media files include inline files that launch players on the visitor's system, plug-in programs that visitors can download, or ActiveX controls that are automatically available with recent versions of Internet Explorer or that can be downloaded like plug-ins.

As I mentioned at the beginning of this section, when media runs smoothly it adds a whole new dimension to Web sites. But media files require programs outside of normal HTML to run, and therein lies the rub. Browsers must be able to associate an application to run embedded media files. To present the headache side of the contradiction, Figure 12.36 shows the same Web page displayed in Figure 12.35, but this time opened in Netscape Navigator instead of Internet Explorer.

As you can see in Figure 12.36, only one of the delivery methods, the QuickTime movie plug-in, even displays in the Netscape Navigator browser

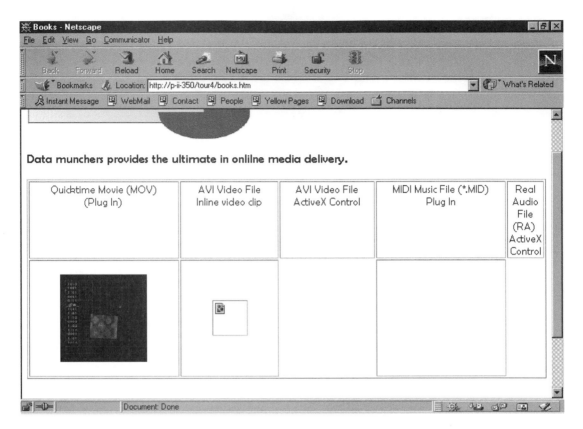

Figure 12.36   *Media compatibility headaches.*

window. That's not a knock on Navigator. I designed a Web site that takes advantage of many of the media delivery options available in FrontPage that are not recognized by Netscape Navigator 4.5. The solution to this problem would be to include links at the Web page for visitors whose browsers would not interpret the media players, so they could download the media players. Assuming a visitor is motivated enough to follow the link, download the media player, and then troubleshoot any problems associating the media player with his or her browser, that's all it would take to deliver the media file.

Having given you a sense of the challenges of delivering media in FrontPage (in the off chance you haven't already bumped your head against the wall on these problems), we can now explore how to implement media in FrontPage.

At the beginning of this section, I divided the problem of presenting media into two parts, which could be rephrased as creating a media file and implementing the file in a Web site. In a basic sense, the first problem is not your problem. As a FrontPage Web administrator, developer, or consultant, you will most likely not be the person developing media files. You might be, but if you are, you are an expert in two different fields, and you've got yourself a thick stack of books on developing media content in your media authoring program of choice, like Macromedia's Flash or a MIDI composition program.

In a sense, as a FrontPage Web design expert, your role is that of a photo developer. The art, media, or sound folks provide the media, and your job is to make it accessible via browsers. Here, we will focus on four ways to present media files:

- Embedded background sounds
- Inline video clips
- Plug-ins
- ActiveX media controls

Embedding Page Background Sounds

FrontPage allows you to embed one, and only one, audio file in a page background. These files must be in the *.wav or midi (*.mid) file format. You can elect to play the sound file once, many times, or continuously.

These embedded background sound files have a number of drawbacks. They aren't interactive, in the sense that a visitor can elect to play them or turn them off. Not only that, a visitor has no indication that a sound file is attached to the Web page (unless you include text on the page to the effect of "This page has a sound file that's about to play. Quick! Reach for the volume dial on your speakers!"). Embedded sound files slow down page loading dramatically. Most *.wav files are large enough to add a minute or so to download time on a 56K modem. That doesn't mean that the page will take an extra minute to display, but it means that the background sound will blast off quite a bit after a visitor has downloaded the rest of your page content.

With all those limitations, background sound files can provide an appropriate accompaniment to your Web page. An audio file that says "welcome" can greet visitors. A chime can introduce your page. And, once a sound file is downloaded, it can be looped to play over and over without reloading.

To embed a background sound in a Web page:

1. With your FrontPage Web open, and your page open in the FrontPage Editor, select File, Page Properties.
2. In the General tab of the Page Properties dialog box, click on the Browse button to locate a sound file in the *.wav or *mid file format, as shown in Figure 12.37.
3. Use the Loop spin-box to define how many times you wish your sound to play. Select the Forever check box to loop your sound file continuously.
4. When you have defined your sound file, click on OK. You can test the sound file in the Preview tab of the FrontPage Editor, or in your browser.

At this writing, embedded page background sound files do not play in Netscape Navigator. Since background sound files are not essential to most page content, that's not a drastic drawback to including page sound files.

Embedding Inline Video Clips

FrontPage can embed *.avi format video clips in a page without the need for plug-ins or ActiveX controls. These video clips play in Internet Explorer, but not Netscape Navigator.

To insert an inline video clip:

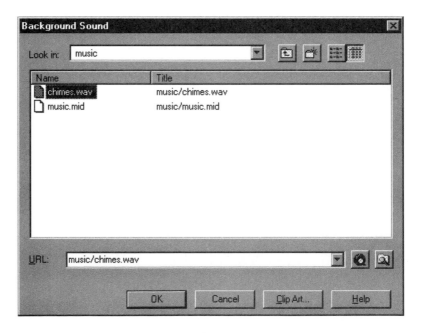

Figure 12.37 *Embedding a background sound in a page.*

1. With your FrontPage Web open, and your page open in the FrontPage Editor, click to place your insertion point where the video will appear in your page.
2. Select Insert, Active Elements, Video.
3. In the Video dialog box, navigate to an *.avi format video file, as shown in Figure 12.38. Click on OK to insert the video into your Web page.
4. Right-click on the video in the FrontPage Editor, and select Image Properties from the context menu. You can define many of the same image properties that you can define for a normal (non-video) image, in the General and Appearance tabs.
5. In the Video tab of the Image Properties dialog box, use the Show Controls in the Browser check box to display start, pause and stop controls with the video. Use either (or both) of the check box options in the Start section of the dialog box to start the video when the page is opened (On File Open), or when a visitor moves his or her mouse over the video (On Mouse Over).
6. Use the Repeat controls to loop the video a set number of times, or to run it forever. In Figure 12.39, the video is formatted to run once when a visitor points to it. After you define video options, click on OK.

You can test your embedded inline video in the Preview tab of the FrontPage Editor, or in a browser.

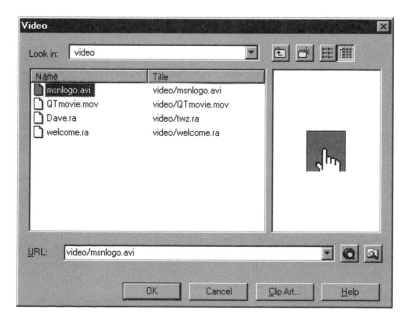

Figure 12.38 *Embedding an inline *.avi format video.*

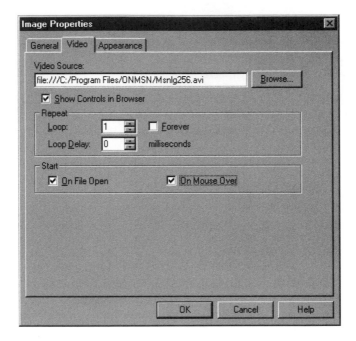

Figure 12.39 *Defining video play options.*

Presenting Media with Plug-ins

Plug-ins represent both the most reliable way to present media content and the method that can be the most annoying for visitors. Why this paradox? All modern browser versions are capable of downloading plug-ins to play media. All purveyors of media (like Apple QuickTime, Real Audio, etc.) supply free player software at their Web sites that can be downloaded and associated with any major browser.

Downloading plug-ins, and following the directions from the plug-in creator and your browser to make them work, is a lot of hassle. On the other hand, it usually works. Embedded *.avi video files pop right up in IE, and in that sense they are easier to use and see. But, of course, they only work in IE. So, plug-ins are more work, but they are more universally accepted and more reliable if you expect your Web site to be visited by folks with older versions of IE, or with Netscape.

To insert a plug-in for a media file:

1. With your FrontPage Web open, and your page open in the FrontPage Editor, click to place your insertion point where the media plug-in will appear in your page.
2. Select Insert, Advanced, Plug-In.
3. In the Plug-In Properties dialog box, use the Browse button to open the Select Plug-In Data Source dialog box, and navigate to a media file. Click on OK to insert the video into your Web page.

What if your system does not have a plug-in file installed for the media file you wish to present? Normally, you will want to download the plug-in file for the media object you are using, so you can test the plug-in on your own system. Plug-in files for media files can be found at the Web sites of the companies that produce them, and a quick visit to your favorite search engine will find a site that provides downloads for viewers that work with nearly every audio and video format in existence.

4. In the Message for Browsers Without Plug-In Support, enter a helpful message for visitors who do not have a plug-in with which to view your media file.

In the Size and Layout areas of the Plug-In Properties dialog box, you can define the size, border size, and alignment of the plug-in. After you do that, click on OK to insert the plug-in.

You can preview your plug-in in the Preview tab of the FrontPage Editor, or in a browser. In the Normal tab of the FrontPage Editor, the plug-in will be marked with a plug-in icon, as shown in Figure 12.40.

Plug-ins provide online controls like start, stop, and pause buttons that are not available in embedded, inline audio and video files.

Presenting Media with ActiveX media controls

ActiveX controls are similar to plug-ins. While Netscape has promoted plug-ins, Microsoft has developed ActiveX controls. Microsoft has an advantage of being able to create ActiveX controls for its own applications and include them in Internet Explorer. However, ActiveX controls can be downloaded from Microsoft for use in Netscape Navigator as well.

Different ActiveX controls are associated with different types of media files. For example, in Figure 12.41, the ActiveX control for the AVI video file has a Play, Pause, and Stop button and a Seek Bar. The control for the Real Audio sound file has a volume slider, a Start/Pause button, and displays information about the sound file.

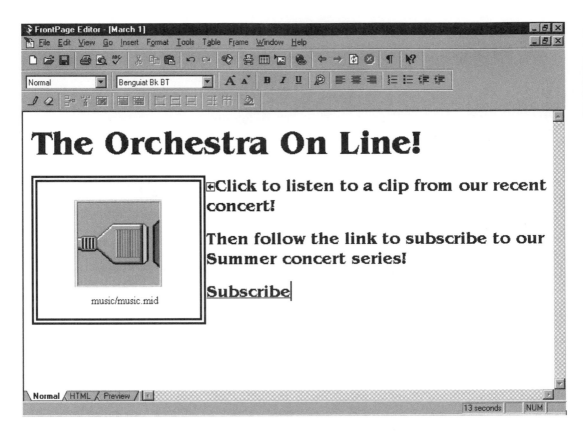

Figure 12.40 *Plug-ins are represented in the FrontPage Editor by a plug-in icon.*

Since ActiveX controls are different for different types of media delivery, you'll have to do some experimenting to define controls for different types of media. Here, I'll walk through two examples: an ActiveX control for an AVI sound file and for a Real Audio file.

To define an ActiveX control for an AVI video file:

1. With your FrontPage Web open, and your page open in the FrontPage Editor, click to place your insertion point where the AVI ActiveX control will appear in your page.

2. Select Insert, Advanced, ActiveX Control. The ActiveX Control Properties dialog box opens.

3. From the Pick a Control drop-down menu, select ActiveMovieControl Object. Click on the Properties button to define the file to associate

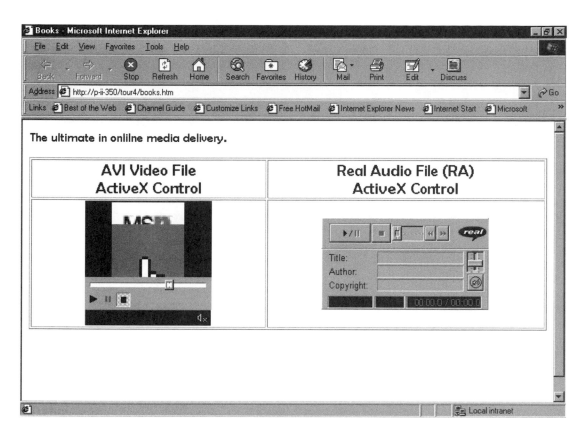

Figure 12.41 *Different strokes for different folks: ActiveX controls depend on the type of media file with which they are associated.*

with the control. The Properties are displayed both in a graphical window and a Properties dialog box, as shown in Figure 12.42. The graphical design window is used to size the control, while the Properties dialog box is used to define the content of the control.

4. Click on File Name in the Properties dialog box, and enter the file name of the AVI video file. If the file is not in the root directory of your site, enter the path name (for example, media/movie.avi). Then, click on Apply. Click on OK to finish defining the control properties.

5. The (other) ActiveX control Properties dialog box, shown in Figure 12.43, can be used to define the position, size and spacing for the control, as well as an HTML page to display in browsers that do not interpret ActiveX controls.

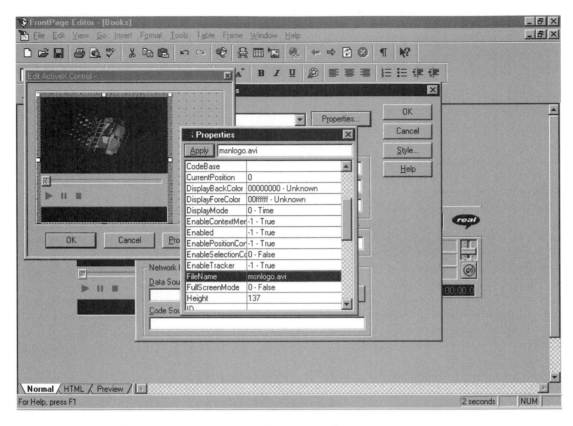

Figure 12.42 *Defining an ActiveX control for an AVI video.*

You can test your AVI ActiveX control in the Preview tab of the Front-Page Editor, or in your browser.

Real Audio ActiveX controls differ from AVI video controls mainly in that they are defined not by file name, but by "Source," which must be a URL.

To define an ActiveX control for a Real Audio sound file:

1. With your FrontPage Web open, and your page open in the FrontPage Editor, click to place your insertion point where the Real Audio ActiveX control will appear in your page.

2. Select Insert, Advanced, ActiveX Control. The ActiveX Control Properties dialog box opens.

3. From the Pick a Control drop-down menu, select RealVideo™ ActiveX Control (32-bit) Object, or a different Real Audio or Real Video option on your system.

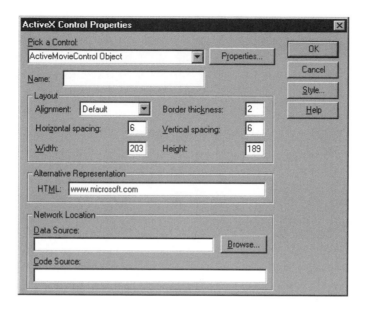

Figure 12.43   *Just to keep things from getting dull, there are two different ActiveX Control Properties dialog boxes.*

4. Click on the Properties button to define the file to associate with the control.

5. Click on Source in the Properties dialog box, and enter the complete URL of the Real Audio file, as shown in Figure 12.44. Unfortunately,

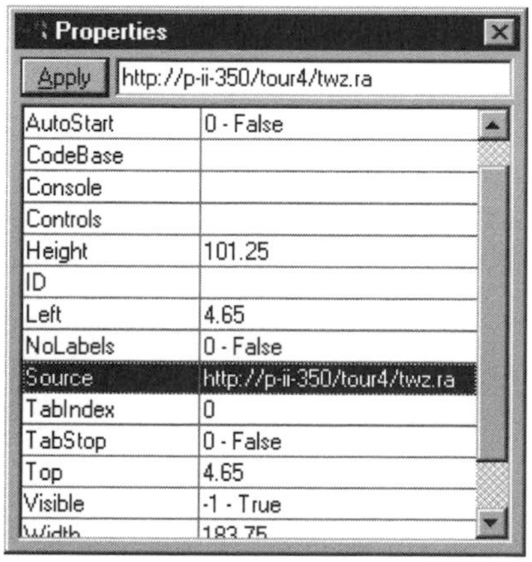

Figure 12.44   *Defining a source URL for a Real Audio ActiveX control.*

you can't browse to the file, so you may have to jot down the exact URL so you can type it accurately. When you have entered the URL for your Real Audio file, click on the Apply button in the Properties dialog box. Then click on OK in the ActiveX Control window. The by now familiar ActiveX Control Properties dialog box appears, and you can edit the display of the control, then click on OK.

Like other ActiveX controls, the Real Audio control can be tested either in the Preview tab of the FrontPage Editor, or in a browser.

The world of implementing media in FrontPage Web sites continues to be charted. For more information on including media in your Web site and incorporating plug-ins, see the following resources:

1. *The FrontPage 98 Bible* by David Elderbrock with Paul Bodensiek (IDG) has one of the more extensive discussions of media and plug-ins in Chapter 16.
2. *Special Edition Using Netscape Communicator 4* (Que) by Mark R. Brown explains how plug-ins work in Netscape in Chapter 14.

Study Break

Embedding an *.avi Format Video File in a FrontPage Web Page

Start by locating an *avi format video file on your hard drive or on the Web. You can use the Windows Finder (right-click on the Start button and select Find) to search for files with *.avi file name extensions, or you can save an *.avi file from a source on the Web to your hard drive. For sources of free *.avi videos, check out:

http://www.d1dpa.com/d1non-s-video.html
http://www.sigma.net/capt_am/media/clips.html

or search the Web on your own.

Once you have located an *.avi video file, embed it in a FrontPage Web page.

Define the video to play when a visitor moves his or her mouse over the video, and define the video to display controls, and play just once.

Finally, save your page, and preview the video in Preview tab of the FrontPage Editor.

■ Summary

In this chapter we surveyed tables, graphics, and media—a rather extensive array of FrontPage features that contribute to providing page layout, graphics and media to a Web page.

Tables can be used to display rows and columns of data as they are in a spreadsheet or word processing table. But tables are also a fundamental layout tool in Web pages, making up in part for the fact that HTML does not support column layout.

FrontPage makes the process of embedding images in a Web page very simple. Any image that can be copied or imported into FrontPage will be converted into a Web-compatible image. And FrontPage even includes rudimentary graphic image editing tools that can be used to create transparent backgrounds, assign image map properties, or alter image appearance.

Finally, FrontPage provides several options for embedding sound and video files, ranging from humble but functional animated GIF images, to embedded *.avi format video clips.

▲ CHAPTER REVIEW QUESTIONS

Here are some practice questions relating to the material covered in the "Incorporating Tables, Graphics, Animation and Media" area of Microsoft's *Designing and Implementing Web Sites Using Microsoft FrontPage 98* exam (70-055).

1. *Image transparency can be assigned to which of the following image file types? (Select all correct answers.)*

    A. GIF files

    B. JPEG files

    C. AVI video files

    D. MIDI files

2. *Image files can be added to a Web site through which of the following methods? (Select all correct answers.)*

    A. Scanned directly into FrontPage with a TWAIN compliant scanner

    B. Imported in the FrontPage Explorer

    C. Copied through the Windows clipboard

    D. Embedded as page background images

    E. Inserted from a File in the FrontPage Editor

3. *Real Audio files can be presented in ActiveX controls.*

    A. True

    B. False

4. *Tables are one of the most reliable techniques for formatting Web page content in columns.*

    A. True

    B. False

5. *FrontPage includes some image editing properties, but not the ability to assign transparency to images in a graphic design program.*

    A. True

    B. False

6. *Which of the following techniques can be used to define tables? (Select all correct answers.)*

    A. They can be drawn with the Draw Table tool

    B. They can be merged from data forms

    C. They can be saved as embedded images

    D. They can be generated from text

    E. They can be imported from spreadsheet programs

7. *Which of the following are limitations of displaying media files as ActiveX controls? (Select all correct answers.)*

    A. ActiveX controls can be displayed only in Netscape Navigator, or with browsers that have ActiveX plug-ins

    B. ActiveX controls require FrontPage 98 extension files on the Web server

    C. ActiveX controls can be displayed only in Internet Explorer or with browsers that have ActiveX plug-ins

    D. ActiveX controls require an associated ActiveX control for the type of media file

    E. ActiveX controls require at least some experience with JavaScript coding

8. *Transparency can be applied to images in the Save Embedded Images dialog box .*

    A. True

    B. False

9. *FrontPage's ability to embed inline video without plug-ins or ActiveX controls is restricted to the AVI file format.*

   A. True

   B. False

10. *You cannot see the display of a plug-in in Normal view of the FrontPage Editor.*

    A. True

    B. False

11. *Background coloring can be assigned to tables, but not to individual table cells.*

    A. True

    B. False

12. *Which of the following changes can be made to images in the FrontPage Editor?*

    A. Image coloring can be edited

    B. Text can be added to images

    C. Image size can be cropped

    D. Transparency can be added, but only to JPEG images

    E. Images can be edited with compatible plug-ins

13. *Cell padding can be assigned to tables, but not to individual table cells.*

    A. True

    B. False

14. *You can change the file type of an embedded file in the Image Properties dialog box.*

    A. True

    B. False

15. *Table width can be defined in which of the following increments? (Select all correct answers.)*

    A. Inches

    B. Picas

    C. Percent

    D. Pixels

    E. Bytes

Using Style Sheets and Templates

FrontPage 98's array of Web and Page templates provides powerful development tools for Web designers. Like templates in other applications, Web and Page templates provide design tips, and even supply generic content that can be used or adapted in Web sites. But FrontPage templates also include more substantial features, like the ability to generate Webs with discussion forums, input forms, search boxes and tables of contents. Page templates create pages with frames, defined feedback forms, and corporate directories. As a FrontPage expert, you will need to be aware of which templates generate which Web objects in order to advise, train, and troubleshoot for Front-Page Web designers.

FrontPage also includes features to assist in creating styles. These styles provide formatting features unavailable through standard HTML. Styles can be local (applied to specific text), page-wide (style sheets), or applied from external files that can be used for multiple pages.

341

In this chapter we'll explore both templates and wizards that generate Web sites and pages, and we'll look at how FrontPage works with styles and external style sheets. At the conclusion of this chapter you will be able to:

- Be familiar with FrontPage's selection of Web templates.
- Connect FrontPage features with the Web templates that include them.
- Use Page templates.
- Create new page templates.
- Create external style sheets.
- Use an external style sheet with multiple Web pages.

MCSD 13.1   Using Web Templates

In FrontPage 98, Microsoft places unusual import on using templates and wizards to generate Webs. In fact, in almost every case, FrontPage Webs are initiated by some form of Web Template or wizard, even if only the modest "Empty" Web template is invoked.

In the case of the Empty Web Templates, the purpose is not to create Web site content, but instead to generate the folders and files needed for functional FrontPage Webs.

FrontPage Web templates and wizards also automate the process of creating Websites. For many developers, generating and adapting these features via Web templates and wizards is all that is required to create a relatively sophisticated Web site.

For all these reasons, Microsoft expects those of us who are deployed under FrontPage 98 MCP or MCSD status to be quite familiar with the features of the different Web templates.

Of course, you need to understand that even with wizards there is a tremendous amount of page editing required to create real content for Web pages, as well as a need to revise and modify the Web structure. However, to help with that process, some Web templates or wizards also generate a list of unfinished work in the Task view of the FrontPage Explorer.

The FrontPage 98 Explorer provides five templates and two Wizards. First, I'll quickly list them, and what they do. Then we'll look at some important features of the more sophisticated templates and wizards.

The Empty Web Template only creates the necessary folders for FrontPage Webs to function. That's a big "only!" FrontPage administrators should insist that developers who create Web sites from scratch begin with the Empty Web Template. Figure 13.1 shows the Empty Web template being selected in the FrontPage Explorer.

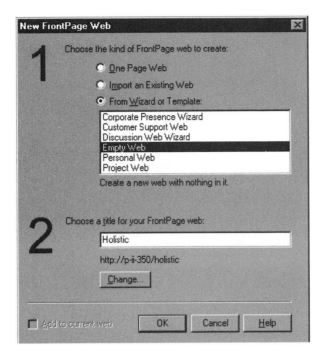

Figure 13.1 *The Empty Web Template will create folders and files required for FrontPage Webs.*

The Learning Web Template is required only when using the tutorial that comes with FrontPage 98. If you will be using the tutorial as part of your training plan, you will use the files in this template. File this information under "training" in your FrontPage problem-solving database.

The Personal Web Template comes with content to create a site that shares personal information. However, this template generates a good structure to start many relatively basic Web sites. The value of this template as a starter template is that it creates a basic navigational structure, applies a theme, and generally sets a beginning developer off in the right direction.

The navigational structure and pages generated by the Personal Web Template are illustrated in Navigation View of the FrontPage Explorer in Figure 13.2.

The Corporate Presence Wizard creates a very sophisticated site that can be defined for a wide variety of organizations or companies. The user enters data describing the corporation or organization, and the kind of look and feel he or she wants to assign to the Web site.

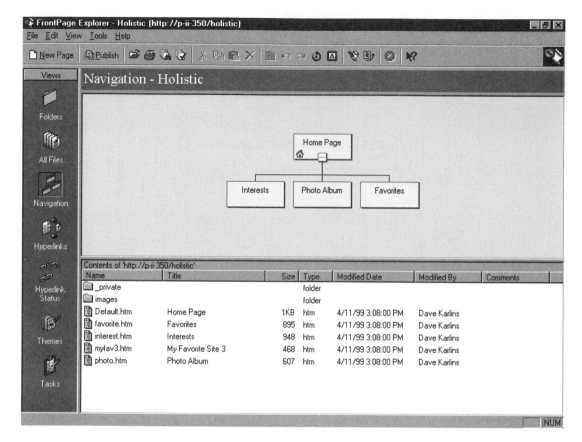

Figure 13.2   *The Personal Template creates a structure with a home page, and three linked pages.*

The Customer Support Web Wizard can be used to produce a very complete Web site for responding to customer support questions about a product. The site comes with two developed sections:

- Input forms to collect questions
- A template Q&A page and pages to display product information

The Discussion Wizard fashions a Web with a discussion forum for visitors, where they can post comments and read each other's comments. This wizard can be used in conjunction with existing Web sites to create sub-Webs or linked Webs that provide the discussion facility for a linked Web site.

The Project Template creates a Web site that displays the structure, personnel, schedule and status of a project. It is very specifically oriented toward display data from a project manager, and not a template you would be expected to be intimately familiar with. The template includes:

- A Home Page
- A Members Page that sets up to list project team personnel, and provides hyperlinks to their e-mail addresses
- A Schedule Page that posts tasks due this week and next week, and provides a list of project milestones
- A Status Page that includes a structure for monthly, quarterly, and annual status reports
- An Archive Page that includes links to documents authored by project members, to software programs, and components developed by the project
- A Search Page
- A Discussions Area that is not a full-blown discussion forum but instead a page that provides information on the project

Figure 13.3 shows the structure of the Web produced by the Project Web Template.

All Web templates and wizards are launched from the FrontPage Explorer. Now that we've quickly reviewed the Web Templates and Wizards, it is necessary to closely examine a few that you will be expected to be more familiar with, the Corporate Presence Wizard, the Discussion Web Wizard, and the Custom Support Web.

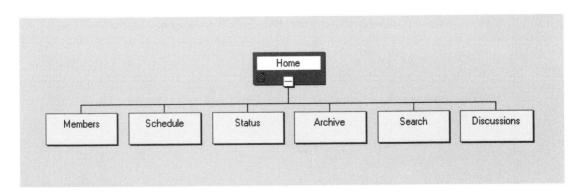

Figure 13.3 *The Project Template creates a structure with a home page, and six child pages.*

The Corporate Presence Wizard

The Corporate Presence Wizard is a significantly more sophisticated wizard than the other Web templates and wizards. It is a very effective tool for generating all kinds of corporate (and organization) Web sites, and includes many options. As such, it is a significant part of FrontPage, and worth some in-depth exploration.

To generate a FrontPage Web with the Corporate Presence Wizard, follow these steps:

1. Start by opening the FrontPage Explorer, and choosing Create a New FrontPage Web from the Getting Started dialog box. What if the dialog box isn't visible in the FrontPage Explorer? You can use the menu option File, New, FrontPage Web instead.
2. Click on the OK button in the New FrontPage Web dialog box, and choose the From Wizard or Template radio button in the New Front-Page Web dialog box.
3. Click on Corporate Presence Wizard in the list of templates and wizards. This launches the wizard, and begins a series of wizard windows which I'll discuss next.

Warning

Before you click on the OK button in the New FrontPage Web dialog box to generate a Web, type a Web title in the Choose a Title for Your Front-Page Web area of the dialog box. If you are publishing the Web to a different server than is selected by default, use the Change button in the New FrontPage Web dialog box to assign a new server.

When you launch the Corporate Presence Web Wizard, the first Wizard dialog box you see will just introduce the wizard. Click on Next to move to the next window.

The next dialog box provides a set of check boxes that allows you to select any or all of the five main pages that you can create, in addition to your home page. The check boxes for those pages determine what pages will be included in your Web site. As shown in Figure 13.4, the options for pages are:

- Home page (required)
- What's New page
- Products/Services page
- Table of Contents page
- Feedback Form page
- Search Form page

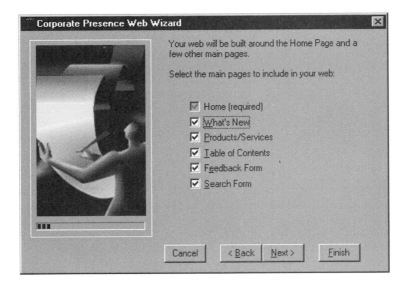

Figure 13.4 *Options for the Corporate Presence Wizard.*

For each page you select, you will be prompted for what content to generate on that page. For example, the (required) home page can have an Introduction, a Mission Statement, a Company Profile and Contact Information.

After you define the contents for your corporate presence Web site, you will be prompted to select a Theme for your Web. You must click the Choose Web Theme button in order to open the Choose Theme dialog box. Themes assign color schemes and graphic elements to your Web. You can preview each Theme in the final Wizard dialog box. When you have assigned a Theme, click on the Finish button to complete the process and generate a corporate presence Web site.

Themes and templates tend to conflict with each other. The color scheme applied by a Theme can clash with the colors in a page template, for example. The Theme vs. Page Template conflict is an argument for waiting until your site is designed to experiment with Themes.

Figure 13.5 shows one possible (typical) Web structure generated by the Corporate Presence Wizard.

The Corporate Presence Web Wizard also creates a task list in Task View of the FrontPage Explorer. The Tasks View has a list of tasks that need to be completed before the Web is done. You can right-click on a task and select Do Task from the shortcut menu to complete the missing work

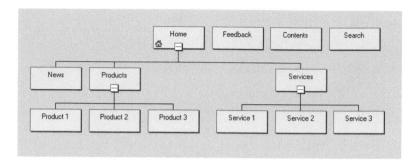

Figure 13.5 *Possible result of the Corporate Presence Wizard.*

needed to finish your site. In Figure 13.6, I am opening the task of customizing a search page for a site generated by the wizard.

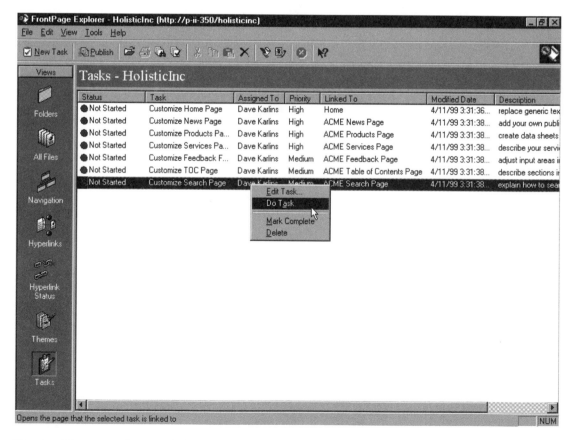

Figure 13.6 *Finishing Web developing using the generated Task list.*

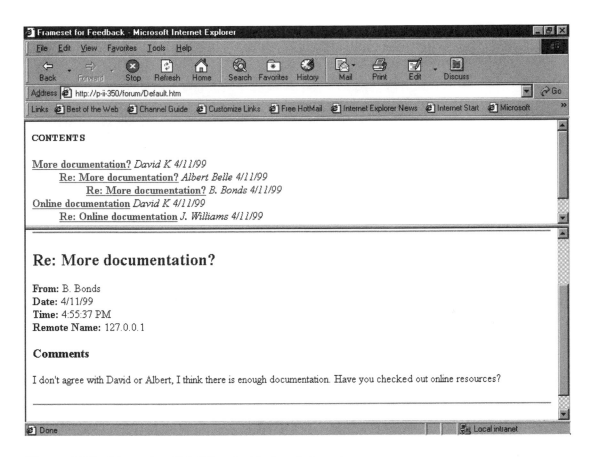

Figure 13.7 *Discussion Web Wizard with threaded postings.*

Using the Discussion Web Wizard

Discussion Webs are one of the most powerful and complicated elements you can create in a FrontPage Web. Figure 13.7 shows a discussion Web as viewed in a browser, with threaded (hierarchal) postings, grouped by topic.

The Discussion Web Wizard plays a unique role in that it is normally used to create Webs that supplement existing Webs. Those Webs can be saved to a sub-folder of the root Web folder, or to another folder at the Web site, or even another Web site.

As you run the Discussion Web Wizard, the second Wizard dialog box prompts you to enable features for your forum. Those features are:

- The Home Page is required.
- A Table of Contents lists pages in the Web site.

- The Search Form page creates a page with a Search box. When your Discussion Web collects a large list of articles, visitors will want to use a Search Box to find ones relevant to their interests.
- Threaded Replies. If you select this check box, you create a Web site with a threaded discussion page. Discussion Webs with threads present visitors with a choice of replying to an existing article, or starting a new "thread." A non-threaded discussion page simply lists articles that have been submitted. Visitors can add a new article at the end of the list, but they do not participate in individual discussions, or threads, within the page.
- The Confirmation Page option generates a page that lets visitors know that their article was received.

The Discussion Web Wizard generates the discussion page as a framed page. Frames, or framesets, as two or more framed Web pages are called, are discussed in detail in Chapter 7, "Creating User Interfaces." Near the end of the Discussion Web Wizard, a dialog box provides options for the frameset configuration, or creating a discussion Web with no frames.

Visitors to your Web site using Netscape Navigator 3 or higher or Internet Explorer 3 or higher will be able to view Discussion Web sites with frames. But others will not. If you want to make your discussion forum accessible to non-frame-compatible browsers, you can use the Dual Interface radio button in the Discussion Web Wizard (shown in Figure 13.8). This helpful option will create a Web site that has an alternative view for visitors with older browsers who cannot interpret frames.

Creating a Customer Support Web

The Customer Support Web template generates a Web site with a home page and seven main pages:

- What's New—a place to put announcements for users of your product.
- FAQ—A Frequently Asked Questions page with places for questions and linked answers.
- Bugs—includes an input form to collect customer bug reports.
- Suggestions—includes an input form to collect customer feedback.
- Download—A page that connects to an FTP (File Transfer Protocol) site, for use if you are connecting to an already existing FTP site.
- Discussion—A threaded discussion Web that lets visitors talk to each other.
- Search—provides a page with a search box.

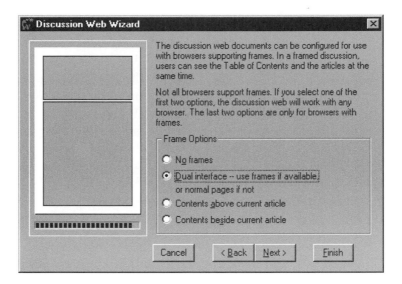

Figure 13.8 *Discussion Webs can be generated in framed and non-framed versions.*

The Customer Support Web is a complex template. Many of the main pages, like the Bugs and Suggestions pages, are linked to other pages that support input forms, confirmation pages, and other pages needed to support the site. If you use this template, you will create a site that is quite large. Editing the structure of the Web generated by this template is tedious.

Study Break

Creating Web Sites Using Web Templates

Practice what you have learned by generating a Web site using the Corporate Presence Web Wizard.

After you generate the Web, perform the first task in the generated task list, and open the Home Page to customize it. Delete the navigation buttons at the top of the page. Change the banner graphic to text.3. Replace the purple comment text with real content (make some up). Edit the information in the shared border at the bottom of the page.

Close the Home Page. View the generated navigational structure in Navigation View of the Front-Page Explorer.

Test the generated in Web site in a browser. What elements are included in the site? (Make yourself a list.)

MCSD 13.2 ## Using Page Templates

FrontPage 98 includes dozens of templates for creating Web pages. To initiate a page using a template, select File, New from the FrontPage Editor menu. The New dialog box supplies a description of every page template.

Figure 13.9 shows the New dialog box, with a page template being previewed in the Preview area. Not all templates come with preview thumbnails, but all templates display at least a description in the New dialog box.

Page templates generally break down into two types—design assistance and content assistance. Design aid includes existing tables, images, and formatted text. Other templates come with content, and can be used as a starting point for a Web page. Many of these pages include hyperlinks.

Finally, page templates are used to generate framed pages. Frames are explored in detail in Chapter 7.

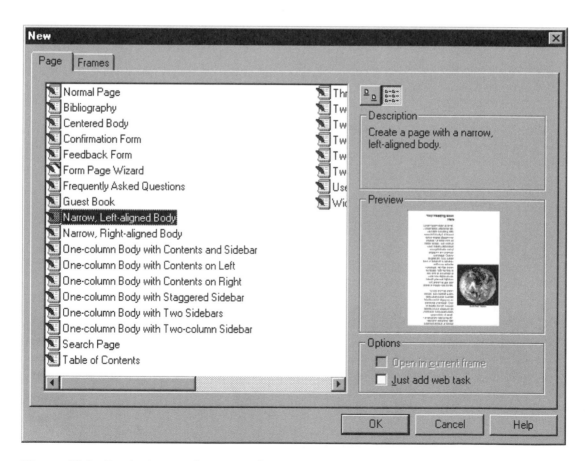

Figure 13.9 *Previewing a Web page template.*

While a familiarity with design-oriented page templates is valuable for a Web designer, the real meaty content is found in page templates that include content. Following is a list of some templates that include substantial FrontPage content:

- The User Registration Page template has a real User Registration Web page with content that describes the purpose of registering as a product user. All you have to do is substitute your Web site name. Figure 13.10 shows the template input form. The comments in the template page explain how to plug the form into a user registration system for your Web site that provides users with usernames and passwords that enable them to access your site.

- The Employee Directory template has hyperlinks on the top of the page and bookmarks to which they are linked in the body of the page.

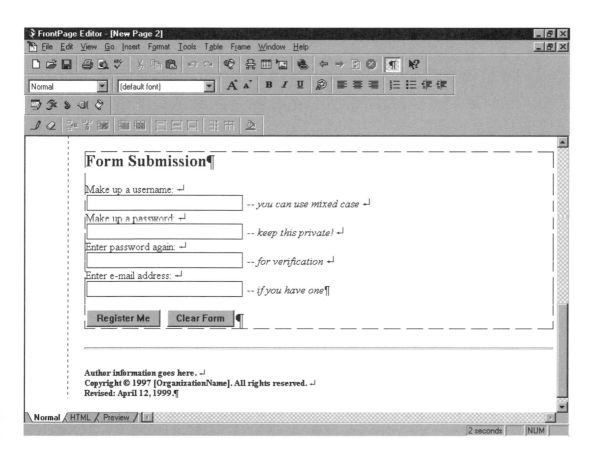

Figure 13.10   *Using a template to create a user registration form.*

- The Feedback Form template creates a Web page with an Input Form. The form fields have been defined, using radio buttons, text boxes, a check box, and Submit and Reset buttons. Figure 13.11 shows part of the feedback template in the FrontPage Editor.

Study Break

Using Page Templates

Practice what you have learned by creating an empty Web site and adding content with page templates.

First, use the Empty Web template to create a new FrontPage Web.

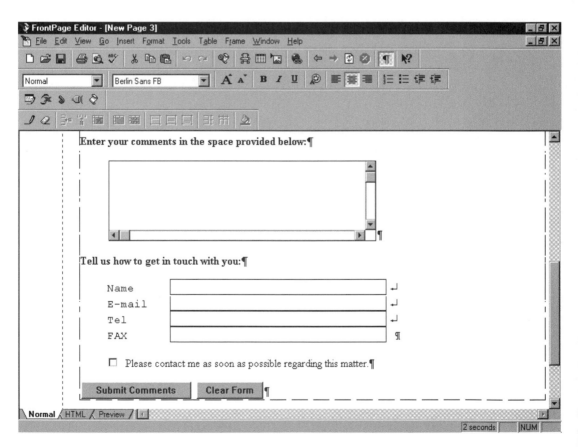

Figure 13.11 *An instant feedback form, courtesy of the Feedback page template.*

Next, create an Employee Directory. Replace the dummy data with some names of your own.

Add a Feedback form, using the Feedback template.

Finally, save the new Web pages, and test them in a browser.

MCSD 13.3 Creating Page Templates

You can create your own page templates. These templates might be used to store the basic elements of a page design (like background color, logos, images, and blocks of text) that you use frequently. Once you create a page template, it will be listed along with FrontPage's built-in templates in the New dialog box, and you can use it to generate new pages.

A user-defined template can include images, text, navigational links, formatting, and any other element that can be placed on a Web page. In a large-scale development environment, user-defined page templates can play a key role in systematizing and speeding up page design.

To create a user-defined page template, follow these steps:

1. Design the Web page that will be used as the template.
2. Select File, Save As. The Save As dialog box appears.
3. In the Save As dialog box, click on the As Template button. The Save As Template dialog box appears, as shown in Figure 13.12.
4. In the Save As Template dialog box, enter a Title, Name, and Description of your template.
5. Click the OK button. You can close your template and use it later to create more Web pages.

When you are ready to use your template, just select File, New from the FrontPage Editor menu.

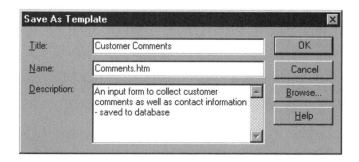

Figure 13.12 *Defining a template.*

Study Break

Defining a Page Template

Practice what you have learned by creating your own custom template.

First, open a FrontPage Web (or create a new one), and select File, New in the FrontPage Editor. Add a bit of text.

Next, save your page as a page template.

Finally, create a new page using the template you just defined.

MCSD 13.4   **Embedded Styles and External Style Sheets**

Styles allow you to apply font and paragraph attributes to text. There are three basic "levels" at which styles can be applied. The most basic level is local styles that are applied only to selected text on a Web page. These styles allow you to add attributes like alignment, line spacing, and borders to selected text.

The next level of style is an embedded, or page-wide style sheet. These embedded style sheets work like style sheets in a word processing or desktop publishing program. You can define style attributes for paragraphs like spacing, alignment, font, color, and borders. Then, you can save those attributes, and apply them to any selected paragraph.

The highest level of style is an external style sheet. An external style sheet is, as its name implies, a file external to the Web page to which it is applied. External style sheets are powerful formatting tools because they can be applied to many pages. And, when an external style sheet is edited, the formatting changes are automatically applied to every Web page to which the style sheet is applied.

When the styles assigned to a page or to text contradict each other, local styles take priority, then page-wide styles, and finally external style sheet attributes apply. For example, if you apply a page-wide style sheet to a page that assigns Arial font to Normal text, you can still select that text and apply a different font to it using a local style.

In this section of this chapter, we'll examine all three types of styles.

Assigning Local Styles

The most basic way to apply styles to text is to use the Style button available in many of the dialog boxes in the FrontPage Editor. These Style buttons are available from the Font dialog box (select Format, Font from the FrontPage Editor menu), the Paragraph dialog box (select Format Paragraph from the FrontPage Editor menu), and many other dialog boxes, including those for Input Form fields. These style buttons in various dialog boxes open the Style dialog box.

The options in the Style dialog box provide some intriguing formatting features not available from the Formatting toolbar or from the Font, Paragraph Properties, or Page Properties dialog boxes. You can assign formatting attributes to selected text without defining (or redefining) embedded styles that apply to an entire page.

The Style dialog box has six tabs for local styles. They are:

- The *Class* tab allows you to apply style that is defined in an embedded style sheet assigned to a page, or from an external style sheet or a style sheet. We'll explore embedded and external styles later in this section.

- The *Alignment* tab defines top, bottom, left and right margin size, padding (around an object), and text wrap attributes.

- The *Borders* tab allows you to assign various combinations of border styles and thickness to the top, bottom, left, and right of objects to which a style is applied.

- The *Font* tab allows you to select a font, font size, and a secondary (backup) font for visitors who do not have your primary font installed. Use standard fonts as secondary fonts.

- The *Colors* tab allows you to define both a background color and a color to assign to the foreground. For example, if you wanted Heading 1 text to be red, with a yellow background, you would select yellow as the background color, and red as the foreground color.

- The *Text* tab allows you more detailed control over how text will display. Features include small caps, text alignment, and the ability to micro-define character spacing and line height.

Styles applied to selected objects on a page are referred to as local, as opposed to embedded style sheets that apply to an entire page.

Defining and Applying Embedded Styles

FrontPage allows you to define and apply styles in the FrontPage Editor that function in a similar way to styles in word processing or desktop publishing programs. You can assign text and paragraph attributes to styles, like font size and color, alignment, etc. Then, you can apply these styles to paragraphs.

A limitation of this process is that the styles you define are applicable only to the page for which they are defined. We'll address that limitation in the next section of this chapter.

The following steps are used to define a style sheet that can be applied to a single page in FrontPage 98:

1. In the FrontPage Editor, select Format, Style sheet. The Format Style sheet dialog box opens, as shown in Figure 13.13.
2. FrontPage will generate code for style attributes, using (generally) recognized standards for style sheets (or CSS, for Cascading Style Sheets). To define a style to which the attributes will be applied, you need to know a bit of HTML code. Here comes the shortest course on HTML you'll ever see: the BODY style defines attributes for a whole page. The styles H1 through H6 define styles Heading 1 through Heading 6. You can define a style by entering BODY, H1, H2, H3, H4, H5 or H6 after the

```
<style>
<!-
```

lines in the dialog box. (Click after the `<!-`, press Enter, and then enter a style to define). This bit of HTML will allow you to experiment with FrontPage's style sheets.

Figure 13.14 shows all six heading styles, plus the BODY style entered.

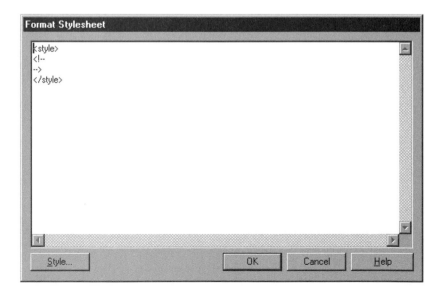

Figure 13.13 *Defining a style sheet for a single page.*

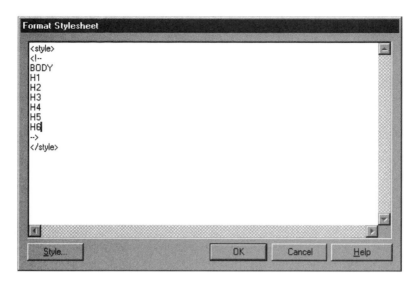

Figure 13.14 *Preparing to define six heading styles and the BODY style for a page.*

3. Click after one of the style names (for example, after BODY, or H1). Then, click on the Style button in the dialog box to define style attributes. The Style dialog box, shown in Figure 13.15, opens, with five tabs for defining various style elements.

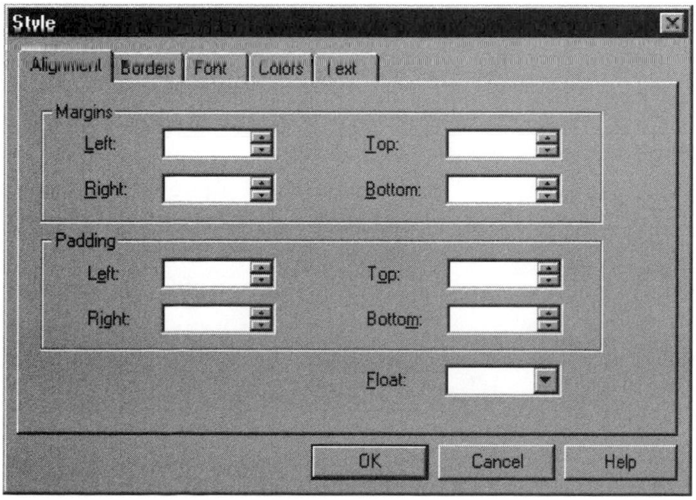

Figure 13.15 *The Style dialog box.*

4. Use the five tabs in the Style dialog box to define attributes for the style to which you are assigning attributes. The tabs are the same as those available for local styles, except that the Class tab is not available because it is used to assign style attributes from style sheets, and here you are defining a style sheet. You might, for example, want to assign a small font for H6 style, and a much larger font for the H1 style. A style sheet that uses the same font (but different sizes and colors) for each style will be the least distracting to readers, while a style sheet that applies a wide variety of fonts and other attributes to styles will add "pizzazz" to a page.

5. After you have defined all the attributes for a selected HTML object (like BODY or H1, for example), click on OK to close the Style dialog box. Figure 13.16 shows the Format Style sheet dialog box, with seven styles defined.

After you define styles for a page, you can apply those styles to elements on a page by selecting text, and then selecting a style from the Change Style drop-down menu. In Figure 13.17 I've applied the six heading styles to text, and the BODY style was applied to the whole page defining the background and foreground (text) colors.

The BODY style is applied automatically to the page as soon as you close the Format Style sheet dialog box.

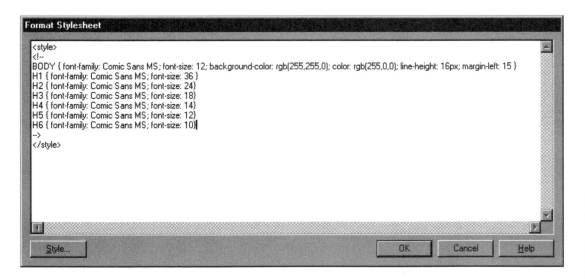

Figure 13.16 *Defined styles.*

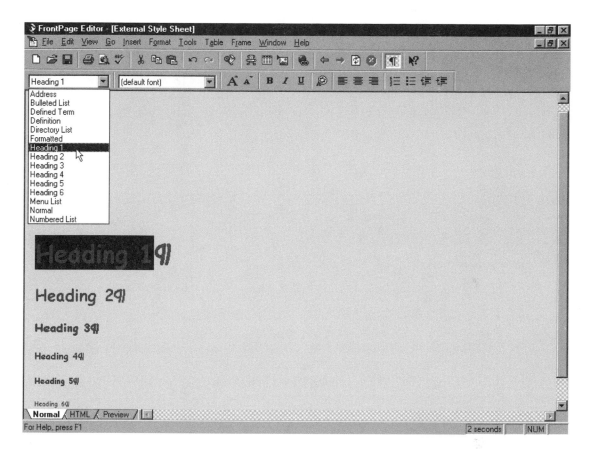

Figure 13.17 *Styles are applied by first selecting text, and then choosing a style from the Change Style drop-down menu in the Formatting toolbar of the FrontPage Editor.*

Compatibility Issues with Styles

The style attributes available in the Style dialog box provide a level of formatting way beyond that allowed by HTML. That would seem to be the answer to a page designer's prayers—minute control over text formatting just like with a high-powered page layout program.

But how compatible are these extra formatting features? I'll let you be the judge. Figure 13.18 shows a page with defined style sheets in Internet Explorer 5 and Netscape Navigator 4.5. You can't tell from this black and white figure that the colors didn't translate, but you probably noticed that the fonts and page background were not interpreted by Netscape.

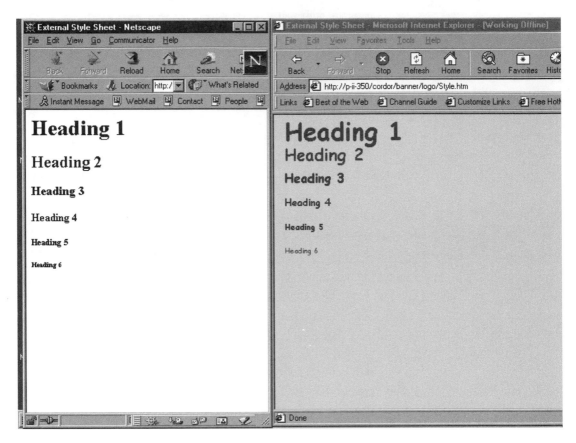

Figure 13.18 *Many elements of FrontPage-generated styles are not recognized by Netscape Navigator 4.5.*

Furthermore, versions of IE prior to version 4 do not provide full support for styles generated by FrontPage 98. In sum, regular HTML formatting assigned in the FrontPage Editor is much more reliably interpreted by browsers, and there are major compatibility issues with assigned styles if visitors are using browsers other than recent versions of IE.

Study Break

Defining and Applying Embedded Styles

Practice what you have learned by creating embedded styles and applying them to a page.

First, open a page in the FrontPage Page Editor, and select Format, Style Sheet.

Next, define three styles: BODY with a blue background and a yellow foreground; H1 with Comic Sans MS font, size 36, and H2 with Comic Sans MS font size 18. Save the page.

Finally, enter two lines of text, and apply Heading 1 style to one and Heading 2 style to the other. Note the display in the FrontPage Editor Preview tab. Preview the page in both Internet Explorer and Netscape Navigator if you have either or both of them installed on your system. Save this page. You'll use it in the next Study Break.

As you probably realized, defining really complex style sheets requires both some detailed knowledge of the features in the Styles dialog box and some HTML code to identify objects to which to assign style attributes. Following are some resources for those two elements of defining style sheets:

- For a complete discussion of FrontPage-defined style sheets, see *FrontPage 98 Bible* by David Elderbrock and Paul Bodensiek (IDG), Chapter 10.

- For a quick introduction to just enough HTML to define styles, see *HTML for Dummies Quick Reference* by Deborah S. Ray and Eric J. Ray (IDG).

- For a detailed discussion of using styles in input forms, see *Teach Yourself FrontPage 98* in a Week by David Karlins, Chapter 10 (Sams).

- For a discussion of creating Netscape-compatible style sheet coding, see *Special Edition Using Netscape Communicator 4*, Chapter 27 by John Simmons (Que).

MCSD 13.5   Creating and Using External Style Sheets

An external style sheet is a file that contains the same kind of information you just learned to define for a single page. The difference is that the style attributes in this page can be applied to any page to which it is linked.

FrontPage 98 does not include any wizards or menu options to generate the required files and coding to define an external style sheet page, or link that file to Web pages. However, now that you've seen how FrontPage can generate style coding to define styles, you can use that feature to set up external style sheets that can be used for multiple Web pages.

Here's the routine for defining an external style sheet file in FrontPage, and then using that file for multiple Web pages:

1. Start by creating a style sheet for a single page, as outlined in steps 1–5 in the previous set of steps in this chapter. Your style sheet should look something like the one illustrated back in Figure 13.16.

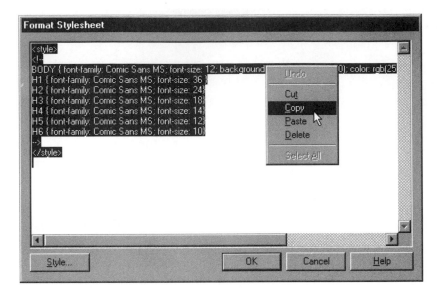

Figure 13.19 *Copying style sheet coding.*

2. Click and drag to select the entire contents of the Style dialog box. Right-click on the selected code, and choose Copy from the context menu, as shown in Figure 13.19.
3. Open a new file in a text editing program, like Notepad.
4. Select Edit, Paste to copy the style sheet coding into the text editor.
5. Save the text file with a *.css file name extension, like styles.css, for example.
6. After you have saved the *.css file, import that file into your FrontPage Web. Be sure you import the file into the same folder as the pages that will access the styles. An imported CSS file is shown in the FrontPage Explorer in Figure 13.20.
7. To apply the external style sheet file to a page, enter the following code at the beginning of the page, after the first <head> code in the HTML tab, substituting your style sheet file name for xxx.css:

```
<link REL="stylesheet" HREF="xxx.css" TYPE="text/css">
```

8. After you enter the line of code in HTML tab, save your page. External styles will be reflected in the FrontPage Editor. You can apply the linked external styles by selecting Styles from the Change Style drop-down menu in the Formatting toolbar.

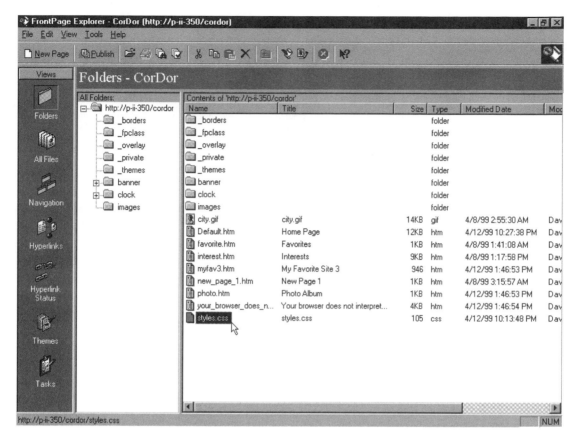

Figure 13.20   *An imported style sheet file.*

Defining and Applying an External Style Sheet

Practice what you have learned by creating an external style sheet, and applying the styles in the CSS file to Web pages.

First, open the page in the FrontPage Page Editor that you used in the last Study Break to define a style sheet for a page. Select and copy all the coding in the Style sheet dialog box for that page.

Next, open a text editor like Notepad, and paste the copied code into the text editor. Save the text editor file as style.css. Import that file (style.css) into the FrontPage Web using the File, Import option in the FrontPage Explorer.

Finally, Enter the following line of code after the first <head> code in the HTML tab:

```
<link REL="stylesheet" HREF="style.css" TYPE="text/css">.
```

Save your page, and view the page in Normal view of the FrontPage Editor. Note the effect of the attached external style sheet. Copy the line of style sheet code from the HTML tab in your page to other pages in your Web site to apply the external style sheet to those pages as well.

■ Summary

FrontPage's Web and Page templates are more than just a way to get quick page layout help. Web templates generate sites with complex and editable features like discussion forums, input forms, search boxes, and tables of contents. Page templates create pages with frames, defined feedback forms, and corporate directories.

FrontPage generates three levels of style attributes: local, page, and external. Add a bit of HTML coding, and you can use FrontPage's style sheets to generate and apply external style sheets. Local styles apply only to selected objects. Local styles apply just to selected text. Embedded styles apply to an entire page. External style sheets can be applied to multiple pages.

▲ CHAPTER REVIEW QUESTIONS

Here are some practice questions relating to the material covered in the "Using Style Sheets and Templates" area of *Microsoft's Designing and Implementing Web Sites Using Microsoft FrontPage 98* exam (70-055).

1. *If a Web site requires user registration, the User Registration Web wizard will help generate the necessary Web pages.*

    A. True

    B. False

2. *Which of the following are generated by the Corporate Presence Web wizard? (Select all correct answers.)*

    A. A Search page

    B. Learning files used with the FrontPage tutorial

    C. A Schedule Page that posts tasks due this week and next week

    D. A Feedback page

    E. A Products/Services page

3. *Internet Explorer version 2 presents a compatibility problem for external style sheets.*

   A. True
   B. False

4. *If you needed to include a Discussion Forum in a Web site, the easiest way to generate it might well be the Discussion Page template.*

   A. True
   B. False

5. *Page templates can be used to generate user registration forms, framed pages, and an employee directory.*

   A. True
   B. False

6. *Which of the following can be generated directly in the FrontPage Editor? (Select all correct answers.)*

   A. External style sheets
   B. Style sheets that apply to the selected page
   C. Local styles that apply only to selected text
   D. Netscape-compatible external style sheets
   E. Style sheets that detect firewall penetration

7. *Which of the following elements of a FrontPage Web site will likely present compatibility problems when the site is viewed in Netscape Navigator 4 or higher? (Select all correct answers.)*

   A. Web pages generated from FrontPage 98's Personal Web template
   B. External style sheets
   C. Local styles
   D. Page-specific style sheets
   E. FrontPage Themes

8. *Embedded style sheets apply to an entire Web site.*

   A. True
   B. False

9. *FrontPage will generate external style sheets in the Style sheet dialog box of the FrontPage Editor.*

   A. True
   B. False

10. *HTML styles like H1 and BODY can be redefined using external style sheets.*

    A. True

    B. False

11. *Styles provide formatting control beyond that available in HTML.*

    A. True

    B. False

12. *Which of the following types of pages can be generated by templates? (Select all correct answers.)*

    A. Discussion forums

    B. Collapsible outlines

    C. Page transitions

    D. User defined custom pages

    E. Themes

13. *The Customer Support Web generates a download page that can be used with an FTP server.*

    A. True

    B. False

14. *Which of the following Web templates generates a Feedback form? (Select all correct answers.)*

    A. The Empty Web template

    B. The Personal Web template

    C. The Customer Support Web

    D. The Discussion Web wizard

    E. The Feedback Form template

15. *Styles applied to specific selected text take priority over which other styles? (Select all correct answers.)*

    A. Style sheets assigned to a page

    B. Styles applied from an external CSS file

    C. Formatting applied directly from the Formatting toolbar

    D. Browser-compatible Java applets

    E. Text files

Publishing and Testing a FrontPage 98 Web Site

One of the more critical areas of FrontPage Web development is posting and updating Web pages to servers. A Web site is not much good if it cannot be made accessible via an intranet or the World Wide Web! In Chapter 14 we'll walk through the procedure for posting content to servers with FrontPage extensions, and also to Web sites without FrontPage extensions. In Chapter 15 we'll develop a routine for maintaining a FrontPage Web, including maintaining site organization, locating orphaned pages, and identifying and fixing broken hyperlinks. In Chapter 16 we'll look at new technology issues, including publishing Web channels with FrontPage. And finally, in Chapter 17, we'll look at access and security challenges, including administering Web access, using the Registration page template, and configuring FrontPage for a proxy server.

Publishing a FrontPage Web Site

Few elements of FrontPage Web management cause as much chaos and confusion as publishing Webs from one server to another. Most developers, even experienced Web site managers, are not used to the method by which FrontPage publishes and then transfers published Webs from one server to another.

In this chapter we'll walk through the process of moving FrontPage Webs from server to server, and I'll share some experiences troubleshooting this procedure.

We will also examine the options for controlling who can post content to a Web site. And, we'll take a look at FrontPage's somewhat controversial Database Region Wizard, which provides one option for sharing data from a server database with visitors to a Web page.

At the conclusion of this chapter you will be able to:

- Publish FrontPage Webs to Web servers.
- Publish Webs to more than one server.
- Define mechanisms and safeguards for controlling who can publish content to a Web site.
- Use the Database Region Wizard to provide access to database information in a FrontPage Web Site.

MCSD 14.1   Publishing a FrontPage Web Site

If you have spent some time in the trenches troubleshooting FrontPage development, you've no doubt encountered quite a bit of confusion about the relationship between FrontPage Webs and servers. If you haven't spent time troubleshooting FrontPage development, take it from those of us who have—you will. It will be helpful to start out by reviewing the basic concepts and terminology involved in *publishing* a Web site.

Unlike other Web development strategies, where sites are created in components like HTML pages, images, and scripts and *then* those files are uploaded to a Web server, FrontPage 98 *starts with the server*. From the moment a FrontPage Web is initiated in the FrontPage Explorer, a server connection is established and a for-real, Web server-based Web site is created.

In most FrontPage development environments, the initial Web is developed and saved to a local server, either the FrontPage Personal Web Server, the Microsoft Personal Web Server, or Internet Information Server. Once the Web is developed, it can be *published* to another server, typically an online server that provides a connection to the Internet, or a local intranet server.

Finally, be aware that FrontPage users who are new to the whole concept of Web server software will be inclined to think in terms of folders or directories on their operating system instead of looking at FrontPage Webs as being entities that are only functional in the context of the server software. The many files that comprise a FrontPage Web must be saved to, organized by, and managed by Web Server software. You may need to patiently and repeatedly educate new developers that they should not attempt to circumvent the server software by locating, opening, or editing files directly on their local drives as if those files were freestanding files that could be edited by a word processor or other application software. Instead, we must preach the mantra that no element of a FrontPage Web should be tampered with without first opening the entire Web in the FrontPage Explorer.

When you first initiate a Web in the FrontPage Explorer, the New FrontPage Web dialog box actually assigns a server and server folder. The routine is:

1. After launching FrontPage, click on the Create New FrontPage Web option button in the Getting Started dialog box (or select File, New, FrontPage Web from the menu). The New FrontPage Web dialog box appears, as shown in Figure 14.1.

2. Note that in the "2" area of the New FrontPage Web dialog box, underneath the Choose a Title For Your FrontPage Web box, there is a server location. FrontPage could be more explicit about the fact that a server destination is being defined. Perhaps the folks at MS were trying to shield mere mortal users from dealing with server issues, but certainly at our level of expertise, we need to be conscious of the server linkage being defined when new Webs are created.

3. When you click on the Change button in the New FrontPage Web dialog box, the Change Location dialog box appears, as shown in Figure 14.2.

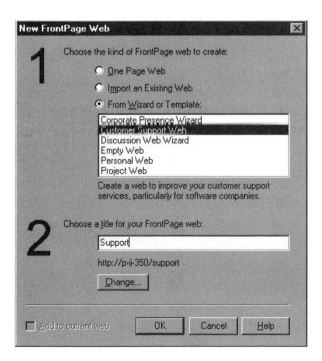

Figure 14.1 *You're not just creating a Web site, you're defining a Server folder.*

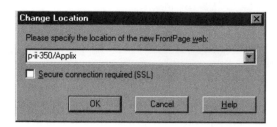

Figure 14.2 *Defining a server destination for a FrontPage Web.*

Here, you can accept a default location (usually a local server), or enter another server address.

4. After noting, or changing the server and folder in the Change Location dialog box, OK all dialog boxes to generate a Web folder on the designated server.

In Chapter 6, "Establishing a Development Environment," we explored the process of installing the Personal Web Server, and FrontPage 98 server extensions. When you use any version of the Personal Web Server or when you develop Webs on other servers with FrontPage extensions, you can implement and test essentially all the features that FrontPage has to offer. To put that negatively, without FrontPage server extensions on the supporting Web server, many of FrontPage's most valuable features like input form data handling and image maps are disabled.

In short, the very act of *creating* a FrontPage Web is *publishing* that Web to a server. Publishing a Web is also the way a FrontPage Web is transferred from one server to another. For example, in a typical development scenario, a Web might be developed first using a version of the Personal Web Server, and then *published* (again) to another server to be accessed from an intranet or the Internet. We'll explore that process in the next section of this chapter.

Troubleshooting Server Issues

Because most developers come to FrontPage from other, less integrated Web publishing systems, it is often necessary to do reeducation as to how Front-Page handles publishing Webs. As a FrontPage expert, your job includes proselytizing about FrontPage's holy trinity: FrontPage Explorer, FrontPage Editor, and a FrontPage Server (often one of the two Personal Web Servers). *All three* components of FrontPage 98 must be running together to create Web sites that will handle the functionality assigned by FrontPage components.

Signs that development is proceeding disconnected from a Web server include:

- Developers are creating Web pages but they do not have FrontPage Explorer running.
- Developers are complaining that features like image maps and form handling are "not working" in FrontPage.
- Developers are asking your advice on how to "upload files" to a server.
- Developers are asking you which disk folders are used to store their files.

Study Break

Identify Your Server

Practice what you have learned by identifying the default server on the computer with which you are working.

First, generate a new Web using the Personal Web template, but do not click on OK in the New FrontPage Web dialog box.

Next, note the current default server in the "2" area of the New FrontPage Web dialog box. This is the server to which your Web will be saved.

Finally, click on Cancel. We won't generate this Web now, we've simply identified the server to which Webs on your computer are saved.

Note

Isn't it technically possible to simply use the FrontPage Editor to create Web pages without the FrontPage Explorer (or a server) running? Yes, it is. And, those files (and embedded images) can simply be saved as HTML files (or image files) in a disk-based folder, and then uploaded to a Web server. Doing that in FrontPage is a bit like using a bazooka to kill a fly, and requires circumventing the built-in connections between FrontPage Explorer, FrontPage Editor, and a server.

MCSD 14.2   Publishing to Multiple Servers

In a typical FrontPage development environment, FrontPage Webs are first published to a version of the Personal Web Server, or Internet Information Server, and then published (republished) to a server connected to the Internet. Other scenarios include moving a FrontPage Web from one Internet server to another, or from one intranet server to another. Finally, there are times when you will want to publish a site from an Internet server to a local computer or intranet server. This last option can be used to back up a site from an Internet server to a local server.

You can publish a FrontPage Web to only one location at a time. You can, however, repeat the process of publishing a Web to upload a FrontPage Web to multiple servers.

FrontPage manages the process of copying all necessary folders and files automatically for situations where both the source and target servers have FrontPage 98 extensions.

Publishing to an Internet or Intranet Server

If you are contracting with an offsite server that supports FrontPage, you need two things from the server provider or administrator:

- A Name
- A Password

Armed with that information, follow these steps to publish a FrontPage Web:

1. Open the FrontPage Web in the FrontPage Explorer.
2. Click on the Publish button in the FrontPage Explorer. The Publish dialog box opens, as shown in Figure 14.3.
3. Click on the More Webs button. The Publish FrontPage Web dialog box opens.
4. Enter the URL of the destination Web server in the dialog box. If you are shopping for a Web site provider that supports FrontPage, click on the Connect to the Microsoft FrontPage Web Site button. That site provides links to hundreds of providers, as shown in Figure 14.4.

Note

The default setting is to publish files that have changes only. If you are publishing a Web to an already existing Web, you can either publish the entire Web to the target location, or just changed pages. We'll explore this scenario in more detail a bit later in this chapter.

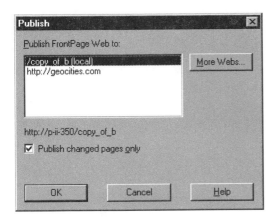

Figure 14.3 *The Publish dialog box.*

5. After you enter a URL for the destination of your Web server, click on the OK button. If you are publishing to a different site, you'll be prompted for a Name and Password, as shown in Figure 14.5.

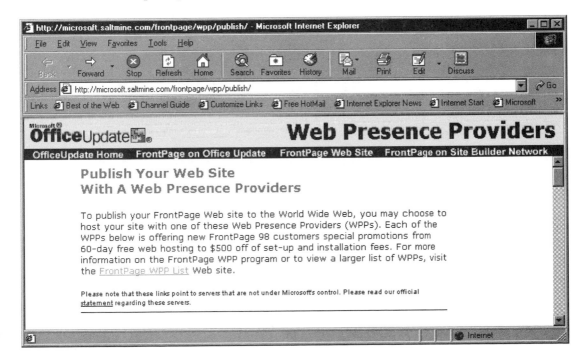

Figure 14.4 *Shopping for Web hosting.*

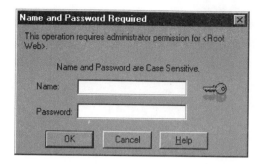

Figure 14.5 *Entering Name and Password is all that is required to publish a FrontPage Web to a server with FrontPage 98 extensions.*

6. After your site is published, you will see a confirmation in the Status bar of the FrontPage Explorer.

Uploading a FrontPage Web Site from One Server to Another

One of the most frequently asked questions/troubleshooting issues at my online FrontPage 98 Forum (at www.ppinet.com) involves problems of moving Webs from one server to another. The following Q&A is slightly edited from one of those exchanges, and will help prepare you to interpret and troubleshoot Web publishing problems:

Q: David, I uploaded my site to server. That went fine. Then I wanted to download it onto my second machine, this worked fine as well. When I tried to then open up the site on the second machine all files etc. were present but there was nothing in navigation view. Is it possible to get the complete working site with all pages intact etc downloaded to my second computer?

A: Your "2nd computer" must have a server with FP extensions installed. You should use the FrontPage Publish Web dialog box to publish your Web to the second machine.

Q: Thanks for the reply, David. I have PWS installed on my second machine, and I was able to download the site after I uploaded from the other PC. The problem is that the downloaded site simply contained all the files etc., it did not contain any structure of the site. Navigation view simply displayed one single home page. If you can, answer the question: Should I be able to download a site in its entirety and then navigate that site exactly as I would any other site on my machine? If the answer is yes, then I have done something wrong.

A: I'm concerned about your continuing use of the term "download." You need to use the *Publish* feature to *publish* your Web from your online server to your local Web server—which is installed on your 2nd machine. Is that what you're doing?

Q: David, I am "importing" the Web from my server to my machine. RESULT: One solitary home page. No structure! But all files are present.

A: Imported Webs don't retain navigation structure, published Webs do. You can either publish your Web from your online server to your local computer or redo the navigation links. You still never explained why you aren't using the *Publish* feature. Is there some reason why this won't work?

Q: Oh. *Publish!*

Publishing Changed Pages

Returning to the frequent scenario where one copy of a Web is on a local server and one is on the Internet . . .what happens if you want to change the Internet version of the site?

There are two options in this situation. You can directly open the Internet version of the site. To do that, select File, Open FrontPage Web in the FrontPage Explorer. Use the Getting Started dialog box to open an existing Web (click on the More Webs button if necessary). The second option is to revise the site offline on your local or intranet server, and then publish (upload) your changes.

To publish changes to a FrontPage Web site from one server to another, follow these steps:

1. Open the version of the Web in which you will make editing changes.
2. Make changes to your source Web.
3. Select File, Publish FrontPage Web from the FrontPage Explorer menu. (You can also click the Publish button.)
4. In the Publish dialog box, select the target Web server using the More Webs button if necessary.
5. You will usually want to select the Publish Changed Pages Only check box, as shown in Figure 14.6. This is the default.
6. Click on OK in the Publish dialog box to send only revised files to the second server.

Study Break

Publishing a Web from One Server to Another

Practice what you have learned by publishing a backup copy of a FrontPage Web.

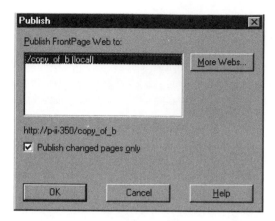

Figure 14.6 *Publishing only changed pages.*

First, open an existing FrontPage Web.

Next, click on the Publish button. Accept the default settings to publish a backup copy of your Web to the same server.

Make some changes in the original Web, including adding some new pages.

Finally, publish only the changed pages to the second Web.

Uploading Files to Servers Without FrontPage Extensions

If you attempt to publish your FrontPage Web to a server without FrontPage extensions, FrontPage will automatically launch the Microsoft Web Publishing Wizard, as shown in Figure 14.7. The Web Publishing Wizard uses File Transfer Protocol (FTP) to transfer your files to the target server. Therefore, you will need an FTP Server Name and Directory Path in order to use the wizard.

After you enter the FTP Server Name and directory path, click on the Next button in the wizard. You will be prompted for a user name and password. Then click on Finish.

As the files upload to the FTP site, you will see a Transferring Files dialog box, as shown in Figure 14.8

After the FTP transfer, you'll see either a confirmation or an error message notifying you that the information you supplied was not correct or complete.

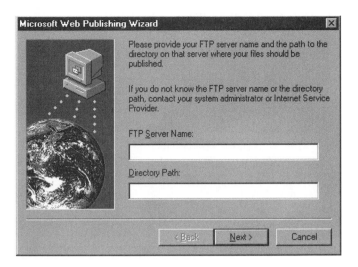

Figure 14.7 *The Microsoft Web Publishing Wizard uploads sites to servers without FrontPage extension files.*

Study Break

Publishing a Web to a Server Without FrontPage Extensions

Practice what you have learned by creating a Web site and uploading it to a non-FrontPage-enabled Web server. As an optional tutorial, if you don't have access to a non-FrontPage server and you want a real-life exercise in using File Transfer Protocol, you can follow the specific steps below to acquire a free Web site from Geocities.com, and upload a FrontPage site there. Otherwise, disregard the Geocities-specific instructions, and test your skills with another server.

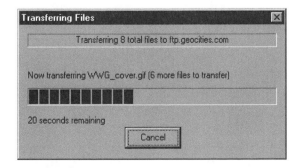

Figure 14.8 *Using File Transfer Protocol to move files to a non-FrontPage Web site.*

First, open a FrontPage Web using a version of the Personal Web server.

Next, obtain an FTP address and path, a user Name and a Password for a non-FrontPage Web server. If you don't have access to a non-FrontPage server, you can sign up for one by following the "Free Site" instructions at www.geocities.com.

Select File, Publish in the FrontPage Explorer. (Make sure you are logged on to an Internet connection). Select File, Publish FrontPage Web from the FrontPage Explorer. Click on the More Webs button in the Publish dialog box, and enter the FTP address of your target server. (If you're using Geocities, the FTP address is ftp.geocities.com). Click on OK. Transfer your Web to a non-FrontPage server.

Finally, make some changes to your Web, and use FTP to move only the revised pages to the server.

MCSD 14.3 Using the Database Region Wizard

The Database Region Wizard creates a *region* within a Web page that displays all or (usually) only a part of the contents of a database saved to the Web server. In that sense, database regions are an active element within a Web page, in that they automatically update to display data based on any changes made to the embedded database. You can use the Database Region Wizard, for example, to keep clients posted on current inventory, based on data in an on-line database.

The Database Region Wizard is not easy to use. The comedian Steve Martin used to do a routine called "How to make a million dollars and not pay any taxes." To start out, Steve told the audience that they should go get a million dollars and he'd walk them through the part about not paying taxes. Using the Database Region Wizard is a bit like that. Once you have all the required elements needed for the wizard, the wizard itself is not that hard. The hard part is creating the components that you need to make the wizard function. All (all!) you need is:

- A server with Active Server Pages extension files
- A database registered as an ODBC data source
- A working knowledge of SQL

That's it. If you have all that, you're ready to create a Database Region Wizard.

Microsoft doesn't expect you to be an expert at database management, but the expectation is that, provided with all of the above, you can provide access to database data using the FrontPage Database Region Wizard.

We'll discuss the required elements and where they come from, and then walk through how to integrate those components into a FrontPage Web page that provides visitors data from a database.

Adding Active Server Pages to a Server

Web pages with Database Regions must be saved as *.asp (Active Server Pages) files, and will be displayed only in a browser if saved to a server with ASP capability.

In order to test the Database Region Wizard, you must have Active Server Pages technology installed on your Web server. If you do not, the FrontPage 98 CD has a program (ASP.exe) that installs Active Server Pages to the Personal Web Server. The executable file that installs ASP is buried in the E:\60 Minute Intranet Kit\60 Minute Intranet Kit\modules folder on the FrontPage 98 CD. The file you need to install ASP is asp.exe.

To install ASP, follow these steps:

1. Double-click on the file asp.exe on the FrontPage 98 CD. The installation program for ASP launches. Click on OK in the license window, and the first install dialog box appears, as shown in Figure 14.9. Then click on Next.
2. If you already have ASP installed, the wizard window shown in Figure 14.10 appears, allowing you to either reinstall ASP, or remove it.

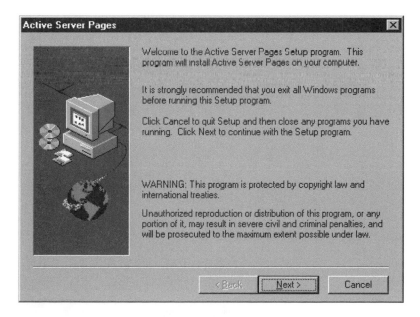

Figure 14.9 *Beginning to install ASP.*

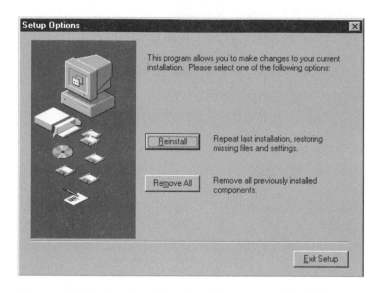

Figure 14.10 *Options for reinstalling or removing ASP.*

3. If you have the Personal Web Server running, you will be prompted to stop it before you can install ASP. Select Yes when prompted to turn off the PWS.

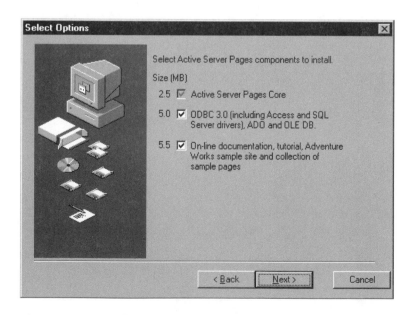

Figure 14.11 *Selecting ODBC components.*

4. When the Select Options wizard window appears, choose the ODBC check box, as shown in Figure 14.11. Then click on Next.

5. When the Select Paths wizard window appears, confirm the default installation directory, or use the Browse button to change it. The Select Paths window is shown in Figure 14.12. You do *not* need to install ASP in any particular directory, or change the default directory, in order for FrontPage and your Web server to detect the ASP software.

6. After you have confirmed or changed the installation folder, click Next. ASP software will be installed on your system.

After you install ASP to your Web server, you have one of the elements in place to test a Database Region—a server that supports *.asp pages.

Registering a Database as an ODBC Data Source

In order to utilize a database in a Database Region, you must import the database table and then register that file as an Open DataBase Connectivity (ODBC) file.

With a FrontPage Web open, import the database file (it can be in any database file format, like a Microsoft Access *.mdb file), follow these steps to register the database as an ODBC file:

1. Select File, Import to open the Import dialog box and import the database file.

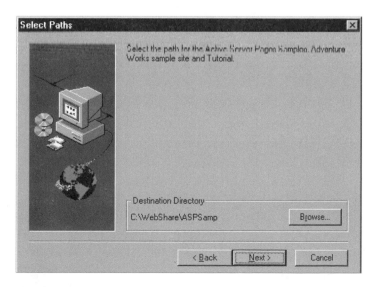

Figure 14.12 *Selecting a location for the ASP software files.*

2. Next, open the Windows Control Panel, and double-click on the ODBC Data Sources icon (may have a slightly different name depending on your operating system) to open the ODBC Data Sources program.
3. In the User DSN tab of the ODBC Data Source Administrator window, select the User DSN tab. This might vary depending on the version of Windows you are using.
4. In the User DSN (or similar) tab, you will see a list of available Drivers. Select the one that matches your database file. In Figure 14.13, I am selecting a Microsoft Access (*.mdb) file. After selecting a file source, click on Add, then Finish.
5. After selecting a file source, you'll see another dialog box prompting you for a Data Source Name. This is a name you make up that will identify your ODBC file later on in FrontPage. Enter a name, and click on OK in the rest of the dialog boxes.

You now have created an ODBC file that you will use in the Database Region Wizard.

Defining Queries in SQL

The final element you need to have ready in order to be prepared to complete the Database Region Wizard is a query that will define what is being

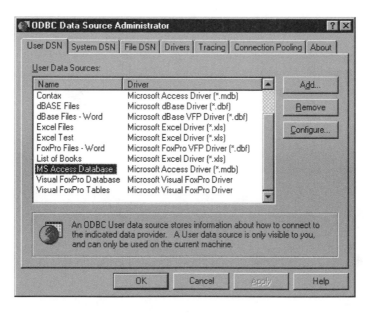

Figure 14.13 *Converting an Access file to ODBC.*

displayed from your database. This query must be described in Structured Query Language (SQL), and we won't attempt a crash course in SQL coding here. However, you can copy or generate SQL queries from some databases.

For example, in Microsoft Access, after you generate a Query from a database, you can select View, SQL View, and view the query you constructed as SQL code. Figure 14.14 shows such a view. If you copy the SQL code into the Clipboard, FrontPage will help out by prompting you to paste it into the Database Region Wizard.

Creating a Database Region Wizard

After you have installed ASP to your server, imported and converted your database to an ODBC data source, and picked up a bit of SQL coding, running the Database Region Wizard is breeze. Here's how to display database data in your Web page:

1. Open a FrontPage Web, import a database, and convert that database to ODBC. The database is now available, on your server, and can be embedded in a Web page.
2. Open a Web page in the FrontPage Editor. Place your insertion point where the data will display from the database, and select Insert, Database, Database Region. The Database Region Wizard appears.
3. Enter the Data Source Name you defined for your ODBC database, as shown in Figure 14.15.
4. Use the Username and Password check boxes and fields only if required by the database file. Then click on Next.
5. The next wizard window asks for a SQL query. Here's where you paste the SQL code you copied from your database. Of course, the other option is that you are, or have access to, an SQL coder. In Figure 14.16, I've pasted some SQL code into the dialog box. After you paste some code, click on Next.

Figure 14.14 *Copying an SQL query into the Clipboard.*

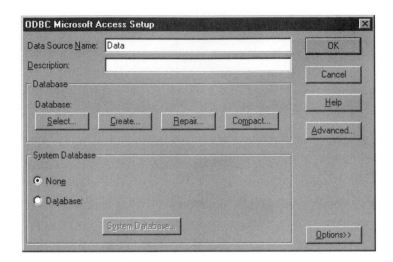

Figure 14.15 *Entering an ODBC Name.*

6. The final wizard window requires that you list the field in your database that you wish to display. You can expect a database developer to provide you with this data, or you can dig into the database and find field names to display. Figure 14.17 shows fields entered into the Wizard to display. Finally, click Finish.

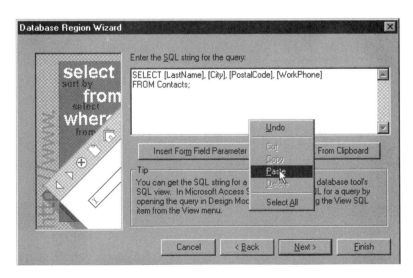

Figure 14.16 *Pasted SQL code.*

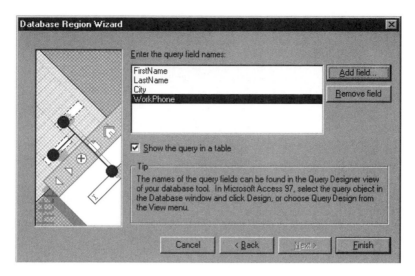

Figure 14.17 *Field names for a database query.*

When you finish generating a Database Region, you'll see a warning that you need to allow scripts to run in the folder to which you save the Web page with the Database Region. There are actually two steps to this: saving the page as an *.asp page, and enabling the Server folder to run scripts. These steps will walk you through that process:

1. After you have embedded a Database Region in your Web page in the FrontPage Editor, select File, Save As. The Save As dialog box appears.
2. In the Save As dialog box, enter a URL with an *.asp file name extension, like the one in Figure 14.18. Then click on OK.
3. In the FrontPage Explorer, select the folder to which the *.asp page was saved. Choose Edit, Properties from the FrontPage Explorer menu, and click on the Allow Scripts or Programs to Be Run check box, as you see in Figure 14.19.
4. You can preview your *.asp Web page in a browser the same way you preview an HTML page: in the FrontPage Editor, select File, Preview in Browser. Figure 14.20 shows a Database Region page in the FrontPage Editor. And Figure 14.21 shows the same page viewed in a browser.

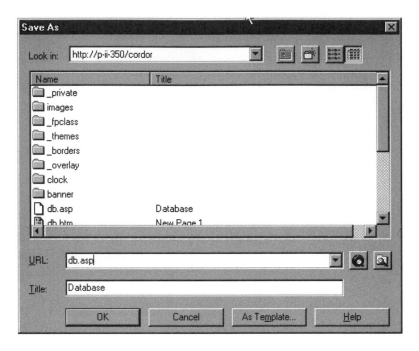

Figure 14.18   *Saving a page as an *.asp file.*

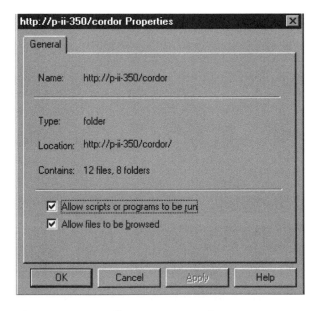

Figure 14.19   *Allowing scripts to be run.*

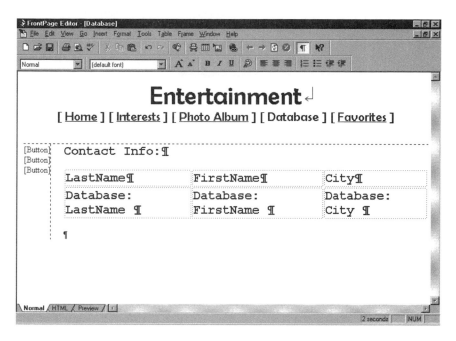

Figure 14.20   *A FrontPage Database Region in the FrontPage Editor.*

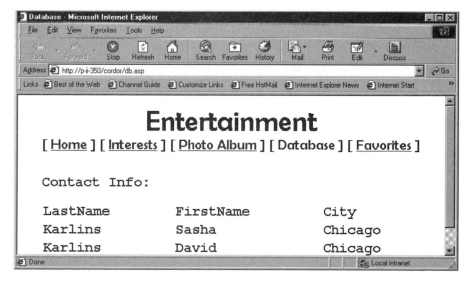

Figure 14.21   *A FrontPage Database Region in Internet Explorer.*

Study Break

Defining a Database Region in a Web Page

If you haven't been supplied with an ODBC file, let alone a source database file and a query, it is quite a bit of work to define a Database Region in a Web page. However, you will be expected to understand how Database Regions work, so walking through this Study Break exercise will be helpful.

First, install ASP on your Web server if it is not installed already.

Then, create a database file, or open an existing one in a database program.

Next, import the database file into a FrontPage Web.

Then, convert the database to an ODBC data source.

Finally, embed the ODBC data source into a FrontPage Web page using the Database Region Wizard.

■ Summary

As long as developers publish FrontPage Webs to servers with FrontPage extensions, the process of publishing (and republishing) FrontPage Webs is graceful and smooth. If developers try to circumvent the built-in publishing features, however, there is a good chance they will effectively disable much of the functionality of FrontPage. FrontPage 98 also offers the option of using File Transfer Protocol to publish Web sites to servers that do not have FrontPage extensions.

In this chapter, you also learned how FrontPage can support Database Regions in Web pages. These regions provide live access to online data. They require that ASP software be installed on the server, that a database be imported into a Web, and that this database be registered as an ODBC file.

▲ CHAPTER REVIEW QUESTIONS

Here are some practice questions relating to the material covered in the "Publishing and Managing a FrontPage Web" area of Microsoft's *Designing and Implementing Web Sites Using Microsoft FrontPage 98* exam (70-055).

1. *FrontPage allows you to publish only changed pages to a server.*

    A. True

    B. False

2. *Which of the following are reliable options for posting FrontPage Webs to a Web site? (Select all correct answers.)*

   A. Using FrontPage's built-in FTP wizard to transfer files to a server

   B. Publishing the files directly to a server from FrontPage

   C. Uploading files from local drive file folders

   D. Uploading files using the Import dialog box

   E. Using the Express dialog box

3. *Database Regions require databases be saved as Active Server Pages files.*

   A. True

   B. False

4. *Database Regions can display data from almost any database.*

   A. True

   B. False

5. *FrontPage Webs cannot be created without publishing them.*

   A. True

   B. False

6. *Which of the following are required to create a Database Region? (Select all correct answers.)*

   A. A Web folder enabled for scripts

   B. A server that runs Active Server Pages

   C. A query in SQL language

   D. An Access database file

   E. An ODBC data source

7. *If a FrontPage Active Server Page is not displaying correctly in a browser, which of the following could be the problem? (Select all correct answers.)*

   A. The page was saved to a folder for which scripts were not enabled

   B. The page has external style sheets

   C. The Web server is not enabled for ASP

   D. The page was not saved with an *.asp file name extension

   E. The Web was not saved with an *.asp file name extension

8. *FrontPage Webs can be published to as many as six servers simultaneously.*

    A. True

    B. False

9. *FrontPage Webs cannot be saved directly to servers that do not support FrontPage extensions.*

    A. True

    B. False

10. *Server locations are defined for FrontPage Webs as soon as the Web is created.*

    A. True

    B. False

11. *Importing individual Web pages from one server to another is the best way to preserve the site's navigation structure.*

    A. True

    B. False

12. *Which of the following are signs that developers have not properly initiated a FrontPage Web before creating Web pages? (Select all correct answers.)*

    A. FrontPage Explorer is not running during page editing

    B. Page formatting is not being applied

    C. Image maps are not functioning when previewed in a browser

    D. Pages are being saved to files with an *.asp file format

    E. Pages are being saved to local drives instead of FrontPage Webs

13. *The only way to define a Database Region is with an SQL query.*

    A. True

    B. False

14. *ASP can be installed from (Select all correct answers):*

    A. The FrontPage Explorer

    B. The FrontPage Editor

    C. The Web Server Administrator

    D. The Web Server wizard

    E. The FrontPage CD

Maintaining a FrontPage 98 Web Site

Today's Web site developer can be responsible for a mind-boggling network of Web pages, with associated links, images, and embedded files. One of the great advantages of development with FrontPage is the program's built-in Web management features.

Simply being able to graphically view (and print) the navigational layout of a site in FrontPage is a tremendous help in communicating and consulting on Web design strategies. Beyond that, Front-Page can automatically check and either identify or fix a disrupted hyperlink in a Web site. In this chapter, we'll explore these automated Web management tools.

At the conclusion of this chapter you will be able to:

- Understand the basic options for managing a FrontPage Web Site.
- Analyze and maintain the organization of a FrontPage Web.
- Locate orphaned Web pages.
- Publish updated Web content.
- Verify hyperlinks.

MCSD 15.1 Managing a FrontPage Web Site Overview

FrontPage provides powerful tools for managing and maintaining a FrontPage Web. Those tools allow you to view your site from several perspectives, including hyperlinks between site objects, file folders and directories in your Web, and navigational structure.

A typical maintenance routine for a FrontPage Web might include the following:

- Periodic testing and updating of internal hyperlinks using the Recalculate Hyperlinks feature.
- Periodic testing and fixing external hyperlinks using the Verify Hyperlinks feature.
- Examining and printing a schematic of all hyperlinks.
- Identify and delete unnecessary orphan pages.
- Printing the site navigational structure.
- Examining file and directory contents and status.
  In this chapter, we'll walk through the procedures for all of these maintenance tasks.

Study Break

Examine Site Maintenance Views

Practice what you have learned by examining a Web using FrontPage 98's site maintenance views.

First, generate a new Web using the Personal Web template.

Next, view the Web in Hyperlink Status view. Note the status of any existing hyperlinks (external hyperlinks cannot be verified if you are not online). Then, examine the site in All Files view. Are there any Orphan files?

Finally, view the site in Navigation View. Select File, Print Navigation View to create a hardcopy printout of the navigational structure of the Web.

You can delete this Web by selecting File, Delete FrontPage Web from the FrontPage Explorer menu bar.

MCSD 15.2   Analyzing and Maintaining Site Organization

The organization of a FrontPage Web can be viewed from three main perspectives: the navigational structure, the file and directory structure, and the hyperlink structure.

If you are familiarizing site developers (or users) with the site layout, you might want to share a printed version of the site's Navigation View, or parts of it.

If you are working with a Server administrator to assess the requirements of a host server, you might want to examine closely the file and directory structure of a site.

And, if you want to identify all targets for hyperlinks from a Web, you might benefit by printing and sharing a hyperlink schematic for your site.

Analyzing Navigation Structure

We examined defining navigational structure in Navigation View back in Chapter 7, "Creating User Interfaces." The FrontPage MCP Exam definitely requires familiarity with how navigational links are defined and edited, so if you're a bit foggy on that, you'll want to review chapter 7. Here, we'll focus on analyzing and sharing a navigational structure.

Scenario: The Information Systems manager has called a summit of everyone involved in developing the corporate Web site. The attendees range from corporate marketing representatives and an outside image consultant, to the company's president. You are expected to present an overview of the Web site. A scenario like this is a perfect opportunity to present the Web structure, not as viewed by a developer, but as viewed by a visitor. Navigation View does just that.

For such a printed presentation (or a live, online presentation), you will want to make liberal use of Navigation View. Use the + and - (expand and contract) symbols that accompany each page that has child links. Figure 15.1 shows a site with three layers of navigational links displayed.

Other Navigation View tools that will be helpful in analyzing and presenting a navigational structure include:

- *File, Preview* presents a preview of a printed navigational structure.
- *File, Print Navigation View* sends the current Navigation View to your printer.

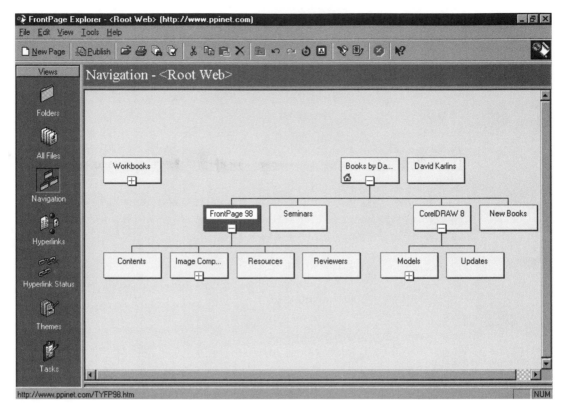

Figure 15.1 *Three levels of navigational links.*

- The *Rotate* button in the Navigation View toolbar toggles your display between vertical and horizontal.
- The *Size to Fit* button in the Navigation View toolbar toggles your display between compressing the flowchart to fit in a single window, and expanding it to full size.

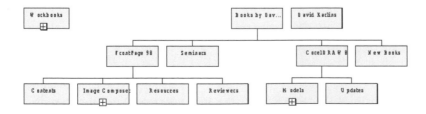

Figure 15.2 *Printing Navigation View*

Viewing and Printing a Navigational Structure

Practice what you have learned by opening a Web and printing the navigational structure.

First, open an existing FrontPage Web (or create a new one). Make sure there are some navigational links defined in Navigation View.

Next, rotate the view, and compress it to fit on the screen (if necessary).

After organizing the Navigation View, preview and then print it.

Analyzing Files and Directory Structure

FrontPage 98 provides two views of files: Folders, and All Files. Folders View shows the folder structure for the Web, with files organized in folder structure. Files view lists all files. Use All Files View when searching for a file when you don't know in which folder (directory) it was saved. Use Folder View to see how files are organized in your Web.

You'll find Folders View in the FrontPage Explorer similar to the Windows' Explorer. You can view the contents of a folder in the right side of the Folders window by clicking (once) on that folder on the left side of the Folders window. For example, in Figure 15.3, I am viewing the contents of the images folder.

Right-clicking on a file or folder opens a context menu that allows you to cut, copy, delete, or rename a folder or file (or see the folder or file properties). And you can click and drag to move a file to another folder, or right-click and drag to choose between moving or copying a file or folder.

To copy a file out of a FrontPage Web and into a local folder, select the file, then choose File, Export from the FrontPage Explorer menu.

Since all this is very similar to the Windows Explorer, you'll have no problem managing files in the FrontPage Explorer Folders View. However, what is more of a mystery is the folder system used by FrontPage for generated Web elements. Table 15.1 identifies some of the more frequently generated folders. The list is by no means complete, as FrontPage extensions generate unique folders for different servers, and some folders are generated only for files used with non-FrontPage standard components (like CERN image maps, for instance). With that disclaimer, you'll find most of the folders you run into in FrontPage Webs in the following list:

Table 15.1 *FrontPage-Generated Folders*

Folder	What's in it
_borders	top, bottom, left, and right shared border files.
_derived	GIF image files for buttons and banners.
_fpclass	Compiled Java (*.class) files for Hover buttons and Banner Ads.
_overlay	Transparent GIF image files overlaid on top of other images used for text in banner images or navigation buttons.
_private	Generated files with data collected through input forms, and other files intended to be accessed by browsers.
_themes	GIF image files, CSS style sheet files, and other files used in Themes.

Hidden folders (preceded with an underscore) are not normally displayed. To view them, select Tools, Web Settings in the FrontPage Explorer, and in the Advanced tab of the FrontPage Web Settings dialog box, select the Show Documents in Hidden Directories check box.

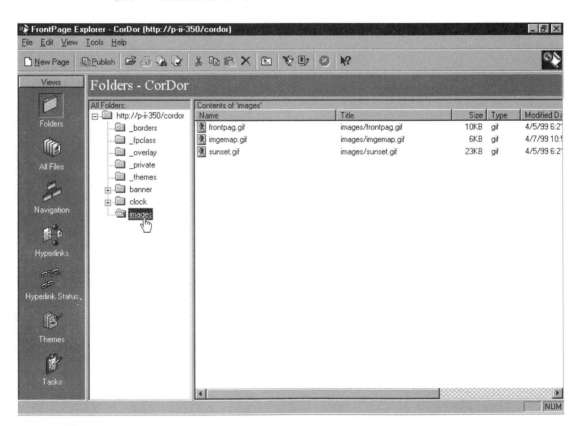

Figure 15.3 *Viewing the contents of a folder in Folder View.*

> As a FrontPage professional, you will always want to display these hidden folders for any FrontPage Web you are developing, maintaining, or supervising.

Study Break

Examining FrontPage Folder Structure

Practice what you have learned by viewing folder structure in a FrontPage Web.

First, open an existing FrontPage Web (or create a new one). Generate a Hover button. Create a small input form (one form field will work well). Test the input form in a browser by submitting at least one data form. Create shared borders. Examine your site in All Files View, and note the size of your files. Try sorting All Folders View by file size, by clicking on the Size column heading.

Next, view your site in Folders View. View hidden folders. Press the F5 function key to refresh the display.

Finally, examine your folder structure. Where are the files with the input form data? Where are the Java applets for the Hover button? Where are the shared border HTML pages?

Viewing Hyperlink Structure

You can examine the hyperlinks to and from any page in Hyperlinks View. Select View, Hyperlinks (or click on Hyperlinks in the View bar to display links). When you open Hyperlinks View for the first time, it displays a split screen, with the page icons and links shown in the right pane, and a folder view in the left pane. You can hide the folder view if you wish by dragging the border between the panes as far left as possible. Hyperlink View without folders displayed is shown in Figure 15.4.

Later in this chapter we'll examine how to verify and fix hyperlinks. For now, we'll focus on using Hyperlink View to examine Web structure.

Hyperlink View can be thought of as complimentary to Navigation view. The difference being that while Navigation view displays only generated links that take advantage of FrontPage's Navigation Bars, Hyperlink View shows all links including those entered manually into a site.

Once in Hyperlink View, you can expand any page by clicking on the + sign on the page. Expanding a page displays all links to and from that page. You can focus on a specific page by right-clicking on the page, and selecting Move to Center from the context menu.

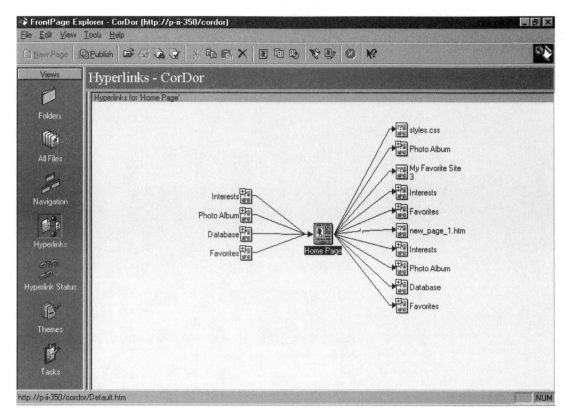

Figure 15.4 *Examining hyperlinks.*

Three buttons in the Hyperlinks window toolbar, shown in Figure 15.5, allow you to control global display of links.

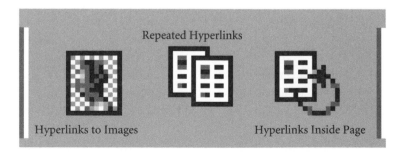

Figure 15.5 *Controlling hyperlink display.*

They are:

- Hyperlinks to Images toggles between displaying image links and hiding them.
- Repeated Hyperlinks toggles between displaying all links from a page or hiding those that are duplicates.
- Hyperlinks Inside Page toggles between displaying or hiding links to internal bookmarks on a page.

Study Break

Examining Hyperlink Structure

Practice what you have learned by viewing hyperlink structure in a FrontPage Web.

First, open an existing FrontPage Web (or create a new one). As long as there are links in the site, you can experiment with Hyperlink View.

Examine links in Hyperlink View. Expand the links from various pages using the + sign, and contract them using the - sign.

MCSD 15.3   Locating Orphaned Pages

Orphan pages are pages which are not linked to other pages within a Web site. Does that mean that all orphan pages are redundant and must be deleted from a Web? No, there are reasons for orphan pages. For example, there may be a page in the Web that is connected to other Web sites through external hyperlinks, but that is not linked to other pages in the Web. This might be a page that, while physically saved to the same server as the rest of the Web, simply has different content, and should not be linked to the rest of the Web.

While not all orphan pages are wasting Web space, some are. Many times, during the process of Web development, pages are constructed and then abandoned, but not deleted from valuable Web server space.

To identify orphan pages, view your Web in All Files View. This way you see every file in your Web. Click on the Orphan column heading to sort pages by orphan status, and to list orphan pages together. Figure 15.6 shows a list of orphan pages.

If you routinely check for orphan pages, you can right-click on them (one at a time), and assign tasks to them from the shortcut menu.

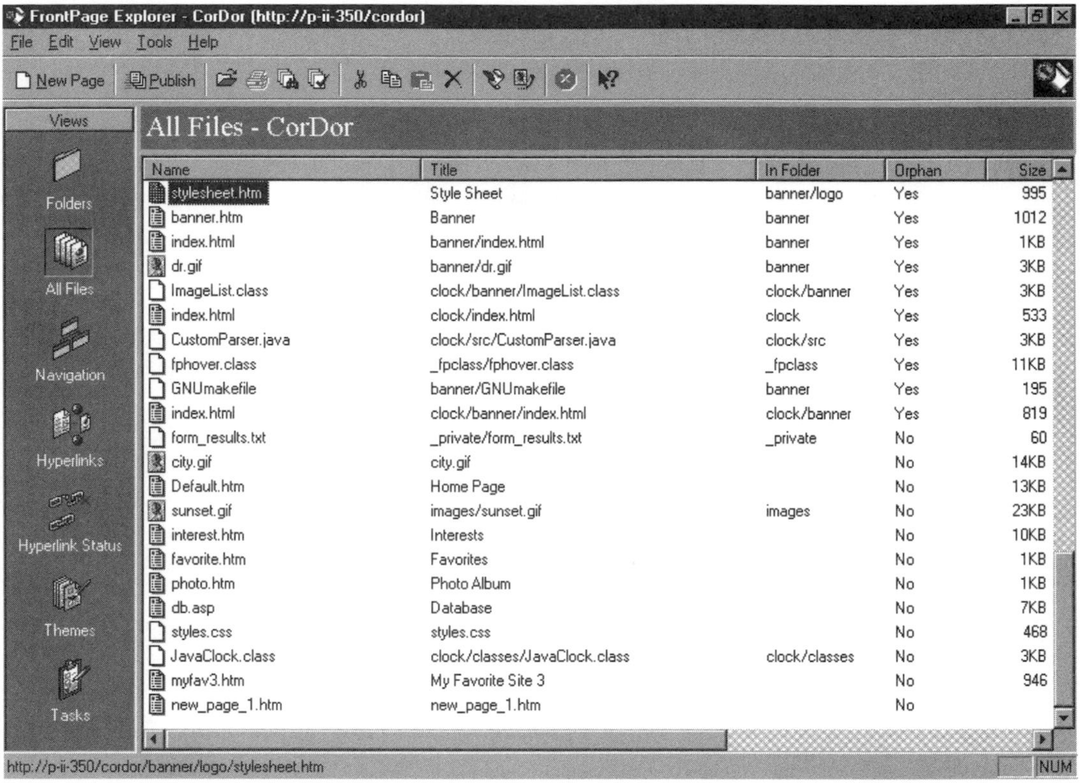

Figure 15.6 *Orphan pages.*

MCSD 15.4   Recalculating and Verifying Hyperlinks

The Internet, as we all know, is an ever-changing place. Is that valuable Web site that lets visitors translate your image text into Finnish still functioning? How about the incredible Java resource page run by a Japanese teenager? The set of links to holistic health sites you dug up two years ago? Even links to frequently-used pages at Microsoft change all the time! So, part of ongoing site maintenance is testing external hyperlinks to see if they are still valid.

Internal hyperlinks within a Web site can also go bad. For example, pages can be moved from one folder to another, leaving behind invalid links.

FrontPage automates the process of identifying and testing external and internal hyperlinks. Internal hyperlinks can be tested and fixed using the Recalculate Hyperlinks feature, while external hyperlinks can be tested using the Verify Hyperlinks command.

Recalculating Internal Hyperlinks

The Recalculate Hyperlinks feature doesn't just test for invalid internal links, it fixes them. I sometimes wish I could see a list of which links were redefined, but I will say that the command has never failed to correct all internal links.

To recalculate internal links, select Tools, Verify Hyperlinks. After you OK a warning dialog box telling you that the procedure might take awhile, FrontPage goes through your pages, and automatically rewrites and regenerates links from one internal location to another.

You might never need to recalculate hyperlinks, because when you move or rename files in FrontPage Explorer, generated links are changed automatically. On the other hand, links to moved pages might get disrupted if a server connection failed while the page was being moved.

More typically, a page author might simply enter a link incorrectly, or create a link to a non-existent page while designing a page. For example, in Figure 15.7, I followed a link on a page in my Web site, and got a "The page cannot be found" message from my browser. Since that link was to an internal Web page, it's time to check the integrity of my internal links!

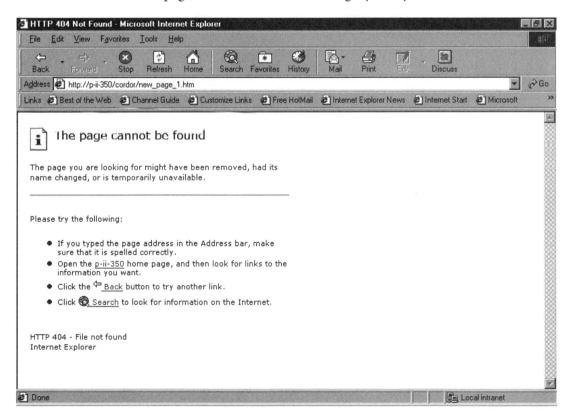

Figure 15.7 *Oops! An internal link is invalid.*

Study Break

Disrupting and Recalculating a Hyperlink

Practice what you have learned by recalculating and repairing an internal link.

First, open an existing FrontPage Web (or create a new one). The Personal Web template will work well for this Study Break.

Next, create a link on a Web page to another page. Once you create the link, the target displays in the Status bar when you move your mouse cursor over the link, as shown in Figure 15.8.

Save your page. In the FrontPage Explorer, move the target page of the link to a different folder within the Web.

Finally, return to the Web page with the original link. Examine the link in the Hyperlink Properties dialog box. *The link has already been recalculated!* Now you see why as long as you manage your FrontPage files in FrontPage using the Create (or Edit) Hyperlink dialog boxes, you will rarely need to recalculate hyperlinks.

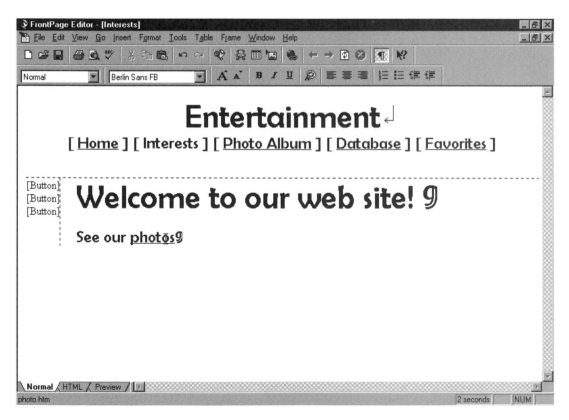

Figure 15.8   *Viewing a link to a page within a Web.*

Verifying and Fixing Hyperlinks

Another very valuable Web maintenance tool in FrontPage is the ability to test all hyperlinks in a Web site. This feature tracks down every link in your Web, tests it, and provides you with a list of which links are no longer valid (and which ones are).

To verify hyperlinks for a FrontPage Web, follow these steps:

1. Open your Web. If you want to test hyperlinks outside of an intranet (to the Internet), make sure you are logged on to the Internet.
2. In FrontPage Explorer, select Tools, Verify Hyperlinks.

Note

While FrontPage verifies your links, update messages appear in the FrontPage Explorer Status bar.

3. When FrontPage finishes verifying hyperlinks, a summary report appears in the Status bar listing the number of broken internal and external hyperlinks.
4. You can sort your list of links by status by clicking on the Status column heading in the Hyperlink Status View. Figure 15.9 shows a set of verified hyperlinks, sorted by status.
5. You can fix hyperlinks by double-clicking on them. You can use the Edit Hyperlink dialog box (shown in Figure 15.10) to fix the link throughout your site, or just for the selected page. The Edit Page button allows you to edit the link right in your Web page. Or, enter a new link with the Replace Hyperlink With box. The Browse button allows you to browse the Internet and choose a new page as a target for the link. After you enter a new page, click on Replace to change the links in your page(s).

Study Break

Testing Hyperlinks on a Web Page

Practice what you have learned by testing hyperlinks in a FrontPage Web.

First, open an existing FrontPage Web (or create a new one). Make sure there are at least a few links on one of the Web pages. Include a bogus hyperlink (like www.dot.dot.dot.com) so that you can get experience identifying a bad link.

Next, select Tools, Verify Hyperlinks in the FrontPage Explorer menu.

After you test the status of your hyperlinks, sort them by status.

Finally, fix the bad link(s).

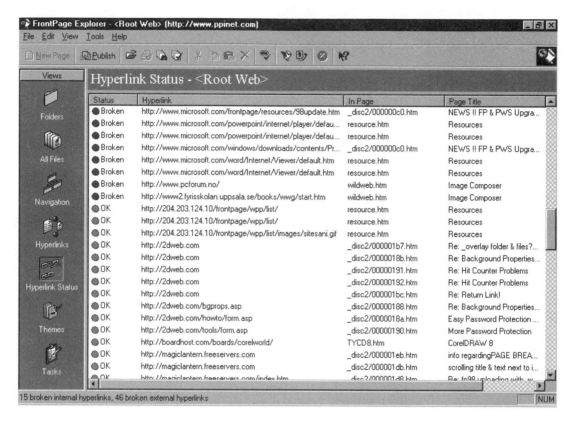

Figure 15.9 *Tested hyperlinks sorted by status.*

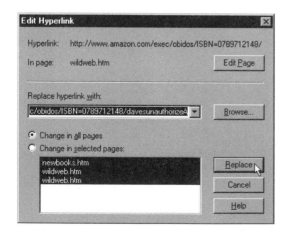

Figure 15.10 *Fixing broken hyperlinks.*

■ Summary

In this chapter, we looked at how FrontPage can be used to manage, test, and maintain an existing Web Site.

You can view a Web from different perspectives. To look at a Web from the perspective of a visitor, you can use Navigation View. To look at the Web's link system, use Hyperlinks View. Folders and All Files Views provide different ways to see all the files in a Web. All Files View is also an effective way to list orphan pages.

Along with viewing Web sites from different perspectives, FrontPage includes maintenance tools that test links and automatically fix broken internal hyperlinks.

▲ CHAPTER REVIEW QUESTIONS

Here are some practice questions relating to the material covered in the "Managing a FrontPage 98 Web Site" area of Microsoft's *Designing and Implementing Web Sites Using Microsoft FrontPage 98* exam (70-055).

1. *Navigation View is a good way to survey hyperlink structure.*

   A. True

   B. False

2. *Which of the following are a problem with orphan pages? (Select all correct answers.)*

   A. They are especially liable to being viewed by unauthorized visitors.

   B. They require FrontPage server extensions

   C. They are always stored in hidden directories

   D. Orphan pages are not linked to other pages in a site

   E. They present special browser compatibility problems

3. *Recalculating hyperlinks identifies and corrects external links.*

   A. True

   B. False

4. *You rarely need to recalculate internal hyperlinks since FrontPage usually takes care of that automatically.*

   A. True

   B. False

5. *Which of the following can be used to analyze a site navigational structure? (Select all correct answers.)*

   A. The Navigation button in Folders View

   B. The Rotate button in Navigation View

   C. The Zoom button in Hyperlinks View

   D. The Navigation dialog box in the FrontPage Editor

   E. The Navigation button in the Publish dialog box

6. *Which of the following are important elements of FrontPage Web maintenance? (Select all correct answers.)*

   A. Testing external links

   B. Deleting extra navigational structures

   C. Publishing corrected or updated Web pages

   D. Updating database file extensions

   E. Updating ODBC data specifications

7. *In which of the following folders would you be likely to find shared borders page files? (Select all correct answers.)*

   A. _shared

   B. _borders

   C. shared

   D. _overlay

   E. borders

8. *To simplify Hyperlink View, you can hide hyperlinked images.*

   A. True

   B. False

9. *Moving pages in Navigation view automatically updates links in those pages.*

   A. True

   B. False

10. *Files used to save data collected from input forms are saved by default to a folder that is hidden.*

    A. True

    B. False

11. *After FrontPage identifies bad external hyperlinks, it automatically fixes them.*

   A. True

   B. False

12. *Which of the following are problems you might address in Hyperlinks view? (Select all correct answers.)*

   A. Identifying navigational structure

   B. Identifying broken links

   C. Identifying folder or directory structure

   D. Locating *asp pages

   E. Locating missing files

13. *One quick way to identify all the bad links in your Web is to sort tested pages by file type.*

   A. True

   B. False

14. *The Navigational Structure of a site can be presented in which of these formats? (Select all correct answers.)*

   A. Printed output

   B. A schematic of hyperlinks

   C. A Web server status report

   D. Horizontal or vertical

   E. As a list of hyperlinks

15. *Folder structure is best viewed in All Files View.*

   A. True

   B. False

Adapting a Web Site to New Browser Technology

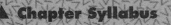
As we near the end of your preparation for the FrontPage 98 MCP/MCSD Exam, we will examine a unique and cutting-edge aspect of Web publishing—adding channels. In addition, we'll survey some other developing aspects of Web publishing, and how to take into account, plan for, and develop new browser technology. Channels allow visitors to essentially create an active, online window to your Web site in their operating system desktop. Not all operating systems support channel technology, but it is a major feature of Windows 98.

Other new browser technology includes the expansion of HyperText Markup Language (HTML), and the rather challenging fact that Microsoft and Netscape appear at this writing to have taken significantly divergent paths in enhancing HTML via competing standards of Dynamic HTML (DHTML). In this chapter we'll explore the challenges of conflicting DHTML standards, as well as other developing browser technology issues.

413

At the conclusion of this chapter you will be able to:

- Understand how channels work.
- Define channel options for a FrontPage Web.
- Be aware of new browser technology and how to adapt FrontPage Webs to match new browser options.

Viewing Channels

Before we examine how to create a channel in FrontPage, it might be helpful to start at the end of the process and examine how channels are displayed and controlled in Microsoft Windows. For our purposes, we'll examine how Windows 98 handles channels, since channel options are enhanced in Windows 98 in comparison to Windows 95.

If you are already a channels guru, you can skip ahead to the next section in this chapter and dive right into the process of defining channel options in FrontPage Webs. However, since channels are displayed in the desktop of an operating system, if you are not familiar with how they work, it will be helpful to review that first.

Figure 16.1 shows a channel window displaying in the Windows 98 desktop. Truly hardcore fans of my Web site (Hi Mom!) need not waste their time logging onto the Internet and viewing my site in their browser. Instead, they can create a live, linked version of my Web site right on their desktop. More real-life examples would include channels to Web sites providing real-time stock quotes, up-to-date industry news, or instant information from a corporate Web site directed at sales personnel.

Web sites that provide channels allow a visitor to add an active desktop item to his or her desktop. If the visitor decides to add your site to a desktop, FrontPage will generate a hyperlink that serves as a "sign-up" button for your channel. When a visitor clicks on that link, a browser dialog box will appear, confirming the channel, as shown in Figure 16.2.

Both the FrontPage Channel Wizard that is used to create these channels, and the Windows operating system, allow a user to define how often the information in a channel should be updated. So, for instance, a user can elect to update his or her view of my Web site every hour, every day, or every week. FrontPage developers can also define update properties, but those assigned by a user in his or her operating system override the update properties defined by a Web site.

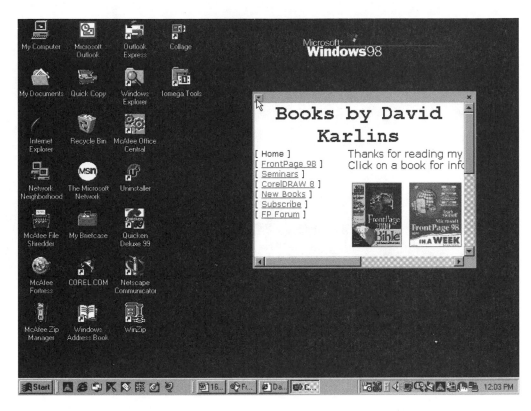

Figure 16.1 *A channel window in the Windows desktop.*

After a channel is defined by a user, he or she can set channel properties in his or her operating system. To set channel properties for a defined channel in Windows 98, a user will follow these steps:

1. Right-click in the Windows 98 desktop, and select Properties from the context menu.

2. Select the Web tab in the Display Properties dialog box. A list of downloaded channels appears, as shown in Figure 16.3.

3. Use the check box(es) next to each downloaded channel to select the ones to be displayed on the Windows desktop.

4. Click on a channel in the list, and click on the Properties button to define how the channel will appear in the desktop. The Web Document tab (shown in Figure 16.4), displays information about the Web site to which the channel connects, and allows you to select or unselect the

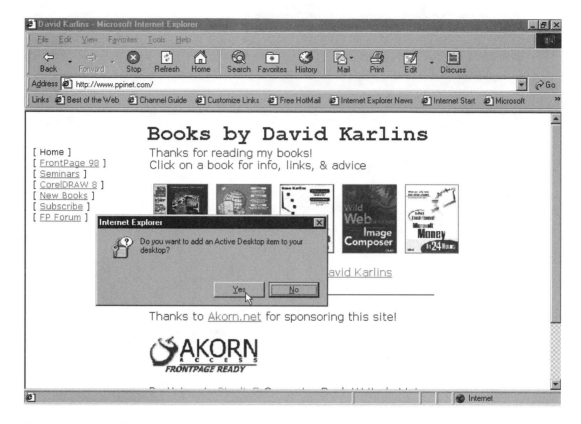

Figure 16.2 *Adding an active Web page to a desktop.*

Make This Page Available Offline check box. Checking the box stores a cache version of the Web site on the user's hard drive.

5. The Schedule tab in the selected Properties dialog box allows a user to decide how often to synchronize (download) the Web site content with his or her channel window. As you can see in Figure 16.5, one of the synchronization options is the schedule that the site developer recommends.

6. The Download tab in the Property dialog box for a selected channel allows a user to define how much of a Web site to download into his or her local cache, and also to define whether or not to be notified by e-mail when the site is changed.

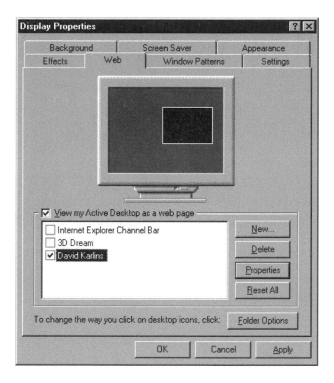

Figure 16.3 *Defining channel display properties.*

7. After properties for any particular channel are defined, click on OK to return to the Web tab in the Display Properties dialog box.

8. Finally, OK the Display Properties dialog box itself to return to the Windows desktop.

In Figure 16.5, it's David Karlins' Recommended Schedule that is a synchronization option. However, that would change, of course, if a different Web site channel were being defined.

Channels aren't for everyone. As with other elements of FrontPage 98 technology, they mesh well with an all-Microsoft, all-up-to-date environment.

Visitors to a Web site whose systems do not support channels will not be able to install channel windows in their desktops.

Figure 16.4 *Saving a cached version of a Web site locally.*

There are two ways that channel properties are defined. The site developer can establish definitions for how a channel is to display on a desktop, and how often it will be synchronized (downloaded). Users also have channel definition options, and those settings override the definitions set by the Web site.

Finally, users can manually synchronize a channel. Figure 16.6 shows a channel window being synchronized in Windows 98.

Study Break

Subscribing to, Synchronizing, and Deleting a Channel

Practice what you have learned by subscribing to a channel. My instructions will work for Windows 98. If you have a different operating system, you can experiment with how channels are defined in your system.

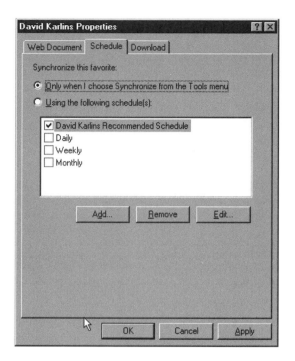

Figure 16.5   *Defining a channel synchronization schedule.*

First, log onto a Web site that has channels. Mine, at www.ppinet.com, will work if you need one with which to experiment.

Next, subscribe to the channel.

Define the channel so it updates hourly.

Finally, test the channel in your operating system desktop. Manually synchronize the channel to provide the latest information. To delete the channel in Windows 98, select it in the Web tab of the Display Properties dialog box (accessed by right-clicking in the desktop and choosing Properties from the context menu), and click on the Delete button.

MCSD 16.1   Configuring and Publishing a Channel

If you read the previous section in this chapter and tried the Study Break exercise, you've got a basic idea of how channels behave for end-users. If you already knew all about how channels work in operating systems, welcome

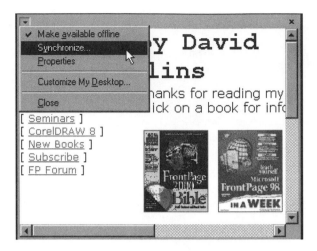

Figure 16.6 *Synchronizing a channel.*

back. In this section, we'll walk through the process of configuring and publishing Web channels with FrontPage.

With a FrontPage Web open, follow these steps to configure and publish a channel link from your Web:

1. From the FrontPage Explorer, select Tools, Define Channel from the menu. The first window of the Channel Definition Wizard (the Welcome window) appears, as shown in Figure 16.7.

2. If you are creating your first Channel definition, you should choose the Create a New Channel . . . option button. If you have an existing channel that you want to edit, choose the Open an Existing Channel Definition file option button, and use the Browse button to find your existing channel. Then click Next.

3. In the Channel Description window (step 1 of 7 in the wizard), enter descriptive information for your page. That information includes:

   • *Title:* By default, this is the title of the Web. You can change it to a descriptive title.

   • *Abstract:* A more extensive description of your channel that displays when a visitor points to the channel logo in the Web site.

   • *Introduction Page:* This is the URL for the page that displays when a visitor subscribes to your channel. You can enter your site's

Figure 16.7 *Defining a new channel in FrontPage 98.*

home page (the default setting), or use the Browse button to define a different page.

- *Logo Image*: Use the Browse button to select an image in your Web. This image should be an 80×32 pixel GIF image. The image will display in visitor's browsers as the channel logo.

- *Icon Image*: Use the Browse button to select the URL for an image file that will be used to identify a page in your channel. This image should be a 16×16 pixel GIF file.

- *Last Modified*: This information is generated automatically based on when you last created or changed your Channel Definition file (CDF). The CDF will be generated when you complete the wizard.

4. After you complete the Channel Description window, click Next. The Choose Source Folder window appears, as shown in Figure 16.8. You should select the Include Subfolders check box if you plan to make folders (directories) within your Web available through a channel. You will select the *actual pages* to make available in the next step of the wizard.

5. After selecting (or not) the check box, click on Next. The Edit Page List (Step 3 of 7) wizard window appears. You can *exclude* pages in your Web from a channel by selecting them in the list, and clicking on the Exclude button.

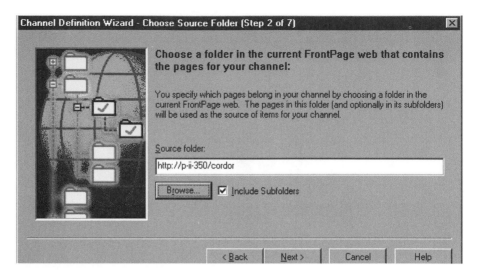

Figure 16.8   *Making folders available for your channel.*

6. After selecting pages to exclude from a channel, click Next again. The Channel Item Properties (Step 4 of 7) appears. For each page, you can assign several options. To assign options to a specific page, first select that page from the Channel Items list, and then configure the page using these options in the wizard window:

   • *Delete*: Here is a chance to remove the selected page from the Channel Items list. If you change your mind, use the *Restore* button to put the page back on the list.

   • *Abstract*: You can enter a description of the page that appears in some browsers (like IE 4 or higher) when a visitor points to the page icon in his or her browser's list of channel items.

   • *Page Cache*: This drop-down provides three options. The first is to allow the settings at a user's operating system to determine whether or not the page is cached on a local drive. This other option allow's you to define a default—either cached or not cached. In general, you will want to make the default cached so that a visitor can store a local version of your site. The *Reset* button simply undoes your selection and reverts to the default setting.

   • The *Specify Usage* option button simply allows the channel to function as a channel, as opposed to the *Hidden* option, which allows a browser to download a selected page for offline browsing, but does not create a channel link. This is appropriate, for example, for pages that are targets of links on pages that are not hidden.

- The *Channel* check box adds the selected page to a list of channel items for visitors.
- *E-mail Notification* sends subscribers an e-mail when your Web page content is updated.
- *Screen Saver* makes the selected page available as a screen saver in a visitor's page.
- *Desktop Component* displays the selected page within a visitor's desktop as a small window within the desktop. If you select this option, use the *Height* and *Width* boxes to enter the size of the window in pixels.

Many, if not all, of the page channel properties you define can be over-ridden by visitors in their operating system. However, you are creating default settings that the user can accept.

7. When you have completed the Step 4 wizard window for each separate page in the Channel items list, click on Next. The Channel Scheduling (Step 5 of 7) wizard window appears, as shown in Figure 16.9. You can define your channel to update with a starting and ending date (the defaults are now and forever), and define a schedule for how frequently (in days) to synchronize channel content between your Web and the local version of the pages. You can also use the Delay Server Checks check box to randomly change the download time so that everyone does not update their channel exactly at midnight (that can put too much strain on your server).

8. After you schedule channel updating, click on the Next button. The Log Target (Step 6 of 7) wizard window appears. Here, you can enter the URL for a special input form that you design to collect data about visitors who subscribe to your channel.

Unless you want to log data on everyone who signs up for a channel, you can leave this field blank. If you do want to define a log target, you will want to create a page that includes a blank form to collect user information. The section "Adding Hidden Fields" in Chapter 8, "Creating Input Forms," of this book discusses how to add hidden fields to an input form. If you wish to design a page that will include a Log Target input form, you can design a form with *no* user-defined input form fields, and just collect *hidden field* information in the form—input fields like Time, Date, Remote Computer Name, User Name and Browser Type. In this way, you can document who is signing up for channels.

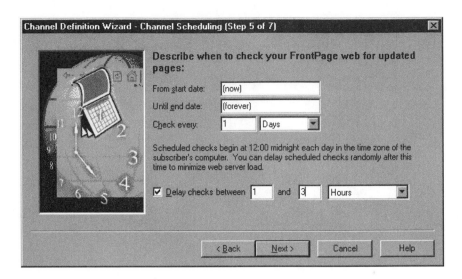

Figure 16.9 *Scheduling channel synchronization.*

9. After filling in (or more likely skipping) the Log Target URL field, click on Next to see the Finish (Step 7 of 7) wizard window. This window prompts you with a default name for the Channel Definition file (CDF) that will hold the channel parameters you just defined in the wizard. You can accept the default name, or enter a different one. The Place a button . . . check box adds a link to channel subscription in your Navigation bar (on every page in which the Navigation bar is displayed). This is a very helpful way to make it easy for visitors to subscribe to your site. The Prepare For Publishing To check box allows you to publish the CDF to a different Web than the one in which it was created. After you complete this final wizard window, click on Save to generate a CDF for your site.

10. You can see the CDF file in the FrontPage Explorer. When you preview your site in a browser, you can use the link generated in the Navigation bar (in Step 9, above), to subscribe yourself to your Web site. This will work even if your site is published to a version of the Personal Web Server.

Configuring and Publishing a Channel

Practice what you have learned by creating a channel subscription link from your site.

First, define a channel for your site. To keep the experiment simple, define only one page for the channel from your site, but enter a complete title and abstract for the page. Accept the default option of generating links in your Navigation bar to subscribe to the site.

Next, generate the CDF and note the new file in the FrontPage Explorer.

View your Web in a browser, and subscribe to your own channel.

Finally, view the channel in your desktop.

MCSD 16.2   Adapting a Web Site to New Browser Technology

The development of new Web technology is expanding at an exponential pace. Just a couple of years ago, features like animated GIF images, plug-ins, even custom font faces and sizes were not supported by most browsers. Internet Explorer version 2 didn't support Frames.

Many of the FrontPage development features explored in this book work only with the latest Web browser technology. I've noted those browser issues in each chapter. Here, I want to focus on browser technology issues in their own right, and outline options for handling them.

The Anarchistic World of DHTML

In Chapter 11, "Incorporating Java Applets, ActiveX, and DHTML," we looked at Dynamic HyperText Markup Language (DHTML) in the context of DHTML components generated by FrontPage. You may recall that Web page elements like collapsible outlines and page transitions and object animation can be assigned directly from the FrontPage menu.

You might also remember that I mentioned in passing back in Chapter 11 that there are major browser compatibility issues with DHTML. Here, we'll focus on that problem in the context of exploring developing browser technology.

If a Web is being designed for an intranet, and you know that everyone on that intranet is using the latest version of Internet Explorer, you can use all the DHTML options available in FrontPage and not worry about a thing.

But if you are designing for the Internet, DHTML presents major browser technology issues.

Part of the framework for understanding the development of browser technology is the fact that Microsoft's Internet Explorer has achieved a level of user acceptance that has enabled Microsoft to take an approach of adding significant interpretive features to IE without worrying about maintaining compatibility with its chief browser rival, Netscape Navigator.

A major arena in which this incompatibility is manifesting itself is in the interpretation (or not) of DHTML. Essentially, DHTML is simply an expansion of the code that browsers can interpret to enable animation and other interactive features in Web pages. Both Internet Explorer version 4 and higher, and Netscape Navigator 4 and higher, interpret their own versions of DHTML.

DHTML allows browsers to support actions like having someone choose an item from a drop-down list and have a description of the item show up in a balloon on the page (effectively a help system). Sometimes DHTML is used to create Web sites where you can "expand" a menu by clicking on it, or sites where the pieces of the main graphic come together in an animated way. The key is that all of the instructions are passed to the browser as text. No plug-ins are required.

The browser technology challenges in this situation are:

- Netscape Navigator and Microsoft Internet Explorer have different object models for how "layers" are positioned and manipulated, so you have to code for both Navigator and IE if you want truly "bilingual" DHTML.

- You have to trap for IE 4+ and Netscape Navigator 4+ if you are doing cross-browser code and serve out one set of DHTML pages for those browsers and another set of pages for non-DHTML browsers. This means, of course, that most designers use DHTML only for menus, entry, or "flash" pages—or for special features (such as a drag and drop "magnetic poetry board" that a friend of mine is designing for a local performing arts center).

- Although there are a number of excellent Web sites (and books) providing code and examples, they tend to use different coding techniques, which can be *very* confusing to someone who doesn't know JavaScript. A quick review of about 13 of these books at Barnes and Noble revealed some brilliant code, but only a seasoned JavaScript programmer would know how to use much of it. The problem stems from the fact that the Netscape Object model (first out of the blocks) is a *lot* cruder than the Microsoft model (which is pretty similar to the model

MS uses for Visual Basic and Access programming). This means that to really know what you're doing you have to know both object models.

How do you trap for FrontPage generated DHTML that is not interpreted in Netscape Navigator (at this writing version 4.5)? One way to identify incompatible DHTML is the warning box that appears when you preview a Web page with offending components. The dialog box in Figure 16.10 identifies a page as containing DHTML elements not recognized by Netscape.

Frames and No Frames

As new generations of browsers replace old ones, frame compatibility becomes less of a browser technology issue and more one of aesthetics and design. In other words, most browsers out there will interpret frames, so the real question is, do you want them?

Nevertheless, a Web site that is technologically compatible with 100% of potential browsers will provide an option for visitors without frames.

FrontPage makes it so easy to provide a non-frame alternative that there's no excuse for developers not to take advantage of it. The No Frames tab in the FrontPage Editor, shown in Figure 16.11, is active whenever you select one of the many Frame templates.

By providing a frameless alternative, you can ensure that every browser will be able to connect with the content at your Web.

What Is "Cutting Edge Browser Technology" and How to Use It

By definition, today's cutting edge technology is tomorrow's standard stuff. Developers tend to categorize every feature supported by the latest version of Microsoft Internet Explorer (or Netscape Navigator) as the limit for their Web design. But every developer should spend some time in the shoes of a typical visitor to his or her Web site, and test sites using a variety of browsers.

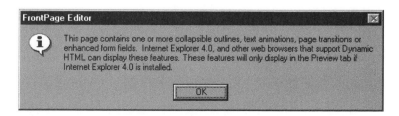

Figure 16.10 *This warning box identifies a page with DHTML not recognized by Netscape Navigator, or versions of Internet Explorer before version 4.*

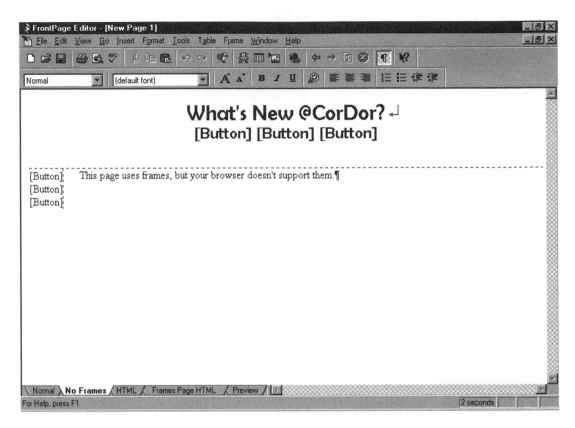

Figure 16.11 *Providing an alternative for browsers that do not interpret frames.*

I consider myself a rather conservative developer when it comes to employing cutting edge Web technology. Yet I had a rude awakening when I had the opportunity recently to visit one of my sites using a friend's Macintosh with AOL 3 installed as a browser. My animated GIF files weren't animated. My style sheet formatting didn't display. And many of the fonts used in my site were converted to Times Roman. The following list identifies browser issues for the three main browsers—AOL, Netscape Navigator and Internet Explorer:

- AOL's browser, version 3, will *not* interpret Database Regions (which require ASP), will not display ActiveX controls, does not display animation in animated GIFs (just the first "frame" of the animation displays). AOL 3 does not interpret Visual Basic or ActiveX, so FrontPage features like the Banner Ad Manager and Channels will not work.

None of the DHTML effects generated by FrontPage are interpreted by AOL 3. And since AOL 3 does not interpret Java applets, FrontPage's Hover buttons won't work either.

- Netscape Navigator, even version 4.5, will not interpret ActiveX controls, Active Server Pages, or channels. In the discussion of DHTML earlier in this chapter, I highlighted major compatibility problems between Netscape and FrontPage's versions of DHTML that prevent the DHTML effects in FrontPage from working in Netscape Navigator 4.5. The Channel publishing features we explored earlier in this chapter are not supported in Navigator 4.5. Attempting to publish a channel from Netscape Navigator provokes the dialog box shown in Figure 16.12.

- Even Internet Explorer version 3 presents compatibility issues with FrontPage-generated channels and DHTML. Older versions of IE did not recognize the MAILTO HTML tag, and won't interpret hyperlinks with email address targets.

The Cascading Style Sheets discussed in Chapter 13, "Using Style Sheets and Templates," are not interpreted by any version of AOL's browser, nor are they supported by versions of Netscape Navigator older than version 3, or Internet Explorer older than version 3.

Given all these browser technology issues, what is a Web designer to do? The moving target of browser compatibility can be addressed using one, or combinations of, the following strategies:

- You can design a low-tech Web site that eschews frames, animation, even font formatting.

- You can provide a low-tech *alternative* to your Web pages that presents your Web content without features that present compatibility issues.

- You can employ cutting edge Web technology in a way that does not prevent older browsers from interpreting the main content of your pages. For example, FrontPage generated DHTML effects will not work

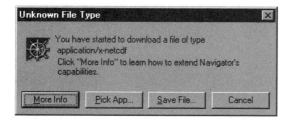

Figure 16.12 *Netscape does not support the Channels publishing feature in FrontPage.*

with Netscape Navigator, but that doesn't prevent the text and graphic content of the page from displaying statically. It just prevents Netscape browsers from interpreting the text and images.

- You can provide links to the Netscape and/or IE download sites, and suggest that frequent visitors download a browser that supports all the features at your Web site.

At this writing, the download sites for IE and Netscape Navigator are:
- **Netscape Navigator (for Windows or Macintosh):**
  http://home.netscape.com/download/index.html
- **Microsoft Internet Explorer (for Windows):**
  http://www.microsoft.com/windows/ie/download/windows.htm
- **Microsoft Internet Explorer (for Macintosh):**
  http://www.microsoft.com/windows/ie/download/mac.htm

Study Break

Exploring Browser Compatibility

You will have to be a bit creative in this Study Break, depending on what kind of browsers you have access to, but the point is to explore browser technology issues.

First, open an existing FrontPage Web. Add an ActiveX control, and DHTML effects (you can review how to do this in Chapter 11).

Next, view the pages with the ActiveX control and the DHTML in Netscape Navigator. If you have an older version of a browser available, test your site with that as well.

Finally, change your home page to provide options for older browsers, including an alternate content page, and download links for current versions of browsers from Netscape and Microsoft.

■ Summary

Every month brings a new headline trumpeting the latest breakthrough in Web technology. As I write this book, downloaded audio files are appearing all over the Internet promising a revolution in the distribution of music. As a FrontPage expert, you will want to stay current through technical journals and updates at Microsoft's Web site. At the same time, you will have to make sober evaluations of what kind of developing Web technology is appropriate, and how it can be supported by FrontPage.

FrontPage 98 comes with built-in and powerful support for channels. Developers who want to provide live, continuous channel options for users can generate the entire channel from FrontPage. FrontPage also includes built-in options for applying Dynamic HTML (DHTML) effects to objects and Web pages. DHTML, however, is one of the least browser-compatible options for Web development, and that has to be taken into account when considering its implementation.

Adapting FrontPage Web development to new browser technology inherently raises issues of browser compatibility. Cutting edge features in FrontPage, like database regions (requiring ASP technology), ActiveX controls, external (cascading) style sheets, as well as DHTML, stretch the current capabilities of browser technology, and also present major browser compatibility problems.

▲ CHAPTER REVIEW QUESTIONS

Here are some practice questions relating to the material covered in the "Testing FrontPage Web Technology" area of *Microsoft's Designing and Implementing Web Sites Using Microsoft FrontPage 98* exam (70-055).

1. *Which of the following FrontPage features present compatibility problems using Netscape Navigator? (Select all correct answers.)*

    A. DHTML

    B. HTML

    C. Channels

    D. ASP

    E. CDF files

2. *Which of the following are options for FrontPage created Channels? (Select all correct answers.)*

    A. FTP

    B. Collecting hidden data about people who publish channels

    C. Generated screen savers

    D. ASP

    E. Page caching

3. *Channels can be used to notify subscribers by e-mail of site updates.*

    A. True

    B. False

4. *Channels can be used to synchronize Web content and a user's desktop.*

    A. True

    B. False

5. *Frames are supported by Internet Explorer version 2 and higher.*

    A. True

    B. False

6. *Which of the following are required to publish a Web page as a channel? (Select all correct answers.)*

    A. A Web folder enabled for scripts

    B. A server that runs Active Server Pages

    C. Either IE 4 or higher, or Netscape Navigator version 4.5 or higher

    D. A URL for the channel definition

    E. A desktop display

7. *AOL version 3 will display frames.*

    A. True

    B. False

8. *AOL version 3 will not display input forms generated in FrontPage 98.*

    A. True

    B. False

9. *Netscape Navigator 4.5 is compatible with the DHTML generated by FrontPage 98.*

    A. True

    B. False

10. *One option for solving browser compatibility issues is to provide browser upgrade links at a Web site.*

    A. True

    B. False

11. *Visitors to sites with FrontPage-generated DHTML probably won't miss out on any essential Web content.*

    A. True

    B. False

12. *Which of the following identify DHTML that requires IE to interpret? (Select all correct answers.)*

    A. A warning dialog box that appears when you publish the Front-Page Web

    B. A warning dialog box that appears when you publish the Web page

    C. Image maps that do not function when previewed in a browser

    D. A warning dialog box that appears when you preview the page

    E. Image maps that do not function when previewed in the Preview tab of the FrontPage Editor

13. *Older versions of AOL's browser do not interpret basic HTML code.*

    A. True

    B. False

14. *Which of the following options for channels can be defined in a user's operating system? (Select all correct answers.)*

    A. E-mail notification

    B. The content of Page abstracts

    C. The content of Site abstracts

    D. The size of a desktop component

    E. Screen saver content

15. *Channel icons are constricted to which of the following? (Select all correct answers.)*

    A. 16 × 16 pixel size

    B. JPEG file format images

    C. 24-bit images

    D. 80 × 32 pixel images

    E. CDF files

Managing Access to a FrontPage 98 Web Site

In this chapter we will explore three different ways of managing access to a FrontPage 98 Web site. First, we'll look at how you can prevent files from being available to all browsers. Second, we'll look at how you can prevent files from being available to some browsers. And finally, we will explore how to function in an environment where a proxy server allows only authorized access to files. Proxy servers are often used as part of a firewall scheme, to prevent unauthorized access to personal or private systems.

In this chapter, you'll learn how to:

- Prevent browser access to files in a Web.
- Set up users and group permissions in Microsoft Personal Web Server.
- Create a system that registers users before they access a Web.
- Control access to the root Web as well as to sub-Webs.
- Control author and administrator access to FrontPage Webs.
- Control access through a firewall or proxy server.

MCSD 17.1 Controlling Access to Data and Objects on a Web Site

FrontPage 98 allows you to define selected folders in your Web as non-browsable. This protects files in these folders from being opened by a visitor. Frequently, you will want to prevent browser access to database files. For example, you may well want to protect data that you collect through an input form from browser access. The names, addresses, e-mail addresses, etc. that visitors to your site enter into input forms might well not be information you want anyone browsing your site to see. Or, if you implemented the database region we explored in Chapter 14, "Publishing a FrontPage Web Site," you might well want to make the imported database unavailable to browsers.

Defining a folder as non-browsable does not protect the data within it from sophisticated hackers. Establishing the security of a Web site from hackers is the responsibility of the network administrator, and may well involve a firewall. In the final section of this chapter, I'll look at how you, as a FrontPage Web administrator, can work within a firewall environment.

Browser access can be defined for specific folders in a Web. In other words, a single folder (like _private, for example) cannot contain both browser-accessible files and files protected from browser access. This means that FrontPage Webs need to be organized so that protected files and browser-accessible files are stored in separate folders. You can, of course, simply move files from one folder to another in the FrontPage Explorer by clicking and dragging on them.

Study Break

Define a Folder as Non-Browsable

Practice what you have learned by creating a Web folder that is not accessible to browsers.

First, generate a new a Web using the Personal Web template.

Next, select Folders view. Click on the root (highest level) folder in the Web, and select File, New, Folder to generate a new Folder. Name the new Folder "Secret." Right-click on the Secret Folder, and choose Properties from the context menu. Deselect the All Files to Be Browsed check box, and OK the dialog box.

Examine your folder structure in Folder view. You have created a new Folder for files that cannot be browsed. Drag the Photo.htm file in the FrontPage Editor, and choose File, Preview in Browser to examine the page in a browser. Click on the Photo Album link in the home page. Your browser will display a message informing you that this page is not accessible to browser.

You can delete this Web by selecting File, Delete FrontPage Web from the FrontPage Explorer menu bar.

To protect a folder from browser access, follow these steps:

1. With a FrontPage Web open, right-click on a folder in the FrontPage Explorer.
2. Select Properties from the Context menu. A Properties dialog box for the selected folder opens.
3. Deselect the Allow Files to Be Browsed check box, and click on OK.

If a visitor attempts to open a file in a browser-protected folder, he or she will see a message in a browser window noting that the file or Web page is not accessible, as shown in Figure 17.1.

MCSD 17.2 Administering User Access to Pages on a Web Site and an Entire Web

In the previous section you saw how browser access can be denied to folders within a Web. You can also allow *selective* access to FrontPage Webs by defining authorized users, or allowing users to register themselves as authorized users. User permissions define who can use a browser to view a site.

FrontPage also allows you to define authoring and administrative access permissions to Web sites. Authoring and administrative permissions define who can use FrontPage to edit a site. User access on the one hand,

Figure 17.1   *FrontPage allows you to prevent pages from being browsed.*

and administrator and author access on the other, are two very different kinds of access. User access just allows someone to browse a Web site. Author access allows someone to edit, delete, or create Web pages. And administrator access allows someone to assign permissions.

In this section, we'll explore assigning browser access to individuals and groups. However, the process you use for assigning browser access is very similar to the process you use to assign author or administrator access.

Defining Web access for users requires some understanding of how FrontPage defines a root Web, and a subWeb. Every server with FrontPage extensions creates a *root* Web. For example, if the server name is ABCO, the default name for the root Web will be http://ABCO. SubWebs can be created in the server, and they are identified by a / symbol. So, for example, a subWeb of ABCO called Projects would have a URL of http://ABCO/Projects. When you open a root Web, FrontPage displays <Root Web> at the top of the FrontPage Explorer, as shown in Figure 17.2.

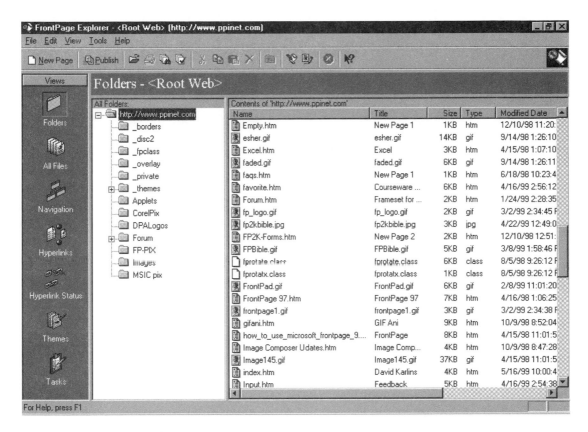

Figure 17.2 *A root Web.*

In the previous chapters in this book, we have not distinguished between the root FrontPage Web, and subWebs. That's because most of the time, the distinction isn't that important. When you create Web pages, define links, etc., a Web is a Web. It is only when you define browser (or author or administrator) access permissions that it's important to recognize the distinction between the root Web, and subWebs.

Access permissions for users and developers are defined for a root Web. However, *unique* permission settings can be defined for subWebs. By default, subWebs maintain the same permission settings as root Webs, unless they are modified. But when unique permission settings are defined for an open subWeb, those permission settings are then applied to that subWeb.

In Chapter 1, "Analyzing Business Requirements," we walked through the process of defining user permissions for individual users. To briefly review, the following steps register a user:

1. Open the FrontPage Web for which you are defining permissions. (If you want to define permissions for *all* Webs on your server, open the root Web.)

2. In the FrontPage Explorer, select Tools, Permissions. (If your menu has Permissions grayed out, your server does not support permissions.)

3. In the Settings tab of the Permissions dialog box, choose the Use Unique Permissions for this Web option button (unless you are in the root Web, in which case that isn't an option because you are defining default permissions for all Webs.)

4. In the Users tab, select the Only Registered Users Have Browser Access options button.

5. Use the Add button to add users to the list of registered users. The Add Users dialog box appears, as shown in Figure 17.3.

6. Enter a user name in the Name box, and enter that user's password in the Password and Confirm Password boxes. Continue this process until you have enrolled all the people who will have browse access to the Web.

When you have defined a site as open to only registered users, every time someone tries to visit that site, they will be prompted to enter a Name and Password, as shown in Figure 17.4. Obviously, the site administrator has responsibility to provide the assigned passwords and user names to people with authorization to browse a site.

In the following sections, we'll explore two other options for defining authorized users: groups, and registration. Groups allow you to assign individual users to a group, and then define access permission for the entire group. Registration allows visitors to register themselves as authorized users.

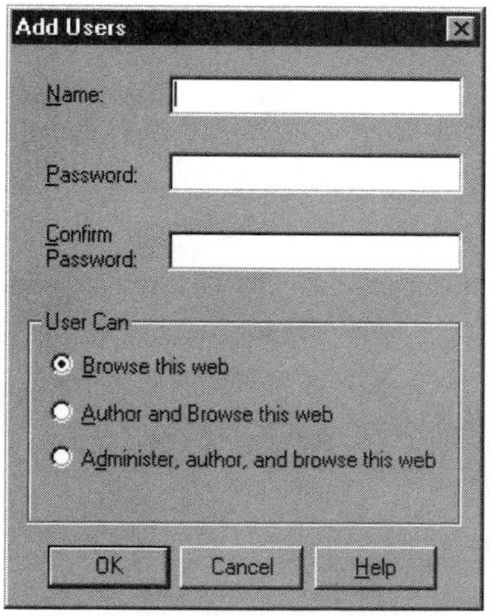

Figure 17.3 *Adding a registered user.*

Figure 17.4 *Accessing a site open only to registered users.*

Defining Groups

A group is a list of existing users who share a set of permissions on the Web server. A user may have different, additional permissions from the group that he or she is in. However, if an entire group has one set of permissions, an individual user will also have those permissions, no matter what user permissions you set. For example, someone who is part of a group that has user privileges can also be given author or administrator privileges *as an individual.*

Groups are defined in your Web server. For example, suppose that you have a FrontPage Web that you want to grant your three systems administrators authoring access to. The first thing to do is to define the three administrators on your Web server. To do that, follow these steps:

1. In the Microsoft Personal Web Server, right-click the Web server icon in the Windows system tray and select "Administer." You'll be taken to the Microsoft Personal Web Server Administration page, shown in Figure 17.5.
2. Click "Local User Administration" to open the user and groups lists. The first tab you'll see is the Users tab, shown in Figure 17.6. Here, you can add a user, change the user's name and password, and remove users from the Web server.
3. To add a user, click the "New User . . ." button at the bottom of the page.
4. Enter the user's name and a password. Give that password to the user so he can log on with his own username, as shown in Figure 17.7.
5. Click "Add" to continue, or "Cancel" to clear the fields.

Once you've created the user list, it's time to create a group for the people on the list. To create the list, follow these steps:

1. Return to the Local User Administration page (you'll be taken there when you finish adding a user), and click the Groups tab.

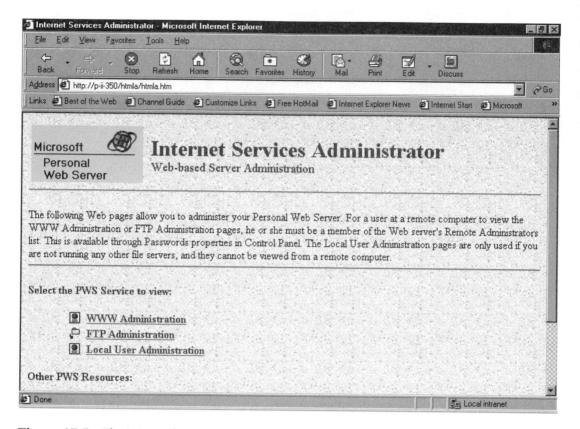

Figure 17.5 *The Microsoft Personal Web Server Administration page lets you make changes to the server.*

2. Click New Group to add a new group,
3. Enter the name of the group in the Group Name box, as shown in Figure 17.8. Then click on the Add button.
4. To add users to the group, select the User/Group tab at the top of the Web page to add and remove users from their groups.
5. Select the name of a person in your group that you want to add in the Users box, and the group to add him to in the Groups box.
6. Click the Add User to Group button at the bottom of the screen, as shown in Figure 17.9.
7. When you've added all the users, go back to the Groups tab.

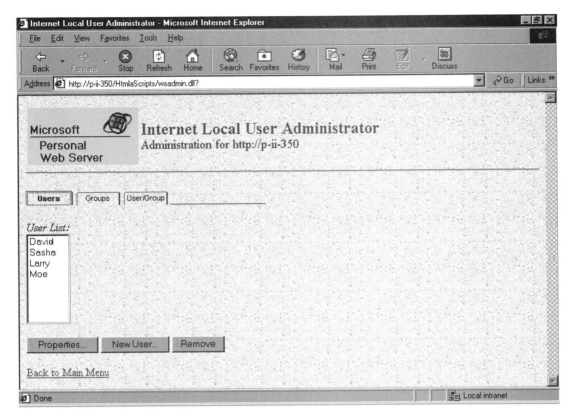

Figure 17.6 *The Local User Administrator tool lets you set up users for your FrontPage Webs.*

8. Select the group you just defined, and click Properties to view the list of users in that group, as shown in Figure 17.10. When you're done, click on OK to return to the Groups view.

Later in this chapter we'll discuss assigning author permission. You can grant any group authoring access, so they can make changes to the FrontPage Web.

You can easily remove users from groups. To do that:

1. Open the Users/Groups tab in the Local User Administration page again.
2. Select a user and a group from the user and group lists.
3. Click Remove User from Group to remove the user from the group.

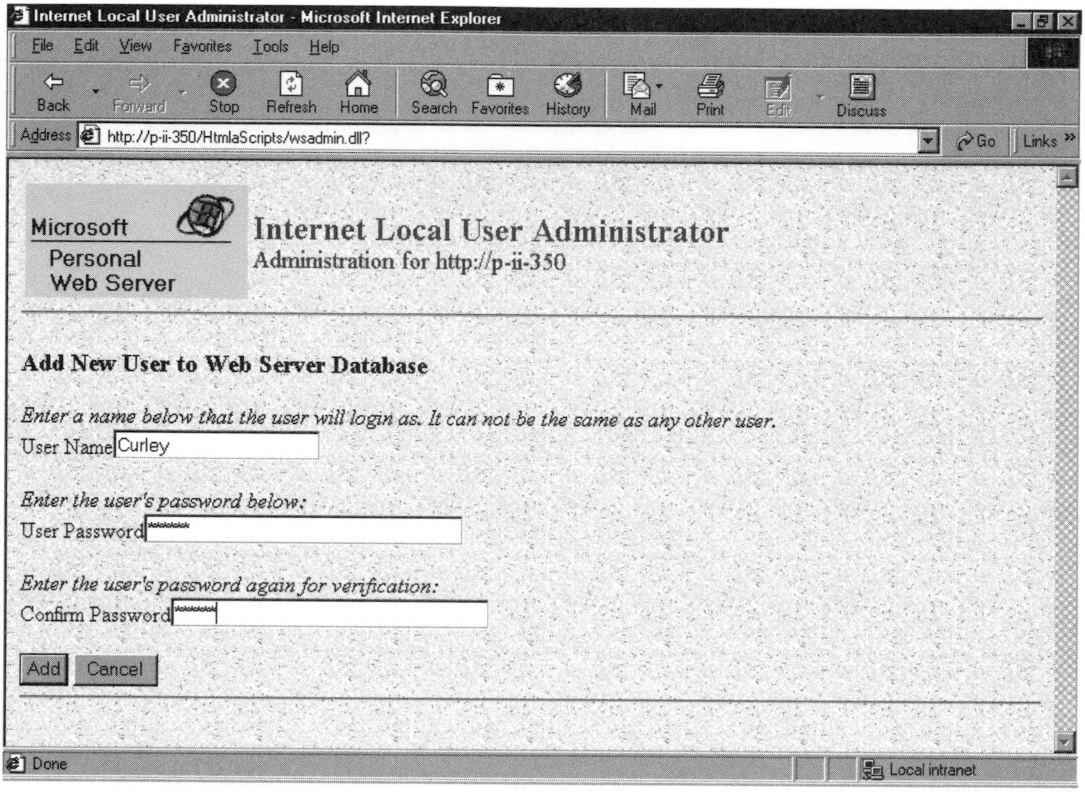

Figure 17.7 *Adding a user to the Web server database.*

Study Break

Adding Users to Groups in Microsoft Personal Web Server

To practice these skills, add a username for several people, using people in your family, including your aunts, uncles, cousins, and grandparents.

Now, create a group called "immediate" and one called "extended."

Add your parents, children, and siblings to the "immediate" group, and everyone else to the "extended" group.

Next, remove your grandparents from the "extended" group and add them to the "immediate" group.

Assign browser permissions to the "immediate" group.

Finally, view the list of members in your extended family by listing the group properties.

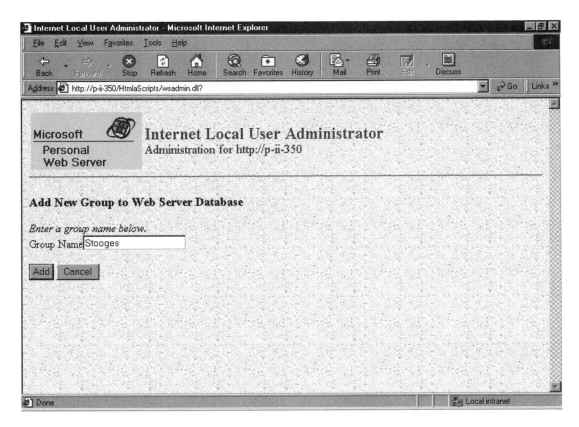

Figure 17.8 *Adding a group is easy!*

Creating a Registration Form

FrontPage automates the process of requiring users to register before they access your site. By requiring users to register, you can collect data about the people browsing your site. For example, you can require that visitors provide their name, e-mail address, and contact information. Or, you can survey visitors to find out where they learned about your Web site, their job, or what kinds of products they are likely to purchase.

FrontPage's registration system has two main elements: defining a Web (or subWeb) as accessible to registered users only, and allowing visitors to register when they visit your site. We've already discussed restricting Web access to registered users in Chapter 1 (with a quick review at the beginning of this chapter). Here, we'll focus on creating the registration form, and allowing visitors to register when they visit your site. Essentially, what this

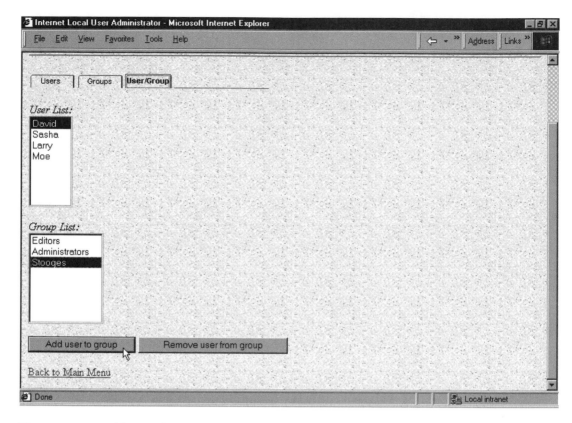

Figure 17.9 *Adding and removing users from groups.*

process does is collect registration information through an input form (like the ones you worked with in Chapters 8–10). This input form sends collected information to a registration list, automatically registering users who fill out the form, and granting them browse permission for the Web. FrontPage includes a page template that allows you to generate this form.

During the registration process, visitors assign themselves a user name and a password. They can then use that user name and password to access the FrontPage Web on subsequent visits.

Unfortunately, no version of the Personal Web Server (neither the Microsoft Personal Web Server, nor the FrontPage Personal Web Server) supports registered end users. You can still walk through the steps below to create a Registration Form using a version of the Personal Web Server, but to actually implement a working registration form you must use Internet Information Server or another professional level server (like an Apache server).

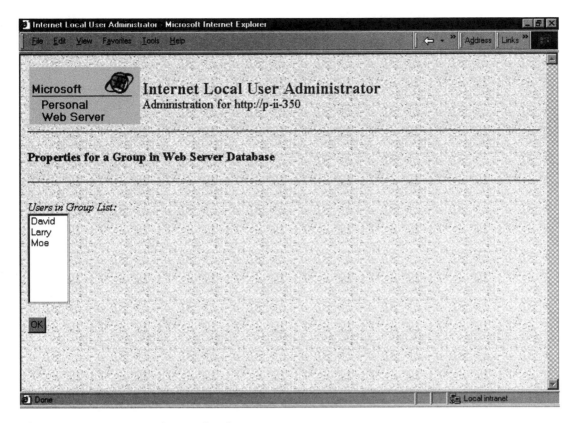

Figure 17.10 *Viewing the user list for a group.*

The following steps restrict a Web to registered users, and create a registration form so that visitors can register and then access a site.

1. Open the FrontPage Web for which you are requiring user registration, and select Tools, Permissions to open the Permissions dialog box.
2. If you are defining permissions for a subWeb, choose the Use Unique Permissions for This Web option button in the Settings tab. If you are defining permissions for a root Web, skip this step, as you are defining default settings for the entire Web.
3. In the Users tab, select the Only Registered Users Have Browse Access options button. Rather than define registered users at this point, just OK the dialog box at this point. You will handle registering users later, through an input form that visitors fill out when they visit the site.

4. If you have a subWeb open, close it and open the root Web for your FrontPage Web (you can refer back to the discussion of subWebs and root Webs at the beginning of this chapter if you need to). Registration pages must be defined in a root Web, even though they may apply to a subWeb.

5. With your root Web open, open the FrontPage Editor, and select File, New to open the New dialog box.

6. In the New dialog box, click on the User Registration page template, as shown in Figure 17.11, then click on OK.

7. Read the comment text at the top of the User Registration page. It explains that "Some Web servers do not allow self-registration. When you save this page to a Web, the FrontPage Explorer will test for this capability, and flag the page with a red triangle in the Hyperlink view if there is a problem."

8. Edit the text on the Registration page—at the minimum, replace occurrences of "[OtherWeb]" with the name of the actual Web for which you are creating a registration page. In Figure 17.12, I'm using the Replace option to change each instance of [OtherWeb] with the name of my actual Web site.

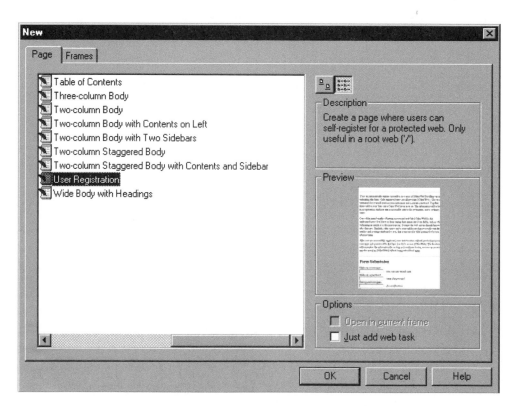

Figure 17.11   *Selecting the User Registration page template.*

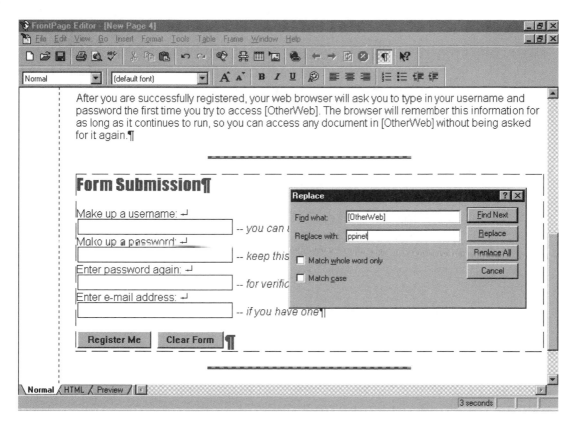

Figure 17.12 *Editing the template Registration page.*

9. You can edit the contents of the input form generated by the template to collect additional data from registered users (refer back to Chapter 8, "Creating Input Forms," for form editing techniques).

10. Right-click inside the input form, and select Form Properties from the context menu to open the Form Properties dialog box. Here, you can custom edit any of the form handling properties using the procedures we explored in Chapter 10, "Processing User Input," (or you can add validation scripts, as discussed in Chapter 9, "Validating User Input."). However, the only property that you need to edit to make the registration form work is FrontPage Web name.

11. Edit the Web name by clicking on the Options button. The Options for Registration Form Handler dialog box appears. In the Registration tab, enter the name of your FrontPage Web in the FrontPage Web

Name box. (The name of your Web is displayed in parentheses in the title bar of the FrontPage Explorer—for example, if the displayed name is http://www.ppinet.com/Register, you should enter "Register" in this box.)

12. Click on OK twice to OK both dialog boxes, and return to the Front-Page Editor.

13. Save the page you created. You might want to select a URL like Register.htm, and a page title like Register.

14. After you complete this process, you need to establish a procedure for notifying potential visitors to your site that you have a registration page that they must use before they access the site.

15. Finally, you can test your registration system. First, attempt to visit your site without registering. Figure 17.13 shows the default message page that is generated by the FrontPage Registration page template. The Registration tab of the Options for Registration Form Handler dialog box allows you to enter a URL for a registration failure page. If you do that,

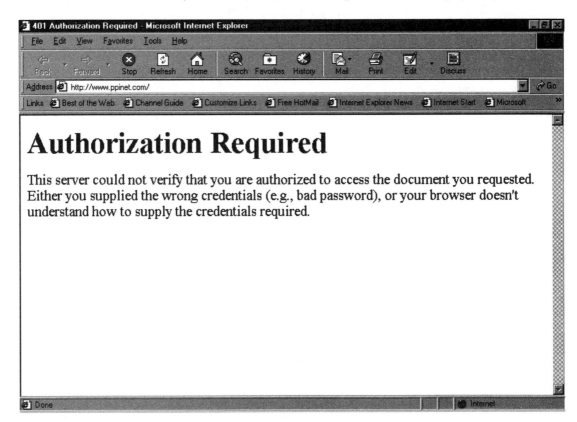

Figure 17.13   *Unregistered visitors are not allowed at password-protected Webs.*

you can define a custom page that includes information to visitors on how to register.

The default settings in the Registration template save registration data to a text file called regdb.txt. This file can be opened in any text editor to see the data supplied by visitors who register.

As I mentioned at the beginning of this section, the FrontPage Personal Web Servers (all versions) do not support site registration. So, while you can walk through these steps using the Personal Web Servers, you cannot test registration with the Personal Web Server.

MCSD 17.3   Establishing Mechanisms for Posting Content to a FrontPage Web

If your FrontPage server allows permission settings (The Microsoft Personal Web Server does, the FrontPage Personal Web Server does not), you can define access to site development, and assign authorization to change site content.

The process for defining permission to post content is very similar to the process for defining browser permission. For example, just as we created user groups with browser permission earlier in this chapter, you can create user groups with author (or administrator) permission.

To assign author or administrator permission, select Tools, Permissions in the FrontPage Explorer. As with user permissions, author and administrator permissions are Web-specific, so you must have the Web for which you are assigning options open.

If you have the root Web in your server open, the Permissions dialog box will control settings for the entire Web. If you have a sub-Web open, the Settings tab in the Permissions dialog box provides for two choices: to define permissions for the specific Web folder you have open, or to assign permission settings defined for the root Web. The Settings tab will not display if you have a root Web open.

After making a selection in the Settings tab (if that is available), select the Users tab in the Permissions dialog box. Click on the Add button in the Users tab.

Choose the Author and Browse this Web options button to define an author, or the Administer, Author and Browse this Web options button to assign administrator access. Then, enter a user name in the Name box, and a password in both the Password and Confirm Password boxes. In Figure 17.14, I'm assigning Author (and Browse) permission to Sasha.

You can enter user names directly into the Add Names box in the Add Users dialog box, or you can use the Add button to enter names that have already been defined in your Web server software.

- *Author and Browse This Web* allows users to browse the Web (only necessary if the Web is restricted to registered users), and to create, edit, and delete pages.
- *Administrator, Author and Browse This Web* allows the user to do all of the above, plus create new Webs.

If you or a Web server administrator have assigned Groups, you can use the Groups tab of the Permissions dialog box to assign one of the three permission levels (Browse, Author or Administrator) to a Group.

Figure 17.14   *Adding an author in the FrontPage Permissions dialog box.*

Study Break

Defining Controls on Web Publishing Access

Practice what you have learned by defining new users, and assigning one of them author privileges, and assigning the other user administration privileges.

First, open an existing Root Web.

Next, define a user and assign that user Author permission for the Web.

Finally, add another user, and assign this user Administration-level permission.

MCSD 17.4 ## Configuring FrontPage 98 to Use a Proxy Server

A proxy server is a type of server that logs and usually controls transactions between computers on either side of the server. They're often used in firewall setups to prevent unauthorized connections from outside the protected computers. They can also be used for logging purposes, and to provide advanced caching options to large organizations.

FrontPage 98 can also be used through a proxy server. You can set up a proxy connection in FrontPage Explorer, through which all your connections will be made by default. The proxy server setup in FrontPage 98 assumes that you are using FrontPage to edit files from behind a firewall onto a Web server outside of one. It doesn't really take into consideration an outside consultant developing a FrontPage Web to be used inside a firewall, needing to connect through the proxy for just one Web server.

You can connect to FrontPage Webs through a firewall one of two ways. Either you're inside the firewall, connecting to a server outside of it, or you're outside, trying to get in. In either case, you'll need to know the name of the proxy server to connect through. That name will be something like http://proxy.domain.com:80, and is available from the system administrator who maintains your proxy server or firewall.

1. To set up a proxy connection in FrontPage, first open the FrontPage Explorer.
2. Select Tools, Options from the menu bar.
3. Click the "Proxies" tab to configure the proxy server.
4. Put the name of the proxy server in the HTTP Proxy field, as shown in Figure 17.15.

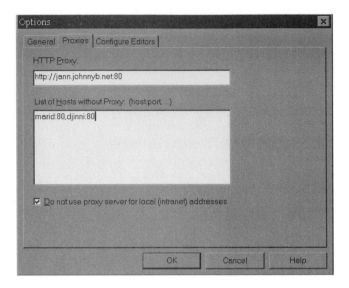

Figure 17.15 *The FrontPage Options dialog box lets you change the behavior of the FrontPage program itself.*

5. Enter any hosts you don't need the proxy server to connect to (such as ones in the same intranet) and their port number (usually 80 or 8080 for Web servers) in the "List of Hosts without Proxy" box.

6. If you want to automatically avoid using the proxy server for other servers in the intranet, check the "Do not use the proxy server for local addresses." box.

■ Summary

In this chapter we've looked at controlling site access to a FrontPage Web from several different perspectives. Files can be protected from browser access by all visitors by placing them in Web folders that are defined so that no browser access is allowed. You can also restrict a Web (or a subWeb) to

When you connect to a Windows NT server through a proxy with FrontPage 98, the connection tries to use the NT LAN Manager services. Unfortunately, these services often fail in this kind of connection. FrontPage will prompt you to turn off NTLM (Windows NT Lan Manager) services at the proxy server, or to disable the proxy settings if they're unnecessary. You'll need to cooperate with your proxy server administrator to get NTLM disabled.

registered visitors only. By doing this, you require that each visitor have an assigned user Name, and Password. User names and passwords can be assigned by a Web administrator, or you can use FrontPage's Registration template to allow visitors to register themselves. When visitors register, they fill out a registration form, and the data is saved to a file that you can open in the FrontPage Explorer.

We also explored the process of defining permission for Web authors and administrators. Web authors can create, edit, or delete Web pages. Administrators can assign access privileges.

Finally, we looked at the process of working on a FrontPage Web at a remote server (other than the one you are working on), using a proxy server to navigate through a firewall.

▲ CHAPTER REVIEW QUESTIONS

Here are some practice questions relating to the material covered in the "Publishing and Managing a FrontPage Web" area of Microsoft's *Designing and Implementing Web Sites Using Microsoft FrontPage 98* exam (70-055).

1. *You can use both File Sharing and Local User permissions in FrontPage.*
   - **A.** True
   - **B.** False

2. *How do you add a user to a group in Microsoft Personal Web Server?*
   - **A.** Set them up in the Permissions settings on a per-Web basis
   - **B.** Open the Microsoft Personal Web Server Administrator pages and use the Users/Groups tab
   - **C.** Use the chmod command

3. *A browse-only restricted Web lets Web users run scripts.*
   - **A.** True
   - **B.** False

4. *What does the Registration Form Handler do?*
   - **A.** Adds users to the Microsoft Personal Web Server
   - **B.** Adds pre-existing users to an otherwise restricted Web
   - **C.** Creates a new user in FrontPage to access an otherwise restricted FrontPage Web

5. *How can you grant access to Web files? (Select all that apply.)*
   A. Change the Web file's permissions using the Windows file manager
   B. Specify a password in a password <META> tag
   C. Change the Web directory's permissions with the file manager
   D. Add a user to the FrontPage Web's Permissions settings
   E. Add a login script to the Web site

6. *What kind of access allows you to delete FrontPage Webs?*
   A. Browse-only
   B. Author and browse
   C. Administrate, author, and browse
   D. No access

7. *You must be an administrator to change a password in FrontPage.*
   A. True
   B. False

8. *How is the root Web different from other FrontPage Webs when it comes to security? (Select all that apply.)*
   A. By default, the root Web's permissions are inherited by all the child Webs.
   B. Root Webs cannot be restricted to registered users only.
   C. The root Web is the only Web that can contain a Registration Form Handler form and make it work.
   D. The root Web must give administration access to "The World."

9. *Windows NT lets you set file sharing and set up Web permissions in FrontPage.*
   A. True
   B. False

10. *UNIX and FrontPage are incompatible. You should not use them together to develop your Web sites.*
    A. True
    B. False

11. *What's the best way to grant browse-only access to an intranet for your company's staff of 20 people in FrontPage on the Microsoft Personal Web Server?*

    A. Create a user account called "staff" and distribute its password

    B. Check the "Restrict Access to Registered Users Only" button on the Users tab

    C. Create user accounts for each staff member and create a group in the Local User Administrator. Add the group to the Web's group permissions

    D. Create user accounts for each staff member and add them all to the Web's user permissions

12. *FrontPage 98 does not work through a firewall server, just for proxies.*

    A. True

    B. False

13. *What kinds of setups do the proxy settings permit you to make? (Select all that apply.)*

    A. Connect from the Internet to a FrontPage Web on an intranet

    B. Connect from an intranet to another FrontPage Web server on the intranet

    C. Connect from an intranet to a FrontPage Web outside the firewall

    D. Connect from outside a firewall to another Web outside the firewall

14. *How do you set up a proxy server connection in FrontPage 98?*

    A. Select Tools, Options from the menu and click the Proxies tab.

    B. Use the Proxy settings in your Web browser

    C. Ask your system administrator for the IP address of the Proxy server and manually enter it using chmod

Answers to Chapter Review Questions

The following answers to the end-of-chapter review questions are provided to help you in your exam preparation.

Chapter 1

1. B.   Search counters can be generated without programming in FrontPage 98.

2. D.   FrontPage extension files can be installed in all major types of servers, and are required to utilize all of FrontPage's features.

3. A.   FrontPage Web sites can be password-restricted.

4. A.   FrontPage doesn't include SSL, but it is compatible with SSL server sites.

5. B.   FrontPage extension files can be installed in all major types of servers.

6. A and B.   Multimedia content and expected hits are factors in determining bandwidth demand.

7. E.   SSL (Secure Sockets Layer) encryption protects data sent over the Internet.

8. B.   SSL does not prevent visitors from seeing public Web site content.

9. B.   The highest level of authority in the permissions hierarchy is Administrator.

10. A.   You can define password access to a Web site in Front-Page.

11. A.   PowerPoint presentations can be included in FrontPage Web sites, although visitors will need to have Power-Point or download the PowerPoint viewer to see them.

12. A, B, E.   AVI files are large and take up much disk space. If they are downloaded frequently they place significant demands on bandwidth. Older browsers cannot interpret AVI files.

13. B.   FrontPage Web sites can be interpreted by IE, or by Netscape Navigator.

14. B, D.   ActiveX content and AVI files are not interpreted by all older browsers.

15. B.   Alternative pages can be displayed for browsers that do not interpret frames.

Chapter 2

1. B.   Simply assigning a proxy server does not create fire-wall protection.

2. A, C.   All Web browsers interpret HTML files, and will display *.TXT files as unformatted text.

3. B.   Keystroke data entry can be facilitated by defining a tab order between fields, but not by assigning hot keys.

4. B.   Importing pages through page view bypasses the Explorer. The most reliable way to import Web files is through the Import dialog box.

5. A.   The Database Region wizard requires a DSN file.

6. A.   SQL queries are part of defining a database region with the wizard.

7. B, D.   You must enable scripting for folders containing ASP pages, and the server to which the site is published must have ASP extensions.

8. A.   ASP server files are available on the FrontPage 98 CD.

9. A.   You can save files in the FrontPage Editor with ASP extensions.

10. A.   Proxy Servers allow you to work on a Web site from a remote location.

11. B.   A Proxy Server can exist when a site is not published to a FrontPage server.

12. B. Proxy settings are defined in the Options dialog box in the FrontPage Explorer.

13. B. Scripting can be enabled or disabled for any selected folder.

14. B. Databases can be queried interactively with FrontPage Web sites only if they are published to the Web server.

15. A, B and E. Alternate text displays when pictures are disabled in a browser, and can sometimes be used by software that interprets images Web pages for sight-impaired browsers. Alternate text functions as a caption when a visitor hovers over an image.

Chapter 3

1. B, C. FrontPage has no script debugger per se, but you can debug scripts in Preview tab and in Web browsers.

2. A. You cannot mix VBScripts and JavaScripts in a page, but you can put them on separate pages.

3. A, B. JavaScript code can be written or borrowed, but Java applets and VB Scripts are not JavaScript.

4. A, D. Java applets are different than scripts in that they are generally saved to files, not embedded in HTML pages.

5. C, D. FrontPage PWS cannot handle much Web traffic. It is designed for development and testing purposes.

6. B. VBScripts can be published to a server through the Scripts dialog box, but not JavaScripts.

7. A. Netscape Navigator requires a plug-in to interpret VB-Scripts.

8. C. Java applets are files, not embedded scripts.

9. B. FrontPage server extensions are available for Netscape servers, providing full support for FrontPage development.

10. A. Several FrontPage components and active elements work only on Web site published to servers with FrontPage extensions.

Chapter 4

1. A. Click on a page in Navigation View and press the F2 function key to edit the page title.

2. B, D. Navigation layout and Navigation bar properties combine to define generated links.

3. B.   Use a *page template* to create a framed page, not a Web wizard.

4. A.   You can do a replace throughout a Web site in Front-Page Explorer.

5. B.   Manage the Task list in Task View.

6. D.   Hyperlink Status View displays the status of links.

7. A, B.   The answer here is a bit subjective, but generally speaking shared borders, input form fields, and hyperlink status can wait until the production stage of defining a site. Task assignment and navigation logic are early decisions.

8. A.   You can spell-check an entire site (or selected pages) in the FrontPage Explorer.

9. B.   You can have up to four shared borders in a site.

10. A.   Shared border pages are saved to a hidden file called _Shared.

11. B.   Navigation bars can be placed anywhere on a page, or not placed at all.

12. A, C, D. Page templates and search strings are never generated by templates.

13. A.   Navigation links must be defined in Navigation View for any site, new or imported.

14. C.   You can track your own files in the Navigation View window from the file list in Navigation View using the right-click method.

15. A.   Printing Navigation View is a good way to present a Web site overview.

Chapter 5

1. A, C and E. Search forms use page titles, text and navigational links to identify matching pages.

2. B, E.   Navigation strategies start from an evaluation of site content and audience.

3. A.   Text marquees are not interpreted by Netscape Navigator.

4. A.   Hover buttons are Java applets..

5. B.   Banner Ad Manager Active Elements are Java applets.

6. A, C.   HTML can either be entered in the HTML tab, or in an HTML Component dialog box.

7. B.   FrontPage extension files are required for many Components and Active Elements.

8. B.   Confirmation fields are used for confirmation pages associated with input forms.

9. A.   Most browsers display HTML source code, which reveals comments that do not display in the normal browser window.

10. B.   Components remove the need to do scripting or coding.

11. A.   Custom confirmation pages include Confirmation Field Components.

12. A, B.   Substitution Components insert fields and Scheduled Include Page Components insert pages for scheduled periods. Both can be revised, with the changes appearing in each page in which they are embedded.

13. B.   Hover buttons can be interpreted by IE, or by Netscape Navigator.

14. A, C, D, E. The Personal Web Template is the only template or wizard in this list that does not include an option for generating a Search Form.

15. B.   Page Banner Components reflect the title assigned to a page.

Chapter 6

1. C.   Microsoft ships only its own browser, Internet Explorer, with FrontPage.

2. A, B, C, D, E. You can install FrontPage extensions to all these servers.

3. A.   By default, FrontPage installs servers, and server extensions to Port 80.

4. B.   Once FrontPage is installed, server extensions normally need to be updated only when a new version of FrontPage is installed.

5. B.   SourceSafe does not provide firewall protection.

6. C, E.   Microsoft PWS and IE are installation options.

7. B.   FrontPage extensions are required for many FrontPage Web features.

8. A.   SourceSafe is mainly intended for large projects with many developers.

9. A.   Microsoft PWS comes with features like user registration and passwords not available in the FrontPage PWS.

10. A.		Port 8080 is the default second server port for Front-Page installation.
11. A.		Features like image maps and input form handling are controlled by FrontPage extensions instead of CGI scripts.
12. A, B, C, E.		Hover buttons are the only feature on the list that do not require FrontPage extensions.
13. B.		FrontPage can be adapted to develop sites for non-FrontPage servers.
14. A.		The TCP/IP test identifies whether a computer is configured to connect to the Web.
15. B, C, E.		SourceSafe monitors and logs file revisions, but does not protect against viruses or unauthorized entry.

Chapter 7

1. B, C, and E.		No Frames pages provide alternate content for visitors without frame-compatible browsers. Links to upgrade browsers will solve the frame-compatibility problem for visitors. Frames often clash with shared borders in that they provide similar functions and use up browser window space.
2. C.		Pages can have a maximum of four shared borders: top, bottom, right and left.
3. D.		Shared borders are demarcated with dotted lines in the FrontPage Editor, but those lines are not visible in browsers.
4. A, B.		Shared borders are Web pages that are saved in a hidden folder called _borders.
5. A, B, C, and D.		All answers describe real challenges in using framesets.
6. B, D.		Navigation bars display only links that are consistent with the types of links you select in the Navigation Bar Properties dialog box. And, they display only links that reflect page relationships defined in Navigation View.
7. A.		Page titles assigned in Navigation View are displayed in Navigation bars.
8. C.		Labels for Next and Previous pages are defined in the Navigation tab of the FrontPage Web Settings dialog box in the FrontPage Explorer.
9. B.		Shared borders can, and usually do, include navigation bars.

10. A, C, D.	Shared border pages are found in the _borders folder, Java Applets (when they are included in a Web site) are found in the _fpclass folder, and Themes files are found in the _themes folder.

Chapter 8

1. A, B.	Drop-down menus can be defined to allow for either multiple selections, or just one selection.
2. C.	Labels are not recognized by Netscape Navigator.
3. A.	Browser type is one hidden field option.
4. B.	One-line text boxes are limited to 999 characters.
5. A.	Groups of radio buttons are identified by a common group name.
6. D.	Scrolling text boxes collect unlimited data.
7. A, D.	Password fields hide data on a monitor, and can only be assigned to one-line text boxes.
8. B.	Password-type fields only hide input on a monitor. They provide no encryption protection.
9. A.	Form field data is collected through Forms.
10. A.	Labels make radio buttons and check boxes easier to use, but are not recognized by Netscape Navigator.
11. B.	Radio buttons cannot collect text data.
12. C, E.	Drop-down menus, as well as radio buttons, can restrict visitors to one selection in a list.
13. A.	FrontPage generates a _private folder to hold input data.
14. B, D.	Date and Browser type are hidden field options.
15. A.	Scrolling text boxes do collect large amounts of data, but not password data, options, or images.

Chapter 9

1. B	A single radio button cannot be a required field, but a group can.
2. A, B, C, D.	Text box fields can validate for letters, numbers, white space, and additional characters.
3. A	Validation scripts can apply greater than or equal to criteria.
4. B.	Drop-down menus provide preset selections and don't require validation.
5. B.	FrontPage generates client-side validation scripts.

6.	C, D.	Check boxes and hidden fields cannot have validation scripts applied, and labels are not a form of input field.
7.	A.	Validation scripts depend on the browser interpreting them.
8.	A.	You can change the default scripting language for validation scripts from JavaScript to VBScript.
9.	B.	Check boxes cannot be required fields.
10.	A.	Text data types can accept letters, numbers and symbols.
11.	A.	Number data types can display a value as either 100,000 or 100.000.
12.	A, B, D.	Zip codes can use data value constraints to restrict values that are too high or low (like 00001), or too short or long, that include decimal places, or to reject form fields that are left blank. There is no need for grouping constraints in zip codes since they do not use commas or decimal places.
13.	A.	Netscape Navigator does not recognize VBScripts.
14.	B.	Form fields are defined in Validation dialog boxes.
15.	C.	Default scripting languages are defined for specific Webs.

Chapter 10

1.	A, D.	E-mail data processing sends input directly to an e-mail address, and saving files to a _Private folder protects them from search boxes and navigation links.
2.	C, D.	HTML files display input data for visitors, and require an *.htm or *.html file name extension.
3.	A.	You can assign each input form separate from handling properties.
4.	B.	There is no limit to the number of forms on a page in FrontPage.
5.	B.	Some versions of the Microsoft Personal Web Server and the FrontPage Personal Web Server do have FrontPage extensions, and do handle other input options, but will not manage e-mail.
6.	A, D, E.	Web pages, text files and e-mail are the three basic ways to collect form input.
7.	B.	FrontPage extension files take the place of other server-side scripting for processing input form data.
8.	B.	Data is managed with server-side scripts.

9.	A.	You can assign an optional, second file to receive input data from a form.
10.	A.	A page with an input form (or more) can share a frame with a page that displays input data.
11.	A.	Definition lists display form fields and form data in an easy-to-read format.
12.	A, B, D.	FrontPage needs a URL, and encoding type and an installed CGI script on the server to process data using CGI scripts.
13.	A.	You can test form management for text files using the Personal Web Server before publishing a Web to an Internet or larger intranet server.
14.	B.	E-mail is the one type of input that cannot be tested using the Personal Web Server without modifying the default installation.
15.	C, D.	Delimited text files (text files with each field separated) work well for importing into Excel.

Chapter 11

1.	C, D.	DHTML and ActiveX present the most browser compatibility dangers.
2.	A, C, E.	Java applets do not present compatibility issues in IE4 or higher, and since they are client-side applications, there are no server issues.
3.	A.	The difference in positioning models is a key reason why FrontPage generated DHTML is not interpreted correctly in Netscape Navigator.
4.	A.	Collapsible outlines utilize an IE-dependent version of DHTML.
5.	B.	*class files are compiled, and cannot be edited in FrontPage.
6.	D, E.	Page transitions and ActiveX controls can be generated in the FrontPage Editor.
7.	E.	FrontPage-generated HTML is IE specific.
8.	A.	Java is more universally recognized than ActiveX.
9.	A.	The collapsible outlines generated in FrontPage rely on DHTML.
10.	A.	You can preview a Java applet in the FrontPage Editor.
11.	B.	IE4 has no problem with Java applets.
12.	B, E.	Neither Netscape Navigator version 3 nor IE version 3 interpret DHTML.

13.	A.	Netscape 4.5 does not support ActiveX controls.14.
14.	A, B, C, E.	There is no option for an alternate display *folder*, only alternate display text.
15.	C.	Transitions can be triggered when a page is entered, or exited, or a site is entered or exited.

Chapter 12

1.	A.	JPEG images cannot have transparency applied. AVI and MIDI files are not image files.
2.	A, B, C, D, E.	All five methods can be used to place images in Front-Page Web sites.
3.	A.	ActiveX controls are available for Real Audio files.
4.	A.	Newer methods for floating images in a Web page are not as universally recognized by browsers.
5.	B.	Transparency can be applied to images in the Front-Page Editor.
6.	A, D, E.	Tables can be drawn, generated from text or imported from spreadsheets, but not merged from data or saved as images.
7.	C, D.	ActiveX controls are difficult to use with Netscape Navigator, and do require that there be an associated control for the embedded file type.
8.	B.	Transparency is applied in the FrontPage Editor using the Transparency tool in the Image toolbar, or in the Image Properties dialog box.
9.	A.	Only AVI files can be reliably embedded as inline video in FrontPage.
10.	A.	Plug-ins must be viewed in Preview tab, or a browser to be tested.
11.	B.	Background color can be assigned to specific cells in a table.
12.	B, C.	You can edit image properties, but not coloring. FrontPage does not support image-editing plug-ins, and JPEG images can never have transparency.
13.	A.	All cells in a table share padding properties.
14.	A.	File type can be changed to GIF, JPEG, or PNG in the Image Properties dialog box.
15.	C, D.	Pixels or percent are the only two options for defining image size.

Chapter 13

1.	B.	There is no User Registration Web wizard.
2.	A, D, E.	Learning files and a Schedule page are not options for the Corporate Presence Web.
3.	A.	IE version 3 does not interpret all style attributes generated by FrontPage 98.
4.	B.	There is no Discussion Page template.
5.	A.	All these features are available from Page templates.
6.	B, C.	External style sheets require coding outside of FrontPage. FrontPage styles are not fully compatible with Netscape Navigator, and have no relation to firewalls.
7.	B, C, D.	All FrontPage styles present compatibility issues with Netscape Navigator.
8.	B.	The term embedded styles is used to refer to styles attached to a page. Styles are applied to an entire site through external style sheets.
9.	B.	FrontPage cannot generate external style sheets without additional tools and coding.
10.	A.	HTML styles can be redefined with external style sheets.
11.	A.	Styles do provide more formatting control than HTML.
12.	D.	You can define your own user-defined custom page templates, and use them to generate pages in the FrontPage Editor.
13.	A.	The Customer Support Web template generates a page that links to an FTP site.
14.	C, D.	The Customer Support Web template and Discussion Web wizards generate Feedback pages.
15.	A, B.	Styles assigned to specific text take precedence over other styles, but not over other formatting.

Chapter 14

1.	A.	The Publish dialog box includes a check box to publish only new or changed pages.
2.	A, B.	You can either use FTP to transfer pages, or Publish directly using FrontPage.
3.	B.	Pages, not databases, are saved as *.asp files.
4.	A.	Many database formats support ODBC conversion.
5.	A.	Saving a Web is publishing it.

6. A, C, E. An ASP server is required to *display* a Database Region, but not to create one. ODBC files can be created from other sources besides Access files.

7. A, C, E. ASP pages must be saved to folders for which scripts are enabled, saved with *.asp file name extensions, and saved to servers that support ASP.

8. B. You can publish a Web to only one server at a time. However, you can repeat the process to publish a Web to multiple servers.

9. B. FrontPage Webs can be transferred with FTP to sites that don't support FrontPage extensions.

10. A. The New dialog box prompts you to assign a server.

11. B. Publishing a Web preserves navigational structure, importing pages does not.

12. A, C, E. Page formatting and saving pages as *.asp files can still take place without a FrontPage Web being properly defined.

13. A. Database Regions require SQL queries.

14. E. ASP is installed from a file on the FrontPage 98 CD.

Chapter 15

1. B. Hyperlink View shows hyperlink structure.

2. D. Orphan pages are not accessible from links on other pages in a site.

3. B. Recalculating repairs *internal* links.

4. A. FrontPage does usually update internal links as files are moved.

5. B. Navigation View can be rotated.

6. A, C. There's no such thing as an extra navigational structure, and database file extensions and ODBC specs do not need to be updated as part of routine maintenance.

7. B. Shared borders files are stored in the _borders folder.

8. A. You can hide images in Hyperlinks View.

9. A. Internal links are updated when pages are moved in Navigation View.

10. A. Input data is saved to the hidden _private file by default.

11. B. Internal links are fixed automatically. You must identify new target links to fix broken external hyperlinks.

12.	B.	Neither navigational structure, file types, missing files, nor folder structure are easily viewed in Hyperlinks View.
13.	B.	Sort tested links by status to identify bad links.
14.	A, D.	You can print, or rotate Navigation View.
15.	B.	Folder structure is more easily viewed in Folders View.

Chapter 16

1.	A, C, E.	DHTML, Channels and CDF (channel) files all present compatibility problems in Netscape.
2.	B, C, E.	You can collect hidden data from subscribers, allow the Channel to function as a screen saver, and cache downloaded Web pages.
3.	A.	E-mail update is an option for Channels.
4.	A.	Web content and a channel can be synchronized.
5.	B.	IE 2 did not support frames.
6.	D.	Answer C is incorrect because Netscape does not support FrontPage channels. Only a URL is required for a channel.
7.	B.	AOL 3 supports frames.
8.	B.	AOL 3 supports input forms.
9.	B.	Netscape 4.5 uses different DHTML standards than FrontPage.
10.	A.	Upgrade links are one option for browser compatibility.
11.	A.	Content displayed by FrontPage's DHTML effects is usually still readable without the effects.
12.	D.	The DHTML warning appears when a page is previewed.
13.	B.	Basic HTML is interpreted by all browsers.
14.	A, D, E.	Only abstract content cannot be defined in a user's operating system.
15.	A.	Channel icons should be 16×16 pixels.

Chapter 17

1.	B.	Local User Administration and File and Print Sharing are incompatible.
2.	B.	Add users and groups to the Microsoft Personal Web Server in the Local User Administration.
3.	A.	FrontPage bots can be run by browse-only users.

4. C.   The Registration Form Handler relates only to Front-Page Web users, and does not add users to the Microsoft Personal Web Server.

5. A, C, D. Web permissions can be set using the file manager or FrontPage permissions.

6. C.   Only administrators can delete a FrontPage Web.

7. A.   Only administrators can change a FrontPage password; individual users can change their own scripts in Windows NT and UNIX.

8. A, C.   The root Web's permissions are inherited by all other Webs, and Registration Form Handlers must reside in the root Web in order to work.

9. A.   You can set both file permissions and FrontPage Web permissions in Windows NT.

10. B.   FrontPage extensions are available for most UNIX servers, and all FrontPage features work on those servers.

11. C.   The easiest way to manage large numbers of users in the long run is to create a group for them.

12. B.   A firewall is a type of proxy server, and there is nothing inherently impossible about using them with FrontPage. Some firewalls may be configured to prevent all incoming connections, and so connecting to a FrontPage Web server from outside the firewall will not work.

13. A, B, C. FrontPage's proxy settings allow you to use a proxy for connections through the proxy in either direction, and to not use the proxy server for specific connections, and intranets.

14. A.   The proxy settings are available through the FrontPage Explorer Tools, Options menu.

INDEX

473

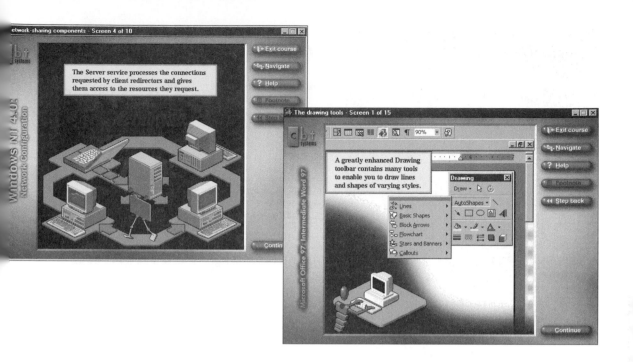

Other curricula available from CBT Systems:

- Cisco
- Informix
- Java
- Marimba
- Microsoft
- Netscape
- Novell

- Oracle
- SAP
- Sybase
- C/C++
- Centura
- Information Technology/ Core Concepts

- Internet and Intranet Skills
- Internetworking
- UNIX

CBT SOFTWARE LICENSE AGREEMENT

IF YOU DO NOT AGREE WITH THESE TERMS AND CONDITIONS, DO NOT INSTALL THE SOFTWARE.

This is a legal agreement you and CBT System Ltd. ("Licensor"). The licensor ("Licensor") from whom you have licensed the CBT Group PLC courseware (the "Software"). By installing, copying or otherwise using the Software, you agree to be bound by the terms of this Agreement License Agreement (the "License"). If you do not agree to the terms of this License, the Licensor is unwilling to license the Software to you. In such event, you may not use or copy the Software, and you should promptly contact the Licensor for instructions on the return of the unused Software.

1. **Use.** Licensor grants to you a non-exclusive, nontransferable license to use Licensor's software product (the "Software") the Software and accompanying documentation in accordance with the terms and conditions of this license agreement ("License") License and as specified in your agreement with Licensor (the "Governing Agreement"). In the event of any conflict between this License and the Governing Agreement, the Governing Agreement shall control.

You may:

a. (if specified as a "personal use" version) install the Software on a single stand-alone computer or a single network node from which node the Software cannot be accessed by another computer, provided that such Software shall be used by only one individual; or

b. (if specified as a "workstation" version) install the Software on a single stand-alone computer or a single network node from which node the Software cannot be accessed by another computer, provided that such Software shall be used by only one individual; or

c. (if specified as a "LAN" version) install the Software on a local area network server that provides access to multiple computers, up to the maximum number of computers or users specified in your Governing Agreement, provided that such Software shall be used only by employees of your organization; or

d. (if specified as an "enterprise" version) install the Software or copies of the Software on multiple local or wide area network servers, intranet servers, stand-alone computers and network nodes (and to make copies of the Software for such purpose) at one or more sites, which servers provide access to a multiple number of users, up to the maximum number of users specified in your Governing Agreement, provided that such Software shall be used only by employees of your organization.

This License is not a sale. Title and copyrights to the Software, accompanying documentation and any copy made by you remain with Licensor or its suppliers or licensors.

2. **Intellectual Property**. The Software is owned by Licensor or its licensors and is protected by United States and other jurisdictions' copyright laws and international treaty provisions. Therefore, you may not use, copy, or distribute the Software without the express written authorization of CBT Group PLC. This License authorizes you to use the Software for the internal training needs of your employees only, and to make one copy of the Software solely for backup or archival purposes. You may not print copies of any user documentation provided in "online" or electronic form. Licensor retains all rights not expressly granted.

3. **Restrictions**. You may not transfer, rent, lease, loan or time-share the Software or accompanying documentation. You may not reverse engineer, decompile, or disassemble the Software, except to the extent the foregoing restriction is expressly prohibited by applicable law. You may not modify, or create derivative works based upon the Software in whole or in part.

1. **Confidentiality**. The Software contains confidential trade secret information belonging to Licensor, and you may use the software only pursuant to the terms of your Governing Agreement, if any, and the license set forth herein. In addition, you may not disclose the Software to any third party.

2. **Limited Liability**. IN NO EVENT WILL THE Licensor's LIABILITY UNDER, ARISING OUT OF OR RELATING TO THIS AGREEMENT EXCEED THE AMOUNT PAID TO LICENSOR FOR THE SOFTWARE. LICENSOR SHALL NOT BE LIABLE FOR ANY SPECIAL, INCIDENTAL, INDIRECT OR CONSEQUENTIAL DAMAGES, HOWEVER CAUSED AND ON ANY THEORY OF LIABILITY., REGARDLESS OR WHETHER LICENSOR HAS BEEN ADVISED OF THE POSSIBILITY OF SUCH DAMAGES. WITHOUT LIMITING THE FOREGOING, LICENSOR WILL NOT BE LIABLE FOR LOST PROFITS, LOSS OF DATA, OR COSTS OF COVER.

3. **Limited Warranty**. LICENSOR WARRANTS THAT SOFTWARE WILL BE FREE FROM DEFECTS IN MATERIALS AND WORKMANSHIP UNDER NORMAL USE FOR A PERIOD OF THIRTY (30) DAYS FROM THE DATE OF RECEIPT. THIS LIMITED WARRANTY IS VOID IF FAILURE OF THE SOFTWARE HAS RESULTED FROM ABUSE OR MISAPPLICATION. ANY REPLACEMENT SOFTWARE WILL BE WARRANTED FOR A PERIOD OF THIRTY (30) DAYS FROM THE DATE OF RECEIPT OF SUCH REPLACEMENT SOFTWARE. THE SOFTWARE AND DOCUMENTATION ARE PROVIDED "AS IS". LICENSOR HEREBY DISCLAIMS ALL OTHER WARRANTIES, EXPRESS, IMPLIED, OR STATUTORY, INCLUDING WITHOUT LIMITATION, THE IMPLIED WARRANTIES OF MERCHANTABILITY AND FITNESS FOR A PARTICULAR PURPOSE.

4. **Exceptions**. SOME STATES DO NOT ALLOW THE LIMITATION OF INCIDENTAL DAMAGES OR LIMITATIONS ON HOW LONG AN IMPLIED WARRANTY LASTS, SO THE ABOVE LIMITATIONS OR EXCLUSIONS MAY NOT APPLY TO YOU. This agreement gives you specific legal rights, and you may also have other rights which vary from state to state.

5. **U.S. Government-Restricted Rights**. The Software and accompanying documentation are deemed to be "commercial computer Software" and "commercial computer Software documentation," respectively, pursuant to FAR Section 227.7202 and FAR Section 12.212, as applicable. Any use, modification, reproduction release, performance, display or disclosure of the Software and accompanying documentation by the U.S. Government shall be governed solely by the terms of this Agreement and shall be prohibited except to the extent expressly permitted by the terms of this Agreement.

6. **Export Restrictions**. You may not download, export, or re-export the Software (a) into, or to a national or resident of, Cuba, Iraq, Libya, Yugoslavia, North Korea, Iran, Syria or any other country to which the United States has embargoed goods, or (b) to anyone on the United States Treasury Department's list of Specially Designated Nations or the U.S. Commerce Department's Table of Deny Orders. By installing or using the Software, you are representing and warranting that you are not located in, under the control of, or a national resident of any such country or on any such list.

7. **General**. This License is governed by the laws of the United States and the State of California, without reference to conflict of laws principles. The parties agree that the United Nations Convention on Contracts for the International Sale of Goods shall not apply to this License. If any provision of this Agreement is held invalid, the remainder of this License shall continue in full force and effect.

8. **More Information**. Should you have any questions concerning this Agreement, or if you desire to contact Licensor for any reason, please contact: CBT Systems USA Ltd., 1005 Hamilton Court, Menlo Park, California 94025, Attn: Chief Legal Officer.

IF YOU DO NOT AGREE WITH THE ABOVE TERMS AND CONDITIONS, SO NOT INSTALL THE SOFTWARE AND RETURN IT TO THE LICENSOR.

About the CD-ROM

The enclosed CD-ROM contains the following computer-based training (CBT) course module:

Microsoft® FrontPage® 98

The CD can be used on Windows 95/98 and NT systems. To access the CBT course, launch the SETUP.EXE file. For further information about installation, read the README.TXT file on the CD. At the Start menu select Run, and type in D:/readme.txt (where D is your CD-ROM drive).

Technical Support

If you have a problem with the CBT software, please contact CBT Technical Support. In the U.S., call 1(800)938-3247. If you are outside the U.S., call 3531-283-0380.

Prentice Hall does not offer technical support for this software. However, if there is a problem with the media, you may obtain a replacement copy by e-mailing us with your problem at: disc_exchange@prenhall.com.